Pearls of Wisdom: Surviving Against All Odds

Book Two

Pearls of Wisdom: Surviving Against All Odds

Book Two

Marie Davis and "Survivors"

A Better Be Write Publisher
New Jersey

This book is written by anonymous writers and all names used in each story have been changed to protect the anonymity and privacy of all people concerned.

First A Better Be Write Publisher edition 2005
Copyright © 2001 by Marie Davis, Monroe Township, NJ

All rights reserved. No part of this book may be reproduced in any form or by any electronic or mechanical means, including information storage and retrieval systems, without written permission from the publisher, except by a reviewer who may quote passages in a review.

ISBN: 0-9767732-6-0

Published by A Better Be Write Publisher
PO Box 1577
Millville, NJ 08332
www.abetterbewrite.com

Covers by Pamela Key
Manufactured in the United States of America.

Pearls Of Wisdom Series © Copyrighted By Marie Davis,

Monroe Township, New Jersey, July 2001

~Dedication~

This book is dedicated to the people who made us what we are today!

"Some people, no matter how old they get, never lose their beauty—they merely move it from their faces into their hearts."
— Martin Buxbaum

~Preface~

~

    The Pearls of Wisdom: Surviving Against All Odds Series was developed for several reasons: I wanted to give other, especially younger, people a look at, and the chance to learn from, the mistakes other people, who are over the age of fifty, had made in their lives; I wanted to give all people the chance to realize that other people had gone through the same trials and tribulations that they had and how the writers had handled the same situations; and finally, I wanted to hopefully let people in trouble gain the courage to change the situations that they might be in and to realize that others had accomplished the feat of solving the problems that go along with change. These brave anonymous writers I call "Survivors," and I hope that you will enjoy the stories contained in this book. If any story helps you, or just makes you take a look at your life, or smile in remembrance, then we have all done what we set out to do.

~Thank You All~

    I would like to thank each of my "Survivors" who had the courage and compassion to come forward and to write their autobiographies of their personal lives, laying themselves and their feelings naked to the entire world in the hope that someone may identify with them or that someone may learn from their mistakes. I thank each and every one of you for your honesty in your story, for your openness of feelings, and for your courage to write it the way it was, which I am sure was painful at times for you to do. Lastly, I thank you for your trust in me that this book would come to pass! And to "Lynetta Marie," who helped me to correct all the errors in this book at a time in my life that was so hectic and overbearing, there are no words of thank you that can show you how much your help meant to me! You are all very dear to my heart!

TABLE OF CONTENTS

Leigh Anne's Story	1
Emily's Story	71
Sandra's Story	143
Dolores's Story	173
Lynetta Marie's Story	249
Updates from *Pearls of Wisdom* – Book One	327

"Leigh Anne's" Story

~Chapter 1~

Life is all about choices, and the choices we make determine the direction our lives take. Some choices I made because I thought it was the proper thing to do. Some I made because I thought, right or wrong, that they would make my life better. But it seems that my life always takes the wrong direction because, no matter how hard I try, the choices I make always seem to be the wrong ones.

I was born in a small town in Texas, just outside of Dallas, in September 1948. My father, Richard, went to barber school on the GI Bill and became a barber shortly after I was born. My brother, Richard Jr., was four, and my sister, Sheila, was sixteen months old. My father was from a large family of nine kids and had grown up in the country. My mother, Gladys, was from New York and had only one brother. Her mother had died just weeks after her birth and she spent her life being shuffled among aunts and uncles. Her father remarried two or three times and she never got along with any of her stepmothers. She left home after graduation from high school and traveled around the country from state to state. She and a friend of hers moved from one state to another. They worked as waitresses in small cafés and, when they got tired of one place, they moved on to another. She said it was her goal to visit every state in the union, but they only made it to about two-thirds of them. I guess they just had wanderlust or something.

At one point she was in Miami Beach, Florida. She worked in a little café there, which was down the street from a bowling alley. My dad was there at the same time working part-time in the bowling alley as a pinsetter. He walked past that café every day going to and from work; but they never met. Months later, my dad was transferred to an Army base in Illinois and, as fate would have it, my mother just happened to be in the same place at the same time. That is where they finally met and fell in love. He won a wedding and engagement ring set in a poker game and decided they might as well use it…so they got married.

My parents were good parents. They made sure we had plenty to eat and clothes to wear. We were taught to be respectful and polite. We learned at an early age not to cheat or steal, and to be honest. It was just that they didn't participate in normal childhood organized activities with us. Our parents never came to the PTA meetings, the holiday programs or even open house. I don't think either of our parents ever met any of our teachers after we were in about the third or fourth grade. My dad worked hard all his life in his barbershop. He always planted a garden, so we had an abundance of fresh fruits and vegetables to eat all year round. We always had a cow and all the fresh milk and milk products you could ever want, and chickens and fresh eggs. My mother was a great baker and always made homemade bread, doughnuts, cakes, cream puffs, and the like, which helped her make extra money by selling the baked goods, as well as milk and eggs. I guess we were poor, but I didn't realize it until years later. I didn't know that most people didn't have to heat their water on the stove, or that in most families you didn't have to share bath water.

It seems as though I have spent my entire life chasing an elusive, unattainable dream. I spent most of it waiting for my knight in shining armor to ride in on a white charger and take me away to a life filled with happiness and love. Instead, all I got was heartbreak and unhappiness. I never felt as if I fit in anywhere. I never thought that anyone cared about me. I can be in a room full of people and still feel alone. I remember once when I was very little, I was sitting on the step that went down into the kitchen. My mother was cooking and I asked her if she had wanted me. She said sure she did. I persisted and said, "You always say that two kids are a perfect family, so why did you have me? You didn't want me, did you?"

Finally, she got exasperated and said, "No, I never planned on having more than two kids, but I got pregnant with you and there wasn't much I could do but have you."

Well, I think she could have handled the situation a little better than she did, but that was the end of it. Even when I was grown up and had kids of my own, I would think about that conversation and wonder if she really meant that she never wanted me or if I had taken it the wrong way.

When I was in fifth grade, right before the end of school, a girl named Pam went home after school and found her mother dead on the floor. Her mother was only twenty-nine years old and had died from a brain hemorrhage. I was horrified! I couldn't imagine not having a mother. I remember going home and telling my mother about it. Instead of comforting me, she proceeded to tell me about how her aunt had died of the same thing when my mother had been fourteen. I didn't want to hear about other people dying. I just wanted my mother to tell me that she wasn't going to die. But, she didn't tell me that. For months after that, if my mother gave me money to buy ice cream I would keep it for weeks because she had touched it.

My older brother and sister always seemed to have some sort of social life. They got to sleep over at friends' houses and go to parties. But, when I asked to go somewhere, I was always told that I was too young. I am probably the only person alive who didn't sleep over at a friend's house until she was twenty years old! When I told my mother I was spending the night with Missy, she wanted to know why I would want to do that. I just told her that we wanted to go out and have some fun and I didn't feel like coming home afterwards.

We lived out in the country on an acre of land. We had few close neighbors and lots of empty space. We had chickens, turkeys, pigs, pigeons, and a cow. There was always something to do. We helped feed the chickens and gather the eggs and it was always a thrill to go with my dad when he milked the cow. We would stand behind him and he would tip the cow's teat up and squirt milk into our mouths. We thought that was just great. We liked to sneak fresh vegetables from the garden and eat them when our parents were not looking. We never thought about dirt and germs. We would just pull the radishes from the ground, wipe them off and then eat them. Sometimes we would take a saltshaker and sit beside the garden eating the tomatoes we picked from the vines.

There were wild grapevines growing at the end of our driveway and, when they were ripe, we would pick them. My mother would make tons of fresh grape jelly out of them. One year, my dad decided to try making wine. He put all the ingredients into a large barrel and left it to ferment, only he left it too long and we ended up with gallons of vinegar. We also had to take turns helping churn the butter. None of us kids liked doing it with the old churn, but then they got one with a crank and that was much easier. After the butter was done, the buttermilk was put in the refrigerator to chill, and then we drank it.

During the summer we spent all day long outside playing cowboys and Indians. We also climbed trees and jumped rope. Sometimes we had ball games that included the few neighbor kids who lived around us, and our parents joined in and played.

Sunday was always a fun day. After church we always went to the drug store, where my dad bought a newspaper and chatted with his friend, the pharmacist. We were allowed a roll of lifesavers each. Then it was on to the icehouse, where my dad rented a locker for storing the beef when he slaughtered a calf. There he would always buy us a soda. I remember I always had to have a Woosie lemon drink. Then he would buy a gallon of ice cream and two family-sized Coca-Colas so that later that night we could have ice cream floats. That was the only day of the week that we were allowed to drink sodas. Most of the time, Sunday evenings were spent with the family playing games or working jigsaw puzzles, where there was always a race to see who would put in the last piece of the puzzle.

When my siblings and I were little, my dad always mailed us funny birthday cards from his barbershop. It was always such a thrill to get some mail. We each got to pick what Mom would fix for our birthday dinner. It's funny but, when I think back, it seems everyone always wanted fried chicken. We always had a homemade birthday cake, but never a birthday party. The first birthday party I ever had was my seventeenth birthday and

I wouldn't have had that, if my sister and I hadn't begged my mother. It was sure a lot of fun. My sister was already married then, and her husband played a guitar and sang pretty well. He and some of his friends came over with their instruments and amplifiers and we invited some other friends. We had a blast, but that was the one and only party that I ever remember being held at our house until my wedding.

Some things from my childhood remain as good memories. For instance, one Christmas my sister and I got grown-up teenage dolls for Christmas. Mom spent hours at night sewing clothes for them. She even made them dress coats with fur collars and cuffs. Dad built a closet for the clothes and even took wire clothes hangers and made them into hangers small enough for the doll clothes to fit on them.

Then, there was the time that my dad's young bull calf got out of the pen and he tried to stop it by jumping on its back. Well, the bull kept running with my dad astride him. He ran down the length of the clothesline, which extended practically the whole width of the acre we lived on. We all stood at the back door doubled over with laughter as the clothespins went "blip, blip, blip" on Dad's head as they hit. He didn't think it was quite as funny as we did.

We had a collie/shepherd mix dog that liked to sit on top of his dog-house and bark at the rain. Once we had a storm and it was hailing. Of course, the dog was on top of his house barking and then yelping as the hail hit him in the head. My brother decided he would go out and get him into his house, so he donned a pith helmet and took off. The hail was about quarter size and by the time my brother made it back in the house, his ears were ringing. They rang for several hours and we thought it was hilarious. Of course, the next day my brother's ears hurt and the poor dog had a sore head.

I also remember going to my grandmother's house on Sundays. Back then it took about two hours to drive there and I always got carsick. I would spend most of the time at Grandma's lying down. We always left really early in the morning. If we left at the right time, Dad would pull over at one point in the road where there were railroad tracks. We would all get out and watch the old steam engine train coming down the track. The engineer would always toot the train's whistle and he and the caboose man would wave at us. It was quite a disappointment to us kids if we missed that train. Today, it amazes me that such a small thing was so exciting to us kids back then.

My mother was Catholic and my father was a non-practicing Protestant. We went to the Catholic Church until I was about four or five and then stopped going altogether. After that, if we went to church, it was when we went to church with a neighbor. I never established a religious connection anywhere. When I was a teenager, I attended a Baptist church for a while, but dropped out of it because no one else in the family would go with me.

I was always a chubby little kid and very shy. For some reason, I was scared to death of old people and men. When I was a baby, I wouldn't let anyone except my mother hold me until I was six months old. I remember as a little child, the old man from down the road who would come over to work on our well. He loved kids…had eight of his own. He would try to talk to me and I remember running and screaming if he just got near me. I have never figured out why I was so afraid of old people and men.

My mother tells me that when I was really small, they had a couple staying with them because the husband was going to school and they didn't have a place to live. The wife babysat us for my mother when she went some place. One day they came home and I was screaming my head off. My sister and brother told her that the lady had locked me in the closet and made me stay there for a long time because I was being bad. My mother told me that she and my dad had told the people that they would have to leave and that they did. I am claustrophobic now, and I sometimes think that this experience might have caused it.

There was a field behind our house that consisted of about fifteen acres. It was sometimes used as a pasture. The grass was left to grow and twice a year the owner would come out with a big combine and cut it down for hay. At the other end of the field was a fence that enclosed peacocks and sheep. One day, when I was about three or four, my brother and sister decided to take me for a walk to see the peacocks. I remember walking forever and then, when we got to the fence, my brother and sister took off running back home and left me there. I tried to follow them, but was lost and crying and screaming out of fear. When they got back to the house, my mother asked where I was and they told her I was back there. Well, she was so angry and she came through the field and found me. That day was so traumatic for me! For years, I wouldn't go near a peacock or a sheep without quaking in fear. It also made me scared to death of getting lost. It is like a phobia. Anytime I have to go some place where I have never been before, I am afraid to go alone because I am afraid of getting lost. Just the thought of going to some strange place alone, gives me butterflies in my stomach and I break out in a sweat and shake. Sometimes I am on the verge of tears.

I always wanted to be accepted but it seemed as if I was always in the way. My brother and sister never really had a place for me in their lives. I would do anything for them to gain their acceptance, like letting them stand me up against the garage wall spread-eagled so they could use me for a target and throw dirt clods at me. When we played cowboys and Indians, I always had to either be the bad guy or the Indian. And, of course, I was the one who always ended up getting killed in the gun battles.

When I was a child, kindergarten was not mandatory. Only rich kids went to kindergarten. Other kids just started school in the first grade. Well, my birthday was too late in September, so I could not start school until the next year when I would be seven. This made my mother mad, so she said she would just teach me herself and she did. By the time the next school year came around, I could print, write in cursive, read and do math.

I will never forget my first day of school. As I said, I was always so shy that I was afraid to talk to anyone. I would not get out of my chair, even for lunch or to go to the rest room. I remember sitting in my chair and wetting my pants. There was a big puddle on the floor and the teacher said the roof must have leaked the night before when it rained so she had the janitor come in and clean up the floor. I remember eating my lunch on the bus on the way home from school because I was afraid to go to the lunchroom.

I only spent six weeks in the first grade before I was moved up to second grade. I don't think I will ever forget when my first grade teacher realized that I could read. I would go to the bookshelf and get a book and read it. She noticed that I spent a lot of time "looking" at the books before taking them back and asked why I spent so much time on them. I told her because I was reading it. She said, "You can't read!" and I told her that I could, too! So, she asked me to read to her and I did. Then, she called the principal down to the room and asked me to read for him. He thought that I had just memorized the book so he picked one out and asked me to read it to them and I did. They were both amazed.

When they asked me to write my name, I asked, "Do you want me to write it or print it?" They said both, and I did that, also. Then, after a conference with my mother, it was decided that I belonged in the second grade and they moved me up a grade. A lot of the kids in my new class made fun of me because I was really only a first grader they felt I didn't belong there.

Cowboys were the heroes of the day, and we played a lot of cowboy games, since we didn't have a lot of money, and didn't always have a lot of store-bought toys. I remember one time my mother carved a play gun for us out of wood. We would run around on our stick horses, chasing each other and shooting at the bad guys. In the westerns we saw on the TV, the cowboy characters always shot at the bad guys until their guns were empty. Then, they would usually throw the gun at the guy and run. Well, one day, my brother was chasing me with the wooden gun and shooting at me. When it "ran out of bullets", he threw it at me and it hit me square in the nose. It didn't break my nose, but I remember it bleeding forever and swelling up something awful.

There were baseball games on Sunday afternoons, and sometimes the neighbors joined in. One Sunday when I was about five, my brother hit the ball and threw the bat before he ran for first base. The bat hit me right in the mouth and knocked both of my front teeth loose. It was a good thing they were baby teeth. The dentist pulled them out because they had already been knocked loose from when I fell down the step that went into our kitchen from the dining room.

The one thing I had going for me was that I was smarter than my siblings were. They always came to me to help them with their homework. When we played school, I was always the teacher and they were the students. The only problem with being smarter was, more was expected of me. When report cards came out, my brother and sister were always praised if they made good grades. But, when it came to my report card, if I got an A, my parents would always say something like, "Why isn't it an A plus?" Although I always excelled, it seemed that I could never please them.

I spent a lot of time with my mother because it seemed as if no one else ever had any time for me. I learned to crochet when I was four. When I was nine, I started sewing my own clothes. When I was eleven, I started cooking dinner for the family every night and I always had it ready when my parents came home from work. Funny, my sister was majoring in homemaking in school, and I was the one who had to do all of the cooking. Figure that!

One night I had dinner cooked, except for the biscuits. It was snowing and the streets were bad so my parents were late getting home. I had opened a can of biscuits and put them in the pan, but decided to wait to put them in the oven until my parents got home. So, not thinking, I sat the pan on the back of the stove and covered it with a paper towel. You guessed it. The heat made the biscuits rise, and then fall. When my parents got home, I took off the paper towel, which was stuck to the biscuits and it removed part of the tops of the biscuits when I took it off. Being naïve, I didn't realize they would stay flat. I cooked them and put them on the table. Dad said, "You made peanut butter cookies, too?" I was so embarrassed, but for years we always got a good laugh over my "peanut butter cookie biscuits!"

I believe my parents were good parents. They kept us fed and clothed. We never really wanted for any of the important things, and I know we were loved. But, when I look back, I don't remember either one of them ever putting their arms around any of us and saying, "I love you." There were never any discussions about much of anything. They were the adults and we were the kids and what they said ruled. We were not allowed to have opinions that differed from theirs. There was never any "mealtime table talk" except for the grown-ups. We kids were supposed to eat and be quiet. Any conversation at the table was between our parents. Anger wasn't allowed. You could get mad at someone, but you were not allowed to express your anger out loud. As I grew up, I learned to keep all of my feelings inside. Even if I went to a funeral, I wouldn't cry because I thought it would be bad if someone saw me express sadness. It took me years to learn that it is all right to cry if you are sad and even yell if you are mad. As I look back now, I think I probably learned this much too late in life.

~Chapter 2~

Everyone wants to think that his parents are perfect and I guess I thought mine were, too. I heard all my life how they had only known each other a month when they got married. They never fought. I don't think we ever heard them have an argument. It was only when I was a grown woman that I realized they never fought because my dad was very passive. He would just shrug things off and go on his merry way. My mother would get mad and rant and rave about things and he would just ignore her. I'm sure they had disagreements but they kept it private.

I guess because I never saw them handle problems, I never learned how it was supposed to be between a husband and a wife. When I was older, I still couldn't understand some of the things they did. If my mother went to the store and bought groceries, she would give the receipt to my dad so he could reimburse her. He would go through the list and mark off things that he didn't tell her to buy and then subtract that amount from what he paid her. I never could understand this because I thought married people shared things, including their money and expenses. When I look back at this relationship, I can understand some of their actions because of the way they were raised. My dad's father, who died before I was born, was a very stern man. He was the man of the family and, therefore, the boss. He showed no emotions. He had never even bought my grandmother a Christmas present before my mother went to stay with them during the war when my dad was overseas. My dad only spent money that needed to be spent and the rest went into the bank.

My mother has always been one of those people to brag that everyone likes her. Well, for years I was angry because it always seemed as if, when I had a problem...and I had many with my husband...I would go to her and talk to her about it. She would always agree and tell me I was right. But then, my husband would bring up the same subject with her later and she would agree with him and tell him *he* was right. I could never go to her to try to solve a problem because I knew she would just go along with anything I said and never really offer any advice. For years I thought she was a back-stabber, but now I realize she just never wanted to get involved.

It's hard when you have a family that doesn't help you when you are in a crisis. When you are in a situation of abuse like I was, you can't dig your way out unless there is something or someone willing to give you a shovel! And, like I said, my dad was very passive and he refused to get involved in other people's problems. So, you could talk to him about your problems and he was a great listener, but he never offered any advice, either.

When my brother was in the tenth grade for the second time, he got tired of going to school because he wasn't passing anyway. So instead of attending his classes, he started going fishing at a little pond every day. I guess he wasn't smart enough to realize that our parents knew he wasn't going to school when he was getting sunburned every day. One day my brother told them he was dropping out of school. My dad told him he could either stay in school or join the service. He decided to join the Air Force.

Once, after my brother joined the Air Force, my parents and my sister and I went to South Texas to visit an Air Force buddy of my dad's. They had a daughter my sister's age. They planned a little get-together for us and invited a bunch of the daughter's friends over. I had never even been to a party and did not know how to act. You would think my big sister would have helped me, but she was too busy flirting and gloating over the attention she was getting. Well, I was overweight and very shy and my sister was skinny and outgoing. It seemed as if no one wanted to talk to me, so I finally went back to where the adults were and sat and watched them play cards. It probably would have helped if they had insisted that I go back and join in with the people my own age. Instead, they just shrugged and said, "She's so shy. She'll grow out of it when she gets older." I didn't know that it would take so many years. I still have a terrible problem with shyness and I don't know how to socialize. The extent of my conversation when I meet someone is "Hi. Nice to meet you." After that, I can never think of a thing to say.

Even though I was always overweight, I don't remember other kids being particularly cruel. I always had lots of friends. I remember watching the movie "Never Been Kissed" and feeling so in touch with the character that Drew Barrymore played. Oh, could I relate to her! I even did homework for the football players so that they would pass, and the cheerleaders and the drill team members were all my friends. Even the class officers were my friends and I was elected an alternate representative for the freshman class student council. I was on the school's first interscholastic volleyball team. Most of us had known each other since first grade. It was just that, even though I had lots of friends, I never had a date with anyone I went to school with. I was never invited to parties. I was always just one of the guys, fun to be around. I never went to a school dance or a prom. And, like I said before, I was twenty years old before I even slept over at a girlfriend's house!

When I was allowed to date at sixteen, the first guy I went out with was twenty-five years old. He was a friend of a girl I knew from school.

When I was in my junior year, I went on a trip out of town for an interscholastic league competition. A group of kids from the school rode buses to Wichita Falls, which is about three or four hours away. I was in the short-hand and typing competition, but there were people there for gymnastics, reading, art and other competitions. We had a very good time on the trip. When we got there, we checked into our hotel rooms and then we were told we could go out and explore for a couple of hours. This was a very small town so there really wasn't much to see or do. We walked around and "helped" a little old lady parallel park. Once we managed to get her car into the parking spot practically sideways, we ran away. Then, we went back to the hotel and ordered pizza and just sat around and ate and laughed. Only a couple of people from our school won any awards in the competitions, but it was a great experience and we all had a good time.

I was twelve years old when I first saw him...the man of my dreams. He looked just like a young Michael Landon. His father owned the service station where my dad bought his gas. His name was Jimmy Lee Williams. He was seventeen, and the first time I saw him, I just melted. He was the first guy I ever had a crush on. Every time we went to the station, he would flirt with my sister and me when he pumped the gas and washed the windows. I made up my mind that when I got old enough, I would marry him. I thought he was my Prince Charming and one day he would take me away and I would live happily ever after. I thought about him all the time. His father eventually sold the station. I just knew that I would not see him again, but I knew I would never forget him.

And, I will never forget the summer I was thirteen. We drove up to New York State to visit my mother's family. This was the first time she had seen any of her family since before her marriage and it would be the first time we would meet them. We stayed with the aunt and uncle with whom she had lived for the better part of her teenage years. They had a little cottage on the Niagara River. We met her father, stepmother and half-sister and brother and all of her aunts, uncles and cousins. Her one cousin, Eliza, came to the cottage with her kids. She had three boys and a girl. Her oldest son was seventeen and he was also very shy, so we hit it off really well. One night he announced that he was taking me snipe hunting. Well, everyone thought that was such a great idea, that I went. I didn't know that it was a joke and snipes were only found at the seashore! We spent a couple of hours wandering through the brush making stupid noises and calling the snipe to come out. Finally we sat down and he started laughing hysterically. I realized then that it was all a big joke.

We sat and talked for a while and then he leaned over and kissed me. I was shocked and scared because I didn't know what was going on. He stood up and apologized and said we needed to go back to the house. I asked him why he had kissed me and he said because I was so sweet and I understood him. I never told anyone about that night but it stayed with me for a long time. A short time after we returned from New York, my mom heard that Eliza had remarried and moved her family to California. We never heard from any of them again.

Then, one day when I was seventeen, my dad came home from work and said, "Guess who I saw today?" When I couldn't guess, he told me he had stopped at a gas station on his way home and Jimmy Lee Williams was running it. My dad said he had talked to him about letting me get gas on credit and he would pay for it on Fridays. Wow! I was so excited. I couldn't wait to go to the station to get gas and see Jimmy Lee again. The next afternoon after school, I drove to the station. I was so nervous. I couldn't believe my eyes when I saw him. He was just so darn gorgeous.

I pulled up to the pump and when he came out to the car, he looked at me and asked, "So, where's your chubby little sister?"

I laughed because he thought I was my sister, and I said, "That was me!" We talked for a long time and he asked me to stop by again the next day. I did that day and every day after school. I even found excuses to tell my parents so that I could go see him on weekends by volunteering to go to the Laundromat and to the store for them. Of course, I always made a detour across town to see him. He always wanted me to stay around. I think he just wanted a young girl there to draw male customers to the gas station, but I didn't care. I wanted to be near him. We never could go on a date because he worked until eleven at night and I had a midnight curfew.

One day Jimmy and I came up with what we thought was a great scheme. I would get my sister and her husband let me spend the night with them, so Jimmy and I could go out. I talked my sister into it, and Jimmy picked me up at her apartment after he closed the station. It was really too late to go any place, so we went to the apartment of a girl my sister and I had gone to school with. The guy she was living with was a friend of Jimmy's. The four of us sat around and listened to records, talked and kissed a little. The guys drank beer but the girls didn't. We didn't get back to my sister's place until around two in the morning. She met me at the door and said Mom and Dad were on their way over. When I asked her why, she said that she had gotten worried because I wasn't back yet, so she had called Mom and Dad. I thought for sure I would be dead after this night! I couldn't imagine what my dad was going to do, so I went to the bathroom and locked myself in. It took them an hour to get me to come out. When I did, they just said we were going home. We drove home and went to bed and never a word was spoken about that night. I wanted them to yell at me, scold me, anything, but they just ignored it. Their actions that night only reinforced my feelings that they really didn't care. If they had, I thought, surely they would have said something about it—anything!

Jimmy was so afraid my dad would say something the next time he went to the station to get gas, but he never mentioned it to him, either. Jimmy said not to worry about it, that it just meant that they trusted me and we could still see each other. After that night, I would make it a point to come in late just to see if my parents would say anything to show they cared. They never did.

I was so in love with this guy that I couldn't stand it. At this time, I had only had three or four dates and I was a very shy, naïve and inexperienced virgin. One Sunday, Dad asked me to go buy a gallon of milk and, of course, I went to the station to get it. We were in the station talking and Jimmy suggested that we go to the place next door and talk for awhile. It was a place where they raised catfish to sell. It was closed, but he knew the owner very well and he had a key.

Like I said, I was very naïve. We went in and he showed me around and explained to me how everything worked. Eventually he cornered me and we started kissing. Things got out of hand and, before I knew it, he was tearing my shorts off and forcing me to have sex. I fought him but I didn't scream or anything because I would have been so embarrassed if someone had come in. And because I was so hungry for someone to want me, I really didn't want to fight him. I thought he felt the same about me and, in my young, immature mind that seemed to make it all okay. Afterwards, he told me how sorry he was and that he hadn't meant for things to go that far and I believed him. He had broken the zipper on my shorts and I had to staple them together before I could go home.

For five long years, I had dreamed of nothing but Jimmy as my knight in shining armor whisking me away to a wonderful life. I was so dumb and so confused. In my mind, I knew that he had meant for it to happen, but I loved him so much that I followed my heart and let myself believe what he told me. I went home and acted as if nothing had happened. Even though I felt the way I did about him, I was afraid to go back to the station. Then, one day my turn signal arm came off and Dad told me to take it to Jimmy's station and see if he could fix it. I didn't want to go there but I did. I got there early in the morning and he told me he would fix it in a little while. Well, he kept me there all day using all kinds of excuses, until closing time. Then, it took him only five minutes to fix it. Afterwards, he asked me to go out with him. Finally I told him I would and we ended up at his apartment.

Of course after we had been there for a while, we starting kissing and one thing led to another. The next thing I knew, we were in bed making love. I loved him so much but I was filled with such guilt that I just didn't feel anything when we were making love. After that, we made love every place we could—even in the back room of the station. After a while, I decided that he only wanted to see me for one thing and I just quit going to the station to see him.

One day I was at home cleaning my car when Jimmy drove up our driveway. My heart stopped. I couldn't believe he had come to see me. He wanted to know how I was and I told him okay. He said he had come by because he hadn't seen me for a while. He wanted to know if I was pregnant and I told him I wasn't.

He said, "You know, you're probably pregnant." I asked what made him say that and he said because I had been a virgin and we had made love several times and he was a pretty virile male. He said, "I come from a very large, fertile family."

I looked at him and said, "And what if I am?"

"Well," he replied, "I guess I'd just have to marry you."

For some reason, when he said that, it just rubbed me the wrong way. He sounded so cocky and arrogant and I just got mad. I looked at him and said the words that would change my life forever. I said, "I wouldn't marry you if you were the last man on earth! And, besides that, I'm too young to even think about getting married. After my sister had to get married, my parents would just die if I did that to them!" He didn't know what to say and I knew I had not said what was in my heart, but neither of us spoke. Finally he said he had to go and left.

After that, I only saw him when I went to fill up my car. Then, one Friday, I stopped at the station to pay my weekly bill and he sent his cousin out to my car instead of coming to the car himself. I asked where Jimmy was and his cousin said, "Jimmy asked me to tell you that he is getting married next week."

I was dumbfounded. I looked away and composed myself before I asked who he was marrying. He said Jimmy had met a woman at a bar who was seven months pregnant and he felt sorry for her so they were getting married. I told his cousin to tell Jimmy that I hoped he would be happy and I drove away. As I drove off, I looked into the station and saw Jimmy standing there watching me leave. By the time I had pulled out of the station, the tears were flowing, but I was proud of myself because I hadn't let his cousin see how hurt I had been.

After that, I felt as if I hated Jimmy, but I hated myself, too. I was determined to get back at him. I wanted to hurt him the same way he had hurt me. What fools we are at seventeen! This started what I refer to as my "love 'em and leave 'em" stage. I went out with two of his cousins and slept with them. In my naïve way, I thought that when he found out, he would be hurt. I never realized that I was only hurting myself. Then I started meeting other guys and going out with them. I was playing a very dangerous game. I would tease them and make promises to them that I knew I would never keep. Then, just when they were getting really serious or were at the point of expecting more than petting and necking, I would drop them like a hot potato. I wouldn't even take their calls. I guess I was trying to get back at the whole male population for what one man had done to me. I spent a lot of time the next couple of years going from one relationship to another, feeling empty inside and hating myself more and more.

    I just couldn't stop thinking about Jimmy and how he had betrayed the love I had for him. I even convinced myself that the only reason he had married that woman was because she was pregnant and that would keep him from being drafted and going to Vietnam. For years, I believed that to be the reason and it made my heart a little less heavy to believe it. All I ever really wanted since I was just a small child was to be loved and needed. I guess I wanted a knight in shining armor to come and whisk me away to a never-ending happiness. Instead of that, I was alone and miserable.

~Chapter 3~

I really wanted to become either a schoolteacher or a lawyer, but I knew there was no way I could afford the cost of college. My dad told me he could borrow the money, but he had worked so hard all his life, I just couldn't bring myself to make him go into debt. So, I settled for going to business school. Near the end of my senior year in high school, I took a test given by one of the business schools in Dallas and scored a hundred. My picture was on the front page of the hometown newspaper with an article about me, because I was the only person who had ever made a perfect score on the test. Jimmy couldn't believe my picture was in the paper until I showed it to him. He was so impressed. The business school was about one mile from my dad's barbershop. I didn't have the money to pay to park my car in a parking garage or lot every day, so the only way I could even afford to take advantage of the scholarship I had been given was to drive to Dad's shop, park there and walk to rest of the way to the school. It was not easy to walk that far in the hot Texas summer sun in high heels. I did it for three months and then decided it was not worth it because it was just a review of everything I had spent four years learning in high school, so I dropped out. I wanted to get a real job and earn some money. During the time that I went to school, I was also working part-time in the evenings at a discount department store.

After I quit business school, I got a job at the gift shop at the airport. I worked there with Darla, a friend from school, and Mellie, a girl from Mississippi. We worked from two in the afternoon till ten in the evening, and then partied after work nearly every night. It was because of Darla and Mellie that I started going to bars and drinking. The alcohol helped me to forget the pain I felt after Jimmy got married.

My mother's uncle and aunt who had raised her now lived in Florida. One day we got a call that her uncle had had one of his legs amputated due to his diabetes. It was decided that my mother, father and I would drive to Florida to visit them. At the time, I was dating a pilot named Jay, who worked for American Airlines, and whom I was really crazy about. My friend, Darla, was dating his brother, Frank, who worked in the luggage handling section of American Airlines. The four of us double-dated. I was gone for a week and when I came back and went in to work, Frank stopped by the gift stand and welcomed me back. I noticed that he and Darla didn't speak at all, and I asked him about it. He said to meet him for lunch and he would tell me all about it. At lunchtime, I met him in the café. Because I hadn't seen Jay all day long I asked Frank where he was. He said that Jay was probably avoiding me. When I asked why, he said that Darla and Jay had been seeing each other and sleeping together every night since I had been gone. I was so angry I didn't know what to do. Here I thought she was my friend and she had betrayed me!

Darla worked in one gift shop and I worked in the other. After lunch, I went to where she was and confronted her. I said that I thought she and Frank were a couple and she laughed and said she had only been dating Frank to be near Jay. She admitted that they had been dating but that he didn't mean anything to her any more. She said that if I had wanted him so badly that I should have slept with him like she did. I was so angry I was shaking. I hated both of them at that moment and I told her, "First of all, if I have to sleep with a man to keep him, I don't need him. But I thought you were my friend...I trusted you! I'll get back at you some day. Until then, steer a wide path when you see me coming because I don't know what I might do to you if I get close enough to get hold of you." I started walking away and stopped. I turned back and told her, "Oh, and one other thing. I wouldn't have a man who had slept with you behind my back. You can have him." Then I went back to work.

Later that evening, Jay had the nerve to come by the gift stand and talk to me. He acted as if nothing had happened and wanted to know if we were going out that night after I got off. I just looked at him for a couple of minutes before I was composed enough to speak. First, I gave him the alligator belt he had asked me to get for him in Florida. Then I looked him square in the eye and told him I would never go out with him again. He acted so innocent and asked why I was acting that way. I told him that I knew about him and Darla.

He said, "Oh, I just used her to have sex. You know how I feel about you." He made it so easy. I laughed, which made him mad. Then I said that maybe he needed to continue to use her because he wasn't going to use me. I turned my back and said I needed to get back to work. He just stood there for a few minutes. I guess he didn't know what to say and he had probably never had a woman break up with him before. I was hurt and angry and yet a little proud of myself because I had stood up to both of them. I told Mellie that I needed to go to the restroom. I went in and locked myself into a stall and cried. After a few minutes, I was composed enough to go back to work. Jay stopped by the gift stand several times after that day. I was polite but cool towards him and he eventually stopped asking me out.

There was a security guard named Phil at the airport who always wanted me to go to dinner with him. He was tall and skinny with red hair and a big long pointy nose, which he seemed to talk through. I was not the least bit interested in him but he just would not leave me alone. I got off work at six P.M.

The girls I worked with kept telling me to go. They said I could get a nice dinner for free and after that I could tell him I just didn't want to see him anymore. Well, it sounded like a plan to me, so I told him I would go. He was to pick me up at my house around seven-thirty that night. I told my parents to tell him that I had a ten o'clock curfew and he needed to have me home by then. I was a little old for a ten o'clock curfew but they told him that and he believed it.

After work, I went home and changed into a nice dress because I assumed we would be going to a nice restaurant. He picked me up and we drove into Dallas. I asked him where we were going to eat and he said it was his favorite place. Imagine my surprise when he pulled into the drive-up window of the Pig Stop and ordered both of us a hot dog and coke! I was stunned. This was the great dinner he had wanted to buy for me all this time? I couldn't believe I had let my friends talk me into going on this date with him. After we ate, we drove around and talked. He wanted to go "parking" and I told him that I had a headache and wanted to go home. At least he was a nice person and he took me straight home.

The next day at work everyone wanted to know how the dinner was and where he took me. They couldn't believe that he had taken me out for a hot dog! Of course, everyone got a big laugh out of it and I told them I would never listen to any of them again. It seems that Phil used that line on girls to get dates because he was such a dork that no one wanted to go out with him.

After the incident with Jay, Darla avoided me, I assumed because she was afraid I would hurt her. Little did she know that I was all talk and it hadn't taken me long to get over it and soon started dating someone else. Mellie and Darla moved into an apartment together and Darla and I agreed to be pleasant to each other whenever we were all there.

At this time, I was dating three different guys: Roger, Mike and Smitty. I liked all of them, but didn't know which one I liked the best. None of them knew that I about the others. Then one weekend, Mellie and Darla decided to have a party. I had invited Smitty to the party but he didn't know if he would make it or not. So Darla and Mellie got the bright idea that they would also invite Roger and Mike, without telling me, and that out of the three of them, surely one would show up.

Everything was going great about an hour into the party, when the doorbell rang. Imagine my surprise to find Roger and his twin brother at the door. I thought to myself that since Roger was already there that now, hopefully, Smitty wouldn't show up. A few minutes later, the doorbell rang again and there stood Mike. I didn't know what to do. I couldn't figure out how either one of them had found out about the party and I certainly didn't know what to say to either of them. Roger was cool about it and said he would just wander around and find someone else to spend the evening with, but Mike was angry. I was trying to explain to him that I didn't know that the girls had invited him and that I had invited Roger.

Just when I thought I had things smoothed over with Mike, in walks Smitty and gives me a big hug and kiss. When he realized that I was with Mike, he told me that he couldn't stay and just wanted to pop in for a minute and he left. I was so hurt and embarrassed. I finally realized that out of the three guys, Smitty was the one that I really wanted there and he was the one who was walking out.

That was the last straw. I turned and walked over to Mellie and Darla who were having a good laugh. I told them I couldn't believe they had done that to me. When they saw how upset I was, they realized that the joke wasn't as funny as they thought it would be. They tried to apologize and said they would straighten everything out but I ran into the bathroom and locked myself in. I sat in the bathroom and cried and tried to figure out a way to get out of the situation but I couldn't think of anything. I stayed locked in there until the party ended. When I finally came out, Darla and Mellie told me they were so sorry about inviting Mike and Roger. They said they had done it because they were afraid Smitty wouldn't show up and I would be alone. They said I should have come out of the bathroom because Roger and Mike ended up being cool about the whole situation and everyone had a good time. I dated Roger a number of times after that, but Mike and I never dated again, and, as for

Smitty, he was seeing someone else anyway so I didn't see him that often after that night.

After the incident with Jay and Darla, and then with this party fiasco, I decided that having women friends wasn't all it was cracked up to be. They stab you in the back at the drop of a hat. After that, I never let myself get close to another woman. I have had female friends over the years but have never let myself confide in them or get too close. I don't trust women and I won't work for a woman. I just can't bring myself to be in a situation where another woman has the upper hand.

Mellie and I usually partied together because Darla was dating a married man and she was with him most of the time. One day Mellie and I decided we could make more money if we danced at a club. Well, what an eye-opener that was! The first interview we went on, the guy handed us these skimpy little bikinis that barely covered anything. He said to go into the restroom and put them on and then come out and show him what we had. Well, we took the bikinis into the restroom and started laughing from embarrassment. Finally, we decided that this just wasn't the job for us so we left the costumes in the bathroom and went out the back door.

Mellie and I frequented a bar called the White Cloud where I met Joe. Joe was quiet and had a lot of interesting friends. We got along really well together, except that he drank too much. One of his friends was Harry Havana, whom we nicknamed Harry Banana. He was a pool shark and a member of the local Mafia. He taught me how to play pool and the three of us would go to different bars and hustle pool for money. I thought it was all really exciting. We would go into a bar and Joe would get into a game and not play well. Then, he would set up a game and ask me to be his partner. I would say something like: "I'm not very good, but I'll play."

We very seldom lost. One night, Harry took us to a place we had never been before and he set up the game. We ended up winning five hundred dollars and then said we had to go. The guys we were playing with then realized that they had been hustled and one of them pulled out a gun. Harry confronted the guys and we ran out. That incident put an end to my pool hustling days. For some reason, the sight of a gun pointed at me made the game a little less exciting. Or maybe too exciting!

~Chapter 4~

There was a band at the White Cloud and Mellie and I became friends with the band members and their girl friends. The leader, Jamie, was Hispanic and he and I started talking a lot. He would sing special songs just for me. One night we ended up at his house and I spent the night there. I didn't know that he lived with his mother until the next morning when we got up. Here I was looking a mess, no makeup, clothes all rumpled, and we walk into the kitchen. There stands his mother cooking breakfast. I was so embarrassed that I didn't know what to say or do. Then I realized that she couldn't speak English and I couldn't speak Spanish, so we couldn't really communicate. She fed me breakfast and I left as soon as possible after that. I think that was probably the most humiliated that I had been in a very long time. I could just imagine what she thought of me and what she was saying to him about me when I was there and couldn't understand her.

Jamie and I dated for only a short time after that. One night he came over to the house to pick me up for a date. My parents were there and I knew my mother did not like it because he was Hispanic, so I laid it on thick. I sat on his lap and we cuddled and smooched. Then I looked at him lovingly and said, "You know, we could just go off and get married. Wouldn't that be fun?"

He said, "Yeah, we could do that. We'll talk about it later." Right after that we left for our date. Neither of my parents ever mentioned the incident, but I know my mother, at least, was rattled by it. I thought it was so funny. Of course, I would have never married him because he was on the rebound and I knew it was just a matter of time before he and his ex would get back together again.

There was another patron of the White Cloud that I used to drink with. His name was Dino and he was a pastry chef at one of the big department stores in downtown Dallas. He was a big, sexy Italian guy whom everyone joked with about his ancestry. Every time he came in someone would say, 'Never let a Dago by' and he would laugh along with everybody else. He was in his late thirties and was married to a woman who looked to be about fifty. Her name was Sheila. Dino was fascinating to talk to. He liked me, but not in a sexual way. We were just friends. We talked a lot about food and cooking and he loved to share his recipes. Sheila told me that she was also a chef. I thought it strange that she was a chef and yet she would be out of town for two weeks every month. What kind of place let a chef work only two weeks a month? I finally found out.

One day, Dino said he had to take a ride across town to check on some business, and asked if I wanted to go along. I was kind of afraid to go with him, but he promised nothing would happen and said he just wanted some company. Finally, I said I would go. When we got to our destination, it was a sleazy bar with strippers and nude dancers, which was not an acceptable hangout for decent people in the sixties and seventies. I was ashamed to walk into the place, but because of the location of the bar, there was no way I would stay behind in the car by myself. I asked him why we were there and he replied that he had to check up on his girls. I was so naïve. I asked what he meant and he said he had girls that worked there, they were his harem and he managed them. I just assumed he was like a talent agent. How wrong I was!

Later, when we returned to the White Cloud it all came together for me. After Dino dropped me off, I was having a drink and asked Jerry to come over and sit in my booth. He asked me what I had been doing with Dino and I told him. He said, "Stay away from him. It's okay to talk to him in here, but don't ever leave with him again."

"But, Jerry, Dino's a nice guy," I countered back.

He laughed and said, "Yeah, he's a nice guy, but he's trouble and you don't need his kind of trouble."

I replied, "Okay, 'Dad,' but tell me this. Why does Dino have a harem?"

He laughed and said, "Boy, you really are naïve. He's a pimp and his harem is the whores that work for him."

I couldn't believe what he was telling me. "You're kidding," I replied, but from the look on his face I knew he wasn't. So, ignorant me, I asked the next stupid question. "So, what does Sheila think about him being a pimp?" Jerry just looked at me for a minute and then burst out laughing.

When he finally quit laughing, he said, "Honey, Sheila is his biggest money maker! He sends her off to a whorehouse down in San Antonio once a month. She stays for two weeks and then comes back. Where did you think he got all the money they are always throwing around on clothes and jewelry and things? You didn't really think that chefs made that much, did you?"

I felt really stupid. I didn't know how to answer him because, yes, I did think they made their money working as chefs. While Dino really was a chef, Sheila wasn't. I was just in shock. I couldn't believe that I had been associating with a pimp and his whore and didn't even know it! After that, I avoided both of them. I was just so ashamed to think that someone might see me with them and know how they made their money and associate me with them.

One night Dino came over and sat across from me in the booth. He said, "I've noticed you have been avoiding me. I talked to Jerry and he said he told you about me. And that's okay. But, I just want you to know that you don't have to avoid me. I like you. You're a good kid and I have the utmost respect for you. If I had a daughter, I would want her to be just like you. I would never, let me repeat, *never*, try to get you to join my harem. I just want to be your friend."

Like I said, Dino was a really likeable person. He sounded sincere and I said "Okay…friends." After that, if we were at the White Cloud at the same time, I would talk to him and we would joke around like before, but I made a point of moving away from him as soon as possible without being rude.

The thought never occurred to me that if I hadn't been hanging out in a place I really had no business being in, I wouldn't have had to worry about the type of people I was associating with. It wasn't until a couple of other incidents occurred that I finally realized that these were not the types of people I really wanted to be with. It was just that, at that point in my life, I needed to be a part of a group and these people had always treated me like I was one of them. The older ones were always very protective of me and I felt safe and secure when I was with them.

The owner of the White Cloud, Jerry, was in his forties. He and his wife treated me like a daughter. When they separated, he moved in and shared an apartment with Gary and Roy. One night he invited a group of us over after the bar closed. A couple of us were cooking breakfast for everyone when Roy started shooting a pistol in the air in the parking lot. They got him into the apartment before the police came and took the gun away from him. Someone stuck it down behind the cushion of the sofa to hide it. Of course, when the police came, everyone said they didn't know anything about a gun and the police left.

Jerry also had a girl living with him. She was the daughter of a hooker he knew. I found out later that she was only fourteen. Her name was Carla and she was there that night sitting on the arm of the sofa. At some point, someone reached behind the cushion to retrieve the pistol and it went off. She jumped up and kept saying, "I've been hit! I've been hit!" No one believed her because there wasn't any blood. Finally, I looked and sure enough there was a hole in her thigh. We called an ambulance for her and, of course, the police arrived with the ambulance. The bullet had gone into her thigh and traveled up into her stomach cavity. When the police came, no one would say anything about what happened, so we all got to take a trip to the police station. Everyone kept saying, "Just tell them you don't know what happened. You don't know anything." I didn't know what to do. Here I was, nineteen years old and the only crime I had ever committed was underage drinking and a little pool hustling. Heck, the only traffic ticket I had ever gotten was for going over the speed limit to pass a tractor! Now I was facing the possibility of going to jail just for being at the wrong place at the right time.

The detectives took each of us to a separate room and questioned us. The one I talked to was very nice. It didn't take him long to convince me to "sing like a bird". He said to tell him what really happened and we could all go home. So, I told him just what did happen. Not long after that, we all got to leave. No one knew which one of us told, because the detectives didn't tell anyone. The detective told me to take a good look at the people I was hanging out with, because they could get me into a lot more trouble than what I had been into that night. Since it had been an accident, no charges were filed against anyone. When we left the station, we all went to the hospital to check on Carla. They had to cut her open to remove the bullet and check to make sure nothing had been damaged. Fortunately, it missed all of her vital organs and the baby she was carrying. We found out that night that Jerry had gotten her pregnant. She carried the baby to full term and gave it up for adoption when it was born.

I figured I should call my parents and tell them what was going on. When I called and told them that Carla had gotten shot and we were at the hospital, I figured they would be worried or something, but they were just upset that I had called and woke them up so early in the morning.

~Chapter 5~

Sometimes I would tend the bar for Jerry when he didn't have anyone to work it. One night I was behind the bar, and in walked Smitty. I hadn't seen him in over a year and I couldn't imagine how he had found me there. He told me he had called the house and my mom told him I was at the White Cloud. He stayed until the bar closed and then we stood by our cars and talked. He said that he had just wanted to see me. His mother lived with him and she was dying and he wanted someone to talk to. He asked if I wanted to go to his house and have a pizza. I told him that I would. We ate the pizza and then sat on the sofa and talked. Smitty was twelve years older than I was. I had met him when I was seventeen and we had dated a few times. He had always been a perfect gentleman and he always took me to the movies and to nice restaurants. We made out just like any other couple, but he had never tried to force himself on me. We were never intimate, but there had always been something special between us.

I felt so sorry for him because of his mother. He was crying and I put my arms around him and kissed him. I knew that this night was going to be different. He needed me that night and I wanted him so badly. Nothing could have stopped us. It was an experience I can't describe. I thought by loving him I could take away all the hurt he was feeling, even though I knew in my heart that I would probably never see him again after that night, I never did.

Once Joe told me he loved me and if I would lose thirty pounds, he would marry me. Well, I really thought I loved this man and I went on a diet immediately. One night I reminded him that he had said he would marry me if I would lose thirty pounds and that I had lost fifty. Joe said,

"I love you and you look great, but I don't want to get married. I've been married once and I'll never do it again." I didn't know what to say, so, of course, I said nothing. I should have just told him it was over then and walked away, but I didn't.

We continued seeing each other for almost two years. Eventually, I realized that even though he had a steady job, the only thing he did was work, drink and party. He smoked pot and popped pills which was something I never even considered doing. Once when we were at the bar, he asked me to drive him down to the drug store. We went in and I bought a couple of things. He told me to go on out and he would be out in a minute. Well, I paid for my things and went out to the car. When I started to get in, some kid ran out and said, "I wouldn't get in that car if I were you." I asked why not and he told me that some guy had just stolen a bunch of sunglasses and put them in the glove box.

I told him, "Well, this is my car and I don't want those glasses." I opened the glove box, pulled out the glasses and handed them to the guy. Then I drove off. I went back to the bar and found out later that someone had dared Joe to steal the glasses and he ended up getting arrested for it. Fool that I am, that still didn't do it for me. I continued to see him until one day he asked me to drive him to a park across town. When we got there we went over and sat on the swings. I asked what we were doing and he told me we were waiting for a friend of his. Then the guy finally showed up. He was this scroungy-looking Hispanic guy. Later I found out that I had taken Joe to the park so he could buy a bag of marijuana. That did it for me. I finally told Joe that it would probably be best if we started seeing other people. He got mad and left.

Even though I was the one to make the break, I was upset and it took me quite a while to get over it. I still hung out at the White Cloud and we ran into each other there often—but I avoided him when I could and he did the same. One night I was really upset over breaking up with him. Jerry was off that night and said he and Gary were going out club hopping and that I should join them to get my mind off of Joe. I bought a fifth of Windsor Canadian and we went to the Pussy Cat Club.

We ran into Harry Havana. He had his saxophone with him and started playing songs for me because he knew I loved the sax. After he quit playing, he came over and joined the three of us at the bar. I usually drank bourbon and coke, but that night the guys kept trying to get me to take shots with them. I really didn't like shots because I don't like the taste of straight liquor. Finally, they bet me that I wouldn't tip up the bottle and take a big swig. Never one to back down, I finally tipped up the bottle and took a big drink. It burned my throat and brought tears to my eyes. I set the bottle down and said, "There!" The bottle was brown and you couldn't really see how much was in it so none of them realized how big a drink I had really taken. They kept goading me and saying that I hadn't really drunk any. After a couple of minutes, I was really feeling the liquor. They kept saying things like, "You stuck your tongue in the bottle and just pretended to drink. Do it again and this time take a big drink." Well, I was drunk and so I did it again. When I set the bottle down this time, it was half gone. I had drunk one half of the fifth in two drinks.

A few minutes later, I had to throw up and went to the ladies room. About fifteen minutes later, I passed out. Jerry and Gary had to come into the ladies room and carry me out to my car. They put me in the backseat and I never woke up all night while they went and partied. They left me lying in the back seat and went to two or three other clubs before going back to their apartment. By this time, I was awake enough for them to get me out of the car and into the apartment. I vomited in the car, on the ground and all over the floor in their apartment. They finally made me lie down on the sofa with an ice pack on my head. They went to bed.

About five A.M. I woke up and thought I should call my parents. I told my dad that I was sick and I was going to stay there until I felt better and then I would be home. My brother was living at home after returning home from the Air Force and my dad said they would come and get me. Why of all times he decided to do this, I don't know. At any rate, they drove all the way across town and took my car and me home. This was early on a Sunday morning.

The following Friday my brother was getting married and I was to be in his wedding. I was sick all week and could barely stand up during the wedding ceremony. My parents never guessed that I was sick because of drinking too much. They thought it was just a stomach virus or something and I never told them the truth. When I thought about what I had done, it occurred to me that I could have died from alcohol poisoning. After that, just the thought of having a drink was enough to make me want to vomit. I didn't drink anything after that for quite a while. In fact, I quit going out at all.

I stayed away from the bar for a week and then went back. The people there were the only ones I knew how to socialize with, so I went back to be with them. Joe was sitting at the bar and I said hello to him as I walked past, but he just ignored me. He finished his drink and left. About a week later, I was sitting in a booth when he came in and he sat down across from me. He asked how I had been and said he understood why I had broken up with him. He said he wanted to be friends and wanted for us to both be able to be in the bar without problems. So we agreed to be pleasant to each other. Sometimes it was hard being there and seeing him and not being with him, but the worst time was if he was with someone else. I would get upset and usually left the bar. It took quite a while, but I eventually got over him.

One night Jerry and Gary asked a group of us over to their apartment when the bar closed and we all agreed. We had only been there for a while when Jerry said they were all going to go back out to a club that was still open. I decided I would just go home instead. I went to the bathroom before leaving and when I came out, everyone was gone except Roy. Since the incident with the gun, I really didn't want to be around him, so I went to get my purse and leave but he blocked my way. He asked me to stay and talk to him for a little while. I told him I really needed to go, but he grabbed my arm and said I was going to stay. He shoved me into his bedroom and down onto the bed. I was terrified to do anything because I knew he had a gun in there. He started kissing me and putting his hands all over my body. I cried and asked him to stop, but he just laughed and said, "You know you want this as much as I do."

I tried to get away from him and he grabbed my hair and yanked my head back and said that I shouldn't do anything foolish. I wasn't sure what he meant by that, but I certainly didn't want to find out. He started undressing me and I started crying and asking him to just let me leave. Of course, he didn't. He just climbed on top of me and had his way. Afterwards, he got angry because I didn't have an orgasm! He slapped me across the face and called me a bitch. I started crying and told him I was sorry and asked him not to hit me again. He called me a bitch and shoved me off the bed and told me to get the hell out of there and not to tell anyone or I would be sorry. I hurriedly got dressed and ran out of there and got into my car.

Once in my car, I locked the doors and cried my heart out. I wanted to tell someone, but I was afraid that he would come after me and shoot me or do it again, so I just went home. And besides, I didn't think it would do any good to tell anyone anyway. I thought back to the time when I was seventeen. All the kids hung out at the Dairy Mart. That is where girls and guys met each other. I had met a guy there by the name of Larry. We had gone out on a few dates and he hadn't made any sexual advances toward me, so I never expected what happened one night when I ran into him. He was standing beside my car and the window was down. We were talking and out of the blue he said to me, "Let's go fuck." At this time, I was still a young innocent virgin. That was a word that was never used around me and I was quite offended. I did what I had seen the modern day movie heroine do. I slapped his face and told him not to talk to me like that. Wrong move! He jerked my door open, kicked me in the ribs and walked off. Well, I went home and told my parents what had happened and my mother said we would go to the doctor the next day. Dad said nothing. The doctor determined that I had two broken ribs. I wanted to file charges against him and my parents told me to go ahead and do it. They wouldn't go with me, however. I went to the City Attorney's office and filed the charges but later dropped them, because I was afraid to go to court by myself and my parents didn't seem interested enough to go with me. So, I figured it would be useless to tell anyone what had happened to me tonight with the rape.

After that night, I quit going to the White Cloud and quit hanging around the people I knew from there. Mellie had moved back to Mississippi and I didn't really have anyone to go out with, so I just stayed home. About a month later, I was watching the news on TV. The news reporter came on with an announcement that the First National Bank in downtown Dallas had been robbed that morning. The reporter said that the bank robber had walked into the bank wearing a bright red sweater. He had the teller put the money in a paper sack and took off down the street. Well, it didn't take them long to catch him. That red sweater really stood out in the crowd. I couldn't believe my eyes when they showed the robber. It was Roy! I just couldn't understand why anyone would rob a bank, much less someone like Roy. His father owned a car dealership and he had all the money he wanted. I guess he did it for the attention. I did feel a little satisfaction, however, in knowing that he would be going to prison for this crime. At least he would be off the streets and not able to hurt anyone else the way he had hurt me, at least not for a number of years.

~Chapter 6~

Here I was, once more alone and lonely. My brother was married. My sister was married. I was single and spending the best years of my life living at home with a father who sat around in his underwear watching television all night, and a mother who had decided a couple of years earlier to drink her way through menopause. I had a job and made decent money, but couldn't afford to move out on my own. I had a car to drive, but if I moved out I would have to leave the car behind. It wasn't mine. It was just mine to use. While I made good money, I didn't make enough for a car payment and rent, too, so I seemed to be stuck.

Several months after this incident, I decided to go to the White Cloud just to see some of my old drinking buddies. While I was there, someone told me that Joe had been asking about me and he had asked them if they would give me his address if I ever came in again. I took the address, but never meant to use it. After a couple of drinks, I decided to go home. Of course, I had to drive by the apartment complex where Joe lived just to see where it was. Once there, I decided I would go to the apartment and see if he was home. He was there and told me he was watching television in the bedroom and asked me to go back there with him. I knew I shouldn't do it, but I did. He started kissing me, telling me how much he had missed me and, of course, we ended up having sex.

Immediately afterwards he told me I had to get dressed and leave because he was living with a woman and it was almost time for her to come home from work. I was so hurt, humiliated and disgusted all at the same time. He asked if I would come by again and I looked at him and said, "Not in this lifetime!" I think a little part of me died that night when I realized that he was only using me for sex, and I vowed I would never let that happen again. I vowed that no man would ever use me again. If only I had been able to keep that vow!

I was working as a secretary in downtown Dallas and decided to try to find a job closer to home. I found one that paid much more than the one I had. Imagine my surprise when I walked in the office the first day and there sat a girl named Flo. Flo had been a patron of the White Cloud and had also been a dancer at the Purple Onion. We had gone to watch her dance one night and she had danced in almost nothing—a little g-string and pasties. I just didn't know what to say to her. I never expected to meet one of those dancers working in an office. At break time, Flo came over, pulled me aside and said we needed to talk. She explained to me that no one there knew about her dancing. She said she did it for extra money to pay for school and they would fire her if they found out. I told her I wouldn't tell anyone and I never did.

I really hated my new job and the man I worked for was a real jerk. Today, I could probably file some kind of discrimination charges against him, but back then you just had to "grin and bear it." I had worked at this job for only a month when I got ill. It seems that Mick, my brother-in-law, had caught hepatitis from someone at work and didn't know he had it. My sister, brother-in-law and their kids all came to visit. A few days later I got very sick and found out that I had contracted hepatitis from being around Mick when he had it. I didn't think I would ever get rid of it and I ended up being housebound for three months.

After I was off work for a month, I received a letter in the mail saying that my job had been terminated. I really wasn't that upset because I had hated the job and I got some satisfaction in knowing that everyone there had been required to take a painful shot because they had been exposed to hepatitis.

During the time I was sick, I decided it was time to make a change in my life. After recovering, I enrolled in cosmetology school. I went to school from eight to five during the day and then worked the soda fountain at a hamburger place from six to midnight and on Saturdays and Sundays. That is where I met Keith.

He worked at the service station next door and came in every day to eat. We started talking and, eventually, started dating. We had only known each other a couple of months when he suggested that we get married. Well, I liked him well enough and sex with him was like "wham, bam, thank you, ma'am" and it was over, so I wouldn't have to be concerned about performing for him and faking orgasms. After the bad sexual experiences I had encountered, I still enjoyed sex but never seemed to climax. After a while, I realized the quickie sex with Keith was not enough. It left me sexually frustrated and I didn't know how to fix the problem. But marrying him would get me away from my dull existence and I wouldn't be alone, so I said yes. Fatal mistake! We met in August and got married in November. We had a small wedding at my parents' house. It was on my mother's birthday, a day we selected because it was Keith's day off and because it would be an easy anniversary date to remember.

Well, being married to Keith was no picnic. It's really true that you don't really know someone until you live with them. I found out quickly that he drank too much and he was abusive. I would go to the grocery store and come home and he would say that I had gone to meet some man even though I came home with bags of groceries. Then, he would shove me around and put his hands around my throat and try to choke me.

When he was late coming home from work, I always knew he was drinking. On those nights, I never went to bed before he came home because I was afraid I would fall asleep and he would do something to me while I was sleeping. I felt that it would be better to be awake when he came in. I would try to appease him by offering to fix him something to eat and get him something to drink, but it never worked. He would start accusing me of having an affair and then start shoving me into the walls and hitting me. I always thought he did this because he was, in fact, seeing other women and it helped him to get over the guilt by accusing me of doing what he was doing. There were times that I had to wear long-sleeved shirts in the summer time to hide bruises on my arms. I was ashamed and embarrassed and I did not want anyone to know that he hit me. But, my generation was brought up to believe that marriage was forever. No matter what the situation, when you got married you stayed married. So now I was trapped.

~Chapter 7~

At the time we got married, I was working in a beauty salon and Keith was working at a service station. I worked days from eight to five and he worked from ten in the morning till midnight. We never got to see each other, so he wanted me to quit my job and I did. We had only been married a month the first time he didn't come home from work. I assumed he was out drinking. No one knew where to find him. After three days, I left our apartment and went back to my parents' house. After a week, I moved all of our things out of the apartment. When he finally came back to the apartment and found it empty, he was fit to be tied. He couldn't understand why I had moved everything out. I told him I didn't think he was coming back and I couldn't afford the apartment on my own.

    I stayed with my parents for a couple of weeks and then found out I was pregnant. Well, as soon as my mother found out, all she could do was ask when I was going back to Keith. She said I really needed to think of the baby and try to work things out. Finally, against my better judgment, we decided to try it again and we rented a house. It was a horrible old house that had cockroaches and rats and no air conditioning.

    Shortly after we moved in, Keith's older brother, Lou, showed up from Illinois and Keith invited him to stay with us. Of course, I was expected to cook for and clean up after him, as well. Let me tell you, Texas in the summer with the temperature hitting over one hundred degrees every day with no air conditioning is not pleasant; to be pregnant and have to put up with two drunks on top of it is definitely enough to put one over the edge. I don't know how I kept my sanity. They were constantly drinking and, of course, Keith would have to put on his big-man drunken act for his brother. He would start pushing me around and being a jerk to show off for Lou. I didn't have a car, so I was stuck sitting at the house all day with his brother, while Keith was at work...when he worked.

    Keith had been working at a service station when I met him. Before that he had been a truck driver. During the course of our marriage, he held jobs driving a dump truck for a gravel pit, working as a carpenter's helper, a plumber's helper, laborer for the electric company and the gas company, siding installer, sprinkler system installer, car salesman, mechanic and he drove a truck for a soft drink company, among others. He never stayed at any job more than a few weeks because he couldn't stay away from alcohol. He would do well for a couple of weeks and then the next payday would come. He would go to work that morning and then I wouldn't see him for two or three days or until his check was totally spent on alcohol. I found out that when he came back to Texas after our divorce, he was working as a grave digger for a cemetery until his heart condition made it impossible for him to do any kind of hard labor type work and that was all he had ever learned to do.

    When I was seven months pregnant, I pulled into a service station one night to get gas. I almost fainted when the gas attendant walked up to the car and it was Jimmy Lee. I was speechless. Neither of us could believe our eyes. We talked for a long time. He told me he had missed me. Then he asked me to leave my husband and go to Oklahoma with him. He said we could start over and have a good life. I said I thought he was married and he said he was but it just wasn't working out. I told him, "I'm seven months pregnant. My family just wouldn't understand if I did something like that. I need to try to work things out and make a life for my baby."

He asked me again to just go with him and said he would make a life for my baby and me. He asked for my phone number. He said to think it over and he would call me, but I just couldn't bring myself to be unfaithful even though I wasn't happy. I wanted to say yes, but all I could think of was what people would say and what my family would think if I had run off with him. Over the years I have often wondered what my life would have been like if I had followed my heart and said yes to him that night.

Unfortunately, I didn't waiver in my conviction and I drove off—back to my life of hell. The only thing good in my life at that time was the baby I was carrying. I wanted it so badly, but there were times that I thought it probably would have been better if I had never gotten pregnant. I did not know what the future would bring for me or the baby I was carrying. I faced night after night of being tormented and just trying to stay out of my husband's way. It was like walking a tightrope trying to not say the wrong thing that would set Keith off on one of his rages. All I had to do was answer a question wrong and I could look forward to being hit or kicked or shoved into the wall. I can't tell you how many holes I had to patch in the walls, and the windows and mirrors I had to replace because he busted them out with his fists. One night he came home so drunk he could barely walk and he still wanted to drink. There was nothing in the house, so he got a bottle of rubbing alcohol and drank most of it. It is a wonder he didn't die, but all it did was make him vomit. And, of course, I had to clean that up, too.

I had a beautiful baby girl, Deirdre, whom we called Dee-Dee for short, followed by Jaycie two years later and Shelly a year after her. When I had my first two babies, my mother came to the hospital. She would come into the labor room with me and I would pretend to fall asleep so she would leave. I just couldn't allow myself to let her know that I was in pain. I should have left Keith long before that, but I couldn't move back home. I lived in a town with no public transportation so I was stuck at home all day with three kids, no money and no car. What was I supposed to do?

Sometimes he would come home in the middle of the night after drinking all day and pull me out of bed. He would rant and rave and start shoving and hitting me. One time he started choking me and calling me by his first wife's name. I was finally able to convince him I was not her and was not like her and he let me go. The only problem was that after he was finished with his drunken rages, he was ready to have sex and go to sleep. I can't count the times that he forced me to have sex with him when I didn't want to.

The day I went into labor with my first child it was one hundred and five degrees. I had done laundry and hung it on the line to dry, picked beans at my parents' house and fixed them for the freezer. I was tired, hot and irritable and having labor pains and Keith wanted me to fix him a steak. I told him I thought I would just go lie down. Well, that started him up. Finally, I convinced him that I was in labor and I didn't know what to do. We had not had the money to pay the doctor so I had quit going to see him at my sixth month. He called my parents and my dad said he would pay the bill so I could go to the hospital. I was only in labor about six hours total when Dee-Dee arrived. She was early and only weighed six pounds, but she was the most beautiful thing I had ever laid eyes on.

About two weeks after Dee-Dee was born, Keith's mother, stepdad and younger brother came to visit us from Illinois. They stayed for three days. It was the first time I had ever met any of his family except for his older brother. We got along okay. After they left, things went back to normal. I was stuck at home all day taking care of the baby, being miserable from the heat and putting up with his drunken brother.

The house we lived in was heated by gas space heaters and it was not very warm in the winter. I remember one night in December it was cold and rainy all day. That night a fog set in. I was in the house alone with Dee-Dee all day and Keith never came home from work. I knew he was out drinking and it made me so mad. I don't know why I did it, but I decided to drink all of his beer. He had a whole case of it in the refrigerator and I started drinking it. By the time he made it home the whole case was gone. I had the cans stacked up in front of me like a pyramid. He was so angry that he started hitting me and choking me and I picked up a pair of scissors and tried to stab him with them. That, of course, made him madder. He went in the bathroom and I picked up Dee-Dee and got my purse. I went out and got into the little Ford Ranchero my dad was letting us use and started to back out of the driveway. Well, he came running out yelling and screaming and I finally told him I was leaving and he couldn't stop me because it was my dad's truck. Finally he backed away and I started backing out. He started walking toward the house and at that moment I hated him so much that I put the car in drive and stepped on the gas. I was going to run over him but I hit the brake when I was almost upon him. The truck stopped about two inches from him.

One of the neighbors had called the police because of all of the yelling he was doing. They went inside to talk to him. One of the officers came out and told me that he had all the gas burners turned on in the kitchen (not lit), but they had turned them all off. I told the officer I was leaving and going to my parents' house and I put the truck in gear and backed out. I just barely missed hitting the squad cars that were parked on either side of the driveway.

I drove to my parent's house and one of the policemen followed me there. I thought when I got there that I was going to be arrested for DWI, but thankfully the policeman was a lieutenant and he had been a customer in my dad's barbershop for years. He told my dad not to let me leave that night and then told me I should not have been driving in the condition I was in.

Well, I stayed there that night, but had to go home the next day because my mother kept telling me that she really didn't have room. It's funny how they raised three kids in that house, but after everyone was gone, there wasn't any room for anyone to come back. So I went back home. After I had left, Keith had busted the bathroom mirror and the glass in the front door and knocked holes in the walls in a fit of rage.

When Dee-Dee was eleven months old, we moved to a house that was in a little better shape and didn't have any bugs. Keith got a job not far from home driving a dump truck for a gravel pit. He had slowed down on his drinking some and his brother had moved out with his girlfriend before we moved to the new house. I thought that, maybe, now that we had a baby, things would start getting better. One morning, I was in bed after he had gone to work and I heard a noise. I looked up and saw our landlord climbing in through the living room window. I asked what he was doing and he said he didn't think anyone was home and was coming in to check on things. Well, I told him to leave immediately. As soon as Keith got home from work, I told him what had happened. He was not a happy camper. I thought he was going to go over and kill that old man.

The excuse Keith used for his drinking was that his dad had died in his arms of a heart attack when he had only been thirteen years old. And, he claimed, ever since then nothing had gone right in his life. He had married for the first time at seventeen. He was in the Army and ended up getting dishonorably discharged because he kept going AWOL to go after his first wife because she kept leaving him. She still lived in Illinois with the two kids that he claimed really weren't his after all. He told these stories in such a way that every one felt sorry for him because fate had been so cruel to him.

Before I finished cosmetology school, my mother had started going. After graduating, she worked as an instructor at the school. About the same time the incident occurred with our landlord, my parents bought a house that had a barber and beauty shop on the property with it. Keith talked to my dad and asked him to let us rent the house from them, since I was going to work in the shop with my mother. My father said okay, so we moved in. It was right after we moved into that house that I got pregnant for the second time. Things between Keith and me were sometimes good and at other times they were really bad.

I was working in the beauty shop all day and a teenage girl down the street was babysitting for me. Keith had gotten a job as a mechanic and became friends with a guy by the name of Wally. Wally and Keith both liked to drink and raise hell. They would go out after work on Friday night and drink until either they ran out of money or the bars closed or both. Then, Keith would come home and wake me up and start in on me. He would accuse me of messing around on him while he was at work. Here I was pregnant, working all day, and taking care of a toddler at night. I had no car or money, but I was going out and messing around?

I was working full-time but Keith only worked when he wanted to. Most of the time he would go out drinking on pay day and stay out until his money was gone. I barely had enough money to pay the bills and buy groceries. There was no money for medical insurance or birth control. In order to be able to see a doctor without going to the charity hospital, I enrolled in a program at one of the hospitals where you pay a reduced rate to go through the maternity clinic and someone had to donate a certain number of pints of blood to make up the rest of the fee. Fortunately, Keith had a rare blood type and he was able to donate the required amount.

The night I went into labor, he started driving me to the hospital but had to stop and buy a six-pack of beer. Then he pulled onto a side road and stopped the car. When I asked what he was doing, he said he was going to drink his beer before we went to the hospital. Here I was in labor, my pains coming just minutes apart and he was downing a six-pack of beer. I was a nervous wreck by the time we finally made it to the hospital. I was so embarrassed that he was drunk that I would not even let him come into the labor room with me.

My second daughter, Jaycie, was born early in the morning after a couple of hours of labor. She was so beautiful. I was so worried that I would not be able to take care of my babies the way I should, but I was determined that somehow I would make a good life for my two little girls. I went home twenty-four hours after Jaycie was born. Four weeks after her birth I went back to work. The girl down the street watched Dee-Dee for me, and Jaycie stayed with me at the beauty shop in a playpen. All of the customers helped me take care of her when they were there.

Jaycie had stomach problems and vomited and cried a lot. I wasn't getting any sleep and I was about at my wits' end. I got no help from anyone with either of the kids. Most of the time I was just totally exhausted. When Jaycie was about two months old, Keith informed me that he needed a vacation and he was going to go home to visit his family. I asked what about me and the kids and he informed me that he needed a vacation from everything, including us. Here I was the one working, doing all the cooking and cleaning and taking care of the kids all the time and he only worked enough to earn drinking money and he needed a vacation? He was determined to go and I told him to just go. It was so nice around the house without him there that I kept thinking how nice it would be if he never came back. But, that didn't happen. He came back after he ran out of money and things went back to normal for us.

Not long after Jaycie was born, I discovered I was pregnant again. I didn't know what I was going to do. I didn't believe in abortion so that really wasn't an option that I would consider. I was so ashamed to be in the situation I was in and pregnant with another child. I wouldn't even tell my parents. Keith thought it was just great. He was one of those men who likes his women "barefoot and pregnant," as the saying goes.

It was during this time that things started going from bad to worse in our marriage, if that was even possible. He was drinking more and more and working less and less. It was all I could do to work all day and take care of the two kids I already had. One night when I was about seven months pregnant, he came home after being out drinking all day. He starting yelling and screaming and I was trying to take the kids and get away from him. When he was drunk, he was like a mad man. I knew if he ever got hold of me that I would never get away.

All I could think of was to get an equalizer to defend myself. I found a hammer sitting in the kitchen and I grabbed it as I ran from him. He backed me into a corner, yelling and cursing and threatening me. When I tried to move away he tried to kick me in the stomach. I raised the hammer and hit him in the head with it. It knocked him out. Then I called the police and asked them to come. He had regained consciousness by the time they arrived and, of course, tried to make it look as if I had attacked him. The police had been there enough times before that they knew better, especially when they saw how drunk he was. He refused medical treatment and they wanted to know if they should take him to jail and I told them to just leave him that he would pass out in a little while. They left and he passed out as expected.

I knew that one day, if I didn't get away from him, things would continue to get worse until something really bad happened, but there was just no place for me to go. I was determined to find a way to get out of the mess I was in.

For this pregnancy, the rates at the hospital I had gone to for Jaycie had gone up and I couldn't afford their clinic so I never went to see a doctor at all during that pregnancy. The night I went into labor, I had to go to the charity hospital. Of course, true to form, Keith stopped on the way for a six-pack of beer and pulled onto the street behind the hospital. He sat there and guzzled the beer while I was in agony. Finally, I told him he had to take me now. It was a good thing that we got to the hospital when we did. The doctor who checked me when I got to the labor room said that my blood pressure was extremely high and if I had not arrived there in another few minutes, that it might have been too late.

They got me on the delivery table and gave me two of the most painful shots I have ever had in my life for my blood pressure. The needles were about four inches long and they put one in each hip. I had spasms in my legs for hours afterwards. I was only in labor one hour after getting to the hospital when my third daughter, Shelly, was born. She was such an adorable little thing.

The hospital sent me home the next day. My mother came and picked me up because Keith was out celebrating and no one knew where he was. When I got home, the house was a wreck. Dirty dishes were piled high all over the kitchen with dried-up food stuck on them. There were empty beer cans everywhere. I knew when he came home he would be drunk and I would have to put up with his crap again.

After Shelly was born, I just couldn't afford to go back to work. I couldn't make enough money to pay for babysitting. So now I was really stuck. Finally, when Shelly was about two years old, things were getting really bad. Keith was drinking and partying and messing around with other women and I was growing to hate him more and more every day.

One night after he had been out drinking he came home and brought this big fat slut with him that he had been messing around with. Her name was Jill and he brought her in so I could meet her. Well, I was beside myself with anger and humiliation. I tried not to say anything that would start him off, but I didn't need to. The whole point of him bringing her there was so he could show off in front of her. He started in until he decided that I was not talking to him the way I should. I told him I wasn't going to listen to him and asked him to take Jill and leave. That set him off. He jumped up and came after me with his fists clenched. I knew he was going to start hitting me so I ran. He tackled me and threw me on the floor. Then he put his hands around my throat and I thought he was going to kill me. Jill, at first, thought it was funny. Then, she came over and talked him into getting up and she convinced him to leave with her. I was thankful to her for that but I hated him so badly. I wanted him to just leave and never come back.

When he didn't come back the next day, I hoped he would never come back. Even though I felt the way I did about him and I didn't want him back, I was devastated at the way things had turned out. I was depressed and for a week all I did was feed the kids and lie on the couch all day. I didn't know what to do. I couldn't get a job because I couldn't find a babysitter I could afford. Then a friend of mine told me about a lady who would baby-sit for me really cheap. I called and talked to her and we decided on a price if I found a job. I went to work for a temporary agency. I had several jobs and then I found one at a company that rebuilt Teletype machines.

The job was supposed to only last a couple of months. After I had been there for a short time, the owner decided to downsize his office staff. He let the secretary go and gave me her job full time. I was ecstatic. I had a decent job and things were going pretty good. The only problem was that I was working all day and Keith was sitting around the house most of the time drinking. Bill, who owned the company, was a super nice guy. He tried to help me out by giving Keith odd jobs when he needed things done. But, even then, when Bill paid him, Keith took the money he made and went out drinking.

The worst part was that my mother would go to the house, which was next door to her beauty shop, and drink with him after she closed it up. I would get home from work and there they would be, both of them drunk. Not only did I have to worry about getting the crap beat out of me, but now I had to worry about my mother driving home drunk.

While I was working for Bill, I became pregnant, even though I was taking birth control pills. I miscarried at two months. I was upset because of losing the baby, but I knew it was for the best. I didn't have any money to go to the doctor so my mother took me to the doctor who had delivered both my sister and me. I explained to him that I had been two months pregnant and had miscarried. He did a brief exam and told me everything looked okay. I went home and didn't think anything of it until a couple of months later when I realized I hadn't had a period. I went to the family planning clinic where I had been going for birth control. They gave me a test and said that I was pregnant again. I didn't realize it then, but I had apparently been pregnant with twins and had only lost one when I miscarried. They told me that I had the option to have an abortion, but I couldn't do it. I was just devastated because I didn't know what to do. Of course, when I told Keith I was pregnant, he was totally excited. He got angry when I told him they said I could have an abortion and from then on every time he got drunk during my pregnancy I was accused of wanting to have an abortion to get rid of his baby.

I worked up until about two weeks before my due date and then I stayed home. My son, Keith Jr., was born the last week in January. That winter was cold and we had ice and snow on the ground the day I went into labor. When the pains were about four minutes apart, I convinced Keith to take me to the hospital. It took quite a while to get there and he, of course, had been drinking so I was quite scared. And, as usual, he had to stop for his six-pack of beer. I finally got settled into the labor room around ten-thirty that night. My pains were only about one or two minutes apart, but I wasn't dilating. They made me get up and walk around the hospital. The pains continued to come closer and closer together and I was in terrible pain, but I just wasn't dilating. Finally, after sixteen hours of hard labor it was time to deliver. I had gone to the clinic at the charity hospital in Dallas because I didn't have any money. Back when my children were born, they usually gave you gas in the delivery room, if you needed it, and epidurals were unheard of at that time. With my three girls I didn't need anything, but this baby was different. With every one of my babies, the doctor had had to break my water and then had to cut me and put in stitches. This delivery was no exception. However, my son was a lot bigger than the girls were and I was in so much pain. They told me because it was a charity hospital they were not allowed to give me gas, but I could administer it to myself if I needed it. I felt as if I was ripping in two and I grabbed the mask and gave myself a big shot of the gas.

Finally, the baby was here. He was healthy and beautiful. After the delivery, the local anesthetic that they used wore off before the doctor finished sewing me up. I felt that needle every time he put it in me, but he said he was not allowed to give me another shot. Then, if that wasn't enough, when they are finished they wash you off with a saline solution that is kept warm. I guess their warmer was set too high because it burned me when he poured it over me.

I was only in the hospital for twenty-four hours and they released the baby and me to go home. They brought him into my room around ten A.M., removed his diaper and shirt, and told me to dress him so I could go home. Well, I waited and waited for Keith to show up and bring me the baby's things and take us home. Finally, they came and told me I had to go to check out and go down to the nursery and sign the baby out, so I wrapped him in the hospital's blanket and went down to the nursery. Then, I called my mother and asked her if she could come get us. It was a Saturday and she closed her beauty shop at noon. She said she would be there when she closed up. I sat there in the hospital corridor until two P.M. with my baby naked except for a blanket wrapped around him and waited to go home.

I was very embarrassed and disgusted when my mother got there and Keith was with her. He and his brother had been out celebrating the birth of his son. He would use anything as an excuse to get drunk. If the birth of his son had been so important, why wasn't he there to take him home? I tried not to say anything that would get him started. All I wanted to do when I got home was lie down and rest, but that was not to be. He had invited all of his friends over to see the baby. Of course, all they really wanted to do was sit around and drink. Then I had to cook dinner for them.

When Keith Jr. was six weeks old, Bill's partner called and asked me to come back to work. I told him that I couldn't afford the babysitting. He told me that if I would come back, they would pay for my babysitting for the girls and I could bring the baby to the office with me and Bill would pick me up and take me to work and then bring me home again. It was an offer I just couldn't refuse. For several months I worked for Bill again and took my son to the office. I was the only woman working for the company but everyone that worked there helped out by changing him and feeding him his bottles.

One day Bill came in and handed me an envelope. He had gone to the bank and opened a savings account with twenty-five dollars as a gift to my son. Well, I never heard the end of that. Keith just could not understand why anyone would do something like that. Therefore, he was convinced that Bill was the father of our son and not him. From that time on, every time he got drunk he would accuse me of sleeping with my boss. He even went so far as to tell his friends and family that he was not the father. Bill's business partner made some bad business judgments and ended up ruining the company. Because the company was going downhill so badly, Bill had to let almost everyone go.

A few months after my job ended, I received a call from Bill. He had sold his company and was working for the new owner. He wanted me to come back to work for him. I needed a job and it was closer to home so I told him that I would. I only worked there for a couple of weeks. The owner was rude and obnoxious and one day he started cussing me in front of a group of employees. It was over something that had nothing to do with me and over which I had no control. Well, I told him in no uncertain terms that no one talked to me that way and I didn't need his lousy job. I got my purse and started walking. I walked all the way home, which was about four miles. Of course, Keith wasn't happy because I no longer had a job but he was happy because I wasn't working for Bill any longer.

Most of the time I was able to keep the kids away from Keith when he was drunk. I have to admit that he spanked them too often and too hard and he verbally abused them. But I always seemed to be able to get him away from them before he ever really hurt them physically, even though it meant I would get beat up and choked. I believe that if he had ever treated them the way he did me I would have killed him. I can't say that he was a good father to them, but everyone kept telling me that kids need a father and staying married to him was the right thing to do. So I hung in there and tried to shield them from him and his drunken rages.

I needed a job really bad, but I had no transportation. One day, when Keith Jr. was eighteen months old, Dad offered to let me use his little Ranchero pick-up truck to drive to work if I found a job. I jumped at the offer and finally found a job as a legal secretary for a large financial services company. The pay was good and I could at least pay the bills and buy groceries. We still lived in the house attached to my mother's beauty parlor, so she was paying the electric and water bills as part of the beauty shop bills.

That helped out a lot. The only problem I had was I opened a checking account. Every time I got paid, Keith would get the checkbook and write checks for cash so he could go drinking. I was working and he was spending most of his time sitting around the house drinking all day. Every year in April he decided that he needed a vacation from everything and he would take the bus to Illinois and spend a week up there with his family. Although it was nice to have him gone, I thought how nice it would be to have a vacation myself. After all, I was the one working all day and taking care of the house and kids at night and on weekends.

I had found government-funded babysitting and I was making a good salary. I got a promotion after fifteen months on the job. Then I went in for my check up and my Pap smear came back abnormal. After additional testing it was discovered that I had Dysplasia, which is a condition where abnormal cells have the potential of becoming cancer. I was told that I needed a biopsy done and would probably have to have my cervix removed, and depending on the results of the biopsy, possibly more extensive surgery. I also needed my bladder tied up and the doctor said he could do that at the same time. I was scared and upset, but Keith just couldn't understand that. This is one time in my life that I don't like to think about.

As usual, our car wasn't running and I had to check into the hospital before four P.M., so my sister drove me there. She dropped me off in front of the hospital and drove off. I checked in and was told to change into the hospital gown and wait for someone to come and get me for a chest x-ray. After that all I had to do was sit or lie around all night. I would go into the operating room in the morning for a biopsy. After the biopsy I would go back to my room and wait for the results. Depending on what they found, the hysterectomy would be done the following morning.

Well, let me tell you, I missed my kids something awful and I was so scared. I lay in that bed in that hospital room all alone. Not one person came to the hospital to see me or to give me any compassion or encouragement. Keith called me about nine o'clock that night drunk and said, "Why don't you just get dressed and come home and forget about all this?" and I told him that I couldn't.

The next morning they came and took me to the operating room. The nurse asked if anyone was there with me and I was so hurt and disappointed and even somewhat embarrassed to have to say, "No, I'm here all alone." After the biopsy was done and I woke up, I was taken back to my room. I had nothing to do but lie around and worry about what they would find. The doctor came in that evening and said that there was no cancer, but that they still needed to remove my cervix just to make sure. So, that surgery was planned for eight o'clock the next morning.

I called my mother and Keith and told them. I also called my boss. He said that someone from the office would come to the hospital but I told him I would be fine and they didn't need to do that. I didn't want anyone I worked with to show up at the hospital during my surgery only to discover that no one in my family cared enough to be there for me. So he said he would check back after the surgery to find out how it went.

The next morning I was so frightened. It was the uncertainty of knowing that I could go into that operating room and never come out. Anything could have happened and all I could think of was that no one cared enough to be there with me. Fortunately, the surgery went well. When the anesthetic finally wore off, I was in terrible pain. The doctor explained that even though the surgery had all been done vaginally with no incision, that I had four internal incisions that were causing the pain. He prescribed a pain medication for me. The nurse brought in a pill for me to take. I took the pill and she left. About ten minutes later, my whole body started itching and my hands were swelling up to almost double. I immediately called the nurse who said I was having an allergic reaction to the medicine and she had to give me shot to counteract it. The next morning I woke up with a rash from my bellybutton almost down to my knees. Apparently, I also had a reaction to the Betadine that they had used to scrub me before the surgery.

On the evening of the fourth day at the hospital, the door opened and I saw my darling children standing there. I was as excited to see them, as they were to see me. But, I thought to myself sarcastically, how kind of my mother and husband to finally think of coming to see me. After all, I could have died here all alone. My doctor had gone out of town immediately after the surgery and the doctor who was handling my case for him was a very good-looking young resident. He came into the room on evening rounds while they were there and, of course, Keith was sure that there was something going on between us because I mentioned that he was cute.

I was in the hospital for five days and I was so glad when they said I could go home. I was still in so much pain but I wanted to go home and sleep in my own bed and be with my children. I thought I could leave the hospital and get some much-needed rest. I should have known that nothing in my life is ever as it should be. After we got home, Keith decided to sit and drink, as usual. I played with the kids for a while and made them all lie down to take a nap so I could rest. I went to sleep and then the next thing I knew Keith was in the room cussing, ranting and raving. He was accusing me of having an affair with my doctor and with my old boss and other things. He kept telling me to get my kids and get out. Finally, he started to get violent so I got up and dressed and got the kids up. I took them outside and started trying to walk down the street to the 7-11 store so I could call my mother or my dad to come get us out of there. He kept following me and making me turn back. He kept shoving me and trying to hit me. I kept backing away from him with the kids behind me.

I looked down and saw his tire iron on the ground and I quickly picked it up. I told him to get away and leave the kids and me alone and started walking down the street again. Of course, he followed and grabbed my arm and pulled me around. When I turned around he said something and drew back his fist to hit me. When he did that, I swung the tire iron as hard as I could and broke his arm. I grabbed the kids and told them, "Let's go, now!" We went on down the street to the store and I called my mother. She came and picked us up at the store and we went to her house. I had to get some rest. I could barely stand up and I was in so much pain.

When I would try to talk to my parents about Keith and how he treated the kids and me, they would just tell me that it was in the best interest of the kids to try to work things out. They, like everyone else back then, were convinced that kids need both parents. I guess it didn't matter if one of the parents was an abusive drunk as long as a child had both a mother and a father living with them. They would tell me about how they had only known each other a short time before marrying and how they had never had a fight and how happily married they had been for all those years. Well, that was such a great challenge to live up to. (A little irony and sarcasm there.)

It took me years to realize that sometimes the best interest of the kids is not always keeping the family intact. I finally realized that the majority of the people were wrong. Living with Keith was an unhealthy environment for my kids and me and it had to be better for all of us to not live with him. I honestly believe that, if I had not divorced Keith when I did, I would not be alive today to tell this story. He would have probably succeeded in killing me. And to all those people who say it's best to work out your problems and keep the family intact, I say that there are situations when that is not possible and is not in the best interest of the family. I had really tried to make it work. I kept thinking that he would change. I thought maybe if we could go out together sometimes that it would have helped, but that wouldn't work, because I never had a babysitter. Sometimes I would ask my mom to baby-sit but she would always come back with, "When you kids were little, I never went anyplace that I couldn't take you. Nobody ever baby-sat for me."

Once a year, on my anniversary, she would baby-sit so we could go out and that was it. We didn't do things with the kids much because they always got embarrassed by the way Keith acted in public because he was always drunk. Sometimes, we would go to the drive-in theater or to the fair or something, but that was about it. When Dee-Dee was in the first grade, she was in the Bluebirds, a group similar to Girl Scouts. At the end of the year they had a covered dish banquet for the girls and their families. We were all hoping that Keith would stay home, but of course, he wanted to go. I begged him to stay sober, but as usual, when I got home from work that night he had been drinking all day. He was raring to go! We all went to the banquet, and although he didn't start any fights, we were all embarrassed by his drunkenness and his filthy mouth. We made it an early night and left as soon as the awards were given out. I believe that was probably the last function of that type that we attended as a family. I just quit telling him that the family was invited to functions and just went alone with the kids. I made it a point to go to open house and PTA without him so that he wouldn't do anything to embarrass the kids at school.

For some reason, when we were around my parents, Keith never did much of anything except drink and run this mouth. He never hit me or got belligerent like he did at home. He always waited until we got home. He would go to my parents' house and mow and do yard work and help my dad with things. My parents would come over on Saturday nights and we would play a domino game called Forty-Two and sometimes we played Pinochle and Canasta. He would drink but never started anything until after they had left.

When he was sober, he could be a very likeable person. My uncle owned a cabin on a lake about a hundred miles from where we lived and we would go there for weekends with my parents and fish and have a good time. Of course, he always got drunk, but he never acted badly at these times, except once. My uncle, who was in his early seventies then, stood up and pulled his pocketknife out. He told Keith that if he ever raised his hand to me or any of my kids in front of him again that he would use the knife on him. I guess Keith believed him because, after that, he watched how he acted around my uncle.

~Chapter 8~

Things started to go from worse to intolerable. I would work all day and come home and have to clean up after him and cook dinner. We didn't have air conditioning and in the summer the heat was unbearable. He expected a hot cooked meal every night. Sometimes I would come home and he would tell me he had invited some of his friends over for dinner. Usually, we barely had enough food for him, the kids and me, so on those nights I didn't eat.

After dinner, I usually had to do the laundry, help the kids with homework and then get them ready for bed. While doing all those things, I also had to make sure the kids stayed out of his way so he would not start yelling at them. He never physically abused any of them, but he verbally abused them. Sometimes I would get between them and him and just pray that he didn't start in on me. It got to the point where I was afraid for my life. Sometimes he would come into the bathroom while I was taking a bath and threaten to throw the electric fan or the blow dryer in the tub with me. I didn't know if he would or not, but I didn't want to find out. Once he got drunk and went on a rampage and I left and went to my parents' house with the kids. I went back home the next day and he had busted all the mirrors in the house and kicked in all the cabinet doors in the kitchen.

I remember one night it was only about twenty degrees outside. It was about two o'clock in the morning when Keith came home drunk. I tried to pretend that I was asleep and ignore him, but it didn't work. He started shoving me and slapping me and telling me to get up that he wanted to talk to me. Finally, I got out of bed and went into the living room with him. I kept hoping he would pass out, but he didn't. He got himself all worked up and started beating on me. I got away from him and ran outside. When I went out, he locked the doors so I could not come back in. I ended up spending the night in the garage with nothing on but a pair of pajamas. I ended up missing a week's work because I was sick in bed and nearly had pneumonia. Of course, when I got my paycheck and it was a week short, he was beside himself with anger. It was all my fault! If I had not stayed outside in the cold I would not have gotten sick. He wasn't worried about not being able to pay bills but, rather about not having enough money to drink on.

We didn't have a telephone so I always had to go next door to the beauty shop to use the phone. One night he started hitting me and choking me and I went to the shop to call the police because he was chasing me with a butcher knife. He came over to the shop after me and threw the glass door open so hard that he broke all of the glass out of it. When the police came, he had the knife in his back pocket. He also had blood on him where he had cut himself on the broken glass. They asked him why he had the knife in his pocket and he said he had taken it away from me so I wouldn't stab him with it. I told the police that he was lying and they believed me. He had removed the coil wire from the car so it wouldn't start and the police told him to give it to them. He told them he had thrown it across the street somewhere. We looked, but could not find it. The police asked if I wanted to press charges against him and I told them to just take him away and keep him until he sobered up. I was afraid to press charges, because when he got released he would come after me and I didn't know what he would do then.

On the nights that Keith went out drinking, I would go to bed dreading when he would come home. He would come in at two or three A.M. and wake me up. I would try to pretend that I didn't hear him, but he would start yelling and pushing until I finally had to acknowledge him. Then he would start grabbing me around the throat and accuse me of having an affair with someone. Sometimes I thought I wouldn't live to see another day. Sometimes he would wake the kids up and start telling them how bad a mother I was and how I had a boyfriend and things like that. They knew I didn't have a boyfriend. Sometimes they would pretend to be asleep and he would go away. Other times, he would make them get up and listen to his rampages. Other times he would stop and buy a bucket of chicken or a bag full of hamburgers and try to make everyone eat in the middle of the night.

Usually after he was through with his drunken rampages, he wanted sex. It didn't do any good to say no, because he forced himself on me. After the sex that usually only lasted a couple of minutes, he would finally go into the living room and turn on the TV and pass out. Then, everyone could go to sleep because he would sleep until some time in the morning. I began to be disgusted by the thought of sex with him and couldn't stand it when he touched me, even if he wasn't drinking. I just wanted him to go away and leave me alone. I wanted a normal life with a normal sex life. After a while it got to the point where all I could think of was getting away from him. I knew that I could never get him to leave. I didn't feel like I should be the one to leave because the house we lived in belonged to my parents. I tried to talk to them about making him move, but they wouldn't do it. They said there was nothing they could do. I think they were afraid of him and of what he might do to them and the house if they made him leave. It got so bad that I was staying awake all night trying to think of ways to get rid of him without getting caught.

I can't believe I did it, but one night I made a pot of coffee for him with a whole bottle of aspirins in it. He wouldn't drink the coffee so I ended up pouring it out. After that night, I realized that things had to change before I really did kill him, because things had gotten to the point where I felt as if it was kill or be killed. I wanted to get a divorce, but I still held on to the notion that it was the proper thing to do to stay married.

I think the thing that really made me decide that divorce was the only answer was when one day Keith was really drunk and he backed the kids and me into a corner. He chased us into the bedroom. The kids and I were on one side of the bed and he was on the side by the door. He was ranting and raving and trying to hit me. He picked up a box fan and threw it at me. The fan missed me, but hit my son in the head. He was okay except for a knot on his head, but that was the last straw. I was determined to get out of this marriage one way or another. A couple of days later I found the excuse I needed to convince myself that I had to get a divorce and it was all by accident.

~Chapter 9~

They were redoing the street in front of our house and a guy Keith had worked with a few years before owned the company that was laying all of the sewer and water pipes. He came up and talked to us and after that, he would stop and talk every time he saw I was at home. Well, Richie was a really good looking guy and he knew just what to say to make a lady feel like a lady. He flirted and complimented, and I have to admit, I was smitten. One Sunday, when Keith had gone with my dad to help mow my parents' lawn and the kids were at church, Richie stopped by. He knew I would be there alone. We were standing and talking when all of a sudden he put his arms around me and kissed me. I felt a tingle all the way down to my toes. I wanted this man so badly, but I pulled away. Even though I was being treated so shabbily by my husband I still felt the need to be faithful to him and I told Richie this. He said he understood.

Richie continued to stop by every chance he got. I was so sick of the way Keith was treating me and I just knew that one day he would kill me. I decided, what the heck, if I was going to get killed over a man at least I would make it worthwhile. So one day even though I knew it was a sin, I just couldn't resist him any longer. Sex with Richie was perfect. Although I felt guilty about cheating, I also felt as if a huge weight had been lifted off my chest. All of a sudden I knew that I could not stay married to Keith after cheating on him. I guess that was the excuse I needed to leave him. After that day with Richie, it was all I could do to let Keith touch me. I tried to give him hints, like I would continue to read my book or watch TV during sex. He didn't get the hint even when I told him I didn't want him to touch me.

Now I wanted a divorce in the worst way. I knew, however, if I filed for a divorce he would probably try to kill me or burn down the house or something. Then he started talking about wanting to take his annual trip to Illinois and I came up with the perfect solution. I told him I would pay for a one-way ticket home if he wanted to go. He said okay. I bought the ticket and sent him on his way to visit his mother. He called just about every other day asking me to send him spending money. I sent him a little and then told him I didn't have any more to send. After a couple of weeks he started calling and asking me to send him money to come back home. I told him I didn't have it and if he wanted to come back he should get a job and earn the money. Of course he didn't. While he was gone I went to a lawyer, paid him a down payment retainer fee and had divorce papers drawn up.

Finally, I told Keith one night when he called that I was filing for a divorce. He was livid. I figured he would borrow the money from his mother or brother and come back here and kill me, but he didn't. I sent the papers up to him and he kept putting off signing them. He wanted to make changes to them, which I agreed to. He finally signed the papers and sent them back. After that, all I had to do was pay off the lawyer and then I could go to court and get my divorce. It took me five months to pay the lawyer's fee, and then the court date was set. My lawyer called and said we would go to court on November third. I laughed and told him that was my anniversary and he offered to change the date, but I told him, "No, don't change it. I started this mess on November third and I'll end it on the same date." And I did.

It was such a relief the day I went to court and the divorce was final. I had four kids and the court granted me two hundred dollars a month in child support, which I knew I would never see a penny of.

It seems as if when I divorced Keith, I also divorced his family. We never heard from anyone in his family again after it was final. His mother never acknowledged her four grandchildren. She even quit sending them birthday cards and never again sent them a Christmas present nor a card. I talked to his brothers and his ex-sister-in-law a couple of times after the divorce and then we lost touch.

~Chapter 10~

A couple of years after our divorce, Keith came back to Texas. Shortly after he came back, his thirty-one-year-old brother died of a heart attack. Keith didn't have a job and I felt sorry for him so I paid for a train ticket for him to go home for the funeral. I was so surprised when he paid the money back to me within a month. However, I wasn't surprised that he never paid me one penny in child support. I knew it was fruitless to try to collect anything from him, so I didn't even try.

I always told the kids that no matter what he had done or how he had treated them, he would always be their father. I also told them that whatever had happened between him and me really had nothing to do with whatever type of relationship they wanted to have with him. I wanted them to be able to have a relationship with their father if that was their desire, but it wasn't. He never came to see them nor called them, but spent a lot of time telling all of his friends and family that I had turned them against him. When I saw him once, he made that comment to me and I told him that he had turned them against himself by his actions and that I had nothing to do with it. I told him that I never stopped him from seeing the kids, but that he had never tried and it was his own fault if they didn't want to have anything to do with him now. Really, secretly, I was glad they didn't, but I would have never admitted it to anyone.

After the divorce, things seemed to settle down a bit. Richie still came by and called, but he was married and I knew he wasn't going to leave his wife for me. He liked my kids and would come by on Saturday mornings and take them to McDonald's for breakfast. Sometimes we would meet for lunch. He was a really good friend. I could talk about my problems with him, and he would offer suggestions on ways to handle the kids and would help me with the problems I had with them.

When I was married to Keith, I never had much money to spend for Christmas presents. I had to put things on layaway early in the summer in order to buy them anything. One year when I wasn't working, he had drunk up all of his money and I didn't have any money to spend for Christmas at all. I was so upset because I wouldn't be able to buy anything for the kids. Keith was working with his friend, Wally. Wally and his wife went out and bought some small things and wrapped them for the kids. I was so embarrassed when they came over and put them under the tree. I was so grateful, but felt so bad because I couldn't do it myself. Years later, after my dad had passed away, I found out that my mother had been giving my brother money to buy school clothes and Christmas presents ever since his son was born. He had one child and I had four and my sister had three and my mother had never offered to help either of us girls out. I was so angry that I eventually said something to her about it and finally convinced her that my brother needed to learn to live without handouts from his mother. Though it may sound petty, it was sort of a victory for me because of the hardships I had faced raising my children.

I had been so programmed to keep personal things to myself that I never discussed anything private with people. I had been divorced for over a year before I told anyone at work. I was ashamed and embarrassed and was afraid that people would talk about me behind my back and call me a bad person for getting a divorce. During that time period, a divorced woman was considered "tainted" and was almost as badly thought of as an unwed mother. When I think about it now, I really don't know why I felt so stigmatized about being divorced. After all, my sister got a divorce about a year before me. And when I got my divorce, my brother was on his fourth wife. I guess it was just that we had always had my parents' successful marriage thrown up in our faces that I felt as if I was breaking some sort of commandment or something.

When I attended my twentieth high school reunion, one of the really popular girls, who was very religious and whom I had known since my first year in school, was talking to me. She asked about my family. I told her I had four kids and hesitantly said I was divorced. She put her hand on my shoulder, looked me square in the eyes and said, "Hey, I am also divorced and now remarried. It's not a crime and it's nothing to be ashamed of. So forget about it and get on with your life!" She was right, of course, but until then I had not faced the fact that maybe being divorced didn't make me a tainted woman, after all.

A short time after I divorced Keith, my mother decided to split up the utilities and all of a sudden I had more bills to pay. It was really tough trying to make ends meet. I had to pay for daycare plus pay all the bills and I wasn't getting any child support. I had been paying rent to my dad for the house, but he wouldn't repair anything. The roof leaked and everything seemed to be falling apart. So I just decided to quit paying him rent if he wasn't going to repair anything. He never said anything about it so I had enough money to last from payday to payday, as long as I didn't spend money on any extras. When my mother decided to take early retirement and close her beauty shop, she told me the kids could stay with them during the summer so I wouldn't have to pay for babysitting. That was great. There was a swimming pool across the street from her house and they would spend most of the time there.

I would go over there a couple of nights a week and go swimming with the kids and then pick them up on Friday night and take them back on Sunday night. At the beginning of the summer I would buy groceries to take over there so my parents wouldn't have to buy a bunch of extra food, but that was to no avail because it seems that all she ever fed them was frozen pizza, cookies, ice cream and things like that. At the end of the summer, I always had all the vegetables and other foods to take back home with me. It was pretty lonesome with the kids gone all week, but there was no way I could afford the babysitting cost otherwise.

On the last day the swimming pool was open for the summer, (Dee-Dee was thirteen) a boy shoved her into the pool and she hit her arm on the rope that goes across the pool. She came up out of the pool holding her arm and crying. We didn't know for sure if it was broken. The lifeguard and I were checking it, when all of a sudden she passed out and just slipped down to the ground. As she did, I let go of her arm and it fell on her stomach. We wrapped her arm in a towel and I took her to the emergency room. Her forearm was broken, but it didn't have to be set because it had set itself when she passed out. She had to start school with a broken arm. Thankfully, she was the only one of my kids who ever had any broken bones.

For the most part, my kids did okay in school. Dee-Dee was very artistic and liked to write poetry. Jaycie was athletic and played basketball and ran track. Shelly was quiet and didn't participate in many activities. Keith had a problem with paying attention and was always the class clown. When he was in the second grade, Keith wanted to play Pee Wee Football. I was making enough money at this time and I could afford the cost, so I let him play. I figured it was something that would keep him out of trouble and off the streets. When they were younger, my girls had wanted to play softball and soccer, but I couldn't afford then. When Keith started football, I told the girls they could play a sport, too, but they were at an age where sports didn't interest them as much anymore. Keith had football practice four nights a week and a game every Saturday. It was nice to go to the practices and be outside. The girls took their homework and did it while he practiced. We all went to the games and they found a lot of people they knew to socialize with.

When Keith was eight and I had been divorced about four years, Tommy moved into the house across the street. He was a big guy who was half American Indian and eight years younger than me, but we had a lot in common. He came over one night while I was out watering the lawn and we stood and talked for hours. Tommy was not Mr. Handsome but he was easy to talk to. We talked every chance we could. He and I weren't a couple at that time and I was still seeing Richie sometimes, but we seemed to have so much in common. It was around this time that I started having problems with Dee-Dee. She was lying and we caught her stealing a couple of times.

Every time I tried to talk to my parents about problems I was having with the kids, they would just say that they were good kids, it was a phase they were going through, and that they would grow out of the problems. Well, I wish I hadn't listened to them. Dee-Dee was stealing things from people and telling lies. She even went to the school councilor and told her that Richie would come over and fondle them, which he did not do. I had to talk to the child welfare people because of Dee-Dee's lies. Everything turned out okay. I knew her accusations were not true, but I was afraid of losing my kids, so instead of dealing with her problems, I broke up with Richie. I remember the night I told him he cried and asked me to reconsider and try to get things worked out for Dee-Dee. I stood behind my decision and wouldn't see him any more. It was really hard for me to do, but I did it for my kids. My sister told me I needed to get her into some kind of therapy, but I had been so programmed to not 'air my dirty laundry in public' that I was convinced the best thing to do was just ride it out and it would go away. Instead, the problem seemed to get worse.

It was during this time that Dee-Dee decided she didn't want to live at home anymore. She was embarrassed because our house wasn't as nice as all of her friends' houses and I couldn't afford designer clothes for her.

She started telling everyone stories, like she was an only child and I was her foster mother and I didn't allow her to have people over. She lied to people about where she lived and pointed out houses of people we knew and told them that that was where she lived. She became friendly with the mother of one of the boys on Keith's football team and she would go to their house and have her friends come over and then tell them that her real mother was dead and Janice had adopted her. Then, when she was fifteen, she decided she wanted to move in with her friend's family. She told me that she would run away from home and we would never see her again if I didn't let her do it. My mother told me that I should let her go because she would get homesick and come back soon. So, stupid me, I listened to my mother like the good daughter I was and let my daughter go.

After a while, she said she wanted to come back home and I was delighted. It wasn't long before she decided again that she wasn't happy at home and asked my parents if she could move in with them. All I wanted was for her to be happy and I didn't want her running away or doing anything foolish and, even though I wanted her to stay at home and work out her problems, I let her move in with my parents. I tried to get my parents to tell her she needed to stay at home, but instead of taking my side, my mother told her she would be delighted to have her come stay with them. Dee-Dee would tell her all of these untruths about her life and my mother would agree with everything she said. But then, on the other hand, when I would try to tell my mother that Dee-Dee was lying about everything, she also agreed with me. As to whose side she was on depended on whom she was talking to at the time.

My mother is one of those people who wants to be liked by everyone so she agrees with whomever she is talking to at the time. If I went to her with complaints about my kids, looking for help, she would just agree that anything I said or any decision I came up with was the right solution. However, on the other hand, the kids would talk to her about the same thing and she would agree with them that what they said or thought was the right thing. She should have stood behind me, but she didn't. This caused me a lot of problems with Dee-Dee during this period of time. Later on, I would realize how much it had hurt my relationship with Dee-Dee and I carry some resentment with me for it even to this day.

My sister continued to try to convince me to get her into therapy, but I refused to even consider that option. When I brought the subject up with my parents, they told me she didn't need therapy that time would take care of everything. Years later I would be sorry that I didn't listen to my sister, but hindsight is always better than foresight.

While Dee-Dee was living with my parents, Dad offered to loan me the money to help make a down payment on a house if I found one I could afford. After months of shopping, I finally found one in a small suburb about seven miles down the highway from where we were living. Jaycie, Shelly and Keith had mixed emotions about moving away from their friends, but Dee-Dee seemed really excited and wanted to move back home when we moved. I thought at last everything was going to be good and things would all work out. How wrong I was.

~Chapter 11~

Tommy had moved several months before to the same little town we were moving to and Dee-Dee started asking if she could go stay with him until we moved so she could get to know people. I wouldn't let her do it and Tommy wouldn't either. She was not at all happy about it. We moved into the house on June first and shortly before school started, I found out that Jaycie was pregnant. I was heartbroken and so angry. She was only fifteen and her boyfriend, Bryan, was seventeen. I wanted to have him thrown in jail. She told me she would never forgive me and she would leave and never come back if I did that. Well, I didn't have him thrown in jail. I just, more or less, gave up. My life was out of control and my kids were out of control, and I didn't know how to fix anything.

I was still dating Tommy and we spent a lot of time together. We had been a couple for several years by now and he tried to be a father figure for the kids, but they wouldn't let him. They began to resent the time I was with him. We still went places together and did things, but I didn't like his friends because they all did drugs and he drank too much. He wasn't a violent drunk, but I was just tired of being around drunks, period! It seems like I always felt as if I had to settle for a man because I didn't think anyone decent would be attracted to me. I was quite unhappy most of the time. Then after Jaycie got pregnant, I was embarrassed and felt as if I wasn't a good mother, and that the problems I was having with Dee-Dee, and then Jaycie getting pregnant were all my fault. I didn't even tell anyone at work that she was pregnant until she had her baby. Well, Dee-Dee was beside herself. She just couldn't understand why I didn't just throw Jaycie out on the street because she was pregnant. She said she didn't know why I was letting her stay at home. I told her because she was my daughter and I loved her.

My son was playing baseball on the city league and I went to his practice every night. Usually the girls would go with me. One of his coaches named Kevin was a very attractive married man who was probably in his late twenties or early thirties. I knew that my girls thought he was really cute, but I didn't know how cute they thought he was until later.

We started getting telephone calls and when I would answer the phone the person would hang up. Dee-Dee started getting a lot of phone calls where she would go into a room by herself and talk so no one could hear her. Then she would go out jogging. One day, Jaycie's boyfriend told me that he saw Dee-Dee get into a car with some blonde guy who looked a lot older than her. I confronted her about it when she got home and she denied meeting anyone. I wanted to trust her and believe in her, so I took her word for it.

About mid-season, Kevin quit coming to practice and only the assistant coaches were there. I heard that he and his wife were having marital problems and he was out of town for a while. I found out later that he had been messing around with other women. When I went home and told Jaycie and Shelly about it, they said that Dee-Dee and Kevin had been meeting secretly for quite a while. I confronted her again and she cried and said it was a lie. I didn't know what to do so I finally just let it drop. I was so embarrassed and really didn't want to go to baseball practice or the games any more because I was afraid that everyone there would know that my daughter had been messing around with the coach. I did go, though, but I didn't talk to people as much as I had before.

I didn't know what to do with Dee-Dee. I wanted to believe the things she told me but I knew in my heart that she was lying about everything. I had thought that moving to a new city and making new friends might help her start over with a clean slate, but I guess I was wrong. She was in her senior year in high school and we had ordered her ring, cap and gown and graduation invitations. Then, in March, just three months before graduation, she decided to drop out of school. Well, I was beside myself. I told her she just had three months to go and, since she was always a good student and made good grades, there was no reason for her to not finish the last three months. She wouldn't listen to me and dropped out anyway.

I was so angry. I had spent money I couldn't afford to spend paying for her ring and graduation things. I couldn't get the money back. And I wanted her to finish school. I tried again to talk to her about it, but, as usual, I said the wrong things. I told her if she wasn't going to go to school, that she would have to get a job. I said that if she wasn't attending school and also didn't want to work, she could just find another place to live. I thought that this would work kind of like reverse psychology, but it didn't. The next day I came home from work and she told me she was moving in with Larry, the guy she had been dating for about a month.

She was seventeen and there was not much I could say about it. I told her I didn't want her to go, but she went anyway. Larry lived only a mile from us on another street, but we never saw her. She had gone to him and his family and told them some really outlandish stories about her life at home. It wasn't until later on that we found out some of the things she had told them.

After Dee-Dee moved out and had been gone for a while, I cleaned out a lot of junk she had left behind. While going through some of her old papers, I found an essay she had written several years before for English. In the essay she wrote that she didn't have a father any more and that her mother was an alcoholic who beat her. She said in the essay that her father had broken her arm in a drunken fit of rage and that her mother had thought it was funny and at first refused to take her to the hospital to get it fixed. She said she had repeatedly run away from home and, as a last resort, had contacted an attorney who had gotten her taken away from me and another family had adopted her. None of this was true and it made me angry, it also made me realize how far she had sunk into her fantasy world. It also made me realize why her teachers had treated me so strangely at open house.

Bryan spent a lot of time at our house and I tolerated him because I wanted to keep Jaycie happy. She was embarrassed to go to school pregnant so we enrolled her in an alternative school. She had an easy labor and her beautiful baby girl, Cassandra, was born in February. All of a sudden, I was a grandmother! I was forty-one years old, my youngest child was only eleven years old and I had a grandchild! I think I aged about ten years. Now, I had my four kids plus a grandchild to support. To make matters worse, even though Bryan came around all the time, he didn't give Jaycie any support. She couldn't understand why I was mad about him being there all the time. I was supporting her child and Shelly and I took care of the baby most of the time.

When Cassandra was a couple of months old, Jaycie started going to an alternative school where she could take the baby with her. She didn't have a car and had to rely on other people at the school for rides because I couldn't provide her transportation. She ended up dropping out after just a few months.

Dee-Dee went to the same alternative school to complete her senior year and got her diploma. Jaycie ran into Larry at the school one day and asked him why he wouldn't allow Dee-Dee to talk to her family. He said that we had mistreated and abused her and that she didn't want to have anything to do with us. She told him that Dee-Dee was lying, but he wouldn't believe her.

One of Keith's friends told him that he had seen Dee-Dee on crutches and that she had hurt her knee. I was concerned and called Larry's house to find out about it. His mother was very rude to me. She said she didn't know why I would call and I said because I wanted to know if my daughter was okay. She told me that Dee-Dee had been walking and her kneecap had slipped out of place. I told her that this was inherited from my dad and that I also had the problem. She asked if I was going to pay the doctor bills for her knee and I told her Dee-Dee was living with them and I had not heard from her for a year so I didn't feel as if it was my responsibility. I did, however, tell her that Dee-Dee was still covered under my medical insurance and she could use it to pay whatever it would, but that I did not feel responsible for the rest of the bills. I asked if I could talk to my daughter and she finally quit saying that she didn't have anything to say to me and put her on the phone.

Dee-Dee and I talked for a few minutes about her knee and about how she had been and then she told me she couldn't talk any longer. It was quite a while before I spoke with her again. Larry's parents changed their phone number and she never called me. Then Keith heard from the boy who used to live across the street from us that Dee-Dee was pregnant. Not long after we found this out, she called me to see if my medical insurance would cover her pregnancy, which it did. She found out from me how to file claims on the insurance and then I didn't hear from her again until her daughter was born. When her baby was born, I found out about it because Keith's friend at school told him that his sister had given birth. After her baby was born, Dee-Dee finally called to tell me she had given birth to a daughter whom she had named Lydia.

The same day Lydia was born, Tommy asked me to marry him. I said I would, but that I had some apprehensions, so we decided that he would move in with me and we would have a "trial" marriage. He moved in and things went along okay for a while. I think I was beginning to realize that, even though it was nice to have someone to do things with and to go places with, I wanted someone to take care of me. I didn't have that with Tommy. I was always taking care of him. He was giving me fifty dollars a week to help with the bills. I thought that was pretty cheap, but never said anything about it at first. Sometimes he worked and sometimes he didn't and I was getting tired of that, also. And, he drank a lot. He was never abusive, but he and my kids started not getting along. I wanted to ask him to leave, but wouldn't do it because I was afraid of being alone again so I decided to try to make the best of it.

When Lydia was about six weeks old Dee-Dee showed up at my job with her. The baby looked just like Larry. I held her for a few minutes. This was early November. I didn't hear from her again until close to Christmas. She called and told me that they had moved into an apartment and asked if I wanted to come see her and the baby. I went over there and took her some Christmas presents I had for them. I only got to see the baby for a minute because she was asleep and Dee-Dee didn't want to disturb her. It was nearly a year before I saw Lydia again. At first, I was hurt about this, then angry, and lastly, I just became indifferent.

I always felt lucky because my kids didn't have a drinking or drug problem and never got into trouble with the law. But I was disappointed because of the directions their lives were taking. Jaycie and Bryan kept seeing each other, but didn't want to get married. She ended up getting pregnant again when Cassandra was a little over a year old. She thought about getting an abortion, but decided that she couldn't do it. I am against abortion, so I was glad she made that decision, but not happy that she was having another baby. I wasn't making enough money and had to rely on the food stamps she got to be able to feed everyone. Bryan never paid her support money and she wouldn't take him to court to get it.

Her second daughter, Missy, was born in April. The night she was born was quite interesting. Jaycie was having slight labor pains that evening, but the pains were too far apart, so I finally told her I was going to lie down and to wake me up when the pains got stronger or closer together. I fell asleep and she did, too.

About two A.M. Jaycie came into my room and said her water had broken and she needed to go to the hospital. I asked why she waited so long to wake me up and she said because she had fallen asleep. I was disoriented and couldn't find my shorts. When I did I put them on backwards. I woke Shelly and Keith up and they got Cassandra up and dressed while I called the doctor. We went out to the car and put Cassandra in her car seat. Jaycie decided she needed a Dr. Pepper to drink on the way. Shelly brought one out to the car and tried to toss it into the backseat. When she did the bottle broke and glass and Dr. Pepper was all over the car and Cassandra. We had to stop and clean up Cassandra and the car seat and floor. Then we all took off.

Stupid me, it was two A.M. and no traffic and I was stopping for every red light and waiting for them to turn green. Finally, Jaycie said, "Please run the light". I did and we finally got to the highway. The hospital was about twelve miles down the road. I got on the highway and she started saying the baby was coming and I told her to hold on and not to push. I told her if she had to push I would go to a fire station, but she told me to just go on to the hospital. We finally got to the hospital and I pulled up to the emergency entrance. I ran inside but there was no one around.

I walked around and couldn't find anyone so finally I yelled, "I need help here. My daughter is in labor and she's about to have her baby in my front seat." A nurse and an orderly came running out with a wheelchair. They put her in the wheelchair and started inside while we parked the car. She said she told them there wasn't time to stop at the desk, she needed to go to delivery right then. The orderly was slowly pushing her toward the elevator when she told him that either he could hurry up or he was going to deliver the baby there because she was getting ready to push. She said that he then started running. The doctor met her at the delivery room. We parked the car and went up to her room and Missy was already here. Another beautiful little girl!

I loved my kids and I loved my grandkids, but I was frustrated and discouraged. It was at this point that I just sort of threw up my hands and said the hell with it all. I felt like such a failure. I had failed at marriage and I felt like I had failed at raising my children.

~Chapter 12~

Shelly decided that she didn't want to go to school anymore. So, she would go to school and just not go to any classes. I started getting calls and notes that told me that she was being sent to alternative classes and detention. One day we got into an argument and I told her that she needed to find a job or something because I was getting tired of supporting a bunch of deadbeats. She brought up the fact that Jaycie didn't work and I told her that she couldn't afford to right now. We got into a big argument and finally I told her, "Well, if you don't like it, why don't you just leave?" I came home the next day from work and she was gone. She had gone to her boyfriend's house. She finally called and told me where she was and I told her to get back home.

She didn't come home that night, but the next day I received a call at work from a police officer who said I needed to come to the police station to talk to him about Shelly. When I got there, I found out that Shelly had called Dee-Dee and asked her what to do. Dee-Dee told her to go to the police and tell them that I had kicked her out of the house. Dee-Dee had gone there with her and told the police detective that I had kicked her out, also. Well, when I got there, the police detective started telling me that Shelly was a minor and it was against the law for me to throw her out of the house. I told him what had transpired and that I never really expected her to leave. I also told him that when she had finally called me, I had told her to come back home.

He looked at me kind of funny and asked "What about your other daughter?"

I said, "Which one?"

He replied, "The other one you threw out."

I looked at him and said, "She dropped out of school three months before graduation. She sat around the house until her birthday. She was eighteen years old and I told her either go back to school, get a job or find someone else to support her, and that she chose to move out. Then I said,

"I didn't know there was a law against an eighteen year old moving out." He said that she had told him a different story and that she had made it sound like I had put her out to live on the streets. I was so angry with her that it was a good thing she wasn't around when I left that police station or she would have heard a few words from me.

The police detective reiterated to Shelly that she had to attend classes at least until she was seventeen. If she didn't attend, they could fine me five hundred dollars and make me spend time in jail and I explained to her that, if that happened, I would lose my job and then I wouldn't be able to take care of them and they would be taken away from me. She decided to go to the same alternative school that Jaycie had attended. She ran into Larry there a few times and once overheard him talking to one of the teachers and telling her how I was a bad mother and how I had mistreated Dee-Dee. Well, Shelly had stepped in and told the teacher he was a liar and told him he shouldn't be telling stories without first checking to see if they were true. Shelly talked to him for a while and he told her some of the things Dee-Dee had told him about her life and she told him right out that they were all lies.

Shelly went to the alternative school for a while and then dropped out. She started going out and partying all weekend. She stayed home during the week and helped with the babies, but weekends she partied. She couldn't get a job because she didn't have a driver's license. They had passed a law that if you dropped out of school, you couldn't get a license until you were eighteen, so now she had no way to get to a job. We lived in an area where there is no public transportation, so if you don't have a car, you have no way to get places and most businesses are too far away from residential areas to walk to.

One of Shelly's friends introduced her to a guy named Dwayne. He came over to the house and Shelly thought he was gross and didn't want to have anything to do with him, but Jaycie decided she liked him and they started dating. He was one of those obnoxious and overbearing people. No one could see what she liked in him, but they kept dating and eventually she would move into an apartment with him.

During this time, Shelly had started dating a guy named Adam. I didn't care much for him, but kept quiet because I was afraid she would leave again. She kept dating him and eventually got pregnant. Well, I asked if they were getting married or anything and she said she didn't want to marry him. They had actually broken up when she discovered she was pregnant. Again, here I was with one daughter and her two babies living with me and the babies' father had been staying here most of the time, and now another daughter pregnant and not married. All I kept thinking was, what did I do to deserve this? I had taught my children the difference between right and wrong. They knew about birth control, so why did they do this?

In August, Shelly gave birth to a beautiful baby boy she named Robert. I was in the delivery room with her, and it was really a miracle to experience the birth. Jaycie felt that Adam should know about the birth and called him. Of course, he and his mother showed up at the hospital and stayed there all day even though Shelly really didn't want them there. He tried to tell her what to name the baby, but she told him she had already named him and had filled out the birth certificate. He was not happy about that. When she came home he told her he was coming over and she told him not to. He called a few times, but she didn't want anything to do with him and didn't want him around her son. I found out later that he was into drugs pretty deep and she was fed up with him. She started dating a guy named Danny. He seemed to be a nice kid and he helped her with the baby.

~Chapter 13~

Tommy was having problems with his back and legs and, after a series of tests, the doctors discovered that he had Multiple Sclerosis. He acted as if it was worse than it actually was. Everyone was getting fed up with his play-acting. In fact, my kids thought that he was lying about the whole thing and did not realize that he was just making it seem a lot worse than it was. He wanted everyone to feel sorry for him. He would just lie around the house all day feeling sorry for himself and we were all getting fed up with that and the fact that he didn't do anything but order people around and expect everyone to be his maid.

In the spring, Jaycie and Dwayne decided to get married, but before the wedding, which was the end of May, she discovered that she was pregnant. Even though she was pregnant, I tried to talk her out of marrying him because we all knew he was abusive toward her and the girls. She wouldn't listen to me though. She asked me to make her wedding dress and the bridesmaid dresses. Shelly was one of the bridesmaids and I couldn't get her to let me measure her for her dress. Finally Jaycie called me one night and told me that Shelly was pregnant. I was beside myself. I confronted Shelly and asked her why and she said she just wanted another baby. I told her that was great, but did she ever stop to think that while she was having her babies, I was the one working my butt off to support her and her kids? By this time she and Danny were not seeing each other anymore and she didn't even tell him she was pregnant.

The day of Jaycie's wedding I gave it one last shot and tried to talk her out of getting married, but she wouldn't listen to me. I walked her down the aisle and the wedding went perfectly. She was a beautiful bride. They went away for a week and the girls stayed with me for the first three days and then they spent the rest of the time with his parents because I had to go back to work.

Shelly had Elizabeth exactly nine days after Robert's birthday. I was in the delivery room with her again. She was a beautiful baby. Jaycie called Danny when the baby was born and he came to the hospital to see her and Shelly. He said she looked just like he did when he was a baby and a few days later showed up at the house with one of his baby pictures to prove it. He came around a couple more times and told her he was going to give her money to help out, but he never did. When she tried to get in touch with him she could never find him. After a while, she just quit trying.

Jaycie called me at work one day and said she and Dwayne had stopped by the house and Dwayne and Tommy had gotten into a fight. She told me that I had to tell Tommy to move out. Well, that really made me mad! What right did she have to tell me that? I told her that, and just as she was doing, I would live my life the way I chose. She said she wouldn't come back over as long as I was with him and she hung up. She quit coming over and very seldom called. So, when Dwayne's mother had a baby shower for her, I refused to attend. Shelly and my mother went and I sent her a gift with them. Her son was born in December. She called after the birth and we went to the hospital to see him.

I really think that my relationship with Tommy would have ended a lot sooner than it did if it hadn't been for my kids. Unfortunately, when the girls tried to talk me into breaking up with him early on, I resented their interference. I have since realized that I felt as if they didn't want me to have a life of my own and I continued seeing him more or less to prove to them that they didn't control my life. Unfortunately, I ended up emotionally tied to him and he had me convinced that I couldn't survive without his moral and emotional support.

I should probably say more about my relationship with him. When I met Tommy, I was really quite desperate for companionship. He was a God-send of sorts. I found as I got to know him, that we liked a lot of the same things like fishing, camping, barbequing, etc. He introduced me to horseracing and bingo. When I had problems, he would listen while I talked about them and he often offered workable solutions.

As I said before, it was at this point in my life that it seemed no matter what I did, nothing ever seemed to turn out right. I had given up on my kids and, unfortunately, spent more and more time with Tommy and less with them. I wouldn't say that I neglected my kids. I made sure they had clothes and food and a home. I just, how should I put it? I traded quality time with them for my own comfort and needs.

As I look back at those years now, I realize that I might have been able to prevent some things that happened. But, at the time, I was being selfish and fulfilling my own needs. When my kids tried to get me to stop spending so much time with Tommy, I took offense. I felt as if they were trying to run my life and that made me more determined to spend time with him. I know now that the way I felt then was wrong.

Breaking up with him was really a relief. I actually had thought about it for quite a while but was afraid to do it because I was afraid of being alone. I had known for quite a while that I had stayed with him more out of habit than love. With him around, I had companionship, another adult to talk to, someone to go places with. I think when I really realized my true feelings for him was one night when there was an argument between him and Shelly. I don't remember what it was about but he thought I should take his side and when I didn't he threatened to leave. I told him, "So leave. These are my kids, my family. When you leave, you'll be gone, but they'll still be my kids and my family."

He asked, "Does that mean they are more important to you than I am?"

Without hesitation, I responded, "Yes." And I really meant it. It was after that night that I started reassessing our relationship and my life.

I finally told Tommy that he was going to have to move out because he was coming between my children and me. He was not happy and we got into a big argument over it, but he moved out. For a while after he moved, I started getting hang-up phone calls. Well, this was right about the time they came out with the star sixty-nine telephone feature and I got it installed on my phone. I found out it was Tommy calling. I confronted him about it and he denied it. Knowing him as well as I did, I figured he would try something like having my phone number changed without me knowing it. I decided to call the phone company and have them put a code on my account that only I knew so no one could make any changes to my service except me. A few days later he called and made some comment about me changing my phone number and knew I was planning something. I figured he had called and tried and found out he had to have a code to do it.

We still talked to each other and went places together sometimes, but it wasn't an exclusive relationship any more. We were both free to see other people if we wanted to. We were slowly drifting farther and farther apart. At first, when we broke up, I was upset and lonely and missed having someone to go places with. I stayed home most of the time now because I don't like to go places alone. After a while, however, I began to enjoy life and my freedom. I guess our break-up was harder on Tommy than me, because he was so dependent upon me. He went through some bad times and eventually joined Alcoholics Anonymous and quit drinking. After he quit drinking, his personality changed dramatically. I found that the person he had become was even more obnoxious and overbearing than the person he had been and I didn't like the new him at all.

Jaycie and Dwayne had expected me to kick Tommy out the night of the fight, but, since I hadn't done it and remained friends with him, they were mad. So because Tommy and I were still friends and I still went places with him and talked to him, Jaycie and Dwayne would not come around or call. I didn't see her son again after he was born until he was several months old. I thought she was going to be just like Dee-Dee and never come around. We missed her girls and wanted to see them, but they were not allowed to see us or talk to us either.

In 1994, my dad passed away suddenly. He had emphysema and was not well, but we hadn't expected his death. It was quite a blow and I was devastated. He was in the ICU for three days before they told us we needed to turn the machines off and let him go. There were so many things I wanted and needed to say to him before he went, but now I couldn't. Only two people could be in the ICU room at a time and only for fifteen minutes every four hours. At visiting time my mother went into the room with him and then we kids had to take turns going in there with her. She would not leave and let any of us have a few minutes alone with him and I really resented that.

I felt guilty because a couple of days before this he had been so weak he had fallen while trying to go to the bathroom. I had told my mother to tell him if he wasn't better the next day I was going to take him to the doctor, but I didn't. I knew he didn't want to go to the hospital, so I wasn't prepared to force him. And now he was gone and I felt like it was my fault. For months I relived that day when I had helped him pull himself up to walk to the dining room. I had wanted to ask him if he wanted to go to the hospital and I didn't do it. I thought if I had, he would still be alive even though his doctor had told me at the hospital that he had told my dad he only had months to live the last time he had seen him. He had never told anyone.

All of my kids were at the hospital before Dad passed away, except Jaycie. She got there after he was gone and was mad because we didn't wait for her. I tried to tell her that there was nothing we could do, but she thought we did it on purpose. My son took it the hardest of all of the kids, I think. He was so close to my dad and he was just devastated. After my dad passed away, Keith just quit trying in school. When he reached seventeen, he just signed himself out of school and walked away. He sat around the house for several months not doing anything. I hoped he would change his mind about school, but he never did. Eventually he got a job and started wheeling and dealing with cars until he ended up with the one he really wanted. He is now twenty-five, has a good job and a new truck that he bought without help from anyone.

I was determined that I was going to break the apron strings tying my brother to my parents after Dad passed away. Up until that time, every automobile my brother had ever owned had either been given to him by my parents or they had bought for him. No one had ever bought my sister or me a car, or given us one, and I thought it was about time my brother learned to take care of himself. Finally when he was fifty-eight years old, he actually bought a car without getting money from my mother. Another small victory.

My mother had also been loaning money to my brother just about every week and he very seldom ever paid it back. She even gave him money to buy a house. When his son was about thirteen, his wife became pregnant and had a baby boy. A year later she had a little girl. Now they had three kids and his wife still didn't work. She stays in bed half the day and does drugs the rest of the time. My brother works and then goes home and takes care of the cooking and the house. My mother would feel sorry for him and give him money. I finally told her that he was a grown man, almost old enough to retire, and it was his own fault that he lived the way he did and it was time he learned to live on his own. Finally she told him he needed to start trying to make ends meet because she couldn't afford to keep giving him money. I know she still gives him money from time to time, but not as often, and now she just won't tell me when she does it or how much she gives him.

~Chapter 14~

After my dad passed away, I felt sorry for my mother and didn't want her to be alone all the time. They had been married for fifty-one years and she needed time to adjust to his being gone. I started cooking a big dinner on Sundays, picking her up and taking her to my house to eat. She would spend the afternoon and then go home. I thought this would only be for a while. Boy, was I wrong. After Dad passed away, my mother quit cooking totally. She only ate TV dinners. Seven years after he passed away, I was still entertaining her every Sunday. My sister would go to Mom's house on Mondays after work and takes her out to eat. Most of the time, when she needed something, she would call me. I had to do her Christmas shopping for her and take her to the store. She quit driving a couple of years ago, so someone has to take her every place she goes.

We have tried to get her to go to the Senior Citizens Center to join in on the functions they have, but she doesn't want to be with "all those old people". I keep trying to tell her she might enjoy being with someone her own age and she says she doesn't want to. I want so bad to tell her, "Well, I would really enjoy being with people my own age some time!" but I don't do it because I don't want to hurt her feelings.

I got tired of cooking a big meal every Sunday and running back and forth so we go out to eat on Sundays if I don't cook. One Saturday she wanted to go out to eat and, since then, I have to take her out every Saturday. I wouldn't mind it but I can't get anything done because I have to go at whatever time she decides she wants to go.

Not long after my dad passed away, Jaycie showed up at my house with her two girls. She said she had left Dwayne for good this time and he was on his way to Tennessee with his parents. I asked about her son and she said he was with Dwayne. She said she was tired of him abusing her and the girls and he had started threatening her with a gun. She felt the only way she could leave alive was to let him take the baby. She said she knew he would be okay with Dwayne's mother to take care of him. She was quite upset, but felt she had no other choice at the time.

She finally filed for a divorce and got visitation rights, but she had to go to Tennessee to see baby Dwayne. She had started dating a guy named Charles and they were living together. It had been a year since she had seen her son when Charles drove her and the girls to Tennessee for the weekend so they could see him. She was heartbroken when she had to leave him. Eventually, Dwayne remarried and he and his wife and parents all moved back here. He let her see Dwayne Jr. once in a while when he felt like it. Dwayne's wife was mean to his son and he eventually divorced her.

Shelly started dating Harold and he stayed at my house quite a bit. When Robert was almost two, they moved into an apartment together. He was good with the kids and Shelly seemed to be happy. They had his boys every other weekend. Eventually, after being together about five years, they bought a house. About the same time, his ex-wife got married and moved to Georgia. Now he only gets to see his kids for one month during the summer and at Christmas. Robert and Elizabeth think he is their daddy even though they call him Harold and they think his sons are their brothers. They have been together for eight years now and seem to be content just living together and not being married. He treats the kids as if they were his own and he is good to Shelly, so I am happy for them.

Jaycie and Charles have been together for eight years now. They have had their ups and downs and moved every year it seems until they moved to Abilene two years ago. I didn't think her girls would ever spend two years in the same school system! Bryan has fathered another illegitimate child, got married once and had a child with her, too. When she left him and moved to Georgia, he followed her. But she divorced him and he gave up his rights to the child. He is now living with a woman who has a son and he still only pays child support when forced to. Cassandra and Missy have grown accustomed to living with Charles even though I don't know how they really feel about him. He had a bad life as a child and really doesn't know how to be a parent, but I have to give him credit for trying, whether I like him or not.

Dee-Dee eventually had a breakdown and ended up leaving Larry. I think her biggest problem is that she can't separate fact from fiction. She has told so many lies in her lifetime that she doesn't know what is true and what is not. She had an affair while with Larry and her second daughter, Katrina, was the result. The baby looks nothing like her or Larry, and Dee-Dee has admitted to her sisters and me that she looks just like her real father. She has never told Larry the truth about Katrina. Dee-Dee met Bert through a singles ad in the paper and they ended up getting married. I wasn't asked to help with the wedding or to participate in it, but was invited to it. I debated about it for a while and eventually decided to go. I didn't know what kind of stories she had told Bert and his family about me, but I decided to just hold my head up and go anyway.

Jaycie ran into Larry not long after the wedding and mentioned to him about Dee-Dee getting married. He said, "Yeah, the girls told me about the wedding. I'm glad she finally got the fairy tale wedding she always wanted." They talked for a while and she asked why he wouldn't ever let her come around or bring the girls around. He laughed and told her he had nothing to do with that. It had been all Dee-Dee. In fact, he said he told her she needed to make peace with her family because someday she might need them. During the time she was with Larry, I saw her maybe once a year. Now the girls are like strangers and, oddly but sadly, I have no real feelings for those grandchildren.

A little over two years after she married Bert, Dee-Dee had a little boy. I took my mother over to her house to see him when he was only a couple of weeks old. I didn't see him again until he was six months old. Now I see her and the kids at Christmas and sometimes she shows up with them on Mother's Day. She won't go to my mother's house to visit because it is run down and not good enough for her. She was coming over sometimes on Sunday when my mother was here. I realized that the only time she came was when my mother was here so I stopped having my mother over on Sundays. Cruel as it sounds, if she wants to see me she can come over, but if she wants to visit my mother, she can go to her house or she just won't see her.

One day in 2000, I decided to call my ex-husband Keith's mother to see if she knew how to get in touch with him. I knew he had been ill and probably wasn't going to live long. I thought it would be nice if he talked to the kids. He hadn't seen them in years and I felt that they might want to make peace with him before he died. She took my number and said she would give it to him when she talked to him. A couple of weeks later, the phone rang and it was Keith. We talked for a while and, in my heart I forgave him and was able to make my peace with him. I was able to give up the resentment and hatred I had felt for him all these years.

I told the kids it might be the last time they ever got to talk to him. Keith talked to him and then Jaycie called him, but Shelly wouldn't. Several years before, she and Jaycie had stopped at the house where he was living. He came to the door and said hello to Jaycie and then asked who her little friend was. Jaycie told him that it was his youngest daughter, Shelly. This angered and hurt Shelly. Then when my dad passed away, Keith had come to my mother's house and Jaycie and Shelly were there with me. He started talking to Jaycie again and again asked who Shelly was. Again it angered her. She resented the fact that he didn't recognize her those two times and hadn't made an effort to keep in touch with them, so she had refused to talk to him now.

About three weeks later, I received a call from Keith's mother that Keith had passed away. It kind of angered me that she told me to let her know when arrangements were made for his funeral and what they were. I certainly didn't feel obligated to pay for his burial and the kids really didn't feel as if they should. After all, they hadn't seen him in years and he lived about an hour away. Dee-Dee decided that she would handle everything and pay for it, so we let her. He wanted to be cremated so the funeral home prepared the body for a family viewing and my mother, Keith, Jaycie, Shelly and I went. Dee-Dee was supposed to meet us there, but she didn't show up until after we had gone. It was sad and I felt sorry for him that he had died without knowing his children and never having met even one of his grandchildren, but I also knew that it was his own fault. I felt that the kids needed the opportunity to say goodbye even though they didn't cry. It was as if it just closed a chapter in their lives.

~Chapter 15~

It's funny, but during all these years, I always had such a hard time relating to people and confronting personal problems and problems with my kids, but at work my personality is totally different. I am forceful and dynamic. I don't have a problem expressing myself or facing problems. It's as if I am really two different people. I had the same job for twenty-two years during which time I earned a paralegal certificate.

Two and a half years ago, I fell on some water on the floor of a large discount store and dislocated my knee. All the ligaments in my knee were torn and I was off work for six weeks. I went to therapy for months. I ended up suing the store for my medical expenses. The suit was finally settled a couple of months ago. The worst thing about this accident was that I missed out on a free trip to London with the company I worked for. Shortly after that trip I missed, the company was acquired and my job was done away with. So, after twenty-two years at the same job, I was out of work. I got a good severance package, but it took me fourteen months to find a new permanent job. The job I have pays less money but is close to home. My boss is an attorney I worked with years ago at my old job. However, one good thing did come of my losing my job—my retiree insurance was grandfathered and, if I take early retirement at fifty-five, I can get medical insurance for life. That's one good reason to hope my fifty-fifth birthday comes soon!!

I think it would be nice to find a good man to spend my "twilight years" with, but even now, the thought of living with and being intimate with a man ties my insides up in knots. I try to believe that the time I spend taking care of my mother is the reason I don't have time for a social life, but in my heart I know that I keep myself from having one. I try to lose weight, but to no avail and I believe I hide behind this weight so I don't have to be faced with an intimate relationship.

I often wonder what my life would have been like if things had not happened the way they did. For years I would daydream about my life being different. In my daydream, I had married Jimmy and lived a wonderful life. Now I wish I could face him and tell him what he did to me. I would like to tell him how he had taken my innocence and then, by the actions he took, had broken my heart and ruined my life. I know that everything that has happened to me in my life can be blamed on my actions as much as anyone else's, but I also know that everyone that I ever came in contact with had something to do with shaping my life. If I had learned at an early age how to socialize and mix with people, I would probably be more outgoing. If I had learned to express myself and bring problems out into the open, I would have been able to have a stronger relationship with my children.

It seems that I have spent my whole life working and taking care of people. Don't get me wrong, I wouldn't trade anything for the years when my children were growing up and I really don't mind taking care of my mom because I know she won't be here forever. But, I would really like to have some time in my life that is just for me. When people ask me if I would ever get married again, I tell them I would if I could find a nice man who has a permanent job where he makes more money than me and, preferably, owns a better home and car than mine. At least that way I would know that he didn't expect me to take care of him.

Keith Jr., Shelly and I have been working on starting our own business. We have been making tee-shirts and business cards and such for people and I now own an embroidery machine. I have been making embroidered items that I plan to sell. I am a good seamstress and enjoy doing handicrafts and Shelly is very artistic. She makes wooden yard art and decorated picture albums, as well as ceramics. So, we think we might start a business selling hodgepodge type handicrafts. Who knows? Maybe something will come of it.

My daughter Jaycie's boyfriend told her that he thought they fought too much and she needed to move out. She and her two daughters came to stay with me on my birthday. Less than a month later she found out that her ex-boyfriend had married some nineteen-year-old girl.

Shelly's boyfriend lost his job and collected unemployment, then found a job and quit it within a month. He spent several months sleeping and drinking and finally took another job. Unfortunately, they had problems that they couldn't seem to work out. Things came to a head shortly before Christmas and they split up. She moved into an apartment with her kids and he is staying with his sister and working when he feels like showing up. She found out that he got fired from that job the other day. Her kids are having a bit of a time with the split because he has been a father figure to them for eight years, but I think they will be ok.

I had thought that my girls were all settled and all I had to worry about was my son getting settled into some sort of life. Now, it seems I have to start all over worrying about them being happy and secure in a good life. I know if I were to die today, I wouldn't rest in peace knowing that their futures are uncertain.

The one thing I have learned about all the experiences I have had in my life is that it is definitely true that you should never judge a person until you have walked in their shoes. It is always so easy to criticize people but, until you have experienced what they experienced, you can't judge their actions.

All I have ever wanted for my life was to have someone to love me, to have a nice home, a car to drive, food on the table and enough money to live on. And, most importantly, I wanted my kids to have a better life than I had. I guess there is still hope for me but as I get older, it becomes harder for me to imagine my knight in shining armor coming and swooping me up in his arms and carrying me off to some romantic interlude! But who knows? Anything can happen if you want it bad enough! And I choose to believe that there is still hope for me.

To contact "Leigh Anne": survivorleighanne@yahoo.com

"Emily's" Story

When I Look into My Mirror

When I look into my mirror
At the face that's watching me,
I can see a world of changes
In the woman that I see.
If you look a little closer,
You can stare into her soul,
She's an open book for reading,
Filled with tales, her life has known.
When I look into my mirror
At the smile on my face,
It is there to hide my sorrow,
It is there to hide my pain.
I have lived a life of changes,
But not always for the best.
It just takes a face to wear them
And a heart to let them rest.
When I look into my mirror
At my crystal eyes of blue,
You can't see the tears I'm hiding
Or the way they look at you.
They have seen so many troubles,
But they always seem to shine.
I can mask so many sorrows
If I hide behind my eyes.
When I look into my mirror now,
I see someone that's new.
All the streams of tears have dried up
And my smile is shining through.
My deep blue eyes are sparkling
Like the morning drops of dew,
I have spent my life reflecting,
In the mirror, at my youth.
When I look into my mirror
There's a woman filled with love.
She has learned to take her sorrows
And to make them tears of joy.
She has shared her deep reflections,
With the heart of someone true.
When I look into my mirror,
It's myself that's shining through.
(5/30/98)

~Chapter 1~

We never know how vulnerable we are to the path of unfaithfulness until we find it staring us in the face. I'd like to tell you my story of how I ended up on that path and how it has changed my life.

I grew up in a military family for the first ten years of my life. There were four of us, plus my mom and my dad. My brother, Ted, and me are the oldest—we're twins. Then there's Samantha, who is four years younger than us, and a brother, Allan, who is six years younger. In the first ten years of my life we moved to six different states. Dad was in the Navy and kept getting transferred. From the time I turned six until I was ten, we owned a home in Connecticut, and I've always thought of that home as where I grew up.

We had a fairly normal life like everyone else. Maybe we weren't the Cleavers or the Nelsons, but as children we were all happy. Mom and Dad had their share of problems like all married people. It wasn't easy being married to a man in the service, and in the very early sixties there were lots of conflicts going on in the world, especially with Cuba. Dad got shipped out a lot during that time and was also stationed in Chicago, but he didn't take us with him that time.

Aside from all the moving, I did what most girls my age did. I loved playing with Barbie dolls, listening to records and dancing, and had my share of puppy loves, too. I remember having a crush on one boy, Bobby, who was four years older than me. One day on the way home from school, he jumped in the seat next to me on the school bus and wouldn't let me out. My heart was going a hundred beats a minute; he was just so cute. There was another time when all the neighborhood kids were playing hide and seek in the woods, and I happened to hide under a big, old oak tree that had fallen. I was under the roots and Bobby happened to come along to hide there also. When he saw me he winked and gave me a quick little peck on the cheek. I thought I'd never wash my face again.

When I approached my tenth birthday, Dad helped one of the neighbors move their relatives from Massachusetts to Connecticut, into the same development that we lived in. I noticed some problems not too long after that between Mom and Dad. You see, my dad was not only a womanizer, but he also had a thing for younger girls. The events at that time period in my life contributed to some of the events of my adult life, so this is where my story actually begins.

~Chapter 2~

I've never considered myself a dare seeker or a woman of the world, but was more the meek, girl-next-door type; the one who would greet you with a hello and a smile and various other pleasantries, but never, and I mean *never*, one who would discuss her sexual preferences or practices with other people! That was something very personal to me.

I never had much luck with the men in my life; from the time I was ten years old up to my forties. I was very much intimidated by men, and I found myself living much of the time in my own little shell. My mistrust in men started when I was only ten years old, when I awoke in the middle of the night to find my father fondling me and performing oral sex on me. I had no idea what was happening. He even made me perform oral sex on him, while holding my head down with his heavy hand. My parents had been at a party that night at a neighbor's house and Mom was still at the party when dad came home. I remember him being drunk, but that was still no excuse for what he did to me. That was the one and only time that ever happened, but that one night was enough to scar me for life. I hated what my father did to me. I was hurt, ashamed, and thought I had done something terribly wrong. I knew what he did was wrong because it didn't feel right, but who could I tell? Certainly not my mother. I was afraid that she would blame me. I guess that's what any ten-year-old would think. I hid my shame and anger by eating. It was the beginning of the weight problem that would follow me through life. It was also the beginning of many years of heartache in my relationships with men.

I have never told my mother about what my father did to me; I was too afraid and ashamed. I knew my dad had a problem and my mother knew that he had one, too. She divorced him the following year, only for me to find out years later that she did so because she was afraid that something like what had happened would happen. She felt relieved in her heart that she had gotten us away before it ever did. I could never, and will never, tell her that it was already too late.

Mom moved us to New York, to move in with her sister and brother-in-law and their five children. Four children in my family and five in their family along with three adults in an older two-story home with only three bedrooms was a bit much. All four girls slept in one room. I was the oldest at eleven and I slept on the top bunk; next came my sister, who was seven; then my cousin who was also seven and they shared the bottom bunk; and my youngest cousin, who was only a baby. Her crib was in the big closet. My two brothers had to share a room with my three male cousins. Mom got to sleep on the sofa in the living room. We lived with my aunt and uncle like that for almost two years. That's when my mom was able to get us a place of our own.

My dad and mom were sitting in divorce court the afternoon that President Kennedy was shot. I remember how upset I was that day to begin with, and then this horrible tragedy to our nation happened the same day. I remember being on the bus to religion class when they told us about it. What a horrible day for us all, but for me it held many other memories. Although I was disappointed in my dad for what he had done to me, I still loved him. Crazy, huh? I felt such a deep sense of loss that day; I lost my father, and we lost the President. It was a sad day indeed.

My father had a thing for younger women. In fact, after he divorced Mom, he married my best friend. She was part of that family he had helped move down from Massachusetts. Mary was four years older than me and I found out that my dad had been seeing her before my mom even left him. How could she do that to me? I thought she was my best friend. I have to admit though, that I wasn't too surprised. After all, I knew my father had a thing for younger women, and I should have seen all the signs, especially after what he had done to me. I hated Mary for breaking up my family and I could never and will never forgive her for that. They went to a southern state to get married when Mary turned sixteen. Mary became pregnant not too long after they married, and I have a half-brother named James.

Mom found a new place for us to live in the next town over. It was the bottom floor of a two-family house. We had spent a short year in the school where my aunt lived and now we had to make new friends again. That's where I met Tammy. Tammy was not quite a year older than me, but was a grade ahead of me in school. I was going into the seventh grade so I would be going to the high school. Tammy was the only person I knew in this town, so I had to start from scratch once school started. Being the "new" kid is never an easy thing for a girl in high school. I have always been a full-figured female, and that is probably one of the reasons men always had the wrong idea about me, including the boys. I started wearing a bra at the age of ten, having blossomed much earlier than most girls my age.

I met some really great friends at my new school. I wasn't in the popular crowd or the "black leather jacket" crowd. I was just in with the average kids. I made a big mistake within the first month of school though when I developed a crush on Andy, one of the boys in the popular crowd. The girls in that crowd didn't like that one bit. I started finding nasty letters in my locker and started getting nasty looks from everyone in that crowd. How was I supposed to know he was dating one of the popular girls? Needless to say I backed off from him real fast.

Mom dated a few men during my high school years. I remember her meeting this one man, Joseph. I didn't like him at all. He had never been married. I was thirteen at the time, and there was something about him that I did not like. I would have flashbacks about my own dad and what had happened with him. I was so afraid the same thing would happen with this man because he just gave me that "look". I did everything I could to break them up. I wasn't very nice to him at all and my mom couldn't figure out why. I just couldn't tell her. They eventually broke up and my mother was very angry with me because I wouldn't give him a chance. I couldn't. I was too afraid.

A new girl, Janice, moved to the neighborhood from the Bronx. We hit it off instantly, and became really great friends. Janice introduced me to her cousin, Billy, who lived in the next town. But Janice only attended our school for one year; then her family moved back to the Bronx. Billy and I would get together from time to time to go out and do things. I had a feeling that Billy was gay, but I never asked because it didn't matter to me.

It took me many years to trust a male and boyfriends in high school were not in my plan. In the spring of my sophomore year I met a boy on the telephone party-line. His name was Charlie, and he was one of my teacher's sons. I remember my teacher talking about his son, all favorable of course, so I decided "What the heck!" His father always made him sound so nice.

It was a blind date and Charlie asked me to bring along a friend for his friend. We were going to go to a friend's house to listen to music. Back in the late sixties girls never went out in jeans or pants; it was always skirts or dresses. So I wore a pretty sweater and a nice straight skirt. I had to sit in the back seat with my Charlie and his friend did the driving. As we approached what looked to be a long driveway, the driver signaled and made the turn. We drove down this long dirt road until we came to a lake with no house in sight. I asked where we were and Charlie told me to shut up. Then he opened my door and said, "Let's take a walk." I got out of the car and he took my hand and led the way. We walked to the other side of the lake and he started getting very free with his hands. I told him to stop, that I wasn't that kind of girl. He got very angry and literally pulled me back to the car.

It was getting dark and I told them we had to be getting home soon. Charlie was still very angry with me and was all over me in the car, but I still resisted. He started to chuckle as he unzipped his pants and he pushed my head down, forcing me to perform oral sex on him. When I didn't comply he took out a can of ether and tried to knock me out. Flashbacks of what had happen between my father and I were running through my head. How could this happen to me again? He dropped my friend off at her house then they drove me home, and as I got out of the car he said, "If you tell anyone about this, I will slander your name all over school." I never said a word to anyone, but he didn't keep his word. That week in school there were nasty rumors circulating about me and my 'date.'

The "black leather jacket" crowd would drive past my house yelling words like, slut, whore, and other profanities at me. I was devastated, so much so, that I cut the class that Charlie's father taught for over two weeks. I couldn't bear to hear him praise his black leather jacket, drug taking, "good boy" of a son, again. At this point in time, I had sworn off boys completely.

I met another guy on the telephone party-line…Vito. Vito lived in the next town and was friends with a couple of the girls I knew in school. We talked for a couple weeks and he invited me over to listen to records. Being only fifteen, I told him I could only come over if his mother was there. He told me that she would be. I remember what had happened with Charlie and I didn't want the same thing to happen again. Vito sounded so different. When I knocked on the door, he answered. I went inside and didn't see his mother. He said she was lying down. We went into his room and I sat down. He shut the door and I said, "But …your mother.…" He said he didn't want to wake her up with the music. I was quite naïve back then. I should have known that she wasn't home. Immediately Vito was all over me. He almost ripped off my blouse, but I got up, put myself together and ran out of his house, and I cried all the way home.

I did not hear from Vito again, nor did I want to. My friend, Mary, invited me up to her house after school one afternoon. I wasn't the best of friends with her, but she was in our group and closer to my friend, Jeannie. I heard nothing when I entered her house and I told her that I thought some of the other girls were going to be there. She told me that they were downstairs in the basement and we were going to have a séance. It was very dark as we went down the stairs. When I got to the bottom of the stairs, Mary turned on the light and I found Vito sitting there. He was still so pissed off at me for running out on him that day that he had come to get even. I had no idea Mary even knew him. Mary stood behind my chair and tied my hands behind me. Vito took some straight pins and tried poking my nipples with them. He got me a couple times, but I was crying too hard so he stopped. I was totally humiliated and very angry. I looked at Mary and asked her how she could do this to me! She said she didn't know he was going to do that. I had a feeling that maybe she was drinking or high on something, but I didn't know for sure. I didn't talk to Mary after that, nor did I tell the other girls what had happened.

Needless to say, I didn't date much after that episode. My faith in the male population was really starting to dwindle. My grandfather had the ability to read palms and about this time, I had asked him to read mine. When I asked him what my palms revealed, he replied, "I really don't want to tell you. The only thing I will say is, beware of the first three real relationships that you have with men." I had no idea what that might entail, but that was all he would say.

~Chapter 3~

I basically was a very quiet, naïve girl in high school. Although I didn't date, I did belong to a few clubs. Late in my sophomore year, the head of the music department approached me about my singing voice. The choir teacher wanted me to promise that I would try out for the musical production the following year. I did and ended up with the second lead role in the play. I was slowly coming out of my shyness and I found that I wasn't afraid to stand in front of people to sing or perform. I thank my lucky stars for that teacher because he really brought me to life and I finally felt like I belonged.

Tammy and I had such a great time in high school. We did everything together—we shopped, went to dances, to the movies, and all sorts of things. We would spend hours sitting under the apple trees in her backyard on a blanket with our teen magazines, our bottles of coke, and our transistor radios, just doing what teen girls do best—talking and daydreaming. We listened a lot to the Beach Boys and dreamed of going to the beach and watching the guys surf. The shore was about two and a half hours from us and neither one of us drove yet. We'd sometimes sit in her dad's Chevy Malibu, turn on the radio and sing to the music. We'd pretend we were cruising down at the shore, waving to the guys we passed.

The Beatles had been around a while and were coming to New York City, and oh, how we loved them. Tammy's uncle worked in the city not too far from where the Beatles were going to perform. Tammy and I were dreaming up a scheme to go down to see them. Her yard bordered the train tracks that took the trains down to the city. We planned on jumping a train one day and taking it down, and it was the perfect plan. Unfortunately for us, our sisters tattled on us and told our parents of our plans, so we both got grounded.

Tammy's dad always treated my sister Samantha and me like we were his daughters. If Tammy and her sister got lectured, Samantha and I got lectured along with them. Tammy had an older brother, Brian, whom I had a crush on. Brian and his friends would taunt Tammy and me to no end. We would play touch football with them in her back yard. Their idea of a touchdown was picking one of us up with the ball and carrying us over their shoulders to the goal line. They would put us down on the ground and yell, "Touchdown!" Brian and his friends loved to tease Tammy and me, but they were never far away. When we attended dances, and they were there or at any other functions for that matter, they were always within reach if we had any problems with anyone. They were sort of our guardian angels.

There was an old chicken coop on the property where Tammy lived that we were going to fix up for a clubhouse—a place where we could get away from our sisters and our brothers. Tammy's brother found out about it and one day when Tammy and I were back in the woods working on the shack, Brian and a friend surprised us by showing up. They tied me to the center beam with a rope, and then took Tammy and tied her hands and then put them over her knees and stuck the broomstick between them so she couldn't move. They put her up on an old table that was in there and then they left. They also gagged us so we couldn't yell for help. We just looked at each other in disbelief as they walked out. Luckily for us, our two sisters whom we had told not to follow or bother us, decided to sneak up and see what we were doing only to find out what had happened. They untied us and we were hotter than a chili pepper at her brother and his friend. We told her dad about what happened and he yelled at Brian, but after a while it was sort of funny. After we thought about it, we knew that eventually they would have come back.

Brian and his friends loved to do that to Tammy and me—scare us out of our wits. Tammy and I would sleep out on her big wrap-a-round porch during the summer. We'd have snacks, candles, our teen magazines, a transistor radio and we'd set up our chaise lounges to sleep on. Brian would wait until he knew that we were either sleeping or oblivious to the world before he would sneak home on his motorcycle by walking his bike. Then he'd walk it down the long driveway and jump on the porch to scare the heck out of us. All in all, it was great fun.

Behind Tammy's house was a really big field and at the end of the field was a wooded area. Tammy's brother made a track back there for his car. He and his friends would ride back there, and because part of the track went back into the wooded area, we couldn't see them from Tammy's bedroom windows. Tammy and I would hide back there and watch her brother and his friends and most of the time they didn't know we were there. We found a stash of girlie magazines in a wooden box along with a pack of cigarettes and matches. Tammy's dad was dead set against smoking, so Tammy and I would walk the track back to the wooded area where we would sit and have our cigarettes. We both started smoking at fifteen and neither of our parents knew.

One day when Tammy and I were walking on the track, her brother Brian quietly got in his car and started it up. By this time we were back on the part of the track that was in the wooded area. All of a sudden he was behind us and we started to run. The more we ran, the closer he got. We finally took a dive into the woods to get away from him. With our hearts really beating he came back, stopped the car and said, "Don't let me see you smoking again or I'll tell Dad."

Tammy's dad let her take the car around the track and one day she stopped and said, "Take the wheel and drive." I was so scared but I got behind the wheel of the car and she told me what to do. I ended up in the tall weeds off the track and that was the end of that. Tammy and I always got ourselves into some sort of trouble, but it was always good clean fun. Nonetheless, we never seemed to get away with anything.

When we turned sixteen, Tammy and I worked in the shoe department of a local retail store. I was the first one to get a job there, and then she came after. We had so much fun on the nights that we worked together. We made friends with most of the kids who worked in the store. Most of them were from other towns so we'd get together on Saturday nights for a party at someone's house. We'd dance, have our coke and snacks, (never any alcoholic beverages) and just have good clean fun.

~Chapter 4~

Tammy graduated in June of 1969, and I became a senior that year. That summer we decided to take a trip down to the Jersey shore. I had spent the week at my aunt's house in New Jersey and Tammy and our sisters were supposed to pick me up that Friday night. We told our parents that we had saved up enough money to spend the weekend in a hotel, but we lied. We found a sand pit, parked the car and slept in the car that night. Around four A.M. we heard a lot of noise that really scared us, so we left and found a place to park near the beach. In the morning we were awakened by a policeman who told us that we were not allowed to sleep in the car, so we got out and went on the beach. We all got really sunburned that day and we started back to New York around four that afternoon. We had met some guys earlier in the summer, and they worked at a gas station in one of the nearby towns. When we got back to New York, we went to the gas station to see them. We decided that we would sleep in the car there that night, since they worked the night shift. The boss came around midnight and made us leave, so we went down to the nearby park and slept there. We took turns watching that night, so that at least one of us was awake at all times. After two days of being together, no bath, and now really sunburned, we were all getting a bit cranky, but we couldn't go home yet, as we had told our parents that we would be home on Sunday.

That night we slept in the car again down at that town park. Our friends slept in their car next to us, so we weren't alone. The next morning we had all had about enough of each other. Tammy and I were arguing and so were our sisters, so it was time to go home. We got home around ten A.M. Our parents were really surprised to see us so early. We told them that we had run out of money and just wanted to come home. We had some great adventures that summer, and then it was off to school for me and off to work for Tammy.

I never cut school. I was too afraid. But one day, Tammy, her boyfriend, Roger, me and my friend, Paul, all cut school and went down to the city for the day. We bought some Tango and Southern Comfort before we left. Tammy was driving and I was in the back seat with Paul. We went to the Museum of Natural History. When I tried to get out of the car, I fell back in. I had had too much to drink. We made such a spectacle of ourselves that the security guard asked us to leave. We left there and went to the Museum of Modern Art. We were better there and had a great time. We got home in time so that none of the parents knew that we didn't go to school. Paul, Roger and I wrote each other notes so we wouldn't get in trouble the next day. That was the only time I ever cut school. Guess I was too chicken to do it again.

Being it was my senior year and it was getting close to prom time, I decided to ask Paul to the prom and he said yes. For the next couple of months, though, a new guy had started working with us and I really wanted to go with him. It was Roger's brother, Rich. I asked Paul if he was really sure that he wanted to go and he said yes, that his mother had already ordered his tuxedo and ordered me flowers. I sighed. How I wanted to go with Rich.

The day of the prom was a very exciting day. They let all the seniors leave at noon so we could go to the hair salon and do our last minute preparations for our big night. We would be leaving around five P.M. for our big party. Paul and I would be going with my best friend, Mandy and her boyfriend. We had our hair all done up in curls, and when I came home, I decided to call Paul to go over the details for that evening. His mother answered the phone and when I asked if he was there, she said no. I asked where he was and she said that he had gone away for the weekend! I was dumbfounded. I asked if he had picked up his tux and the flowers and she knew nothing about it. I was crushed! I was stood up the day of the prom. He had never had any intentions of going with me. I called my friend and she suggested that I call my new co-worker, Rich, and see if he wanted to go. I called, but unfortunately he was scheduled to work, so his brother Roger said that he would go with me.

He arrived in a nice brown suit and had picked flowers from his mother's garden. We had such a great time, and I forgot all the hurt that I had been feeling earlier that day. I chalked this up to another learning experience in life. What I had not expected was for Tammy to get outraged that Roger had taken me to the prom. She was convinced that Roger and I had planned on going together the whole time. I was so hurt that she would think that. Tammy didn't talk to me for quite a while after the prom. I was lost without her friendship, and I knew I had done nothing wrong to deserve it.

I had not seen my real dad at all until my senior year in high school. He came for my graduation in June of 1970. He invited me to come home with him and his new wife, Mary, for two weeks as part of my graduation present. At first I was really scared. I still hadn't gotten over what he had done to me when I was ten. Would it happen again? How was I to know? But I really wanted to spend some time with my father, so I said yes. I went back with him and Mary after graduation and spent two weeks. They still lived in the town that I had grown up in, but on the outskirts of it. I had a really nice time and luckily nothing transpired between my dad and me. Sometimes I wondered if he even remembered what he had done to me that night.

I never saw my dad alive again. He passed away that November at the age of forty from a cerebral hemorrhage. I still, to this day, have never told my mom what had happened when I was ten, so why bother now? He got his due. Mary was pregnant with their second child when Dad died. After his death, she put her first son, James, up for adoption. About a month after his death she had another baby boy, Alex, and her mother adopted him and raised him. Eventually Mary got remarried, and took Alex. I've heard from Mary once in all these years. Although I know she's wanted to contact me and remain friends, I just couldn't bring myself to associate with her, especially after what she put my family through, and the fact that she thought so little of my father that after he died she put their sons up for adoption. I never hated my dad for what he did to me, but I did feel sorry for him. I know I never provoked that incident, and I realized that he was the one with the problem. I guess at eighteen I was lucky to realize that. I never dwelled on what happened. I just moved on with my life.

~Chapter 5~

Just before my dad passed away, my mom started dating the ex-husband of an old friend of hers from high school. His name was Wayne. He was a really super guy, and had a daughter three years younger than me. My sister, Samantha, and I weren't very fond of Wayne's daughter, Diane, but we did all we could to get along. After all, it was Mom's happiness at stake. When Samantha and I heard that Wayne and Diane were coming to visit, we would sneak out the back door before she saw us, and run to Tammy's house. We really didn't want to be mean, but Diane was one spoiled brat!

They eventually moved in with us after I had graduated from high school. We moved to the next town into a really big, two-story older home. There was enough room in it for all of us to have our own bedrooms. It was great. Diane was a bit of a spoiled brat being an only child up to that point, and she had a very hard time adjusting to her dad paying attention to four other children. She would make up lies just to get my sister and me into trouble, but we learned to turn the other cheek when it came to her. I remember her spreading rumors about my sister in school, which eventually got my sister beat up by a group of girls. Diane denied having anything to do with it, but we knew better.

Diane still expected to get everything and anything she wanted. After all, she was Daddy's little girl and that is how it had always been. Sometimes, Wayne was very blind to her little schemes, but he eventually started to realize that his daughter was no angel.

Tammy and Roger got married when they turned twenty. They moved up to Buffalo, New York where Roger was attending college, and Tammy got a transfer to the telephone company up there. I didn't see too much of her after that, but we did keep in touch by telephone and letters. I missed her so much during that time. It was like losing my sister as well as my best friend.

I was far from being a promiscuous girl, but my two sisters aged sixteen and seventeen, were already sexually active. Here I was almost twenty years of age and had never had my "first time." We had two guys who lived across the street from us who had moved there from Canada. Jim and I became really close, and my seventeen-year-old sister, Diane, was involved with the other guy, Paul. Jim ended up moving in with us because the man he was renting a room from had decided to move away. Jim would sneak into my room, and we would kiss and lay there listening to music. I was very much taken with Jim. Then one night we found ourselves home alone as everyone else had gone out for the evening, and Jim came into my room. We started to kiss, and before I knew it, he was undressing me as well as himself. He was my very first lover. It was very awkward and not at all what I had expected it to be like, but he was very gentle and made sure I was comfortable.

My seventeen-year-old stepsister, Diane, started going out with Jim. She told me that they were talking about me and my relationship with him. Like a fool I believed her and didn't think anything of it. Jim and I would secretly meet outside the house, so my parents wouldn't know what was really going on. Jim and I talked about getting engaged and one day marrying, but we agreed not to say anything right away to the family.

About three months had gone by and Diane and I were sitting talking. I told her that Jim had asked me to marry him. I expected her to be very happy. After all, that is what she was working toward when she would go out with him to 'talk about me,' wasn't it? When I told her that he had asked me to marry him, she ran up the stairs screaming and crying. I was so confused. She came back down the stairs with her purse in hand, walked out the door, got in her car and drove away. Mom asked me what had happened. I told her that I had told Diane that Jim had asked me to marry him, and that she had gone ballistic. I found out later that evening that the 'talks' that she and Jim were having were nothing more than sexual encounters! She had betrayed me and so had Jim. I confronted Jim with this information and he didn't deny it. I asked him to move out and I never spoke to him again. He moved out of town.

Mandy and I were became regulars at one particular bar. I had made lots of friends there, and was quite smitten with a fellow named Jerry. We would sit together on Friday and Saturday nights at the bar. I would get up and sing with the band (I wrote music and lyrics) and they would back me up on music. Jerry and I would dance, laugh, and just have a really great time. One particular night we all went to another place and Jerry came, too. Mandy was going to give me a ride home but had to leave early, so Jerry told her not to worry, that he would make sure that I got home okay.

I didn't have my driver's license yet, and always had to depend on my friends to get a ride home, which I really hated, but I was too afraid to drive. When closing time came, Jerry asked if I was ready and I said yes. He had told another couple that he would give them a ride home, too. I said that was fine.

We dropped his friends off at their place at three A.M. I was about ten miles away from home. Jerry and I had gone upstairs with his friends for about fifteen minutes and then returned to his car so he could drive me home. When we got back in the car, Jerry leaned over and gave me a kiss, then another, and another. I heard him lock my door, but didn't think anything about it. I had not had another sexual encounter since my time with Jim and I wasn't looking for one tonight either, but Jerry was.

I really didn't want to have sex with Jerry—it was late, I didn't have protection with me and I had a feeling that it was a very fertile time of the month for me and I told Jerry all that.

He forced himself on me anyway. I remember my neck being jammed against the door handle, and I said to Jerry, "What happens if I get pregnant?"

He said, "Don't worry about it. I'll help you out if anything happens." I have to admit that it wasn't a very pleasant experience. I was starting to wonder why everyone said sex was so pleasurable. Up to this time my only experiences sexually were not very pleasant ones. So here I am in the front seat of his car, the door is locked, my neck is jammed on the handle, and Jerry has put all his weight on me so I couldn't move.

I said "No!" but it didn't matter, he was going to finish what he had started whether I liked it or not. I never realized that what had happened to me is now called date rape. I never would have thought to call the police and I just let it pass.

I started feeling sick about a month later, but I never gave it a thought. Jerry and I would meet up again about a month later at our favorite hang out. We danced, had a great time as usual, and he asked if he could drive me home. Don't ask me why but I said yes. We were driving home and he stopped the car in a deserted parking lot. We started to kiss and we eventually had sex again. That was the last time. I knew that it wasn't the right thing for me to be doing. We didn't see each other again after that. It just wasn't the kind of relationship I was looking for at twenty.

I continued to hang out there, but I started going out with the kids I worked with. What a great group of people they were. We even went to parties that our store assistant managers threw. Life was looking up. I still went to the bar with my best friend, Mandy, once in a while, but mostly I hung out with the girls I worked with. The guys that we hung around with were all in college. It was the summer of 1973, and they had rented a place down at the Jersey shore for the summer. The girls and I would go down on Saturday nights and stay over. It was one big party. None of us were dating the guys. We were just one great group of friends.

In October I was offered a new job. When they sent me for my employment physical, the doctor was poking around in my stomach and said, "There's something in there. Is there any reason for you to believe that you might be pregnant?" I guess I knew in the back of mind that I was, but I was too afraid to admit it or to find out if I was. The doctor gave me an appointment to go for a blood test that Saturday. Now the hard part came—I had to tell my mother.

Mom took it better than I had thought. We went to the appointment and found out the next day that, yes, I was indeed pregnant. I was at the end of my fifth month already. I am a full-figured woman, so being five months pregnant didn't show on me at all. It was amazing though, that after I found out that I was pregnant I instantly needed maternity clothes. The next hurdle I had to face was telling Wayne, Mom's boyfriend.

His daughter, Diane, had recently had an abortion because she found herself pregnant, too. The first words out of Mom and Wayne's mouth to me were, "There will be no abortions in this family. You got yourself into this mess—now you will deal with it." I was twenty years old. I hadn't even been sexually active for a year and now I'm already pregnant. Why me? Now the next hard thing came. I had to go to work and tell my new boss that I was pregnant.

Carmine was a great boss, and although I had only worked there a couple of weeks, he said that I could stay and they would work around my pregnancy. My due date was February fourteenth and I still had plenty of time to learn the new job and to save up for the birth of my baby. The next task at hand was to tell the father.

My mom asked me if I knew who the father was. I had had only one other sexual experience after Jerry and that was with Don. It was a one-night stand and happened during the middle of the summer, but I knew who the father was—Jerry. There was no one else that it could be.

I called his house to ask him if he would meet with me only to find out that he was in the hospital. Jerry was a carpenter and had fallen off the roof of a house and was laying in the hospital with two broken legs in traction. I really didn't like the idea of breaking this sort of news to him in the hospital, but I was already five months pregnant and I had applied for medical assistance and was told I had to tell the father first.

Mom took me to the hospital to see him. When I walked into his room he smiled at me. I asked my mom if I could be alone with him, so she waited in the waiting room. His new girlfriend was in the room, too. I asked him if we could have a couple of minutes alone to talk. He said okay and asked her to leave for a couple of minutes. When I told him that I was pregnant with his baby, he went into a rage and started yelling at me. He called me all sorts of names, and asked me to leave. I was devastated. I had no intentions of marrying him, but I wanted him to be part of his child's life.

I left the hospital in tears. Mom started to question me, "Are you sure it's his?"

I said, "Yes, it is." She believed me, as I had no reason to lie. The next night I went out with my friends, and someone came into the place we were at and told me that Jerry's girlfriend was looking for me, that she had been to another place asking if anyone had seen me. It's not easy trying to hide a pregnant girl. My girlfriend, June, took me to another place to be with the other group of friends I hung around with so that they would make sure that nothing bad happened to me. Jerry's girlfriend didn't find me that night, but she did call me the next day. She told me that she believed me, and that she would do everything she could to be sure that Jerry was responsible with helping me.

The group of friends that I was close with always made sure that nothing bad ever happened to me. The guys would protect me when we were out, and everyone was just as excited about the upcoming birth as I was. Jerry wanted nothing to do with anything. He would learn fast that he was going to be part of this even if he didn't want to.

Being I was a new employee, my health benefits hadn't kicked in yet, so I had to apply for Social Services. They would pay for all of my hospital and doctor bills, but I had to file a paternity petition against Jerry, which I did.

My son wasn't due until mid-February, but I developed toxemia and became really sick. I started having labor pains on January twenty-sixth, and the doctor told me to get to the hospital. It was so funny. Mom and I went to the car and Wayne was supposed to bring out my suitcase. It was one o'clock in the morning, and he was just so excited he forgot it. We started backing out of the driveway and I said, "Where's my suitcase?" Wayne looked at Mom, pulled back in the driveway, ran in the house and got it, and we all laughed on the way to the hospital.

The doctor eventually had to induce labor. My blood pressure was sky high. I was in labor for twenty-one hours. My son finally arrived on January twenty-sixth at ten P.M. He was a tiny little guy, only weighed in at three pounds, thirteen ounces and was only seventeen and a half inches long. The cutest little guy you could ever see. I named him Ken. I would later find out that he was jaundiced and was born with a slight heart problem. All my friends came to see me. They bought so much for him that he never had to want for anything. The only one missing was Jerry. He never came to see the baby, not that I expected him to, but it would have been nice. My friends didn't tell me until Ken was almost a year old that the doctor had told my mom that I had been in the stroke range with my blood pressure and I could have died having my son. I had always wondered why all of them were at the hospital to see me, including all the guys in our group. The nurses even let them all in the room to visit.

~Chapter 6~

After Ken was born, I had the blood work done for the paternity petition. The tests all came back positive; Jerry was the father of my child. I already knew that, but he needed to know. He was petitioned by family court to pay child support. He turned down visitation. He wasn't interested. When Ken was three months old, the week before he was baptized, Mom and Wayne got married. They wanted their first grandchild to have real grandparents. It was a small wedding and we had a small party at the house.

My stepfather grew very fond of Ken, and things worked out quite well at home for all of us. I consider myself very lucky to have had such caring parents during such a hard time in my life. My family was there one hundred percent for me and my son. I had asked Tammy and Roger to be his godparents and they said yes. When I went to see the priest about the baptism, knowing that I was a single mom he asked if I'd like a private baptism for Ken, and I said yes. I had been so nervous about not being married and having a son, but the priest told me he understood and that making the decision I had made about keeping Ken, was a brave one and he admired me for it.

As Ken grew, he outgrew his heart problem. Jerry finally started coming to see him when he was two years old. Jerry's parents took quite a liking to him, and it made me happy to see my son having a relationship with his father. That didn't really last too long, though. Jerry's paternal instincts just weren't there. It started to bother me when he would come and pick up Ken and take him to his parents' house. Jerry's mom and I had developed a nice friendship on the phone only. Jerry didn't want to bring me around to his parents' house. Maybe he was afraid they would like me.

I didn't date too much after I had Ken. Most guys always thought the wrong thing about me. They would hear that I was twenty-one and a single mom, and right away they took for granted that I was fast and loose, which was not the case. I can honestly say that I never had sex again until I got married. I was too afraid that the same thing would happen to me again and I wasn't going to let it. A mistake is something you do once, not more than that. I worked a full-time job and spent lots of time with Ken and even had time out with my friends. I still lived home with Mom and Wayne and they really enjoyed having us there.

I landed a new job in the utility company where Wayne worked in 1976. It was a temporary job but it paid well, one hundred seventy-seven dollars a week. With a child to support I decided that this was a great opportunity for me, so I took it. I worked as a temp for only nine months and then landed a permanent position with the company. The only drawback was that I had to work the second shift.

Second shift was from four-thirty P.M. to twelve-thirty in the morning, which worked out great. I would be home all day with Ken, and Mom and Wayne would watch him at night. I was still able to go out with my friends, too. The agreement with my parents was that I could stay out as late as I wanted, but when Ken got up, I got up. I can't tell you how many times I got home and Ken was awake and that would be the end of my sleep, but that was the price I paid for some fun time with my friends.

I really enjoyed motherhood and Ken was the perfect baby. Sometimes it bothered me that I wasn't married, but I knew that one day I would find the right man. As much as I would have loved to have been with Jerry, I knew in my heart that it would have never worked out for us. You can't get married because you have a child. We would have been divorced before the first year was over. I had a very full life and enjoyed every minute of it. I will admit that being a single mom does have its drawbacks, but you learn to overcome them and adapt and move on with your life.

About now a lot of the friends I had worked with at the store were finished with college and working full-time jobs and seriously dating guys. We didn't see each other all that much anymore like we had before.

I was almost twenty-five years old now and I decided it was time that I learned how to drive. I had such a great job, and even though Mom didn't mind taking me to work, and I got a ride home from one of the ladies I worked with, I was tired of depending on everyone. I started taking driving lessons. I continued to take them and finally got my license in 1977.

My new job was going great, and Jerry wasn't really part of Ken's life at all. He and I were in and out of court for back child support. He had lost his job and was unemployed, but luckily for me the judge was a hundred percent on the mother's side, and ordered him to pay me five dollars a week. The judge's theory was, if you can afford a pack of cigarettes a couple times a week, you could afford to give your child something. Even with the judge's leniency, Jerry still got behind, and big time behind. The next time we went to court, the judge told him, "If I see your face here again I'm throwing you in jail, and I won't hesitate. This child is your responsibility and you will pay for him!" He was ordered to pay me twenty-five dollars a week plus twenty-five dollars a week for back support.

There was a security guard who worked the same hours as me named Larry who kept asking me out. I found out that he was married, so I kept telling him no. He was very persistent, but I didn't give in. One night, I was walking through the lobby at work, and the other security guard said hello to me. I stopped and we talked for a while. His name was Mark. This went on for about a week or two and he was really a nice guy, but I hadn't given it much thought. The day after Thanksgiving I was working, and took my normal stroll through the lobby. Mark asked me if I'd like to go out for a drink after work and again I said no. I didn't want to fall prey to the "after work for drinks, and into bed" scheme. I hadn't dated anyone seriously in such a long time, and to be honest, I was afraid to. So I went back to my office and continued to work. About five minutes after I sat down, Mark peeked around the corner and said, "How about coffee instead?" I thought that was so sweet, and giving in, I said, "Okay."

I eventually found out that Mark had taken me out on a bet. Seems that Larry had bet him that I would turn him down if he asked me out, so

Mark went for the bet. Obviously, Larry lost the bet. In fact, they were supposed to meet the following day to go hunting, but Mark never showed up because he came to my house instead. Larry still continued to try and get me to go out with him, even though he was Mark's best friend from high school. I always said no, and even if they hadn't been friends, I didn't date married men.

In the months that followed, Mark and I were inseparable. We worked the same hours and after work at midnight, we'd go to our local Denny's for coffee and a snack. He actually ended up courting me there. Mark would drop me off around one-thirty in the morning and come back around ten A.M. so we could take Ken to pre-school. Then we would either go shopping or do our running around, then we would pick Ken up from school, and Mark would drop us off at home. It gave me a couple of hours to spend with Ken alone before work. Mark would go home to shower and get ready for work, and then pick me up on his way in. This went on every day. I think I saw more of Mark in a week, than I had ever seen of anyone else during any other relationship in my past.

Mark and I became very serious, very fast. He got along with my family...at least I thought my family liked him, and I really loved his. In January, Mark surprised me with a marriage proposal and an engagement ring and I said yes. We decided that we would get married in May on our sixth-month anniversary. I know it seems like we hadn't known each other long enough to be getting married, but I was twenty-five and he was twenty-eight and we saw each other every single day anyway. We both thought it was the perfect thing to do. We had lots of plans to make before the wedding date and we were paying for everything ourselves.

On Valentine's Day, Mark had planned a really special evening for us. We decided it was time for us to see if we were sexually compatible. Mark had made reservations at a local hotel and we made our plans. When we arrived at the hotel we were both very nervous. Mark got the key while I waited in the car. When he came out he motioned for me to come in. We happened to have parked right in front of the room they gave us. As I got out of the car I leaned over and locked his door, then I locked mine. We got in the room and Mark says, "Do you have the car keys?"

I said, "No, you do." Of course he didn't. We had locked them in the car. Thank goodness the hotel had wire hangers in the room, so Mark took one of them and was able to get his keys. Alone at last! Our first time together was very awkward as it was the first time I had had sex since I got pregnant with Ken. I was nervous and so was Mark, but all went well. That was the only time we had ever gone to a motel.

One Friday night in March, we were sitting in my living room watching television. It was about one in the morning, and all of a sudden Mark started breaking out in a sweat and holding his chest. He was in so much pain. I woke Mom and Wayne, and then I called the ambulance.

Mark spent two weeks in the hospital. It turned out that he had a blood clot in his leg that had moved to his lungs. The doctor said had I not called right away, he could have died. I was so happy that he had been with me, and not driving home when it happened.

While Mark was in the hospital, he became very friendly with one of the nurses. I had no idea just how friendly. When he was released from the hospital, he acted sort of funny, but I ignored it. I figured that he had been through a lot as it was and that he just had a lot on his mind.

I continued to make plans for our wedding and one day I got a call from his mother. She proceeded to tell me that Mark had asked one of the nurses out to dinner because he wanted to repay the kindness that she had shown him while he was in the hospital. My future mother-in-law had intercepted the call and told the girl that Mark was getting married in two months and wouldn't be taking her anywhere. The nurse was quite surprised to hear that. When I confronted Mark, he didn't deny asking her out, but said it was only because she had been so good to him in the hospital. I should have taken that as a warning sign, but I didn't.

Mark and I decided that we wanted to buy either a condo or a mobile home and started looking around. We found a cute two-bedroom mobile home in the next county, and bought it. We had the closing on April first, and decided to move into it on April fifteenth. We were getting married on May twentieth, and it seemed like the right thing to do. By this time Mark had started a new job and was going to be working on the day shift, eight A.M. to four-thirty P.M. I was still on the second shift, but there was talk that something was going to come up on the day shift. Luckily for me, it opened up just before we moved into our home. It all seemed to be working out great. We found the perfect babysitter for Ken. She was a sixty-year-old grandmother who lived next door to us.

Mark always had an eye for women and there were times I could have sworn he was seeing someone else. I could just tell by the way he was acting. I had been forewarned by one of the girls that I worked with not to marry him. She was, in a round about way, related to him and knew a lot about him. It was also about then that my mother came to me and told me that they were not comfortable with Mark, that they felt that I could do better in my life and shouldn't get married right then. But I was too anxious and I had already spent so much money. My dress was bought, everything was ordered and paid for, and we had our mobile home. It was only a month before the wedding and there was no way I was calling it off...so like a fool I went through with it.

Mark and I got married on May 20, 1978, on a beautiful hot day. The day couldn't have been more perfect. Ken was there to witness his new daddy and his mommy getting married, along with all our friends and families. It was a perfect day, and I couldn't have been more in love, but still in the back of my mind was the episode with the nurse. My grandparents couldn't attend the wedding. My grandmother had breast cancer and was too weak to come, so after the ceremony, I, Mark, my maid-of-honor and our best man, went to visit my grandparents before we went to the reception. My grandmother was overjoyed when we arrived. I wouldn't have let her miss out on the most important day of my life. I loved my grandmother so much. She meant the world to me.

Everyone had such a great time at our reception. It's funny, but I don't remember too much of it, I was so busy trying to make sure it all ran smoothly. The important thing was that everyone else had a good time. Mark's family talked about our wedding reception for years to come.

Mark and I didn't go away on a honeymoon. We went back to our mobile home alone. Ken was staying with my parents, and we had two nights alone. He had to return to work on Monday morning even though I was on vacation. I should have known then that this was how our life would be. I should have been more insistent about a lot of things at that time of my life, but I was too caught up in the thought of being married and being a wife. I left myself wide open for the marriage that I would encounter.

I was supposed to start my menstrual cycle the day of our wedding, but it never came. We waited another week and still nothing, so I had a pregnancy test done. It came back positive. I was two months' pregnant. Mark and I discussed it and decided that I would have the pregnancy terminated. I had had so many problems when I had Ken that it was just too risky for me to have another child, plus we had just gotten married and we were not ready to have another baby. We decided not to tell our families about it.

Jerry was still not a part of Ken's life, and was getting behind in his child support again. Mark and I discussed our future and Ken's and how Jerry would fit into it. We decided that we wanted a normal life for Ken, and Mark decided that he wanted to adopt him as his own. The next time that I went to court, the judge was making rulings on Jerry's back support and that's when I told the judge of our intention. He asked Jerry if that was all right with him and reminded Jerry that he would be giving up his parental rights. Jerry said it would be fine. The agreement was that instead of Jerry having to pay the back child support he owed me, he would pay for the adoption. Jerry agreed, all the papers were drawn, and Ken legally became Mark's son. I had thought that by doing this that we would be more of a family. Unfortunately, although Mark tried very hard, he just didn't seem to have any paternal instincts. It was an awkward relationship between them at best.

~Chapter 7~

Our first couple of years of marriage were happy ones. We struggled financially but we made ends meet. Ken was flourishing in school and we were a family. Mark and I had discussed having more children, but Mark really didn't want anymore, so we had left it at that. I have to admit that I really wanted another child, but we had agreed that it just wasn't feasible.

We owned a small speedboat and Mark's parents owned a cabin cruiser. We would spend our weekends at the marina, picnicking and cruising on the Hudson River. We had such a great time and Ken really enjoyed it, too. Holiday's were never very happy for some reason. Mark hated them and made sure that we all knew that.

Tammy and Roger eventually divorced. Roger became a manic-depressive and it was just too much for Tammy to take. She met a really nice guy, Kenny, who was a singer in a band. They dated for about six months before they got married, and then she seemed really happy. Her mother was unable to attend her wedding because she had breast cancer and had also developed a tumor in her brain. It was really great to see Tammy's family again.

I had always been very close to my maternal grandmother. I was the oldest grandchild and had always been my grandmother's favorite. Grandma had been suffering from breast cancer for the past five years and she was getting weaker, so she wanted me to take her diamond ring the week before Mother's Day in 1979. I told her, "No, Grandma, I'll take it when the time comes, not now." On Mother's Day Grandma died. I was devastated. Besides my mom, Grandma was the most influential woman in my life. I loved and adored her, and I still miss her so much. Before Grandma passed on, I had told her that Mark and I were not going to have any more children. She had said, "Maybe one day you'll change your mind."

Mark and I had our ups and downs during the next couple of years. He became very verbally abusive and our tempers were always flaring. I figured it was all just part of the adjustment of matrimony. I never said anything to my family about the way Mark would talk to me. He would belittle me and call me names and although I hated it, I let it slide off my back. Mark and I had a pretty good and active sex life, but I knew that sex was not the answer to our problems. Mark decided to join the local fire department and that seemed to calm him down a bit. He became really dedicated to it.

Things started to settle down and we were getting along a lot better. Then I started getting sick at night. I had the strangest feeling that I could be pregnant and I told Mark. The next morning I did a pregnancy test at home and it was positive. Mark was so happy and excited that he threw open the door early in the morning and yelled, "I'm going to be a father!" I had never seen him so excited. So were my in-laws.

I did all the right things during this pregnancy. I took very good care of myself, and I still worked my full-time job. Ken was so excited at the prospect of having a little brother or sister, as he was seven years old now. My tummy was quite large and I had to leave work at the beginning of May. Seems the baby was getting caught in the contractions and the doctor had to perform an emergency C-section. Michael was a perfect baby. There were no medical problems and he weighed in at eight pounds, fourteen ounces and was twenty-one and a half inches long. He was so big compared to Ken when he was born. Before Michael was born, I had asked the doctor about tying my tubes and he had said that he preferred to wait at least six months to make sure the baby was okay first. When the doctor saw the problems that I was having with delivery, he asked if I still wanted them tied and I said yes, so during the C-section he tied my tubes.

Mark was the perfect "new" daddy. He did so much for me; got up for feedings during the night, bathed him, and fed him. I couldn't have been happier. Mark even took care of my incision for me. Ken was such a little man and he helped me so much with his new baby brother. I was so happy in my life that nothing could have changed my feelings at that point.

I was awakened from my sleep one night, about three in the morning. I saw my grandmother standing before me. I said, "Grandma, I have another baby boy."

She said, "I know. He's there because of me." Then she disappeared. I cried for about ten minutes. Was I dreaming or was it real? It felt very real then and it still does.

Although Mark was a good daddy, he started to stay out more and was drinking with the guys from work. He went fishing one night after work, about four weeks after I had had Michael. He told me that he would be home around eight o'clock, but never showed up. At about eleven o'clock I started to get worried, as there was still no word. By one A.M. I was panicking, thinking that the worst had happened. Did someone knock him out and rob him? Was he even alive? I was a nervous wreck so I called the police to see if he had maybe been involved in an accident—nothing. I finally got a call from our town police saying that they had located him, and that he had fallen asleep while he was fishing. When Mark got home he was furious that I had called the police! How could I have done such a thing? This wasn't to be the last time he pulled things like this. Mark had a terrible habit of, 'running to the store for just ten minutes' and not coming home for hours, without even a call to tell me. He became a very inconsiderate man.

Our neighbors were a really close group of people. Our mobile home was on a dead end street and we all did things together. We cooked out a lot during the summer, and met at each other's homes in the evenings. Sometimes though, we were a little too close.

The neighbors across the street, Gina and Matt, had one son who was the same age as Ken. We were pretty close with them and they would come over at times. Gina would always boast to us all about how great her sex life was with Matt. In fact, that's all she ever talked about. Made a person wonder sometimes. I never really discussed my sex life with my husband with anyone. I felt it wasn't anyone else's business. Matt started not coming home on time after work, and Gina had no idea what was going on. Matt and I were pretty close friends and he told me that he was seeing someone else who was a mutual friend of theirs. I promised to keep his secret, and I did. This went on for quite a few months. Gina continued to tell us all how great their life was, how good Matt was in bed, and I knew just the opposite to be true. Matt was sleeping in the living room, and there was no contact, sexually, between them.

Matt was involved in an automobile accident and unfortunately, the other person died. He was very distraught over the whole incident and he turned to his 'friend' for comfort. Gina wasn't very comforting to him, and kept throwing the accident into his face all the time. Matt had had enough, and told me that he was going to tell Gina about his girlfriend and that he was going to file for divorce. The night that Matt told her, she came to my house crying. I knew what had happened and it didn't take Gina long to figure out that I knew all about it. Needless to say, she was quite upset with me, but what was I supposed to do? Tell her that her husband was having an affair? I don't think so. She wouldn't have believed it.

Matt moved out that weekend, and Gina and her son became fixtures at my house. Mark ended up hurting his back at work, and was out on disability. Rumors started flying around town that my Mark and Gina were a two-some, and that they were inseparable during the day while I was working. Seems that Gina couldn't cope with her breakup with Matt and she was leaning on my husband. About that time, there was a popular song on the radio. It was about a relationship between two lovers. I found that whenever it came on the radio, my husband would turn it up loud and start singing, and I realized it was about his relationship with Gina.

I had gone on a diet (I've always had a weight problem) and I lost seventy-five pounds. I had a feeling that something was going on between Mark and Gina because Mark hardly noticed how good I was looking, although his buddies at the firehouse did. Some of those "buddies" were looking to have a relationship and approached me on more than one occasion, but I declined each one. I confronted Mark about my suspicions about him and Gina and he told me that I was crazy. Gina even took me out one night for dinner, to prove to the town that she and I were still friends and that nothing was going on. Boy, did I play the fool! In the meantime Mark's friend, Larry, would call the house and was still trying to get me to see him. I continued to ward off his advances.

One very cold and icy January night, Gina came over to the house. She was so drunk she could hardly stand. It was all starting to get old—she wasn't cooking for her son and all she was doing was drinking and crying. It was getting late and Gina asked Mark if he would walk her across the street. It was eleven P.M. and he said that he would. I told him to go ahead but to please hurry home. He said he would. I sat and waited, and waited and waited some more and finally at one A.M. I thought, the heck with this and put my shoes and jacket on and walked across the street. I knocked on the door, but no one answered. I knew her son was sleeping so I opened the front door and stepped in. I didn't see anyone, so I walked down the hall. When I approached her bedroom, I opened the door and found my husband on top of her. I know he had his shirt on, but I didn't see anything else. I shut the door and ran home crying. He soon came home and said that nothing was going on. I said, "Bullshit, I know what I saw!" He swore that he didn't have sex with her, but I knew in my heart that he had.

The next couple of months were very stressful. The two of them tried everything to convince me that nothing was going on. Again Gina tried to take me out to try and calm things over, but I told her to go to hell. I started going to marriage counseling, trying to cope with what I felt inside. Mark kept denying any wrongdoing, as did Gina, but I knew in my heart something had been going on. I had seen the glances between them—those of lover to lover. I felt like Gina was getting even with me for not telling her about Matt's affair, and that this was her pay back to me. Mark was very bad at hiding his feelings and he was lying through his teeth. I even found out after the fact that Mark had bought Gina a gold locket. My mother-in-law sprang that one on me and Gina still has it to this day. As much as I wanted to end my marriage, I didn't want my boys to go through life without their daddy like I had to. I was going to try and work things out.

My brother-in-law started calling the house more frequently, and he knew that his brother and I were having marital problems. He was having problems with his wife also and at one point he had said to me, "I think you married the wrong brother." We always got along really well—maybe too well. I was very vulnerable at this time, still trying to get over the incident between Mark and Gina. Mark became the "neighborhood father," as everyone was either separated or divorced by now and he took it upon himself to take the children places. It was really wearing on our relationship. He was spending more time with the other kids than his own.

Mark decided to take the boys and the other kids on a camping trip for the weekend. Michael was almost two, so he went to my parents' for the weekend. This sort of gave me a weekend alone to sort things out. Mark and the kids were gone about an hour when the phone rang. It was Mark's brother. All I heard was, "Hi, sexy. What are you up to?" I told him that Mark had taken the kids away for the weekend camping and he asked if he could come over and I said yes. He came over and I started crying. He held me and told me everything would be all right, and then he started kissing me. I guess I had felt it coming. He would call and talk to me but I never expected to sleep with him. We never spoke about what we did. We just sort of let it ride.

I continued with counseling, trying to cope with my marriage and with Gina. I needed guidance. I was so afraid of being a single mom with two children now, ages nine and two, and I didn't want to live near Gina anymore. I still didn't believe Mark that nothing had happened. The counselor told me to ride it out, and not to do anything yet. But I wanted to give Mark an ultimatum—either he told Gina to go to hell and to never talk to him again, and become a faithful husband, or he had to move out and I would file for divorce. I gave him one weekend to make up his mind. He told Gina that they couldn't be friends anymore and we continued on with our life.

It was now July of 1983 and we had an opportunity to buy our own home. I knew that I had to move out of the neighborhood, as I couldn't stand being neighbors with Gina anymore, or any of the other women in the neighborhood for that matter. They all knew what had been going on and no one had said a word. So Mark and I went to look at the house. It was small, but it would be ours. Again I told Mark, either we buy this house and move away from Gina or I'm leaving, so we bought the house.

Matt, Gina's soon-to-be ex-husband, started to visit us more often. Mark started getting extremely jealous, but that was just too bad. I was getting a very vengeful attitude. I had never wanted to cheat on Mark. What had happened between his brother and me had just happened. It wasn't planned, and it never would happen again. I felt very guilty over it and so did he. But Matt was a different story. I have to admit that after years of hearing Gina say how good Matt was in bed, I wouldn't have minded finding out for myself. Besides, Mark had been with Gina, why not me with Matt?

Matt would come over in the evenings, and as it was summertime, we'd stand outside by his truck talking. Mark was very good friends with the police chief in town, and the chief kept telling Mark to be careful, that he thought that Matt was coming onto me. Mark confronted me and, of course, I denied it. When Mark would go fishing, Matt came around and we would stand outside and steal kisses whenever we could. I was becoming quite desirous of him. This went on for months. No one had a clue—at least not a concrete one. Then one evening Matt stopped by and I was home alone. Mark and the boys had gone to his mom's for the afternoon, and were due home later in the evening. Matt started to kiss me. It was like something I had only seen in the movies. I had never felt so much passion as I did when Matt kissed me. It was a hot evening and I had on only a sundress and panties. Next thing I knew, Matt had me leaning against the table and we made love. It was one of the most exciting experiences in my life, sexually. I had never felt the way I did with Matt, nor at anytime during my marriage with Mark. And the funny thing is, we did it at the spot on the table where Mark eats. I had finally, in my mind, gotten back at him for what he had done to me with Gina. Although Mark would never find out about it, in my mind, I had repaid him.

Matt continued to stop by from time to time and Mark never had any idea of what had transpired between us. We would all sit at the kitchen table and Matt would play footsies with me. Mark started to get a little annoyed about Matt coming by and began to become more verbally abusive to me. The more he said, the more I denied, and the more I couldn't wait to see Matt.

One evening, Matt and his son came over to visit. Mark had bought our boys a small pool table and had put it in the basement. When they came over, Mark took the boys downstairs to play pool and Matt and I stayed upstairs and watched TV. We were very devious in our brief affair and that evening, while they were all downstairs, we made love on the couch right above their heads. No one knew—ever.

Matt continued to call me and started pressuring me to leave Mark. I think I would have at that time until Matt explained that he wasn't looking for any permanent relationship, just one that would involve maybe a night or two at his house and then I would have to go home. I started to cool things off with him. If I was going to leave Mark, I wanted something more than just a casual relationship.

Mark continued to flirt with every woman who looked his way. My trust in him was about nil, and I was feeling guilty about what I had done, too. Our marriage continued to go downhill. Mark was always in and out of hospitals. The doctor would put him in for two or three weeks only to say, "I can't find anything wrong with him." It seemed that Mark was in the hospital almost every year for something, and every time he went in he'd be out of work for at least a month with no pay. I found myself losing the love for him that I had when we married. No matter how hard I tried to make ends meet, it never quite worked and Mark did nothing to help me with the bills.

Our finances were really bad and bill collectors were always calling. We re-mortgaged the house. Our sex life was starting to falter. Mark was sleeping more and more on the couch. He said it was his back. I had started dieting again, and lost a lot of weight. I looked really good, and other men were really noticing. Mark still didn't give me the time of day and I found myself taken with my boss, Philip.

~Chapter 8~

Philip was ten years older than me, divorced, very cultured, and the nicest man you'd ever want to meet. We got along wonderfully. We could get into stares and never have to say anything. Our eyes would say it all. We each knew what the other was thinking. It was the coolest thing. I would have given anything to spend some time with him, other than work time, but he told me that he would never come between my husband and me. I don't know why I didn't divorce Mark then, but I just kept on trying to make it work. So foolish we are sometimes.

I loved my job so much. It was my whole life, second only to my children. I always felt so lucky to have such a great position, as far as work went. I always tried to put my children first but I was also a career woman. It wasn't easy juggling both at times but it had to be done. Sometimes my job was the only sane thing in my life. I don't know where I would have been through all that had happened, had it not been for my job.

I had spent the last seven years as a keypunch operator in a room with ten other women. Whoever said it was easy working in a room full of women should have their head examined. I took a new position in the computer room of our company as a tape librarian making less money, but it was the best move I could have made. With all my problems at home, I needed to save my sanity someplace, and I found that in my job.

My duties were very diversified and I had the best boss in the company. Over the sixteen years that I worked with him, we became very close and had a great working relationship. I have some really great friends, too, who had helped me through the Gina episode. Julie became my best friend and continues to be. My life has been so enriched by her friendship. There have been times that Mark has gotten jealous over how close Julie and I are.

She had been through a bad marriage also, but she was smart and got out of it. Her husband, though, was more physically abusive than just verbal. I guess I was lucky I didn't go through what she did. Her ex-husband was also an alcoholic, and a drug abuser.

In September of 1988, Mom and Wayne decided to move near us and they bought a mobile home in the same park. It was so wonderful having them living so close and I really enjoyed having them up here. I would find out real soon, just how lucky I was that they had.

It was April of 1989. Our town was having their annual cleanup, and being the civic-minded person that I was, I helped. About a week or two after the cleanup day, I noticed a red ring of rash on my wrist. It burned and was really hot. I asked my doctor about it and he said that it was only a spider bite and I let it go at that. I started to feel sick and had developed some flu symptoms.

Then on May twenty-fifth I woke up and found the right side of my face feeling numb. I decided to go to work anyway. At least I would have people around me if something was terribly wrong. Philip asked me if I was okay, and I said yes, but he had a concerned look on his face. Then another co-worker, Susan, called me to see if I was okay because Philip had told her that I didn't look too well. She came back to see me and I started to cry and as soon as I did my right eye flew opened and the right side of my face drooped down. I couldn't close my eye or smile. The right side of my face was paralyzed. They called Mark at work and told him he needed to come and take me to the hospital, but Mark said, "I'm too busy, I can't come." I was devastated! He has no idea how much he hurt me that day! My co-worker took me to the emergency room, and left me there by myself.

I was sitting in the waiting room watching TV and I felt like such a freak with my eye and droopy face. On TV there was a show with Geraldo Rivera. It was a show about people with Lyme's disease who were misdiagnosed. I sat and listened and realized that it sounded just like what I had been going through. I told the attending physician what I thought and his reply was, "It's not Lyme's disease. There is no Lyme's disease here."

I was sure that's what it was, but he said it was Bell's Palsy and put me on steroids for two weeks. He assured me that I would be better by then. Steroids destroy the immune system and here I am with a rampant infection racing through me, and he puts me on steroids! Needless to say, my face did not go back to normal after two weeks, and I was developing more and more problems.

The day after this episode was Mark's birthday. It was his fortieth birthday and I had planned a big party for him. I wasn't sure whether to have the party or not, but everyone said that they would help me out. A few people didn't come because they had heard what happened with my face and were convinced that I had had a stroke. I was only thirty-seven years old so I believed that there was no way that I had a stroke. I had the party, and I'm really happy that I did. It helped to calm me down a bit from what had transpired the day before. Thank goodness Mom and Wayne lived nearby.

I wasn't able to work for four months. I had to keep a patch over my right eye so it would not dry out and get infected; and I had to hold my mouth up in order to talk or eat. I was becoming very sensitive to light and sound and was suffering from terrible headaches. I experienced mini-seizures when I tried to fall asleep at night; and I was so weepy and cried all the time. I would pass a mirror and see my face and I'd start to cry. I was so devastated. I started to experience anxiety attacks. I couldn't walk across the street or sit in a small room or even drive the car.

My first anxiety attack occurred while I was driving and it almost cost me my life. To this day I do not drive out of town because I still suffer from them. So what was wrong with me? Was I dying? Did I have a tumor? It took me many visits to many doctors and many tests until I finally met up with an Infectious Disease doctor who finally diagnosed me with Lyme's disease. Julie took me to all those doctors and for all those tests. It amazes me how very solid a close friendship can be. She meant more to me then than my own husband. She was always there for me, he never was! And she continues to be here for me to this day.

I was put on a portable intravenous pump and given mega doses of antibiotics. At the end of the second week I was finally able to shut my eye, and my face started to come back, but because so much time had elapsed until I was finally diagnosed and treated that I have been left with residual effects from the paralysis and continue to suffer from chronic Lyme's Disease.

My life with Mark was really becoming strained. I harbored some really angry feelings toward him now because he hadn't been there for me when I really needed him. I had to depend on everyone else to take me to the doctors and to offer me support. I even joined a Lyme's support group with another friend with Lyme's and we would attend the group meetings together. I had to give up so many of the things that I enjoyed because of my disease. My children really had no mother that summer as I was too sick to do anything. My anxiety attacks were worse than ever. I couldn't go out in the sun. The littlest noises sounded like thunder to me. I couldn't sleep; I couldn't eat; I was a total wreck; and cried all the time.

I have no idea how my family even survived that summer. I couldn't do housework, I was too weak to cook, and I hardly went out of the house except to do some shopping with my husband. Our bills started to really get behind because my short-term memory was affected so badly by the Lyme's that I would forget to write out the checks for them. I was too embarrassed and upset to be seen by other people. I felt like a freak with my distorted face. My children suffered from my lack of attention and not being able to take them any place or to do anything with them. In fact, even today Michael reminds me how he missed out that year.

Mark continued to be verbally abusive toward me, and there were times I wanted to spit in his face for some of the things he said to me. He would call me a 'lard-ass', and remind me that no one would want a woman with a distorted face. But I was so weak and I knew that I couldn't make it on my own. He knew that, too. I felt so imprisoned—and so alone.

It's not easy being sick and living with a man who is verbally abusive. It makes you feel like a piece of shit, and being in the physical and mental state that I was in because of my illness, I just let the words hit me and bounce back off. I really had no choice but to put up with the abuse, as there was no place for me to go. There was no sex in our marriage for over a year. I felt so ill that there was no way that I could even think of sex. Mark did not understand the illness that I had nor did he want to. Instead he would tell me that there was nothing wrong with me and that the doctor was a quack. I wasn't driving at all now. I couldn't even drive up the street to the store without having an anxiety attack. I was losing more and more of my independence and it was really taking its toll on me.

Even though I had been going through so much, after the first treatment of antibiotics I returned to work. I worked full time and only took time off when I was on IV therapy. In total to date, I have been on the IV nine times. Lyme's disease is a very debilitating disease if not properly treated. I was so lucky that I found the right doctor when I did or I could have been a lot worse off.

It was April of 1991. Mom and Wayne had come over for Sunday dinner. We were watching TV when one of Ken's friends stopped by and asked if he wanted to go for a ride with him and he said yes. After they left I turned to Mom and Wayne and said, "That's funny. I didn't think Ken's friend had a driver's license."

Wayne said, "Oh, you worry too much. Let him be. He's old enough to know better." About ten minutes passed and an ambulance call came over Mark's police scanner. There was an overturned car in the woods. One person was thrown from the car; the other was still inside it. My heart sank. I just had this feeling. Mark and Wayne said that they would take a ride and check it out.

About thirty minutes went by. Mom and I were listening to the commotion on the scanner. Then the call came telling us that it was Ken and his friend. They were taking him to the military hospital in town because that was the closest hospital. Mom and I went to the hospital and a neighbor took care of Michael for me. The doctor said that they had taken x-rays and they would have them in a little bit. When the x-rays came back they called us into the room. It seems that Ken had broken his pelvis in six different places. They transported him to the county hospital where he spent the next eight weeks in traction.

Wayne, Mom, Mark and I took turns going to see Ken so that he would have a visitor every night. Ken had a tutor come to the hospital so he wouldn't fall behind in his studies. He healed and mended in record time, and when the eight weeks were over, he left the hospital in a wheel chair. Once home, he did his exercises and went to physical therapy. He used a walker for only three days and then went on crutches. The doctors were amazed at how fast Ken's body mended. He even managed to pass with his class and move ahead to his senior year. Ken took a different look at life after his accident. In his senior year of high school, he decided that partying was more important than studying, and he had a hard time getting through it, but he managed. He spent his senior summer in summer school and received his high school diploma in September 1992.

I received a tearful phone call from Tammy that October. She proceeded to tell me that she had breast cancer and that Kenny had left her because he couldn't bear to see her this way. I can't understand how a man who is supposed to love you can just walk away when you need him the most. Tammy was left with two young children to face this dilemma alone. So many nights she would call me crying in pain. I had wished so much that I could just jump in the car and go help, but my anxiety attacks just wouldn't let me drive out of town and she lived two hours away.

In December of 1992, Mark and I both developed a bad case of the flu. Neither one of us was able to go to work for almost a week. Mom and Wayne had said they would take Ken grocery shopping so they could get some groceries into my house. Upon their return from the store, Mom and Ken were carrying the groceries in while Wayne sat out front of our house in the car. On Mom's third trip out, she came running in the house hysterical. She said that when she got back outside she had found Wayne slumped over the steering wheel not breathing. I told Mark to call 911, and I ran outside to see if there was anything I could do. When I opened the door Wayne had already lost his color and I heard his last gasp. His body was getting cold and I had no idea what to do. I panicked. It took the police department over thirty minutes to get to my house. Mark was furious and wanted answers. The ambulance was there at least fifteen minutes before the police, and proceeded to perform CPR. Of course it was too late. Wayne was gone.

I felt so guilty about sending them to do my shopping. I felt so guilty that I couldn't do anything for him when I went out to the car. I was sick and panicked and had no idea what to do. His funeral really enlightened all of us. He had belonged to his local fire department for many years, and firemen from every company in the county, and even some from the next county, had come to pay their respects. It was all very moving.

Wayne had been the father I never had. We had our ups and downs and differences of opinions, but he was more of a dad than my own was. He wasn't the kind of man who openly showed his love, but you felt it. I felt so bad for mom. She had already been through so much in her life and now this. I spent the nights with mom for the first week after Wayne passed away. She needed someone to be with her. Mom and I had always been close and this brought us even closer. She continued to work a full time job and managed living alone. I'm so happy that they had moved up by me. At least I could keep an eye on her.

In the summer of 1993, Tammy decided to sell her home in New York and move to Florida with her two children. She filed for divorce from Kenny and moved away. My son Ken moved out on his own in October of that year. He was now nineteen years old. My baby was leaving home. I cried for a week after he moved. Mark's grandmother passed away and Ken asked his grandfather if he could move in. They decided that the house would be better with someone living in it, so Ken and two of his friends moved in. They only charged Ken two hundred dollars a month, just so he could have his independence. It worked out wonderfully.

I was starting to feel better with my Lyme's so I started to drive a little. My relationship with Mark was still very strained and I really wanted to divorce him. For some reason, every time I've decided that this is it, something else happened. It was like someone was telling me, "You will never leave him" and that thought made me very depressed.

I decided that maybe we could make things work and approached him amorously to see if, maybe, just maybe, there were a few sparks left. We tried having sex again. It had been quite a few years since we last made love. I felt really bad that there was nothing there. It was more of a chore. There was no enjoyment. He was having problems performing, and there was no pleasure or satisfaction in it for me. Our attempts at intimacy ended almost as fast as we tried to rekindle it. Mark would go back out on the couch afterwards. It got so bad that I finally said, "Please don't ask me again."

When I told him that I wanted a divorce he said, "Who wants you? You're face is distorted and you're a cripple, so who would want you?" Mark and I were not sleeping with each other at all. It was October of 1993, and aside from the couple of times that we had tried, it had been about four years since we had had a real sex life.

Mark's brother was having problems in his marriage as well, and was spending a lot of nights at their mom's house. Mark invited him to come up and stay with us for a few nights. I was a little uncomfortable with it, but I didn't say anything. One particular night his brother came and asked if he could take us up on it. He had no idea that Mark and I were not sleeping in the same bed. When bedtime came, I went to my room and shut the door. Mark laid down on the couch and told his brother he could have the recliner. His brother said that was okay. I remember lying in bed listening to them talk. When Mark started to snore his brother said aloud, "Oh no, I forgot how bad you snore!" That woke Mark and his brother said, "I'm not sure I'll be able to stay here. Your snoring will keep me up and I have to get up at four A.M."

With that, Mark said, "Go in and sleep with Emily. She won't mind, I'm sure." I couldn't believe my ears! Was he crazy?

I heard his brother say, in a shocked tone, "Are you sure?"

Mark said, "Yes, by all means. I trust you."

His brother opened the door and came into my bedroom. I looked at him in disbelief. Scared and shaking, I moved over. His brother got into bed with me and we didn't say a word. Then, I said, "I can't do this."

He replied, "It will be okay." We tried to go to sleep, but we couldn't. I could hear Mark snoring out in the living room on the couch. His brother leaned over and kissed me.

I said, "Please, it's been so long." I really didn't want to start anything with him. We kissed for a while and caressed, and I said to him, "I can't do this. It's too awkward; it's not right." He understood and we both fell asleep. I wanted to kill Mark for letting his brother sleep with me. How could he? Did he feel that little for me to allow such a thing? I was so confused and very bitter. How dare he allow anyone to sleep in the same bed with me! It just wasn't right. His brother and I have never talked about either of the two incidents that we had. I've carried a lot of guilt over that first one, and wished it had never happened. Being vulnerable really causes a person to do strange things…things that we normally wouldn't do if our lives were happy.

I was having a problem with my feet swelling from the Lyme's. Sometimes the water retention would make it hard for me to stand on my feet for too long or to put my shoes on. I was on and off IV therapy for my chronic flare-ups, but I continued to work full time, take an active part in my community and in my son Michael's education.

In July 1994, we introduced Mom to a nice widower named Roy from the fire department that Mark belonged to and they hit it off right away. Before a year went by, Mom gave her mobile home to my sister and moved in with Roy.

Mark started showing me a lump that he had on his right elbow that was growing and getting quite large. His doctor told him that it was just a cyst and to not worry about it. He started to worry when he noticed that his hand would go numb whenever he used that arm too much and that the lump was getting larger. He told the doctor, but the doctor insisted that it was probably just resting on a nerve. Mark finally took it upon himself to go see a surgeon in December and asked him to take it off. The surgeon said he would.

Mark was told that it would only take a little time to remove the cyst. When the doctor opened his arm, he found that Mark actually had a cyst that had turned cancerous. The reason his hand was going numb was because the cancer had sent out feelers that had wrapped around his nerves. The operation took a lot longer than had been expected.

After Mark's surgery he waited for all the test results to come back in. It was definitely confirmed that he did had a cancerous cyst. Mark would have to undergo six months of radiation and physical therapy. Our finances weren't the best now either. I had great health insurance from my job, but Mark's wasn't the best.

Mark's attitude about life changed drastically after his surgery. It was almost impossible to live with him, and more than once I had thought of just asking him to leave. But how could I when he was going through cancer treatments? I bit my tongue and tried my best to get him through this. It wasn't an easy task though, because he was becoming more and more verbally abusive, and he was also getting very comfortable with staying home and letting me support the family.

Mark worked as a warehouseman and his arm had to be back to one hundred percent before he could go back to work. They did not offer him any sort of light duty, so Mark started to really milk the time off. He was enjoying being home and me being the sole breadwinner. I started to resent the fact that I had to do everything. Besides the bad attitude, Mark also refused to do any housework.

After six months of being off, Mark's disability payments ran out. Now I was totally the only breadwinner and my check didn't go very far. I had a car loan and an unsecured loan being deducted from my check, as well as other deductions. It was getting very difficult to make the house payment, let alone trying to put money away for taxes and all the other bills that go along with running a house. Thank goodness the credit union at my job where I had the two loans let my loan payments slide for the period that Mark was out of work or I don't know what I would have done. Our budget was set up with two people working, not one, and it was now extremely difficult.

I felt pretty good that I had only gotten behind by a little over a month on my mortgage payment. The year that Mark was out of work was a very taxing time for me, physically and mentally. I had to find my own transportation back and forth to work, so thank goodness Mom lived in town. And not being well myself, all the stress of trying to make ends meet was really taking its toll. To top off the situation, Mark started getting phone calls from a Danielle. I asked many times who she was and his reply was, "She's only a friend."

I could have bought that until Danielle started calling and hanging up whenever I answered the phone. Besides, what was another woman doing calling my husband? I started hearing in town that they were seen together at the stores. When I confronted him, Mark would always say that she needed a ride and he was just being nice. I remember one night after I arrived home from work the phone rang. It was six P.M. It was Danielle on the other end, and when I asked what she wanted, she proceeded to tell me that her car had broken down about three miles from my house and she needed Mark to help her get it started. She said that she needed a jump. I'll just bet she did! I handed the phone to Mark, along with a very disturbed look, and he said to her, "I'll be right there." Did he think I was a fool? So off he went and he returned about two hours later.

I started hearing that Danielle's car was seen at my house during the day while I was working. It didn't matter what I thought, I always got the same answer from Mark, "She's just a friend." I started answering her calls with a very sarcastic attitude, but she was too stupid to catch on. I had never seen Danielle so I had no idea who she was or what she looked like. Then one day I got that opportunity when we ran into her in the supermarket. I had to chuckle as she was not much to look at. Then I started thinking, maybe I'd be lucky and he'd run off with her. No such luck.

Danielle eventually moved out of town and closer to her parents in Connecticut. I thought maybe she was out of our lives for good but not so. Danielle would still come to town and stay at a local motel. Her excuse was something about having to pick up her mail in New York. Her ex-husband didn't know that she had moved out of town, and she would call from the hotel for Mark every time she was visiting. It started to really get to me, but I bit my tongue hoping Mark would leave and go with her.

My boss, Philip, was a great friend to me during this time. He offered his shoulder at work and acted as a sounding board when I needed to blow off steam. My family was there for me also. They stuck with me and helped me through it morally. Julie and I were the closest any two friends could be.

Mark finally, after a year, returned to work in January of 1996. The bills were still mounting and the attitude at the mortgage company was starting to change. I felt like the world was on my shoulders. I needed something to help me hide from the depression I was sinking into.

My job offered interest-free loans for complete computer systems, to be paid by payroll deduction. I knew that Mark had been out of work for a year, but he was back now and I needed something to help me with my sanity. Perhaps I could learn more and eventually make it work for me financially. I could go into desktop publishing, perhaps make up business cards for other people. So I decided to buy a computer. It would only cost me twenty-five dollars a week out of my paycheck. My salvation quickly became the friends I met online and I don't know where I'd be now without them.

My virtual life began to overtake my "real" life. This was turning into a great escape from the life that I was living with Mark. I had no idea how much of an escape it would become. All too fast it became my secret life—looking for Mr. Right on the Net.

~Chapter 9~

The past eighteen years with Mark have been far from happy years...beginning with the first incident with the nurse before we got married, right on up to the incidents with Gina and Danielle. My Lyme's disease made me feel very unattractive, and Mark just wasn't there for me like I was there for him during all of his illnesses. He had been spoiled as a child, had always had everything that he wanted and he expected the same thing in his adult life, too. His true colors had shone up throughout my whole illness. When I developed the anxiety attacks and couldn't drive, Mark really held the upper hand. He thought nothing of not showing up on time when he was supposed to pick me up from work. We worked right around the corner from each other, but he wouldn't call to tell me that he was working late, not worrying that he had to pick me up.

There were so many times that I had to sit at my desk for up to three hours waiting. If he took me to the supermarket, he'd tell me he was running into town to pick up something and would be right back. I'd do the family shopping and then be standing outside waiting for him to return from for hours. He never had any regard for me or his children. Our sex life was never anything to write home about. I never felt satisfied with Mark. He just wasn't the romantic, passionate man that I craved. I would rather go without sex, than to have to fake satisfaction. I always thought it was me, but I learned very fast that that wasn't the case at all.

My first two weeks online I didn't enter any chat rooms. Instead I spent most of my time just surfing the web and playing games. My Lyme's was starting to act up again and the doctor wanted me to go back on my IV antibiotics for three weeks. One morning, after Mark had gone to work and Michael had gone to school, I decided to go into a chat room and was quickly IMd (instant messaged) by a younger man from California, Bobby.

Bobby and I instantly clicked and we would meet every morning for 'coffee' on the net. Bobby was engaged to be married, thirty-four years old, and I was forty-four at the time. Our chat started to get a little steamier and I had always heard about cyber sex, but I had never experienced it. It was amazing how very real your body responds to reading intimate chat. I had never had that kind of feeling before and it put a whole new perspective on my Internet time.

Bobby and I became really close. It's always amazed me how fast relationships are formed online. A week of online or virtual time is almost equivalent to one month of "real" time. You really get to know a person from how they feel in their heart, not by what you see at face value. You get to know the real person, that is, as long as they are not just players. I've always been an honest person, and I have tried not to lead anyone astray online, but you learn real fast that the power of words can also be a dangerous, hurtful thing.

My computer life was starting to really take over my real life. I was coming home from work everyday and immediately putting on the computer before I started dinner. Mark started noticing that I was spending too much time online, and it was starting to cause more problems in our marriage, but I didn't stop. I had met a really nice woman from New Jersey named Jackie. We instantly bonded and started a great friendship. Although she was in her thirties, she was a regular in the Over Forties rooms on AOL.

I started talking to a really sweet man from upstate New York, Don. Don was separated from his wife, had two children and was very lonely, like me. We clicked and found ourselves falling for each other really fast. We would meet at various times during the day online, and then started talking to each other on the telephone. For the first time in many years I finally felt like a desirable woman. My cyber time with Bobby really set me up to the power of cyber sex, and its control over men. I also met a lawyer, but he was so aggressive that I finally told him to not IM me anymore. You learn to pick up vibes from people and to go with those feelings. The lawyer scared me.

Don became very sick and was offline for almost a month, diagnosed with mononucleosis. During his time offline, Joe and I became very, very close. We started calling each other and would talk for hours. I have to admit that after meeting Joe, and with Don's absence, my desire to meet Don was slowly diminishing, but I knew if I didn't meet Don I'd always wonder, what if? Don and I planned our meeting. He would drive the five hours down to see me. I told Mark I was going out with the girls from work and I'd probably stay at Cathy's house if it became too late for her to drive me home. I also told him that she and I would most likely spend the next day shopping or something and maybe go back out on Saturday night, and that our plans were up in the air. He said fine, he didn't care.

I got out of work early that Friday and drove home before Mark. I had my over night bag already packed and a close friend of mine was to pick me up and drop me off where I was meeting Don. Don and I had never seen each other's picture so neither of us knew what to expect. He turned out to be a tall, six foot four-inch man, with big broad shoulders, and nice looking. He was exactly what I expected. We had talked so much about our first meeting and what we desired from each other but I'm afraid our expectations were too high. Maybe it was because my thoughts were on Joe, and Don's thoughts were on the fact that he was with another man's wife. We had a little fireworks, but nothing like we had expected.

Don rolled over with his back to me and went to sleep. When we awoke I expected him to hold me and maybe make love again, but it didn't happen. I took my shower, got dressed, and then Don did the same. There was no intimacy at all that morning. He suggested that we go get breakfast and told me to take my bag with us. We had decided prior to meeting that if things worked well with us, we'd spend the weekend, but in the morning he said that he was nervous about being away from his kids for so long and that it would probably be best this time if we only spent the one night. We went out to breakfast, had a really great time, and then he dropped me off up the street from my house. I went inside and Mark was surprised that I was home so early. It was only ten A.M. I told him that Cathy and I had decided that we were too tired to do the mall thing and that we weren't going out that night. I went into the bathroom and sat and cried. I was so confused and feeling a bit guilty.

Don didn't come online for almost a week. I guess in my heart I knew that I was right, we were not to be. But I had to hear it from him. He finally wrote me an email and said that he didn't feel the sparks that he had hoped for and that he was sorry. This made me feel better though, in an odd sort of way. I had known before I left that night that my feelings were with Joe, but I had to know if there was a possibility of anything with Don.

My friends from the forties rooms wanted to know how things went and I told them. They were sort of happy, too, because they liked Joe so much better. For the next couple of months, Joe and I would meet in the forties rooms and we would also talk on personal IMs and on the telephone.

I had called Tammy in Florida to tell her of my new hobby of meeting men on the Internet and she was so excited for me. She never really cared for Mark and she really hoped I'd meet someone nice who could give me the kind of life I deserved. I could hear a sad tone in her voice though, and when I asked her what was wrong, I couldn't believe what she said. Her cancer had come back in her spine. She hadn't been able to work the past couple of months because she was in so much pain. She told me not to worry about it, that her dad and brother were coming down to help her pack up and she and her children were moving up to her dad's house in Pennsylvania. I never realized how sick she was at that point.

I called Tammy from time to time to talk to her, but most of the time she was too weak to even talk. Her tumor eventually caused blindness. We had been friends since age eleven, and no one else in this world knew me better or cared more for me. Tammy passed away that June. I didn't have the heart to go to her funeral. I wanted to remember the bubbly, full-of-life friend I had had, not the frail woman the cancer had turned her into.

This meeting men online was all so new to me. I had never had so many men paying attention to me all at the same time, and it was just what I needed to boost my self-esteem. It was so wonderful to have men find me desirable again; to feel the romance and passion that I craved.

A new version of AOL had come out and I wanted to install it. I wasn't very computer literate at the time, but I decided to try to install it. When it didn't work the first time, I installed it a second, then a third, and a fourth. My computer was so messed up, every time I signed on it would boot me off. I was dumbfounded. Mark told me that his boss, Randy, was really great with computers so I asked Mark to have his boss look at my computer. Randy came over and started to explore the files on my computer. He started to chuckle when he saw all the versions of AOL that were on it. He explained to me that the computer was in conflict because of all of them. He deleted all of them and then reinstalled AOL for me, and the computer worked fine after that.

While he was checking on some files, he put some kind of command in and all of a sudden all the picture files that I had looked at appeared one at a time on my PC. Oh, was I embarrassed! I had visited a website recently that had pictures of nude men on it, which a girlfriend of mine had told me about. When Randy saw all the pictures flashing across my screen, I almost died. He sat there with his pipe in his mouth and chuckled. I did, too, although I know my face was ten shades of red. He candidly looked at me and said, "My, my, little girl, what have you been doing?" I laughed. That day was the beginning of a really special friendship between Randy and me—one that Mark would never know about nor understand even if he did.

It had been four months since I met Joe online and we were finally talking about meeting in person. Lucky for me, I had a close friend from high school who lived about two hours from where Joe was. My friend, Billy! Remember him? It's funny how old friends creep back into your life. Actually, Billy and I had always kept in touch over the years. Anyway, I got in touch with Billy, explained that I wanted to come to Ohio to meet with someone I had met online. Billy tried all he could to talk me out of it. But he was so excited about seeing me again after all those years he finally said yes. My plan was to fly to Ohio and spend the weekend at Billy's house. Joe would pick me up from Billy's on Monday.

As far as Mark was concerned, he thought I was going to spend the week with my gay friend, Billy. I never expected the reaction I got from Mark. He was outraged at the thought of me spending a week at a gay man's house. Mark was so homophobic and the thought made him crazy. I told him that he had nothing to worry about, or would he like it better if I told him I was going to spend it with a straight man? Mark finally said okay, but with reservations.

Joe and I needed to find out if there was a chance for something more in our relationship. We needed to meet in person to see if there was a true connection. He planned to take a week's vacation and spend the time with me. So I made my flight reservations for the beginning of August. He reimbursed me for my ticket and I set it up for Billy to pick me up at the airport. Billy and I had a great weekend reliving old memories. It had been almost twenty years since we had last seen each other and we were both very excited about seeing each other again.

Joe arrived about an hour later than planned. He called to tell me that he had been in a car accident before he even left his town, but he was okay. When I opened the door my mouth just dropped. He was just so cute, and he looked just like Garth Brooks and had the same temperament. We embraced and kissed and I felt sparks going through me. God, he was more than I had hoped for.

When we got to town we found a hotel that wasn't far from his place of employment. Unfortunately for me, he couldn't get the time off he that had wanted, but promised to spend the nights with me. That was before some really bad problems developed with his oldest daughter. She had run away from home the night before and he felt that he had to stay there to help make things as normal as could be. His children also had arranged for him and his wife to go on a weekend retreat with the church, to try and make things work out at home. I didn't get as much time with Joe those five days as I had planned, but I did get enough to know that I would leave what I had behind to be with him, if he had asked me to.

When we got to the hotel, Joe told me that his hand really hurt from the accident that morning. He left me around three P.M. and said he would be back later in the evening. While he was gone he decided to go to the emergency room. It turned out that he had broken his hand and bruised his ribs in the accident. Another thing that he hadn't known was that he had punctured his gas tank, too. Imagine that! He drove two hours to get me and we drove two hours back in a car with a punctured tank.

Joe came back that evening and we spent most of the night together. He left around midnight so his family wouldn't suspect anything. Joe was such a gentle, kind, and romantic man, the kind any woman would fall for.

I had to pinch myself. I couldn't believe that I had found such a great guy online.

In the hours that I spent alone in the hotel, I called various friends from the Over Forty room to let them know that I was okay. I called California, Wisconsin, Maryland, New Jersey, New York City, Connecticut and even Florida. I never gave the calls any thought as I had used my Sprint calling card.

When Mark picked me up at the airport on my return, he was in a very strange mood. I had expected him to be happy to see me, but what I experienced when I got home, I had never planned on. When we got back home he had a very nasty attitude. He started getting extremely verbal, worse than he ever had been in our whole marriage. He was very, very distraught over the fact that I spent my week with a gay guy. He called me every name in the book, ones I wouldn't have even called my worst enemy. He started throwing things around the house, and it wasn't a very nice scene. For the first time in my years of marriage to Mark, I was truly afraid of him.

Joe and I continued to talk online and on the phone. After the weekend that the children had planned for them, Joe and his wife decided to try and work things out for the sake of the children. Then he told me he would have to give up his online time. I was crushed, but understood why. He promised to call me or come back online if things changed in his life.

I continued to come home from work and spend lots of time on my computer, and Mark was getting nastier by the day. It had been four weeks since I returned from Ohio, and Mark's attitude was not improving. I had never seen him this bad and I had made up my mind that I wasn't going to put up with it anymore. It had been four years since we had had any intimate contact. Things were not changing with us and I needed a change, so I calmly sat him down and told him I wanted a divorce. He became enraged, throwing things and calling me names. Then, finally, he calmed down and I heard nothing. He came out of our bedroom and handed me a piece of paper and walked out the door. I waited a few minutes as he drove away and then opened up the paper. It was a goodbye/suicide note. I panicked!

I called the police and they came to the house. They read the note and asked me which way he had gone and I told them. We live in a very wooded area with lots of side roads...too many, in fact. They asked me to stay off the phone and wait for their call.

It seemed like hours had passed before they called me back. They had found him sitting in his truck with an opened bottle of Draino, and he told them that he was going to drink it. They took him to the psyche ward of the local hospital for evaluation. But I knew that he wouldn't have done anything to hurt himself. It was his way of controlling me again. When the doctors called and asked me what had happened, I told them I had asked him for a divorce and that he went crazy. They told me if I really didn't want him back home that they would keep him there until he understood that and until they found him a place to go. Mark kept calling me, and when I went to visit him, he asked me to please give him another chance. I told him that I would give him one year and if it didn't change, he'd have to go. He agreed.

I really didn't want to save my marriage at that point, but I didn't want to be the one to send him over the edge, either. Mark spent two weeks in the hospital, and then was out of work for three months while he recuperated from his breakdown. He went to therapy and they put him on medicine to mellow him out. I continued to work and once again became the sole breadwinner. I felt my life closing in on me again. I wanted so much to find my Prince Charming, someone to take me away from this life I was living. I knew he was out there in Cyberland! I just knew it, and I planned to find him.

My feelings for Mark changed drastically after his suicide attempt. I harbored some very ill feelings toward him, wondering how he could do that to his family. Neither of my boys had a good relationship with their father, as he just never had the time for them either. We never went away on vacation. We never went out to dinner or a movie. There was nothing special that we did as a family at all. Holidays were never a good time at home either, because Mark would ruin everything. He especially hated Christmas, which was my favorite along with Thanksgiving. Mark made everyone else miserable during those events. I spent most of my holidays crying because he always ruined the spirit of the season.

As far as the bills went, Mark never worried about them, nor did he ever even look at them. In the over eighteen years of our marriage he had never even opened a phone bill—until this September. It was the bill after my trip to Ohio. I was at work when Mark called me, ranting and raving about the telephone bill. "How could you? Who were you calling? I know it was because of the computer! I just know it!" Then he proceeded to tell me that he and his mother had made copies of the phone bill, and that he was going to use it against me. The bill was for twelve hundred dollars! Yikes!! But how could it be so high? Sprint never told me that even if your call doesn't go through, they charge you one dollar each time you accessed your number and that each phone call you did make was fifty cents a minute. All those calls I had made while in Ohio! There were also three hundred and fifty calls made that never went through at all for a total of three hundred and fifty dollars!

My answer to him was, "What can I say? I'll have to pay for it." When I got home from work that night he was furious and out of control. He had hidden my keyboard and when I told him, "Don't worry, I'll buy another one," he proceeded to try and pull the phone wires out of the floor. The neighbors heard him screaming at me and me crying and they called the police. When the two officers arrived they told him that he had to return my keyboard to me and that he had no right to destroy my phone lines. They told him that they wouldn't take him in, but if they had to come again, they would arrest him. They knew my history with Mark and they were not playing games.

I thought long and hard on how to solve the problem with Mark and to be able to continue with my online time, so I set up a screen name for him and introduced him to my friends in the Over Forties room. Fight fire with fire, I thought. Everyone was very cordial to him, and Sam's wife, Diane, sparked up a friendship with Mark. Mark was still out of work on disability for his suicide attempt, and Diane was also a suicidal person, so they thought maybe they could help each other out. I thought that was great, but never expected them to end up with a telephone relationship. That month Mark ran up a seven hundred and fifty dollar phone bill by calling Wisconsin every day. What could I say? I surely had no room to talk, but I was outraged.

Mark's boss, Randy, had to come rescue my computer again. I had somehow messed up some files and it wasn't working properly. Randy and I exchanged email addresses and he told me he signed onto AOL, so he gave me his screen name. We started chatting at night and our friendship started to really grow. Mark had no idea the things that Randy and I shared online. We both made up lists of things we had never done sexually but wanted to do, and then we exchanged them. Our lists were kept privately between us, and we often talked of fulfilling some of those desires—together. Randy knew about my various online affairs and my relationship with Mark. My friendship with Randy actually saved Mark's job, because Randy knew our financial situation and just wouldn't do that to me. Mark had no idea how close he had come to being fired and that I had actually saved his job.

Mark was still out of work. I was starting to feel like he was milking it again. It had been almost three months since his suicide attempt and I figured that he was way overdue and should go back to work. It was the end of October and one day in a Lobby Chat room, I came across a writer from Boston named Dennis. Dennis was thirty-four, a science fiction writer with a couple of books out. We instantly hit it off and our conversations would have made great scripts for a romantic movie. Dennis encouraged me to continue writing. I had written a few poems in my life and had really enjoyed it. He loved what I had to say and helped get me started writing again.

I found myself completely mesmerized by Dennis, and I was completely taken away. He was not like any of the other men I had met online. He always left me in a dreamy, almost trance-like state, whenever we spoke. He was a true source of inspiration to me. I found out real fast, that romance and passion were my forté in writing. He touched a part of my heart that had been surrounded by barbed wire most of my life. He removed that stop sign that had been there for so long and he left me wanting more. He even taught me to write erotically. Dennis encouraged me to let my inhibitions go, and to write what I felt inside. I have to admit that I became very good at it. So good, that I could melt any man who read my erotic prose. I was told that I should write for Playboy, I was that good. This man on my screen taught me so much—he taught me to feel what I hadn't felt before, or was afraid to feel. He mesmerized me.

We would laugh and say how we could make wonderful stories together; any other lovers couldn't match that the passion we felt. He fueled feelings I never knew I had, he made my body tremble like no other man before him. I think, for the first time in my life, I knew what it felt like to be sexually charged by one man. He left me breathless. Dennis would call me at work, and I'd melt every time I heard his voice. He'd send me love letters like no one before. I found myself hungering for him, not being able to wait until he came online. I told Dennis of my plans to go to Florida for a week. We had only known each other for four weeks when I went away. The day before I left, Dennis sent me a story he wrote about us and asked me to promise not to read it until I was on the airplane. I promised.

I lucked out and had an empty seat between me, and the next passenger on that flight. I was sitting by the window and felt more comfortable about reading the story. My eyes welled up with tears as I read the beautiful words Dennis had written to me. It was a love story like I had never read before. It was of him and me. He filled my heart with such passion and romance, and his words were like a gift from the gods of love. I had never met a man who so eloquently penned his words of love, and I felt so lucky to be the recipient of his affection.

When I got to my hotel room, I unpacked and settled down. That evening the phone rang about ten P.M. It was Dennis. He had called to "tuck me into bed", but we didn't get off the phone until one A.M. I told him how beautiful his story was and I started to cry. He told me to not weep, that his words were from his heart and they were written for me to feel happiness and love. I told him they were tears of joy, not sadness.

Dennis not only wooed me in our sessions of chat, but also taught me the art of phone sex. I was amazed at how real it felt, how much passion you could feel from the sound of one's voice. I didn't want to hang up the phone that night. I wanted him with me forever. That evening Dennis called me again. We talked for another two hours, and it was really hard to hang up. He left me feeling quite satisfied and loved. I hadn't felt that way in a very long time.

When I returned home, I found another "gift" from Dennis in my email. It was a sound wave of his voice, reading the story he had written for me. I cherished that wave as it meant so much to me. I have never been so touched by any one man. We continued to talk online and he encouraged me to write and I happened to mention that I'd love to write for Hallmark Cards. So with his encouragement, I contacted Hallmark Cards and asked for a portfolio package. I was so excited when it arrived that I couldn't wait to start. Mark wasn't very keen on me doing it, but then he never acknowledged my writing. In fact, he was convinced that I didn't have what it takes to be a good poet.

I finished my portfolio and sent it off. I waited a couple weeks and got their reply. They said that although my work was good, it wasn't what they were looking for, but to continue to write poetry, and to try again at a later date. Mark was really happy about the fact that I had been rejected. Had I been accepted, I would have had to move to Kansas City, and I wasn't taking him with me. I had really hoped that this would have panned out, as it would have finally been my way of getting out of the marriage.

In the months that followed, I saw less and less of Dennis online. That happens a lot with online relationships and friendships. People just come and go and without a word, they're gone.

The holidays came and went and life at home was the same as always. Mark was in his anti-holiday mood, worse than ever. I have to say that it was the worst Christmas I had ever had in my life. I felt so bad for my boys. I swore it would be the last one I spent with Mark. I decided to see if I could find someone else locally who was in the same situation I was. Dennis contacted me. He was having some really upsetting problems in his life. He promised to talk to me about it when things settled down a bit.

In January, I got hit with garnishments for the bills from Ken's broken leg, an injury he had received from playing football in his sophomore year, as well as some of Mark's medical bills from an old hospital stay. The garnishment's added up to almost ten thousand dollars and for the next two years my paychecks would be short. I asked Mark to please either get a part time job to help me or to take the overtime at work. His answer and attitude was? No. I had no choice but to find a part-time job for myself. I worked my normal forty hours Monday through Friday, and took a part-time job working on Saturdays in a small gift shop in town from nine to five for forty dollars. That money ended up being my grocery money for the week. I did that for over a year. In the meantime, Mark did work his full-time job, but refused to get a part-time job to help me. He also refused to help me around the house while I worked on Saturdays. I'd call the house to find him on the computer instead. I guess I was getting a dose of my own medicine.

I met a nice guy online from my area, Tom. Tom owned his own business, was successful, good looking, and very, very mysterious. We started calling each other and his voice just blew me away. Mine did the same thing to him. Not since Dennis had I felt so much passion with a man. Tom and I would meet online and steal calls whenever it was possible. His wife went to bed really early and Mark went to the firehouse a lot, so at those times we would sneak in a call. Since Mark and I were still not sleeping together or having sex, it was easy for me to take the phone into my room and talk. There was fire between Tom and me—fire I had never felt—passion so strong that it scared us.

We finally decided to meet in person. We were going to have lunch together and he would pick me up at my job. I was so excited that I couldn't wait. I took an extra half hour so I could spend a whole hour with Tom, and eagerly waited in front of my building...but Tom never showed up. I was so hurt and disappointed. He finally called and said he had chickened out...that he hadn't felt right. I understood. This happened two more times. I had given up the thought of ever meeting him and just enjoyed the excitement of our online/telephone affair.

~Chapter 10~

I wanted so much to be held, hugged, caressed, and kissed. I wanted to feel like a desirable woman again. I wasn't happy with all the online affairs I was having. They were strictly online, but they at least made me feel wanted and cared for. Time is not the same with an online friendship. Things happen at a much faster pace. You really get to know the real person. At least, you hope you do.

It seemed like Tom and I had known each other for a long time, but our times online were few and far between. But when we met online—watch out—sparks flew. I had other male friends I talked with, also. Being a writer it was very easy for me to say the right things to fuel a man. I'm not sure if having that knowledge was always a good thing.

I also learned that men loved women who were big busted. I had always thought men wanted 'Twiggy-sized' women, but boy was I wrong! I had the pick of some very handsome, successful men, online. I knew the right things to say, and could have had anything I wanted. I learned why so many marriages were going wrong—wives have no idea why their husbands stray, but I do. The men would confide in me, just like I did in them. My own marriage was falling apart and I wasn't afraid to tell them why. Their marriages were failing the same way. I understood them, and I took the time to talk to them, to really be interested in what they had to say, but I also knew the other side of the coin—the side of the wife in a bad marriage.

For years Mark had pushed me away when I really needed him, only to want my closeness when he felt the need. His years of calling me names wore heavy on my heart and in my mind. I wanted so much to be wanted by a man who would love me for me, not by what I looked like. I found men like that online. I found men who opened their hearts to me, men who weren't afraid to tell me that I was desired, and meant it. I'm not happy with all that I have done online, or the times I met the men I did, but it made me feel like a woman for the first time in a long time. I wished that I hadn't been so afraid of going out on my own and living the life I desired so much. But I was afraid that I wouldn't be able to handle it, especially financially, as well as because of my anxiety attacks when I tried driving. I felt so trapped.

I continued to work the two jobs while Mark did nothing to help alleviate the financial problems we were facing. I made the biggest mistake in the beginning of our marriage by taking on all the responsibility for paying the household bills. Mark had no idea what the bills were, nor did he care that I didn't have enough money to make ends meet. If I threatened to give him the bills and my money, he would tell me, "Great, do it! Then nothing will get paid."

Thank goodness that I had a good job that paid me well. Working saved my sanity and it also gave me a way to fulfill some of my life's dreams. In the spring of 1997, an email was sent to everyone in the company about that year's United Way campaign. They were looking for some employees to learn a song and become part of a music video with the potential of it being shown on TV as part of our county's United Way campaign. I decided, with the encouragement of my department, to try out for it.

About twenty of us showed up for the first practice, and we were told that there would be two practices to learn the song and learn the harmonizing. Then, on the third practice, we would be going to a professional recording studio to cut a record. I almost got one of the solo parts, but was beat out by someone who had a stronger voice. Just being part of this wonderful project was enough.

On the third practice we all met at a local recording studio to cut our record. I have to tell you, that all my life I had wanted this kind of opportunity, and I couldn't believe it was happening. Recording turned out to be very tedious work. The studio had very low ceilings, and it was hotter than hell in the recording area especially with twenty people, plus all the lights and cameras. Take one . . . take two . . . take three . . . and so on. We worked and sang until we got it right, which I think took about five hours but it was so very worth it.

When the final product was done we were all invited to its official viewing. The video itself was really something. It was the actual making of the video, the recording of the song, and all the practices captured on the video, which included all our little nutty pranks plus the nervousness and excitement of doing the recording. The finished product made us all very proud. The video was unveiled at our annual United Way Campaign kickoff breakfast. All the participants in the video were invited to view it along with the other United Way campaign helpers. After they premiered the video, we were all called on stage to take a bow. *sigh* It was like a dream come true.

Then over the next month the video was shown throughout the company to all its employees—all fifteen hundred of them. The twenty of us were given copies of the video and a cassette copy of the song. I still sit and play that tape; the memories are still as real as that day in the studio. It was a lifetime dream that had finally came true.

Our marriage has never been a fifty/fifty relationship. Mark has always done what Mark wants—weekend camping trips with the guys; bowling; and nights at the firehouse. Emily's job was to pay the bills, work and take care of the house and children. I never had time for me. I changed all that after my two vacations to Ohio and Florida, and then started going away for a week during the summer to the Jersey shore with my best friend, Julie.

Julie's been my best friend since I got married. We are inseparable, and sometimes I think our husbands are jealous of the friendship we have. I believe a woman needs a good friend through life, to confide in, to spend time with…not just in the teen years, but also in the adult years. With everything she has done for me throughout the years with my Lyme's disease and my bad marriage, my life has been so blessed with Julie's friendship. Our week at the shore is a time I look forward to all year. We both enjoy the same things—we eat the same way; we totally enjoy being by the ocean; we sit on the beach for hours; then we do some shopping before going off to dinner. Evenings are spent watching TV or maybe just driving around. Neither one of us has ever gone to look for other men, nor to hang out at the local bars. It's just a week of peace and quiet and relaxation. Mark has never wanted to go on vacation, and now he asks, "Can I go, too?"

I say, "Only if you're paying," and that shuts him right up. Between going away and having my online life, I've pretty much given myself my own life, outside of our marriage. My children are getting older and I now have the time for me. I make sure of that.

My full-time job started to become very taxing. The company was going through some bad times publicly, and there was talk that the company was going to be sold. My dream of moving to Florida was starting to look like it might come true—if only I could be one of the ones laid off with severance pay. I was still working my Saturdays in the little shop. Tom and I still talked on the phone and online.

I met a great guy who said he was single, from Upstate New York. His name was Mike. Mike and I had a really fun time online. He was so full of life, a real joy to know. He introduced me to his "online daughter," not a real daughter, just a cyber one. Helen and I took to each other really well, and Mike and Helen and I would meet in a private room to chat and just have fun. Helen kept saying to Mike, "Have you told her yet?"

I was wondering, told me what? After about a month of chatting Mike finally came clean and told me the truth about himself. His name was Nick and he lived in Connecticut and was married. He was afraid that if he told me that he had lied, that I'd quit talking to him. I assured him that that wouldn't have happened.

Helen introduced me to a close friend of hers, Billy, a nice college guy. Billy and I started chatting when Nick and Helen weren't online. Nice strapping twenty-three year old, same age as my oldest son. I was forty-five at the time. Billy was a very ambitious young man. He had finished college and got his master's in journalism. It's nice to have a younger guy to talk to once in awhile. Although I was in my forties, his friendship kept me young at heart.

My life seemed to be moving along. Working two jobs and all the wonderful friendships I had online, all helped me forget my unhappiness with Mark and our marriage. My youngest son was starting to develop a lot of his father's traits, mainly his nasty verbal mouth. I can understand how this all happened, having lived his whole life with a father who verbally abused me, and knowing that our marriage wasn't a normal marriage like those of his friends' parents.

~Chapter 11~

It was a normal February morning in 1998. We had had some snow and ice during the night and the roads were a mess. Mark and I were still driving to work together and when he pulled into the parking lot at my job everything looked clear. He stopped at the sidewalk as he always did, and that also looked clear. I got out of the car and said goodbye and Mark went on his way to work.

As I stepped up onto the curb to go to the sidewalk, I discovered it was a sheet of ice. I slipped and fell on my shoulder and knees. I jumped right back up and continued on into work, too embarrassed to stop and see if I was okay. One of my co-workers had seen me fall and asked if I was all right. I was crying, but I said yes, and walked on into the building to my desk.

On my way to my desk I passed a couple of my co-workers who could tell something was wrong. When I got back to my desk, Susan called to see if I was all right and I told her no. She came back to see me and I told her how my shoulder hurt and that my knee was in a lot of pain, so she sent me back my boss. Philip and William came also to see if I was okay. I told them I was in pain but would wait to see if it got better. Within two hours I couldn't walk on my right leg at all, so Philip said he would take me to the company health center.

At the health center I was seen by the company's doctor and they took some x-rays of my shoulder and knee. It showed a hairline fracture to the knee but nothing broken in the shoulder. I was told to go home and to stay off my feet. If I wasn't better in a week, I was to go back and be checked again. I said okay. Philip took me back to work so I could notify Mark to come pick me up to take me home.

Philip was retiring in a couple months, so his supervisor, Ben, was the one I had to report to. When I told Ben what I was told by the doctor, he started to say to me, "We expect you to be here—" I didn't wait for him finish. I was in so much pain that I just walked out of his office and hobbled to the credit union to take some money out, because I knew I wasn't going to be able to work for a while.

When I returned to the office Ben yelled at me to come into the manager's office, which I did. He shut the door behind me and started screaming at me, "How dare you walk away from me when I was talking". I told him I didn't want to hear the 'We expect you to be here to work' talk that I was in so much pain that it would have been nice if he had just said, 'Please feel better.'

Then he said what he was going to say was, "We expect you to be here back at work. Please take care of yourself and hurry back."

I looked at him and replied, "That's what I had planned to do. I'm not stupid nor am I one to milk the system."

For the next seventy-two hours, I was in so much pain I couldn't even lift my right arm. The only way I could was if I took my left hand and picked it up. My knee hurt so bad I couldn't stand on it and it was throbbing. I called Philip on Monday and told him that I wouldn't be in, and he said that I should take care and let him know what was going on. After the week I went back to the health center and told them about my shoulder and knee and they advised me to go see an orthopedist.

Besides being out of my full-time job, I had to call in to my Saturday job, which didn't make the owners very happy. But what was I to do? I couldn't work there and be out on disability with my full-time job, and there was no way I could be on my feet there all day either, so I told them all that. They got so upset after the third week that I just quit.

I was suffering so badly with pain that I didn't even spend much time online. I wasn't able to use my right arm for typing, and it hurt to sit for any length of time. I did go online to talk to Nick and to Tom, telling them what had happened. It turned out that I tore my right rotator cuff and besides the hairline fracture, my knees were so diseased from the Lyme's disease plus a cyst that they found, I was developing extreme arthritis besides.

The company sent me to an orthopedist to see if he agreed with my doctor's findings. The exam seemed to be going well until he asked to see my C-section scar. I said to him, "I don't think that's necessary. It has nothing to do with my knees or shoulder." I left it at that. His report back to my company read, "I find nothing wrong with your employee that warrants her to be out of work." The doctor lied! This messed up my Workman's Comp case more than I knew. With me out of work now, including not being able to work that second job, our finances started to fail again. As long as I was on sick time, they could still garnish my salary, and they did. Had the doctor done the right thing by me and approved the Workman's Comp, I wouldn't have been in the financial dilemma I was about to face.

Not feeling well, in so much pain and unable to work, the mortgage company started to get very aggressive with me about being behind. But they offered us a way out, to do a "deed in lieu of foreclosure," where we would actually give the house back, not the other way around where they would take it from us. It sounded like our answer. This would be a great time for Mark and I to part our ways. I had always told him that if I ever lost my house because of his failure to help me financially, that I would go my separate way. We talked it out and decided that for financial reasons only, we would stay together until we got our bills caught up.

There was so much to do in the next three months, and being home and in so much pain it wasn't going to be an easy task. I had to call a real estate agent to come and give me a price for our house and to sign contracts to list it. This was one of the agreements with the bank. I made an appointment for a woman to come and do the appraisal.

My friendship with Nick was a very special friendship. Helen asked me if she could come down to visit me. I told Mark about her and he said it would be fine. Nick and I talked about my meeting Helen and he decided that he would come for lunch the one day that she would be there so that we could finally meet, too. Cyber-father, Cyber-mother, and Cyber-daughter. I know how strange that sounds, but we really had a great relationship, all of us.

Helen arrived on a Thursday, and we hit it off great. It was fun having a pretend daughter, being I had all real sons. Nick came on Friday for lunch and he was exactly like I pictured him, kind, and a real gentleman. Helen teased us that she was the chaperone, and didn't leave us for five minutes out of her sight. It was a really pleasant day. We took lots of pictures and talked, and just had a wonderful time. Nick did kiss me goodbye (with Helen's approval), and off he went.

~Chapter 12~

Since my fall, I've been on a writing frenzy, putting out two to four poems everyday. It was like the floodgates opened up and I had to write it all down. I learned to use my writing as a way of dealing with my life with Mark and my online relationships. There's just so much inside me that I've held back for so many years that I needed to write it all down.

I found a new place for the family to move into, and we would rent it starting that May. I had a lot of work to do to try and pack up a house with my bad arm and legs. It wasn't an easy task, but I took it slow and made sure that I didn't strain myself at all. I ended up throwing half of what we owned away. Things were moving on. The new place had three bedrooms and Mark and I decided that we would have separate bedrooms. My desire to have any kind of sexual relationship with him was over for good and he knew it, but agreed to the separate rooms and eventually to us parting ways. Though we were married we didn't share our life and I liked it better that way.

I really enjoyed having my own room, my own space. The bedroom I chose was big enough for all my stuff and there was a nice area for my computer, a desk and a file cabinet. I had my own phone line with my own number, and sometimes I felt like I was a teenager again, getting her first "own" room. It was a nice feeling. Whenever I talked to one of my friends on the phone, it was such a wonderful feeling being in my own space.

It was starting to get very hard for me to walk because of the pain in my knees, so I got myself a cane to help me. My shoulder was just killing me and I was still going through problems with the disability/workman's comp issue. We moved the end of May and after we got settled, I received a letter from my company demanding that I come back to work or I'd lose all my benefits. I was in no shape to go back to work as I couldn't even walk from the car to the house without being in pain, and the doctor had limited me to no excessive walking or standing and no repetitive motion with my shoulder and arm, so how could I work?

I called the company and they were firm on their demand, so with doctor's note in hand and my cane, I hobbled back to work. It had been four months since my fall, and I was supposed to be on light duty. When I returned I was called into Ben's office where he proceeded to tell me what my duties would be. I told him that I couldn't use my right arm at all and that I couldn't stand, and he proceeded to say, "Is that what you want me to tell my boss, that you can't do the job?" I gave him my note and he said that he would have the computer operators help me.

I received help for a day or two but noticed it dwindling down. I was in so much pain and I wasn't getting anywhere. While I was out on disability, Philip had retired and Ben was now my immediate boss. We clashed a few times that first week, and I couldn't figure out why I wasn't getting any help, until Joe (the operator sent back to help me) said, "I shouldn't tell you this, but I was told to let you do your own work because you have been out for four months and had a long enough vacation." I thanked him for his information and stood there dumbfounded. After I composed myself I called in the head of the Union.

By the next day I was just doing paperwork and deskwork. This went on for a couple of days and at the end of my seventh day back to work, I was called into the manager's office with Ben, the head of our labor department, and the head of our union. I was told that it was obvious that they had made a mistake calling me back to work, and to go pack my things and have a good life. I went back to my desk and packed all my belongings. I was now officially on long-term disability.

That week I worked was very trying, both physically and mentally. So many ill feelings are still harbored over my departure from a job that I had held for twenty-four years. I never received a get-well card nor any flowers from my department, and when questioned, the other employees said that Ben told them it wasn't necessary. I never received any recognition at all for my time in that department either. It really hurt. While packing up my belongings, Ben came back to make sure that I wasn't taking anything that belonged to the company. That really pissed me off. Did he think that little of me, especially after working there for so many years? I didn't deserve the sarcasm he threw at me that day. As I packed my stuff, a feeling of relief fell over me when I realized that I was free from here and was starting my retirement at age forty-six.

I wasn't able to write that week I worked, but when I finally settled into accepting the fact that I wasn't going back to work, I continued my writings, and I also continued on my search for the perfect mate. I was feeling less of a woman, disabled and not working, but my male friends online changed that. Nick and his wife decided to work things out in their marriage. It was my decision if I wanted to remain friends or part our ways and I wanted to remain friends.

I started to meet some of my neighbors. Next to us was a couple living together with her two children. Lillian seemed okay but I remembered Brad from the park near my old house. He was always very loud and either drunk or high on something, so I wasn't very happy to see that I had moved right next to him. Lillian and I seemed to hit it off really great. She was only a year younger than me, whereas Brad was in his early thirties. Brad was a physically and mentally abusive man. I could hear him yelling at her and the children all the time, but I vowed to stay out of their business. I learned all too well that lesson from living in the first mobile home park when Mark and I were first married.

Another neighbor, Jake, lived two doors up from us and was a really good friend of Brad's. I learned very fast not to get involved with Jake. He was single, forty, and still living with his mother. He made many advances toward me when we first moved in, but I didn't give him the time of day nor would I. Brad also made a few advances, but I turned them down, too, which is probably why he disliked me so much. They were both a bit sneaky and they always had a scheme of some sort going, so I kept my distance.

I was really depressed and things at home were the same as always. It bothered me being only forty-six and not being able to return to work, but I was starting to really enjoy being home and I loved the place we had moved into. My computer was in my own room, and it sat next to a window. The view was great and the front door was right there. I was happy and contented with my writing, but I really wished that I had someone to fulfill my sexual desires. I was still always looking for Mr. Right.

My closest friends were very envious of the life I was living—a married woman with all these men paying attention to her. They started to call it my secret life. I had friendships with men who came from all walks of life, most were very prominent in their communities, as well as very handsome men. How lucky could I be? I'm a very simple woman who doesn't expect or look for extravagant things in her life. The one thing in life that would make me the happiest would be to find the perfect mate for myself.

I've talked to writers from Boston, California, even had a telephone friendship with a poet from England, have had offers of trips, money, a new life, as I still searched for the perfect mate. My family was well aware of my quest. My mother backed me one hundred percent. Odd, huh? But she knew that I wasn't happy with Mark, she knew the life I lived with him, and she wanted nothing more than for me to be happy. My siblings felt the same way, and my oldest son, Ken, knew of my quest, too. He would say, "Go for it, Mom."

In the latter part of August 1998, I met another man online, Russell. He was a cop—handsome, sweet, and kind. I think that's why I connected with him so well. Russell and I decided to meet down by the river. It was a beautiful September afternoon, a perfect day. We spent five hours together there, talking, holding hands, kissing, and watching the boats and ships on the river. I couldn't have asked for a better day. We spent an hour trying to say goodbye that afternoon, neither one of us wanting to go. Russell is married, too, like me and lacking from the attention he needed from his wife. Russell would kiss me and my knees would get weak. It was very hard for me to stand after that. I had to laugh sometimes, I so felt like a schoolgirl when I was with him. He was perfect but he was married. I knew in my heart that we couldn't have more than what we had, but he filled a void I had inside.

Russell was the only man I was seeing. We would meet on Friday nights down by the river and spend a couple hours just holding each other, kissing, fulfilling that closeness we yearned for in our life. His wife worked at a restaurant on Fridays and Mark was working overtime or going to the firehouse, so it was easy for me to get out. I cherished my times with Russell, as he did, too. Our passions fueled our hearts, the world stood still when we kissed (and we kissed!), and I felt so alive and wanted. My being a Big Beautiful Woman didn't bother him either. He just liked me for me. I smile every time I think of Russell and my heart skips a beat as I sigh.

Our meetings went on for five months, then he landed a new job and had to work second shift. His wife also quit her Friday night job and winter was upon us. We met a few times in the afternoon, but then Russell was offered a second job as a limousine driver. He basically worked around the clock. He was a very ambitious man. We would grab some time online together, but it was almost impossible to meet in person anymore. That saddened me very much.

Through my times with Russell I still kept in constant contact with Nick. In October of 1998, he came online one day and gave me some bad news—he had pancreatic cancer and was going to be operated on in a week. I can't tell you how upset I got. I was so bad that I had to leave my house and I went down by the river where I sat and cried for an hour. I knew the chances he had and they weren't good. Unless you've been online and had a really close relationship with someone, you wouldn't understand the depth that these friendships go. Nick was my best friend and I hurt for him. I wanted to be with him, to console him, to be there for him, but I knew I couldn't. He had a wife and family so there was no place for me. I had to sit and wait and hope that he would return online again.

His surgery went well, and he had given me the name of the hospital and the address so I could send him flowers. He told his wife that they were from a friend online. Although she knew that he had one, she didn't want to know anything about me. I got a chance to call him and talk to him while he was there, too, and that one call lifted so much off my mind. His prognosis was good, but only time would tell.

I often sit and wonder what would have happened had he not gotten well. Being the other woman sometimes has its drawbacks, especially with an online relationship. If something happens to you or the other person, how would you or they know? If you just disappeared off line, how would the other know what had happened to you? That is the biggest drawback and at times it really hurts.

When Nick went home from the hospital we did get to chat once in a while, while he recuperated. Our friendship was a strong one and he knew how important he was to me and how heavy my heart was during this whole ordeal. Russell and I still shared a very close friendship online and although I had no real time intimacy with him, I still had my online time.

I started playing a game online called Acrophobia. I met some really super people in the game and eventually was asked to join one of the teams. I couldn't believe how much in common I had with my teammates. The game was a wonderful pastime for me in the evenings when Russell or Nick weren't around to talk to. I became very addicted to the game as I had with my whole online life.

Mark ended up back in the hospital again in April of 1999. He had a problem with blood clots in his legs. Once again I was home alone but I loved being home alone, having my own time, not worrying whether Mark would walk in on a phone call or looking over my shoulder while I was online.

While Mark was in the hospital I met a local guy online named Josh. We chatted online for over four hours that first day. He was married with a loveless, no intimacy relationship with his wife, just like I had with Mark. Josh was intelligent, well spoken, and was highly ranked in the military. After four hours of talking online I asked Josh if he'd like to call me and he did. We talked another two hours on the phone. We had so much in common that it was unbelievable. Although I still talked to Russell online, it had been over four months since I had seen him. It didn't look like we'd be seeing each other anytime soon either. Russell and I never to this day ever got to the point in our relationship where we had sex. We still talk about meeting someday, but I doubt that that will ever happen.

Josh and I talked a lot online, but did more talking on the telephone. I would call him at the office everyday and our relationship blossomed. We talked about meeting in person finally and we decided that we'd meet down by the river, my favorite place. I was sitting on a picnic table when Josh arrived. He came up behind me and put his arms around me, slowly turned me around and stared into my eyes. I melted. He leaned forward and softly kissed my lips as he ran his hand through my long, blond hair. My body felt like a million currents rushed through it and he left me weak in the knees. He took his hand from behind his back and handed me a bouquet of flowers. That was it! He had me from the get go. I tried really hard to not let myself fall so fast for him as I still had a somewhat relationship with Russell, and trying to juggle two men was not something I wanted. I knew in my heart that Russell and I would only remain friends, but I still tried hard to not let myself be so vulnerable to Josh.

Nick came online with some good news. He and his wife decided that they were going to sell the house and move to Florida. I was so happy for him, things were going good for them, and I give him so much credit for trying to make things work with his wife. I know it sounds odd but a woman can have a great friendship with a man without having an intimate relationship with him. I know! I've proven that so many times in my life. Mark would disagree with that statement. He thinks that any woman who has a friendship with a man is sleeping with him. Simple mind, I guess.

My dreams of moving to Florida one day were intensifying. I went down to visit Mom and Roy again. God, I loved it down there. I had so many friends there, too. It's still a dream of mine, and maybe one day I will be down there.

My teammates from Acrophobia were planning a bash in Kansas. I wanted so badly to go, but I really couldn't afford it, especially after the visit to Mom and Roy. My teammate and best friend, Sandy, the originator of the bash was so disappointed. She even told me to just pay for the flight that she would pay for the hotel room and my bash expense but I just couldn't. There was always next year.

Josh and I were really getting to know each other quite well. Our calls on the telephone got longer and more intimate. His voice went right through me. We would meet down by the river and steal an hour or two together, but that wasn't enough. Our touches became more personal and we needed and wanted privacy to explore our desires. The nice thing about Josh was that we could meet during the day when no one would suspect anything. Mark would be at work and Josh's wife would be at her job also. Being of higher rank in the military, Josh was able to get time off when he needed it. It was the perfect relationship for us.

It was fall and the telephone rang one morning. It was Josh and he wanted to know my plans for the day. I didn't have any. He told me that he was going to get a room at one of the local hotels for us and he would call when he got there. I was so excited. We had been talking and seeing each other for six months and we had waited so long for this. I quickly showered and got dressed and eagerly waited for his call. He finally called at one P.M. and I went to meet him. Josh was the most gentle, passionate man I've ever met. He did everything to make me comfortable, and he pampered me like I had never been pampered before. When we made love I felt things I had never felt before with any other man. To say that he had captured me would be less than the truth. He totally mesmerized and enchanted me and I felt like I had finally found my Prince Charming. Sexually, he lifted me to heights I have never known. I hated so much to leave that afternoon, but I knew that I had to go home.

My online time was basically spent with Josh, Russell and my online teammates. I no longer went into chat rooms and I wasn't looking to meet anyone new. My poetry writing was really blossoming. I had so much to write about, so much inspiration from the romance I had finally found in my life. I have absolutely no guilty feelings for what I do. Had Mark been there for me or had I not caught him that night with Gina, things in my life might not have led to this. I truly have a secret life and I'm not ashamed of it. A person needs to find his or her own happiness no matter in what form it comes to them. I have never let Mark find out anything about what I've done or whom I have seen. I have not and do not do this to hurt him in any way. My decision to get a divorce one day is still there, it has not been forgotten, and there is still no intimacy between Mark and me. He knows that will never happen again between us.

My relationship with Josh really got intense. I was completely consumed by the passion I felt. I was a much happier woman and it showed in my writing. My friends saw a new glow in me. He was always in my thoughts. All he would have to do is say, 'Come with me', and I would have been there. Although there were no commitments between us, I felt in my heart that one day we would be together. Russell and I did meet again in the fall of 1999. We met down by the river. We spent the afternoon together, talking, kissing, caressing, but it didn't quite feel the same any more. I knew in my heart that we had both moved on. He no longer was looking for that little 'extra' in his life, and my heart was with Josh. It was a sad feeling for me to realize that, but also a comforting feeling knowing that we would be friends for life.

The fall of 1999 was not a good time for either Mark or me. We got word that Mark's father had bladder cancer, and then Mom called to let us know that Roy had lung cancer. Mark spent three weeks with his mom while his dad was in the hospital and then home recovering. I asked Mom if she wanted me to come down to Florida and she said that she would be fine, to wait a while.

While Mark was at his parents' house, I had gone out to lunch with an online friend that I had helped out of a personal dilemma he was having. I had told Mark about it and he said that it would be okay with him. When Mark came home the following weekend from his mom's house, it was dinnertime and he was outside on the deck cooking steaks on the grill. I heard a couple voices and looked out the window. It was Brad and Jake. They just couldn't wait to tell Mark that I had a visitor while he was gone. Mark already knew the story about my friend, I had told him and he was fine with everything.

Brad and Jake said to him, "I don't know how you run your marriage, but your wife had a guy here while you were gone, and we just thought you should know." The next morning at breakfast Mark asked me who the bimbo was that I was with. Boy did that piss me off! I picked up my bagel with cream cheese, and when he had his back to me, I hurled it at him. The bagel hit him in the back of the head! He was stunned. I had to chuckle because there was cream cheese all over his hair. He dropped the subject after I told him to stop listening to them, that he knew the whole story from me and that was the truth, so to take it from the source. Mark seemed fine with that and apologized.

~Chapter 13~

I had a lot of problems with my neighbor, Brad, because of my friendship with his girlfriend, Lillian. Brad was very jealous of our friendship and forbid her to talk to me, and if she did she always paid for it. Brad was an alcoholic and a drug abuser, and he physically and verbally abused Lillian. He figured he could talk to me the same way, but he was wrong. I can't begin to tell you how many times he's been verbal to me. He even got so mad at her for talking to me on the phone that he pulled the phone out of the wall, then came outside and started throwing things at my deck and calling me names. I didn't call the police because she would get the bad end of that deal, and to be honest, I was afraid of him.

One night while Mark was at his mother's house, Brad came over and knocked on my door and wanted to borrow twenty dollars. Brad didn't work, so anytime he borrowed money, you either didn't get it back or Lillian had to pay it back. I told him I didn't have any money, but he put his foot in the door and came in. I was dressed in my nightgown and feeling very uncomfortable. I said, "I'll give you the money tomorrow when I go to the bank."

He said, "Let's go to the bank now." I was babysitting my niece and nephew and told him I couldn't leave.

"Jake will watch the kids," he answered back. I didn't have my car. Mark had taken it when he went to visit his parents. I told Brad that I had no car, but he said I could use his. I had twenty dollars in my wallet but I didn't want to give it to him.

He was really making me nervous and scared so I said, "Let me look and see what I do have. Oh, I do have twenty dollars." I took it out and gave it to him.

He said thanks, but then he got in my face and put his hand up to me and said, "If you tell anyone about this, you'll be sorry." I know I should have reported it to the police because what he had done was shake me down in my own home! But I didn't call them. I was too afraid.

My online teammates were planning their second bash, which would be held in July of 2000 in Las Vegas. Oh my, Las Vegas! Never in my wildest dreams did I ever think I'd get to Las Vegas, so I booked my room at the Flamingo Hilton and booked my flight. My teammate and best friend, Sandy, invited me to come visit her in Washington. I decided to go visit her in April of 2000. We were going to be sharing the hotel room in Vegas, so we both thought that it would be a good idea if we met first. The same day that I was flying to meet her, Josh was flying on one of his missions. We knew we'd be in the sky at the same time and made a point of looking out the window of our planes at the same time, and blowing each other a kiss even though there was no way that we could actually see each other. Josh was very romantic that way.

I had become an old pro at traveling although it was getting harder because of my knees and shoulder. It had been over two years now since I fell, and I was receiving Social Security disability and my company disability. My traveling meant using wheel chairs in the airports. Although I felt like an invalid at times, I knew that it was better for me. The attendants have always been very helpful and pleasant so it made it much easier for me. That is the one thing that has always amazed me about the men I've met online since my fall, it doesn't seem to bother any of them that I have to walk with a cane. I really thought that would make a difference. To me, that's a sign of sincerity.

I had such a wonderful week at Sandy's and we got along so great that it was like we had known each other our whole life. I couldn't imagine the beauty of the state of Washington. It was like being in God's country. I never saw so much greenery and moss in my life. The water was crystal clear in the streams and lakes! We even took a two-day trip to the Pacific Ocean. It felt very strange for this East Coast shore person, to see tall evergreens at the sand's edge; strange and beautiful. Sandy lived in a logging community as her dad used to own a logging camp. It's funny how different life is in different parts of our country, yet the people are so much alike. I really had a great time, and I couldn't wait for our bash in July.

When I returned home it was always the same thing. I'd have to listen to Mark complaining about what Michael did or didn't do that week. His attitude was always the same, it never made any difference where I went or with whom. He is a very insecure man and always has to place blame on everyone but himself. Michael was nineteen now, and we were having our share of problems with him. He got mixed up with the wrong kids and developed a real problem with smoking pot. It's not that I disapprove of it, but the law does and I started finding it controlling his life. He finally graduated high school with a special education diploma and he had worked so hard to get this far in his life. His being ADD made things very difficult for him and for me.

Michael has not been an easy child to raise. Things were much easier in his younger days, but only because the schools and doctors insisted on me putting him on Ritalin. When Michael reached high school age he refused to take it any more. We had an incident where we had to put him into a rehab center for two weeks for alcohol abuse and emotional problems. He came home a different boy, but fell back into his old pattern quickly.

My computer and online life has been my escape from the problems at home. I know that and won't deny it, but the people I have met have really been more than I could have ever imagined. From the men I've met to the people on my team, my life has blossomed and I'm a much happier woman. It's reflected in the poetry I write, my heart has been so full of love and care, and although my married life is not a happy one my secret life is. There have been a few other men that I've met but not mentioned, not all left me in awe but some left me lightheaded and weak-kneed. I shared lunch with many of them and that was where it ended. Your heart knows who to trust and who not to, and your fences go up when the wrong man appears.

July arrived and so did the bash in Las Vegas. Sandy and I coordinated our arrival at the airport in Vegas so that we would be there at the same time. She would meet me in baggage claim and then we'd take the same limo to the hotel. We were staying at the Flamingo Hilton. I had never dreamed I'd be in Vegas and here I was! The place was overwhelming! The Flamingo was like a city inside a building. There were over thirty-five hundred rooms, with three casinos, seven restaurants and five pools. Who could ask for anything more? Our room became "Bash Central" and everyone called as they arrived. We had such a wonderful five days that we never wanted it to end. There were no sexual encounters on this trip. It was all friends just getting together for a great time. We were like family. There was no other way to describe it.

One day we basically took over one of the swimming pools for our bash beach party. Around two o'clock, four of us had decided that we had better have some lunch. Fortunately for us the pool that we were at had its own restaurant, so we got a table and waited for a waiter. Well, our waiter brought us our lunches and we were enjoying them when the barmaid popped back to see if we needed a refill on our drinks. As she gazed at our lunches, she looks at mine and said, "Ewwwww, what's that?" referring to the mashed potatoes. She went on to say, "It looks like someone threw up in that bowl," in one of those perky 'Valley Girl' voices, you know . . ."duh".

With that we all replied, "it's mashed potatoes." As I looked at Norm sitting across from me, I noticed his cheeks were full. He had just taken a drink of coke before she said that and was ready to explode. I then looked at Lydia and Karen and noticed their cheeks were full, too, and I could feel the pressure building as we all refrained from laughing. As the barmaid walked away to get our sodas, we all burst out in the loudest fit of laughter. I had been so afraid that I was going to wear Norm's soda. That was over two years ago and we still laugh about it. That one incident has been the topic of conversation since. What a riot! As for the barmaid—we had thought of turning her in but decided not to. What an air-head. I'm sure she enjoyed her summer in Vegas and she sure gave us a good laugh. Our goodbyes were very sad…we all cried as each person left. I never would have dreamed that we would all bond the way we all did.

When we returned home and started playing team games again, it was quite different. In your mind, you could actually hear the person laugh when they laughed, or hear their voice and see their face when they talked. We all were closer than we ever thought. We were only home three weeks and we started making plans for our next bash. It would be held in July 2001 in Niagara Falls, Ontario, Canada. I think we wished one year of our lives away.

~Chapter 14~

My relationship with Josh was a very comfortable one. In my heart, I loved him so much, but there were no commitments and I knew that I couldn't tell him how I felt. In late August, I let him come to my house. It seemed stupid to make him pay for a hotel when no one was home but me. I made sure the nosy neighbors were out first. I didn't need any trouble. Even though we only had an hour together, Josh fulfilled me like no other man. How I wanted to spend my life with him! He was more than I could have ever asked for, as a lover and a friend.

It was October and Julie and I decided to fly to Florida to visit Mom and Roy. We stayed for a week. It was the perfect time to be in Florida. We hadn't gone to the Jersey shore in a couple of years and needed some time away from home. We went to the beach but spent more time at the pool in Mom's development. All the kids were in school and it was like having our own private pool. I called Josh a couple of times while I was away and Julie spent two days with her sister who lived the next town over. Being away always gave me a chance to think of my life and where I'd like it to go with it.

By now Mark and I were just going with the flow. He wasn't as verbal as he had been, so I guess we were mellowing out. I figured if he wasn't bothering me, that I would try to keep the peace, although this wasn't the life I wanted. I was able to pay off some of the debt that we had after we got rid of the house, and was feeling a little more comfortable financially. He still got very angry whenever I went away, but he has never made any effort to take me any place, and that was his problem to deal with.

The Christmas holidays were better than normal. Mark wasn't his cranky self, and we had a decent time…finally. It was long overdue. In January 2001, I finally got approvals for the surgery on my shoulder and knee from workman's comp. For over three years I suffered in pain, and now they were pushing me to have the surgery.

Our plans for the bash in July were really going smoothly. There were about twenty-five of us meeting this time. Sandy wasn't going to be able to attend this year, as her finances were not that great. I almost contemplated not going myself because it would have cost over five hundred dollars just to fly from New York to Canada, and with my bad knees taking a train was out, too. I didn't want to spend nine hours on a train alone. Another one of my teammates, Lori, from Vermont said that she would drive down, stay overnight and we would drive together to Canada and that sounded great. Our plans were shaping up.

In the beginning of March things were getting really bad between Lillian and Brad, so she decided to move out of her house and in with her oldest daughter and her friend. Mark and I helped her pack up her stuff and load the truck. Brad stayed at his mother's that day, but I knew it would be hell once she was gone. I hated to see Lillian leave, but it was for her own safety that she did. She would call to see how I was doing, but it was too hard for her to visit.

Helen's college friend, Billy, and I had finally decided it was time to meet. We had maintained a good friendship over the past three and a half years, and we really were quite excited. Billy was twenty-seven now and I was forty-nine. I felt a bit like 'Mrs. Robinson', but we have always gotten along so well and our ages were never an issue with us. I told Mark that Billy was Helen's brother and that he was going to pick me up to go to the christening of Helen's new baby twins. Helen was from upstate New York and lived about three hours from me. Mark knew that I couldn't drive out of town because of my anxiety attacks, so he thought nothing of it for me to have someone pick me up. He had met Helen twice since I started talking to her so my story was believable.

Billy arrived at my house around seven P.M. on Saturday night. He had gotten lost coming from New Hampshire. Luckily for me, Mark had been called out to a fire call and missed meeting him. Billy and I were quite relieved at that, as it was the one thing that made us both nervous. When I saw Billy for the first time my heart started to beat really fast. Oh my, he was so tall, so muscular and oh, so handsome. He was exactly like I had pictured him. We had exchanged many pictures of each other over the years, so there were no surprises. I have always been very up front with whomever I talk to online.

As Billy and I started on our way we tried to decide where to go. I had called earlier and reserved a room at a hotel about thirty-five minutes from my house. There was no way Mark would see me there so I reserved a room with a hot tub. Billy and I were talking and we related on the same level intellectually. It was amazing. When we arrived at the hotel Billy went to pay and get the key, but they told him they had given that room away ten minutes before we got there but that they had a couple of other rooms. Unfortunately they did not have a hot tub so he asked me if it was okay and I said sure. Billy and I parked in front of the room and looked at each other. The place wasn't exactly what we had expected but we figured the room couldn't be that bad. When we got our stuff together and went into the room we both stood there with our mouths open and started to laugh. The ceiling over the bed and the wall behind it were covered in mirrors. There was a step up to get into the bathroom, which was nothing to write home about. Billy turned to me and said, "This place looks like it is meant for one thing, and one thing only—having sex." I chuckled and said that I had to agree.

We lay down on the bed and started to kiss. Billy took the rubber band out of his ponytail and his long hair fell around his shoulders. He removed his shirt and he had muscles like I had never seen before. Oh my, where was he when I was in my twenties? I still couldn't believe that I was here with him. My disabilities didn't bother him a bit, and he was ever so gentle with my shoulder and me. He is so strong and sometimes he doesn't realize his strength. We had talked about this night for the past three years and our expectations were exactly as we had dreamed. He was my Knight in shining armor that night. We held back nothing. We just went with the moment.

I'm so happy that Billy and I took the opportunity to meet. You always wonder after a meeting if your friendship is going to stay the same as it was. I'm thankful that ours has. We have talked of meeting again someday and I look forward to that immensely. I sometimes feel that I'm living that part of my life that was missing before I got married when I wasn't dating at all, and though I know it's wrong, the fact is, I have no relationship with Mark and haven't for a long time. Maybe I'm going through mid-life crisis, who knows? All I know is that I feel very content with the life I'm leading. I spent a wonderful weekend with Billy. I guess that's all that matters. When I arrived home Mark was out. When he returned he was very calm and didn't question anything about my weekend away. I'm very thankful for that.

I finally had the surgery on my shoulder at the end of April 2001. The doctor said that it was the largest tear he had ever had to repair, and he was hoping the surgery would take, but he wasn't sure. I decided not to have the surgery on my knee—at least not now. The surgery was very iffy and only had a thirty-three percent chance of improvement, and those odds were disappointing. I knew what I had to deal with now, so I decided I'd wait until I really needed it. The shoulder was very painful when I came home, and the doctor prescribed painkillers for me. They would make me very tired, but I didn't get to sleep during the day much because Brad insisted on leaving his dog out all day. On one particular day I had had enough. The dog barked from seven A.M. until midnight, then all the next day. I had no other recourse than to call the police. They came and ticketed Brad, and Brad told me that he'd get even.

One night while Mark ran uptown, I was sitting at my computer and saw Brad stop by Mark's car. He leaned down and then I heard a loud pop followed by the sound of air coming out. Brad had punctured the tire on Mark's truck. I knew it was in retaliation for Mark helping Lillian move and because I had called the police on his dog. Brad was a very vengeful person, that's why I didn't pursue a lot of things against him that I could have. I knew that there would be repercussions. When I called the police they told me that unless I actually saw the knife in his hand, there was nothing they could do. It was dark and I didn't see it. I later talked to the judge that I saw about the barking complaint, and asked him about the incident with the tire. He told me confidentially, "Sometimes you have to lie," and left it at that.

I knew exactly what he meant. Brad became the 'neighbor from hell.' He did everything to annoy me. He would turn his stereo up really loud during the night, yell profanities at me, and he even did a dance one day in the street with his pants down. Luckily for me, I didn't turn around to look until his back was to me. He had yelled at me that day, "Emily, look at this!" I never turned around.

A week after my surgery, Michael went upstate with a friend of his for the night. They were bringing another friend home. He lived four hours away from us and I was very uneasy about him going with this kid. He always got into some sort of trouble whenever they were together. I had hoped that it would be different this time. It was eleven P.M. and the phone rang. It was Michael. They had been stopped on the thruway coming home, and when the state trooper frisked him they had found pot on him and he was arrested. He had the money on him to post bail, but they wouldn't take it. They told me that we had to come up to bail him out. He was over three hours away and I was in a cast on the upper part of my body so how could I go? Saturday morning we got word that my father-in-law had passed away. They had the wake for him one day and the funeral was going to be Tuesday.

I needed to get a bail bondsman to get the money they wanted to get Michael out of jail, but had to wait until Monday to talk to him because of the weekend. He said that he would give me the five hundred dollars needed, but it would have to be on Tuesday. I had no choice, I couldn't go to my father-in-law's funeral and I had to have Ken, my oldest son, drive me up to Saratoga Springs to bail Michael out of jail.

When we arrived to pick Michael up, I was really upset at the condition he was in. He had been so distraught over the whole situation that they kept him in the infirmary because all he did was throw up the whole time he was there. He had thrown up so much that his face was covered with broken capillaries and his eyes were bloodshot from him crying those four days. Although I knew what he did was wrong, I felt the judge had been very unfair by throwing him in jail with a bail of only five hundred dollars. We got a lawyer up there that day and the charges ended up being dropped and he paid a fine of one hundred dollars. I really hoped that this would open up his eyes and set him straight. A mother can always hope and pray.

Josh and I didn't clash on many things, but we did when it came to the way I handled Michael. He said that he would have left him there and I guess he was right, but Josh didn't know the kind of kid Michael was. His ADD really affected him and made him different from others. Mark never saw that either but then again, the apple doesn't fall far from the tree. I know that Mark is ADD, too, but has never been treated for it. They are so much alike that it scares me. Michael has spent so much of his salary on lawyers and fines that you would think that he would learn.

At the end of May, one Saturday morning there was a knock at the door and it was the provost marshal from the local military base. Seems that Michael had been with his friend again and they were picked up with two others for vandalism that had occurred over the past four weeks. I know that Michael had nothing to do with them as he had been working nights when they occurred, but because he was with these boys that particular night he got arrested, too. This was a different situation from the other times Michael had gotten in trouble. This was on government property and the penalties were much harsher. His first court appearance would be in August.

July came and so did the bash. Lori drove eight hours to my house and spent the night. We left at seven A.M. the next morning for our trip to Canada. We had such a great time on the way. We arrived around three in the afternoon, got our room and started calling to see who else was there. Our room became a meeting place there, too. We were located right next to the indoor pool, and everyone would stop by. We all did a lot of sightseeing together and had dinner together every night at a local restaurant. We went to the falls but I was unable to take the ride on the Maid of The Mist because the walkway was too steep for my knees to attempt it, and wheelchairs were not allowed. So, I stayed up top and took in the scenery while I waited for them all to come back.

Our first night there one of our teammates took us all out to dinner in the Skylon Tower. It was a restaurant that revolves and overlooks the falls and all of Niagara Falls. We all had a wonderful time. Our bash dinner on Saturday night was a great success. Our whole trip was wonderful and it was so great to see everyone again, and to get to meet some more of my teammates who didn't make it to Vegas. We all missed Sandy so much. On the night of our bash dinner, before the dinner took place, I invited my teammates in for wine and snacks and we called Sandy on the phone so she could say hi to everyone. It was a very tearful conversation, but it made her feel so wonderful knowing that we were all thinking of her and missing her.

Summer went on and before I knew it, it was time for Michael's first court appearance. The judge ended up being the uncle of my high school friend, Mandy. I never told him who I was. I didn't want favoritism toward Michael's case. He told the kids involved that they would have to go through weekly drug testing and that their results should go down in count every week. If they went up he knew they were still smoking and he would take action. I knew that Michael was going to be in trouble. His world revolved around being high. No matter what I said to him about it, it didn't matter. His next court date was September eighteenth.

My love for Josh was so intense that I wanted so much for him to take me away from the madness of my life. One day during our conversation, he told me that his wife took a job in California and was moving. I asked if they were getting divorced and he never said yes. I thought it odd, but it was his business. I was doing a scan in the member's directory on AOL and came across a profile that fit him to a tee. The only difference was that in the marital status it said recently divorced. I know it was Josh's because the rest of the profile was almost word for word as the one that I met him under. The other disturbing statement was that it also said, "Looking for friends, fun, and romance." What was I, chopped liver? I had a feeling things would change with his new marital status and I figured maybe he didn't tell me because I would want a commitment. To be honest, I didn't expect it. He needed time to get his life in order first.

September eleventh was a really depressing day. It was also a day for reflecting on my life. I realized that day how fast life passes us by and how very fast things can change. A person can be gone in a flash without any warning and it was a scary feeling. I wanted so much to tell Josh how much I loved him, but I didn't. It got harder and harder for us to see each other. With the threat to our country and him in the military, I knew that our times together were going to be few. We continued to talk on the phone whenever we could catch up with each other. I still talked to Russell all the time, too. Our friendship has remained very strong over the past couple of years.

Michael had his court date in September, his count for drugs was up and the judge got very angry. He was all ready to put him in jail but our lawyer got the judge to consider rehab instead. Michael spent two months in rehab and was a changed young man. I was so happy to have the same boy back that I had had before he got messed up in all this. He flourished, but when he came home he knew that it would be hard for him.

While Michael was away, Josh and I did get an opportunity to be together. He came to my home one day, and we got reacquainted, so to speak. Things between us were cooling a little because of our lack of opportunities to see each other. I was starting to wonder if he was seeing other people. I guess in my heart that I knew he was; after all, it had been since July when we had last seen each other. He's a young forty-two-year-old male, and has a very healthy sexual appetite so who was I kidding?

In January 2002, I started to post on various online poetry boards, and that seemed to take up a lot of my free time. I needed to express myself. It's part of me. I've had so many things happen to me in my life that I found the need to write and share them with others. I've met some really great people on the boards. They've encouraged me to write and have shared so much of themselves through their prose. I learned, too, how choosing the wrong words can hurt another, something I never meant to do. There's so much power in words, much more than people imagine.

~Chapter 15~

On Mother's Day I got a sad call from my mother telling me that Roy had passed away. He lost his battle with cancer. Mom and Roy had never gotten married. They had lived and shared their lives for over eight years together. She loved him so much and my heart broke for her. She had lost three life mates.

I still haven't seen Josh. It's been almost ten months. I've cut way back on my calls to him and he hasn't asked why either. I know it sounds crazy, but I still care so much for him. Russell is still a very important friend in my life (we talk a couple times a week). Mark's boss, Randy, and I are still the best of friends. He knows everything I've done and doesn't blame me one bit. He's quite special to me. Sandy and I are still the best of friends, and we spend a lot of time online playing our favorite game.

Julie and I went away again to the Jersey shore this summer, and it was a wonderful week. Our friendship is never-ending and we are unconditional friends. I think she knows more about me than anyone else in my life. We share a friendship that's so special, and she's the angel in my life as always. She's been with me through so much and has never thought any less of me for all that I've done. She's my forever friend.

Mark's still battling with his legs, and he's been out of work now for almost two months on IV medication. I've come back down with Bell's palsy...on the left side of my face this time...but life goes on. I turned fifty back in July and it was a traumatic day for me. I thought of my times with Tammy, about how we always talked about how we would spend our fiftieth birthdays, and I miss her so much.

I'm hoping one day soon to have my first book of poetry published. I've learned so much as a writer, and I want to share my life's hopes and dreams, and my passions with others. We all set our life goals, and as we age we sometimes change them. My goal is to be a writer, a good writer, and I put all my heart and soul into my work, and one day I hope to be able to share the over six hundred poems that I have written, and hopefully they will touch the hearts of others. Only time will tell.

We all make mistakes in our lives and we all do things that we may later regret. I am not disappointed with anything that I have done. I've grown so much in my adult life. I've become an open-minded woman who's not afraid to go after what she wants. I've finally found romance and passion, something I once only dreamed of. I know that one day Mark will be strong enough to handle his own life, and I will have the freedom I've been waiting for. I sometimes wish that I didn't have the heart that I have, that I could just tell him to go, but after almost twenty-five years of marriage I must admit that I care what happens to him, foolish as it all seems. My forties were the best time of my life. I look forward to my fifties. I'm beginning a new journey in my life. I hope it's as adventurous as my years before, but I also hope that they are peaceful ones as well, and that I find the passion in the man that I've waited for all my life.

To contact "Emily": SurvivorEmily@yahoo.com

"Sandra's" Story

~Prologue~

When I sat down to write this story, I thought it would be easy. An autobiography. What could be easier? We wrote enough of them in school. At the start of every new school year we had to write about our summer vacations. How hard could writing this be? Well, I found out. It is not easy going back and reliving your past. Some memories are painful, some are happy, and some things that happened in the past look so different now. Before I started writing this I went back to the area where I grew up, and went to see the house my parents had built. It seemed so much smaller! I also found out that what they say is true—you can never go back and find things as you remembered they were when you were young. I am sure that this story would be different were this being written by my mother or my sister. Each of us has a story to tell. Even you, dear reader. When you finish reading this book, sit down and put your life on paper. Try it. You may be surprised at what you find out about yourself. It has been a learning experience for me.

This is supposed to be the story of how we got to where we are. I never thought of myself as being in the "silver" generation, until last week when I received my Medicare card in the mail. It made me stop and think. Just how did I get here? How did I get to be sixty-five? Just yesterday I was a kid. A bride. A new mom. Then I was getting a divorce, and falling in love all over again.

I think life is something like a train ride; you come on board kicking and screaming, but soon settle down for the journey. You never know what the final destination is, but you do have choices along the way. The stops you take along the way are up to you. So, "ALLLLLLL ABOARDDDDDD!!!! Next stop, the life of Sandra."

~Chapter 1~

I was born in the South. My first train trip was to California when I was two years old. I have been told that I was too young to remember any of it, but I think that this must have started my lifelong interest in travel, and my love of trains. My mother was the youngest in her family. She was eleven years younger than her sister, so she was really the "baby". She says it was like having two moms, her real mom and her older sister. Dad was an only child. My mom was just nineteen and my dad twenty-one when they married, and I came along a year later. I think they were surprised to find me on the way so soon after their marriage.

My father was the one who decided to head for California. He was interested in radio and electronics, and a new thing called television, and wanted to find a job in the industry. Hollywood seemed to him to be a good place to start. He did find a job, and so we moved to North Hollywood. In 1939, North Hollywood was a sleepy bedroom town of Los Angeles and Hollywood.

The first place I remember living was in an upstairs apartment with a Murphy bed. Remember Murphy beds? How they folded out of the wall, and took up most of the room? The apartment was close to downtown, and I remember walking down to the local theatre, having an ice cream cone, and seeing Disney's first color movie.

Our downstairs neighbors, the Whites, were from Alaska. They were true sourdoughs, and had run a riverboat up and down the rivers in Alaska. In case you are not familiar with the term, a sourdough is the name given to the first settlers in Alaska. I guess they must have gone there in their twenties, and lived there about forty years. They were in their sixties when I first knew them, but as a child they seemed so old. They were younger than I am now. What stories they told! They were friends to my parents, and to me, until they died many years later.

We moved from that apartment to a house just down the street and how well I remember the day World War II started. As young as I was, it made an impression on me that I would never forget. I was sitting on the floor playing with a friend, and my parents were sitting around the kitchen table listening to the radio. My friend's parents were there, too. They stayed glued to that radio for hours, waiting for word of what to expect and what had happened. I can only imagine what went on in their minds. They were all in their early twenties, and the country was at war! Who would go, and who would stay? Would it touch our shores? War! At that moment I am sure that they had no idea of what the future would bring to them, or to us, their children.

My parents had friends who were Japanese and one day we took a trip out to their farm to say goodbye to them. They were being sent to a holding camp and though at the time I had no idea what a camp was, I knew that it was a very sad occasion. Their little boy was my age, and we ran around and played outside while our parents talked. I had no idea what was happening, but everyone seemed so sad. These people had geese and chickens, and grew such wonderful things. I ran outside with their children, and we picked strawberries, and the gander chased us. We left their home with baskets of strawberries. They had sold their small farm to a neighbor and were moving the next day. I have no idea what ever happened to them, or where they went after the war. How sad it was that they had to go away to such a place.

My father became an air raid warden. Because of the work he did, he was not called up to join the service. At four years old I really did not understand what he did, but I found out in later years that he was helping with the development of radar for the military. He had been running a radio store, complete with the RCA dog in front. That dog was my pet.

My father was transferred to Santa Barbara, California, for about a year. I started kindergarten in Santa Barbara and I was not an ideal student. I had learned early on that temper tantrums usually got me what I wanted! For some reason, they did not work in kindergarten! Believe me, I tried. More than once my mother was called to the school to come and get me.

There is a train station in Santa Barbara. In front of the station is a huge tree where I spent many hours sitting on a branch, watching the trains go by; freight trains, passenger trains, and troop trains. The tree is still there, and I would love to go sit in it for a few minutes, but I am not sure that I could still climb it at my age.

While we lived there, a Japanese submarine shelled the coast near us, in a place called Goleta. Dad grabbed his air raid warden hat and left to see if he was needed. The blackout curtains were shut, and most of the lights were turned off. Mother stayed glued to the radio waiting for news. I am sure that they thought we were being invaded. I actually don't think much damage was done and the sub got away, but for me it was exciting for a while.

We were transferred back to North Hollywood and when I started school there, I gave up trying to have my own way about everything. I think the teachers and my parents were much happier with me.

Looking back, I had a real childhood. Maybe those of us who grew up in the forties and fifties were the last generation to really be allowed to be children. We learned to ride bikes without a crash helmet, and to skate without shin guards. We went outside to play and no one worried about us until time for dinner. We had toy guns, and played cowboys and Indians, and no one had ever heard of being politically correct. In my neighborhood, the color of one's skin did not matter, and neither did their religion. I think in that respect California was far ahead of the rest of the country.

Children knew what was expected of us, and if we disobeyed, we knew that we would be punished with a swat or sent to our room. Our parents did not worry about damaging our little egos, and no one cared about our self-esteem. There were winners and losers in our games, and we played tag and dodge ball without knowing that it might be damaging to us. The adults, who sat on the porch and drank lemonade in the summer, generally ignored our games. There was no air-conditioning. We ran through the sprinklers to keep cool. We were sent to bed at a decent hour, ate what was put in front of us, and listened to Little Orphan Annie and the Lone Ranger on the radio. I think that perhaps we were the lucky ones. No organized soccer games, with parents fighting in the stands. No little league, just a pick-up game in the street. Yes, we even played in the street!

Santa came every Christmas, and Halloween meant roving for miles and bringing back pillowcases full of candy. We did not have to have the candy and apples checked before we ate them. We just dove in and made ourselves sick! We were all devoted to doing what we could for the war effort. We saved grease in coffee cans, and newspapers in stacks. We had stamp drives at school. We could buy a savings stamp for a dime, and fill a book. When the book was filled, we bought a war bond. We needed ration stamps for just about everything. (I still have a book of them, saved by an aunt at the end of the war).

Our favorite dessert was something called War Cake. War Cake uses ingredients that were available to the average household during World War II.

WAR CAKE

1 cup packed brown sugar	1/2 tsp salt
1 1/4 cups water	1 tsp ground nutmeg
1-cup raisins	1 tsp ground cinnamon
1 cup chopped walnuts, or pecans	2 cups flour
1/2 cup candied citron, chopped	5 tsp baking powder
1/3 cup shortening	

Preheat oven to 350 degrees, and grease a 9 X 13 baking pan. In a large saucepan over medium heat, combine brown sugar and water. Add the raisins, nuts, and citron. Bring to a boil and boil for three minutes, stirring constantly. Remove from heat, and allow the mixture to cool. Sift flour and baking powder together, and add to cooled mixture. Pour into the prepared pan, and bake at 350 degrees for forty-five minutes or until a toothpick inserted in the center comes out clean. Cool on a wire rack, and cut into squares.

Good with whipped cream, but during WWII we did not have much whipped cream.

~Chapter 2~

My parents did have big ideas for me. As time passed, my dad was becoming more and more involved with people in "the business," the movie business. I think my mom had ideas of making a star out of me! One day she sat me down, and curled my hair with a curling iron heated on the stove. (Ouch) I had black patent leather shoes, and a fluffy dress and bows. I thought we were going to a party. When we walked into a room with a lot of other children in the same type of dresses, their hair curled like mine and doting mothers all around, I realized it was not a party. There was a small stage in front, and one at a time we were called up to the front of the room and given instructions. Tap one, two, three, shuffle, shuffle, tap. I said, "No!" And that was the beginning and end of my movie career.

I soon was to discover that I would not be an only child. My sister was born in 1943. She was a blond, blue-eyed chubby baby, and quite different from me. My poor sister. Toward the end of 1945 my aunt and grandmother came to live with us. My sister was their little pet. I, on the other hand, devised many ways to try and get rid of my sister.

As the big sister, I had to look out for her, and as the little sister, she fulfilled her role as tattletale with zeal. I tried to take her blocks away and leave her at strange houses, but she always found her way home. I put hot sauce in her Ovaltine, and that did not work. I finally convinced her that there were bears in the closet, and if she got out of bed and told on me for reading under the covers, or listening to the radio, the bear would get her. She, to this day, must have the closet door closed in her bedroom. Nothing worked. She just grew up anyway, and became a wonderful sister and a good friend!

Because my dad was active in the radio industry, some of the kids in our neighborhood were not your average kids. Some of them were movie stars in their own right. To us, they were just kids, and joined in our adventures, but looking back, I guess they were different. So many of them are now gone. Ricky Nelson: killed in a plane crash. Only one of the

Crosby boys is still with us. I think Bobby Driscoll from Disney's Song of the South is gone, too, and whatever happened to Luanna Patten, who was also in that film? One of the members of the Sons of the Pioneers lived behind us, and his kid had pony rides at his birthday parties. Remember the Sons of the Pioneers? They sang with Gene Autry. Every time I hear "Cool Water" I think of them, and the pony rides.

~Chapter 3~

In 1945, when the war came to an end, the world became a very different place for everyone.

My parents built a new home in an area now referred to as the "Village" in the North Hollywood area. The Village was the name the builder called the housing tract, and it is still called that today. We walked to school or took the red car. We found that if you put a penny on the train track in a special spot, you could stand on it and make the wigwag go, stopping traffic on Laurel Canyon Boulevard for blocks. We never got caught! Remember wigwags? Now they have crossing gates, but it was more fun to see the wigwag waving its red light in the middle of the street to stop traffic.

Things changed for me, also. Until I was nine, I had lived what was called a privileged and very idyllic childhood…but one day I came home from school, and found that my dad was leaving. My parents were divorcing, and things would never be the same again. It was such a shock that even now I have nightmares about that day. I loved both my parents and that day I lost both of them. I don't remember exactly how I felt, but I know that I was totally devastated.

My mother went to work and my father married the sister of a well-known bandleader as soon as the divorce was final. My sister and I were lucky, though. We had a wonderful grandmother who stayed with us and took care of us while my mother worked. My grandmother did most of the cooking. The War Cake recipe came from her. What a treat it was to come in from school and smell it in the oven. Another favorite was her fried chicken and southern biscuits.

My mother is a good cook, too, but I always remember my grandmother's cooking the most. She made a Shepherd's Pie that I still make and my family loves. It's really easy and you can use left over roast beef, or lamb, or a pound of hamburger. Season, and if you have leftover gravy, add it to the meat. Layer it in the bottom of your baking dish and add a package of frozen vegetables, or canned, if you don't have frozen. I like peas best, but anything will do. Spread a can of undiluted tomato soup on next, and then spread on about two cups of mashed potatoes. Put it in a three hundred fifty degree oven and bake till the top is brown and the pie is heated through. It is amazing how much we all associate food with growing up.

I finished grade school and started junior high at eleven years old. I skipped sixth grade. I was just ahead of the class academically, but I was probably really too young to have been pushed ahead in classes!

I think if I could choose to live in any time, it would still be in the forties and fifties. (You might choose this time, too.) Some might call that time almost primitive by today's standards. One car per family, and color televisions were something in the future. IBM was developing the computer. There was no Internet. You had to pick up the telephone and call your friends if you wanted to talk to them. Telephone numbers started with things like Sunset, or Flower, and there was no area code. If you wanted to call long distance, you dialed the operator. Sometimes you had to take the phone into a closet so that your parents could not hear you giggling over the latest new boy in the class. (That is if the phone cord was long enough!) The average annual income was about five thousand dollars, and the Dow average was about two hundred. Things were simpler. We shared things with each other. Milk was under a dollar a gallon, compared to three dollars now. Bread was about twenty-five cents. A new home was about seven thousand dollars, and if you could drive, you usually had to borrow your dad's car. Back to school meant a new outfit that cost ten dollars. Tennis shoes for gym were Keds. We respected our parents. We respected our teachers. We wore poodle skirts and petticoats starched with sugar! Guys wore jeans, and heaven help the mother who washed them.

Most of the mothers did not work back then, but because of the divorce, my mother had had no choice. That is how she met the man who was to become our stepfather. He had two children, a daughter four years older than me, and a son who was two years older. I later found out, after many years, that he also had another daughter who lived with her mother in another state.

I am not sure why, but my mother did not really include us in her new "family." At the time I thought I was just not up to the standards that her husband-to-be and his relatives expected. To compensate I became involved in everything I could at school, just so I would not have to be at home. I was not part of the "in" crowd, but I was not excluded either. I just did not have the time or patience to do a lot of the things they did. I found a lot of the kid things boring. Cars, beer and drag racing were not interesting to me at all. If there was something going on that I found interesting, then I joined. I was very quiet. When I was not involved in school activities, I read anything and everything and I still do.

Like most teenagers, I had a dream. I wanted to become a doctor. Not a nurse—a doctor! I knew early on that it would take a lot of hard work, but I was willing to do whatever it took. I tried to tell my mom of my dream for my future, but I don't think she listened. I knew she worked hard to support us. I knew that my dad helped. My aunt worked, too, and helped support the family. I thought money might be a problem to put me through college, but I would have been willing to work and pitch in if I needed to.

I got my first job gift-wrapping at a small department store, and made all of fifty cents an hour. Shortly after I started high school my grandmother fell and broke her hip. I think she must have been about sixty. Younger than I am now. She was in and out of the hospital after that, and so my sister and I had to fend for ourselves. We became what are now known as latchkey kids. My mother was working, my aunt was working, and they had lives of their own, and much of the time it did not include us.

I think, now, that if I had been able to develop a real relationship with my mother, my life might have been different, but we moved on and the train of life just kept going from station to station, without checking to see if we wanted to stop there. My early life had not prepared me for what was to come down the tracks at each new station.

Mother bought an apartment building, and five of us lived in a two-bedroom unit. My grandmother came home from the hospital for a while. Even with her there, it still never seemed like home. My grandmother went back into the hospital with complications soon after and died from her injuries.

I think it was then that I became kind of a rebel. I knew what I wanted, but I was also aware that under the circumstances, I would probably never have it. I persisted, but it was not to be. I went to summer classes at college, and when I came home, I started talking about becoming a doctor. That is when I was told that girls did not need to go to college, and that girls did not become doctors, but nurses, and that I would not be able to realize my dream. I was sixteen and close to graduation from high school. At the time I was not sure that my mother really thought that it was inappropriate for girls to be doctors, but I knew my soon-to-be stepfather did. His daughter finished high school and became a secretary, and that was what I was expected to do, too, because that is what good girls did until they got married. I learned that no matter what I did, I was just not good enough to please him.

I cannot remember ever having my mother come to a school play, or a dance performance. I was part of the modern dance team, on the drill team, and in most of the school plays. I do remember that she was either working or off somewhere with "Archie Bunker's" family. That is the name my sister and I gave our stepfather later on in life, after the TV series started. Truly, he was an Archie Bunker, in actions and in attitude. As the years passed and I got to know him, I learned that he was a kind man, and eventually I learned to care about him very much. I know he loved my mother. He was eleven years older than she was and now I think she would have been what is referred to as a "trophy" wife. She was very, very pretty. My mother was his third wife.

It took me many years to learn to have a real relationship with my mother. I finally came to terms with my mother when I was much older and realized what she must have been going through when I was young. Living with my aunt was not easy. Mom was divorced at a time when people just did not get divorces. She had to work and I think she would have much rather stayed at home with us. She probably felt that she needed a husband because she was raised in an era when women were married. There were no women's rights, and I seriously doubt if she could even have had charge accounts in her own name. Husbands or fathers had to sign for their wives and daughters in order for them to open any kind of an account. Life must not have been easy for her.

~Chapter 4~

The next station—Love at first sight! Is it possible for a sixteen year old to fall in love? I thought it was. We used to go skating at the Hollywood Roller Rink, and I skated with a young sailor there. He had wonderful brooding eyes, a perfect smile, and he fit the tall-dark-and-handsome picture that is in every girl's dreams. I never knew his name, but every time I went there I would look for him. Then my aunt arranged a date for me. The boy was in the Navy, and the son of her co-worker. He was only nineteen. Although I had dated other boys, I had not found anyone I really liked. I was very nervous and, when the doorbell rang and I opened the door and saw the boy from the skating rink standing there, I knew. I knew that this was more than just a date. I knew that this was that special once in a lifetime love that all the songs were talking about, and he was Prince Charming on a white horse, come to carry me away to live happily ever after.

I have included so much about my childhood, because it had such an influence on what happened next. Maybe if I had not had such a happy childhood until the time my parents divorced, or had not read so many books where all the endings were happy, I would not have really believed in the Prince Charming story, but I did believe. After all, everyone always lived happily ever after. Didn't they?

We dated for about six months before we became engaged. I was seventeen. I had not enough experience to know what I was doing (I needed a Dr. Laura!). My mother encouraged me to date and get married and even though I kept up in school, for my last six months I was job hunting and even went for some college interviews, those things did not seem important any more. At this time he was still in the Navy, and we wrote or called each other every day. I still have those letters tucked away somewhere. All the hopes and dreams of a young girl in love; visions of a home and a family, and a little white house on a quiet street; kids playing in the yard and dinner hot on the table. Everything just as it is in the storybooks.

My dad and stepmother were very upset. They knew I was too young. My stepmother had a daughter my sister's age, and my sister and I spent weekends with them. My dad was working for a large company and also developing a method of color television, and something called kinescope. He worked with the first television station in the Los Angeles area. He did a show called Polka Parade on the old Los Angeles Channel Five. I even got to dance on it once in a while. He did not like the idea of my marrying at so young an age, but with my mother's help, I eloped.

My husband-to-be got out of the Navy and was working. It was May, and a beautiful spring day. Getting married seemed like a good thing to do at the time. We went to San Diego to visit some relatives. My mother was with us, and we decided, with her blessing, to go to Mexico and get married. It was like a game, and we did not have a clue. Neither of us was ready to marry, and we had no idea what marriage was about, but my mother encouraged us, so off we went. I think my mother decided with me gone, that she would have one less problem on her hands. I have often wondered what made her let us do it? I have never asked her, but I think she just wanted to get on with her own life, and with me gone it would be easier for her to do that.

We lied about our ages, and she signed for us. We said, "I do" (in Spanish) and headed for home. My new husband went home to his house, and I went home to mine. I shocked all my friends. He told his mother, which shocked his whole family.

We did not live together for a month or two, because we had no place to live. I was really dumb because my mom had never told me about the birds and bees, and so everything was a learning experience. We took off for a honeymoon in Santa Barbara. We walked on the beach, ate a lot, went to a movie, and generally got to know each other. Then we went back home, each to our own respective homes because we had nowhere to be together. We decided that this was not a good thing, and so my husband changed jobs, so that we could get away from our parents. Living with parents simply did not work!

Our first home was in Idaho. My husband started driving trucks for a construction firm, and he had a chance for a job transfer, and we took it. They were working at the Mountain Home Air Force Base rebuilding the runways. We needed a place of our own. We found a two-room apartment in an old maternity hospital. There was a shared bath down the hall. It was the only thing available, and it was certainly not the house with the picket fence, but there was a rose bush in the front of the building.

I had never paid bills, written checks, planned a menu, been grocery shopping, or even cleaned a whole house on my own. Laundry was a challenge. We did not know where to start. We moved in with what we had in the way of dishes, towels, sheets, and pots and pans. These were all things that we had received as wedding presents, thank goodness. The apartment was already furnished with two chairs, a table, a stove, sink and refrigerator, a shower but no potty, a bed and dresser, and the biggest bugs I had ever seen in my life!

I had to learn to cook. With the exception of War Cake, Shepherd's Pie, and spaghetti, neither of us knew what to do with a pot or a pan. We lived on canned stew and hamburgers and anything else that came in a can. Living in Mountain Home, Idaho, was an experience I shall never forget! I had never heard of "street hostesses" and the town was full of them. Prostitution was one of the leading industries in the area because of the Air Force Base nearby.

I began to realize that the Prince Charming story was a myth soon after arriving in Idaho. Marriage was hard work. I was not able to find a job, partly because of my age and partly because there were so many people in the area looking for work that any job that became available was filled within minutes. I can honestly say that we were happy there. We explored the area on the weekends, made friends, and got to know each other better. My husband would go out after work to have a few drinks with his buddies, but he always came home, eventually. I did not realize that this was the first sign of things to come.

When we went back to California a couple of years later, I began to realize something was really wrong, but I was not sure what. No one ever talked about drugs then—pot, uppers, and downers. The truck drivers my husband worked with used "uppers" all the time to stay awake on the road. I did not know what "uppers" were. It is in the news everyday now, but at the end of the fifties, drug use was not in the headlines.

My husband started running around with some motorcycle group he met at work. I knew he was acting strange, but had no idea why. I was usually left at home and not included in any of their activities. I had succeeded in finding a good job working for an insurance company in downtown Los Angeles, and took the bus to work, so I was gone about ten hours a day. Besides, I just did not fit in with the motorcycle crowd nor did I realize how heavy the drug use was. Not until the day that I found I was expecting a baby, and told my husband.

That was the first time he was abusive. I asked him to bring a vacuum cleaner upstairs to our apartment from a storage closet in the garage. He started yelling at me. He said he did not have time to help me do 'my job', and that it was my job to keep the house clean. He said that men did not do things around the house. He then pushed me down the steps, and I carried the vacuum up the stairs. He took off with his friends, and left me to lose my baby alone. I never told anyone what had happened. I think at the time I was either too scared to tell or ashamed of what my husband had done. There were no support groups back then. Of course, he swore that it would never happen again.

Everyone told me what a wonderful mother-in-law I had, and I thought so, too. But then, after I got to know her really well, she almost succeeded in making me feel like I could never be good enough for her son. This made things hard to deal with and not only that, she also let my husband know that nothing he could do would ever be as good as what his older brother did. This was hard on him. He really wanted his mother to approve of him. She had ideas as to what 'men' should do and not do. Men did not baby sit their own kids, or change diapers, or help with housework, or cook. Even though my husband was not her favorite son, he could do no wrong where I was concerned.

His mother helped him enforce the 'men do not help in the house' rule. She told him every chance she got that housework was woman's work. At the time, she was working, and divorced. Her boys were perfect...at least the oldest one was perfect...and my husband certainly tried to please her. Her boys thought she could do no wrong and I was in the middle. Her visits were heaped with criticism of me and I began to believe what she said and that there was something wrong with me as a wife. I was sure that I was not a good daughter-in-law. I had no idea that this was mental abuse from her. I then did everything I could to avoid her. I loved my job and I was good at it, so even if I were a bad wife, I knew that at least I could do something right. Knowing that one fact is probably what saved me later on.

Even though we were both working, paying bills became a struggle. I did not know where the money was going. I just did not see it. Maybe I just did not want to know, but I soon found out—motorcycles and drugs. My background had never prepared me for this, and I could not go and talk to my mother. She was having her own struggles. My stepdad was ill, and they were starting a business, and I know now that she was having problems living up to what his family expected of her. I was living in a world all my own and of my own doing. I had made these choices and so I thought I had to live with them.

I was expecting another child, and when our beautiful baby daughter arrived she became the light of my life. I was blind to the affair my husband was having with one of his motorcycle friends. Years later I found out that he had been with her the night our daughter was born. Those things did not seem to matter as long as I could hold my baby and cuddle her. I went back to work when my baby was six weeks old. I had to. Babies needed food and diapers, and someone had to pay the bills. I was lucky if even half of my husband's paycheck ever made it home. I kept thinking that things would get better, and that he would love our daughter and change what he was doing, if not for me then for her.

Our son was born a year and a half later. We actually bought a house and we moved to a small town near the ocean. I kept fooling myself. The drug use was getting worse, but I did not want to see it, or admit to myself that there was a problem. Today I would be able to see the signs of drug use, but back then I did not have a clue. The verbal abuse was getting worse, too. I never knew what to expect when, and if, my husband came home. He would walk in, yell and scream, and leave. He offered me to his friends to let them sleep with me. It never happened, but I had to fight off one guy who was supposed to be his buddy!

I still kept thinking that if I were a better wife, maybe things would change. My husband started drinking along with the drugs. Here we were in a beautiful home, with a Cadillac in the driveway, part owners of a trucking company, and giving all the outward appearances of being an ideal family! It was all a farce. It was the sixties. Our neighbors were into wife swapping, a thing of the sixties. There was no way I would get involved in that. My kids were getting older, and I was sure that there was no way out of the situation I had, and I was sure that it was my own fault that I was in this situation in the first place. By this time I had another daughter and a baby son, and with four children to care for, it was almost impossible to work outside the home.

My mother-in-law encouraged us to let my brother-in-law come and stay with us while he was in his last year of college. We had the room, and in her opinion we owed it to the family to help him. He was, and is, a very different kind of person. Encouraged by his mother, he expected me to cook and clean for him, too, as well as care for my children. I was exhausted most of the time. I found a job and went to work part-time, and usually I came home to a mess, but I was not able to depend on my husband's paycheck making it home and we needed the money I made.

My brother-in-law was with us for almost six months, and it was a constant battle. He did not like kids and so I was expected to keep them out of his way. Hard to do with four of them, especially when it is their own home! He finished school and became a teacher. He married a lovely lady, and soon found out that he was to become a father. I must say all that changed his attitude toward children in a hurry! My brother-in-law managed to ignore what was going on with my husband, or perhaps he thought it was okay. I have never asked him about it.

~Chapter 5~

Abuse can take many forms. In my case, it was mostly verbal. There were threats to the children, and threats to me. At one time my husband actually did hit me. He was so out of it that day and he says he does not remember doing it. I do. Abuse is not just being slapped around. It is being degraded on a daily basis. It is being yelled at, and called names in front of your children, and having their dad tell them that you are not a good mother. It is spending your paycheck on drugs before you bring anything home to feed your kids. It is also about making you wonder about your own sanity.

I found out that my husband had started dealing in drugs big time. I caught him counting out pills of some kind in our living room in front of the kids. He swore that there was no harm in them. It was still mostly uppers and downers. He said all the truckers used them. Heaven help those who were on the road if it were true!

He took to disappearing for days on end. It was all my fault, of course. The house was not clean enough, or the kids were in the way, or I was not fun because I did not drink with him. Sex was at a stand still. I thought that this was my fault, too, because I did not want to admit to myself that he had someone else. The abusive behavior not only continued, it escalated. He would disappear for a day or two and I could not explain to the children what was wrong with their father, because I really did not understand it myself. I fed the kids oatmeal for supper, and the only way I kept food on the table was by using a charge account we had at a local market. There were days I would go to his employer, and ask for an advance on his paycheck. It was actually commission, because he worked by the job and for a mileage rate. His boss gave me the money, but then made advances toward me, so I made sure that we were never alone.

I finally went to my mother for help. I remember well her comment. She wondered what I did to make him so angry! If he was abusive, it must be something I did. Neither his family nor mine would believe that he was on drugs and drinking, because when they saw him, he was always acting as the 'good' husband and father. He could put on such a good act. He would brag about being able to do it.

After one very bad episode, I just told him to leave. Much to my surprise, he did. He left and moved in with a woman he had been seeing for years. This was not the end of the abuse. I would never allow myself to be alone with him because I was afraid of what he might do. Every time he got a chance, he would tell his parents or mine how bad I was. Not a good mom, not a good wife, not a good worker. Our parents believed him. They believed him because he was such a damned good liar. He convinced them that any abuse was all my imagination, that he would never do anything that would harm me or his children, and that he would never in his life take drugs. They did not or would not see the signs of drug abuse, even though he might be high on something as he talked to them. He was all sweetness and light to them. It was such a good act, and he would laugh behind their backs because they believed him.

I had mixed feelings during this time, but I have never been a person to act on "feelings." Rather, I was a person who acted on what seemed to be the right thing, and the most logical thing, to do in every situation. Setting "feelings" aside, I realized that I had not caused the situation I was in, but I could put a stop to the mess! Acting on feelings can get you into a lot of trouble! It would be so easy to play the poor abused wife, but the sensible thing is to get on with it, and not let feelings interfere with what needs to be done to correct the situation. No matter what I felt about my husband, I realized that no one could do something to me unless I allowed them to do it! I was allowing this abuse to happen and I could stop it! At any time!

I filed for divorce, and it was granted based on his infidelity. The judge gave me fifty dollars a month in child support, per child. I never received it from him. The judge also gave custody of our oldest son to his dad, because he thought a boy needed his father more than he needed a mom, and because my husband told the judge that as soon as our divorce was final he was going to remarry. My husband brought the lady he was living with to court with him. My younger boy was only two, and so I was allowed to keep him and the two girls. That was hard on all of us, but especially on the children. I had no proof of the abuse, or the drug use, or the drinking. Only my word. My brother-in-law had seen it but he would never speak in my defense. Without witnesses, my word did not count. My husband had always been very careful that there were no witnesses, and I had never aired our dirty linen in public so there were no police reports, nor any hospital statements showing that I had been hurt. Big mistake on my part!

I got a fulltime job. I worked as a sales person in a small shop, and later as a secretary in an insurance company. I was headed for another stop on the road of life—another station I would have to stop at whether I wanted to or not. No one asked me if I wanted to get off the train at each stop, I was just pushed out into it. I was twenty-eight years old. The same age my mother had been when my father left us.

Other things were happening during this time. My sister married at sixteen, and had her first child not quite nine months later, and her second a little over a year after that. Her first marriage also ended in a divorce, and she became a single mom at eighteen. Talking to her later on I found out that she had left home for the same reasons I did. She thought that she was a bother at home, and did not fit in with our mother's new family.

I had a best friend while I was growing up and she shared in all the things we did. She married at seventeen, another victim of the Prince Charming story. The man she married was also abusive. He would hit her and leave her with bruises and marks all over her face and body. There were no women's shelters in those days and she felt she had no place to go for help or to get away. We would talk on the phone and console each other.

Ann was a beautiful girl. She actually looked like Marilyn Monroe—blonde, blue eyed and really sexy by today's standards. Her husband was a police officer. He was about ten years older than she was. He was legally allowed to carry a gun and as a result, Ann never reached her twenty-fifth birthday. He used the alibi that she was having an affair (which she was not), but he actually received a very short time in prison. I have always wondered what happened to him, or to their son. She had been the one person I could talk to during all the years of my marriage and then she was gone and I was alone again.

My next stop was just next door. My neighbor was several years older than me, and worked at an Air Force base nearby. She introduced me to a recently divorced Air Force officer. I had been on my own for about two years at that time, and I was not really excited about meeting another man. She invited me to lunch at the officers' club on base and she introduced me to Jay.

Jay asked me out and we went for coffee, a movie, out to eat, and gradually over the next year we started seeing more and more of each other. My kids liked him, and he liked them. His former wife was in Florida with her family. He had three daughters and he was eleven years older than me. The relationship left me with a lot to think about, and a lot of decisions to make. I did not think of him as a Prince Charming. By this time I knew that that story was a myth. I did know that I was falling in love, but this time I was sure that it would take a lot more than love to make the marriage work. He got transfer orders to New York, and so we took a short trip to the county clerk's office. We did not tell anyone we were married. Jay left for New York, and I was to follow later when we had a place to live. Here I was at the next station in life, standing on the train station platform as a military wife.

~Chapter 6~

Six months after Jay left for New York, my kids and I got on a plane and flew to join him. What an adventure that was. Things were so different! We did not live on base, but rented a house in town. I found a job, a sitter, and enrolled the kids in school. This was another learning experience. In a few short months I learned to drive a Volkswagen, learned that the military had its own sense of humor, and that an officer's wife always had to wear a dress in the commissary. This was the end of the sixties now. Mini-skirts and tie-dye were in style. Remember Nehru Jackets? Hot Pants? Officer's wives did not wear hot pants—at least not any place where the commander's wife might see them!

We went to New York City to sight-see, but only once. We saw all the usual tourist things, but I got the feeling that if I had tripped and fallen on the sidewalk, or one of the kids had, we would have just been trampled into the concrete. People were so busy rushing here and there, oblivious to the people around them.

The Upstate New York area where we were stationed was very pretty, and it was the home of the Mafia. There was an Italian restaurant there that we really liked. There was a table in the back, and around it sat what I now know were some of the Mafia members. Dark suits, sunglasses, and bodyguards. It was something out of a movie script. If a military person came into the restaurant in uniform and they could not pay their bill, it was always 'taken care of'. If nothing else, the men at the back table were very patriotic.

While we were there, the squadron received notice that the base was to be closed down. There was money in the kitty, and so they decided to have a big party to send everyone off. They bought two pigs, with the idea that they were going to roast them, Hawaiian style. Two different people took the pigs home to fatten them up. One of the pig caretakers had kids. The pig became a member of the family, and they began to think he was a pet, like a dog. This was not a small pig and this was long before anyone thought of pigs as pets. One pig was roasted. The other went on to a new home.

Life was good for all of us but I missed my oldest son, and could only hope that his dad was good to him, because there was no communication between us. Letters and gifts that I sent my son were returned, and child support for the other children stopped. I heard very little from my parents and the children's other grandparents never wrote to them. It was as if we were no longer members of either family.

Jay's ex-wife never accepted the fact that we were married, and I am not sure that my family did either. He was an Irish Catholic, and as far as my family was concerned that was just awful! His ex-wife told his children that I broke up their marriage. That was not true. I did not meet him until long after they had separated. We rarely got to see his girls, and that was hard on him. He missed them as much as I missed my son.

Our next assignment was on Cape Cod. Again we chose to live in town, rather than on the base. I loved Cape Cod. I would love to visit there again someday. We went to Boston to the ball games. We went to see the fall colors, something we had never had back in Southern California. We visited Plymouth Rock. We got lost and ended up on a back road in the Kennedy compound. We were very careful when driving at night, because the farmers who raised cranberries drove at night with no lights. We ate lots of wonderful seafood.

I learned that the Canadian Air Force can drink our guys under the table, and the Aussies can out-do the Canadians. I have often wondered about one story I heard while I was there. I was told that some of the Canadians were taking fresh lobster home. I am not sure where they were stowed on the plane, but someone pushed the wrong button in flight and bombarded a small town with lobster. That must have been interesting for the town's residents if the story was true.

I was working for an insurance investigator while we were stationed there. It was a job I really enjoyed. I could work while the kids were at school, and I even got to do some investigative work myself. This was also the time that the Kennedys' Chappaquiddick incident happened. We could see the island from where we lived. The weather was bad, and there was no way that anyone could swim to Hyannis. It was a good story, however, and it worked for Ted Kennedy. Those of us who lived there had our doubts. The press converged on the town, and it was almost impossible to drive through the narrow downtown streets. Rental cars were few and far between, and reporters were offering just about any price to the local residents to let them use a car or a boat.

While we were on Cape Cod, my husband was sent to several other places that were referred to as 'unaccompanied' tours. One was India, and the other was Iceland. What Jay did there was classified, and to this day I do not know what his missions entailed. He spoke about seven different languages, and was very fluent in Russian. Prior to our marriage he had been stationed in France and flew into several "Iron Curtain" countries with supplies for the embassies. I know that he did cryptography. I also know that he was encouraged to mingle with people and just listen to what was said. He was also in Iran, and in Egypt. He never talked about those tours of duty—ever.

His ex-wife also decided to move from Florida to Cape Cod. This made it easier for Jay to see his girls, but harder on me, because she made sure that people knew she was the 'real' wife. In her mind she was, because the Catholic Church had not sanctioned their divorce. While we were on the Cape, "the real wife," as I came to call her, was diagnosed with a very serious illness, Muscular Dystrophy. What made it even worse, their middle girl, Linda, also had it along with the progressive mental retardation that can sometimes accompany it. We took on the responsibility of supporting both families. The real wife could not work, and it was very hard, but we did manage. I think she really thought she was the real wife because she never sought an annulment in the church, and so no divorce was valid in her opinion. We very rarely ever spoke.

The only major confrontation we ever had was over Jay's youngest daughter when the child was sixteen and pregnant. Jay and I took her to our family doctor, and made arrangements to have the baby put in an open adoption. Jay could never accept abortion as an option because of his religion. Things were going well, and the ultrasound showed the baby was a girl. We met the adoptive family and they were really looking forward to having a baby. Jay's daughter was doing well, too. The father was also sixteen and a Catholic. His family was supportive of the adoption. Then Jay's daughter went to visit her mom for a while, and we subsequently got a call. The real wife had arranged for a late term abortion and wanted us to pay for half of it. She was just too embarrassed to have a pregnant, unwed daughter around the house and in front of her bridge club (her words, I swear!). We found out that the abortion had already happened. I yelled at her, asking her how she felt as the co-murderer of her own granddaughter. She said that if she was expecting and did not want it that she would have had an abortion, too. So much for being a good Catholic! I had to tell the adoptive parents. We really never spoke to the real wife again, and there were no more grandchildren during her lifetime. That daughter had a very difficult time as she grew up. She has a child now, but I think she still thinks of the first one. This all happened after we were transferred back to California.

The Vietnam war was ongoing, and we all lived in fear that one of our people might be sent there. News came that the squadron on the Cape was to be closed down, and we would be going back to California. This, of course, led to another 'closing party'. In the military it seems that one is always saying goodbye. It was unusual back then to be in a place more that two years. The squadron decided to have the party to end all parties. They had a mascot, a blue parrot named "Blue". Blue lived in the ready room, and his language left a lot to be desired.

The base commander's wife had a reputation as a heavy drinker, and also as someone not to cross. Heaven help anyone who did not mow their yard to her standards, or whose wife she did not like. I learned just to not be wherever she was. It made life easier. One of the fighter pilots taught Blue to say, "Screw the commander's wife," but he used her name, and screw was not the word he used. I guess it was bound to happen! Blue was the guest of honor at the party. Mrs. Commander walked up to him and, well, you know what he said. For most of the crew, it was the highlight of their tour. Mrs. Commander wanted to have everyone reprimanded on the spot. Her husband escorted her home. Everyone else was rolling on the floor laughing. That was the last time anyone ever saw her. Later we heard that she had entered rehab for her drinking.

The next question was what to do with Blue. The military can be very creative. The officer who gave Blue language instruction was transferred to a base in England. The rest of the squadron decided to get even and sent Blue (C.O.D.) to him! Perhaps somewhere, Blue is still around. They say parrots live for many years.

~Chapter 7~

We headed back to California, kids, turtle, cat, and all. Our next base was to be our last stop in the military. We were in Northern California. My husband was in a plane equipped with a radar early warning system. The planes were old, and leaked hydraulic fluid at every take off. They flew a set pattern off the coast, but exactly where was classified. Then the dreaded orders came for Vietnam. It is hard to say what I felt. I certainly did not want him to go. He went to a base in Thailand, and flew directing air strikes in Nam. His best friend was shot down. He would never talk about any of his experiences there. But we were really lucky. He came home and after twenty-one years in the Air Force, he retired with the active duty rank of Major. His reserve rank was that of Lt. Colonel.

Now we were both back on that train, headed for a new and different station. The real wife followed us to California and now I had his three girls nearby again, as well as my own children. Having that many teenagers at one time was exciting. You never knew what to expect. The seventies were very hard on teenagers, not to mention the parents. LSD and pot were common, and it was hard for kids to say no, even though they had been raised with the idea that drugs were wrong. My husband was a devout Catholic, and through all the years his faith had been an important part of his life, and so it had become a part of mine, too. Our children were taught that no matter what, faith would sustain them, and that God should be an important part of their lives also. We had some problems, but thanks to their faith, and maybe ours, and a lot of luck, and maybe the fact that they did listen to us even if we didn't think so, we got through the teen years without much kid trouble.

Well, that is not quite true. My ex-husband had stayed out of our lives while we were out of California, but when we returned he gave us lots of problems. He decided that he wanted all the kids, and made things look so good at his home when they went to visit him that they asked to stay with him. I said fine, try it. I knew that if I did not let them go, they would never learn what their dad was really like. I did not want to make them hate their father, and I thought that living with him for a while might be a good thing. He was on his third or fourth wife (I never knew for sure.). She was a very nice lady, or so I thought. She was ten years older than my ex, and kind of reminded me of a grandmother. My youngest son and oldest daughter went, but my youngest daughter would have nothing to do with it. My ex's mother and my mother thought it was wonderful that the children would have a real home. I have no idea what they thought we had! A pretend home maybe?

About four months later my oldest daughter got on a bus and came home. She told me that my ex was still abusive and was very mean to his wife, and in turn, she took it out on the kids. She had two grown daughters, and apparently, my children could not live up to the standards she set. This sounded familiar, reminding me of my own experience. My daughter told me that her kids did the usual kid things, but never let their mother find out. She told me that her dad hit the boys, and that she was really upset about it. She said she had tried to protect them from him. She also told me that every day they were told how awful I was, and that it was my fault that they did not have "stuff," or a home with a pool, or new cars, or whatever the subject of the day might be, when they were living with me. They had all those things at their father's. My daughter said it was as if my ex still wanted to get even with me for divorcing him. I just thought how sad for him, and for his wife. And how sad for our children, too. My daughter also told me that they were not allowed to have any letters or gifts I sent them, nor were they able to return phone calls to me.

Then I got the phone call. It was the San Jose Police. They had my son, the younger one, and could I take him. His dad had beaten him and thrown him out of the house. Of course, we went after him. Because I did not have legal custody of the older boy, he was sent to a nearby relative. My ex blamed me for turning him in. I did not do it, a neighbor of his did. I really should have. He left the state, and has never returned to California. Things got back to normal after that, or as normal as things can be with kids in the house.

I found that surviving with that many teenagers requires good health, fortitude, and maintaining a sense a humor. Number one on the list would be the sense of humor! Kids are amazing and what they can come up with is amazing, too. Everything from a snake in a lunch box to fishing worms in pants pockets. Did you know that worms float in the wash, or that given the surprise factor, you can really throw a snake a long way in the house. Pork chops under the bed? Sure, and where do kids come up with what they flush down the potty? And there was our neighbor's three-year-old boy. We told him that he could come in to use the bathroom, and he was dripping wet from running through the sprinklers. He brought the sprinkler into the house with him. That made for a wet room! The cat did not like the water, so we had a screeching wet cat, too. Without a sense of humor, how do parents survive?

My husband and I decided that we should go back to college. He had one degree, and I had taken enough classes during the years to be able to enter as a third year student. He had the GI Bill, and decided to use it. We spent two years working, going to class, rearing kids, and trying to make ends meet.

Jay's oldest daughter was now in her twenties and on her own. The real wife lived near us and we used all of the military retirement to support her and the other two girls. Her illness was progressing, and we only hoped that she would live until the girls were grown. She did not. What were we? In most ways we were an average, everyday, normal family; not the ones who make the newspapers; not the family whose kids ended up on drugs; and not the ones with a hardship nor a heart-rending story to tell. Just your average people next door. With a few problems, yes, but no more than we saw every day, and much fewer problems than the others we knew had. I suppose that this makes my Pearls of Wisdom not quite as interesting as some, but it is perhaps more like the lives of those who read it. Most of us are just the average people next door. We grew up in the fifties, and made it through the sixties without becoming hippies. Now we were venturing into the seventies.

~Chapter 8~

When Jay's ex-wife died, we found out that there really was some question as to who the real wife was!!! It seems that his ex-wife never did actually sign all the final divorce papers. We checked with an attorney and found that even so, everything was legal, and I was really married to Jay. Jay wanted to marry in the church, but that was to come later.

Graduation time came for us and so did a job offer for my husband. We were on our way to another train stop in far northern California. Jay settled down to a wonderful job at a resort. I was not sure what I wanted to do, so I got my license and opened a tax practice. Working at the resort had some wonderful perks, but dealing with the IRS on a day-to-day basis was something else again. We used the resorts houseboats and patio boats as part of the perks that went with Jays' job.

One adventure on the lake stands out. Jay's middle daughter, Linda, the one with MD, came to stay with us for a part of the summer. Her retardation was advancing but she was still able to function on a pretty normal basis. We decided to take a patio boat out and go have a picnic on the lake. We took hot dogs, and all the usual stuff to go with them, and set out on our picnic. We went down the lake for about half an hour and tied up behind a small island. That is when we found out that barbeque on the boat did not work.

So, I sliced the hotdogs, and made sandwiches out of them, and served the chips and salad. Linda would not eat. Her mother told her never to eat anything that was not cooked, and the dogs were not cooked! Okayyy—so eat some fruit and salad! "No," she said stubbornly, "not if I can't have a hot dog." Linda retreated to the back seat of the boat to pout. She pulled some candy bars out of her purse and proceeded to eat those and read a book. Jay and I set off to explore the island and swim. We came back and Linda announced that she had to go potty. She had to have a real potty, no sneaking behind a tree for her! There are floating potties on the lake, and we set off to find one. Luckily, one was not far away. We tied the boat to it and Linda retreated inside. It was like your standard port-a-potty, but on floats. We waited and waited, and she did not come out. The knot that held us to the pot grew tighter. Finally Jay got off the boat, knocked on the potty door and told her to hurry up. About five minutes later, out she came—with the book. By now, we could not untie the boat. We were stuck to the pot, and did not have a knife sharp enough to cut the rope holding the boat and the potty together.

Jay decided that since we were here and could not leave, he would use the pot. I was trying to hold the boat steady, and along came a fast ski boat with a big wake. The wake started us, and the pot, floating out toward the main channel. I asked Linda to hold the wheel of the boat. She told me, "No, my hands would get too tired." I found words I did not know I knew. Jay came back on board, and we finally got loose. We headed back for the docks, and the pot headed for the Shasta Dam. Linda had a tantrum because she did not want to go home. Six months later we were invited to Thanksgiving dinner with friends. One of the couples in attendance worked for the forest service. They were talking about the strange thing that happened during the summer when a port-a-potty floated all the way to the dam. I never told them we knew and that we had been the propelling factor behind the floating port-a-potty!

Accounting and taxes can be really boring. A few interesting things have happened, but not often. I had one case that sticks out above the others though. My clients inherited property in Oakland, California. Their aunt had died and left slum apartment buildings. One building had been condemned years earlier, but the aunt continued to live in it. She died when the building caught on fire! My clients tried to go through the building, or what was left of it, and to see what could be done with the other slum houses.

They were ready to give up when they started getting letters from the IRS and the city of Oakland. Both were demanding back taxes. The clients attempted to explain that the lady was very dead, and that she could not respond to the letters. The city of Oakland threatened to take the buildings for taxes. That would solve the problem of how to get rid of the buildings, but the IRS was relentless. Finally a letter came demanding that the old aunt appear at a specified time at the IRS office or be held in contempt and arrested. We wondered just how they were planning on accomplishing that. The client called and got nowhere, so they took the letter, a large envelope, and some ashes from their fireplace. They put it all in the envelope, with a note saying here she is, along with a copy of her death certificate, and mailed it to the IRS office. They never heard another word. Funny things don't happen very often in a tax office, but I would have loved to have been there to see the agents' faces when they opened that envelope.

Time seemed to fly by. The girls married, the boys went into the military, and they married, too, and our first grandchild came into our lives.

The first thing that made Jay think that there might be something wrong with him was a shadow in his eye that would not go away. He paid a visit to an optometrist, and the next thing we knew we were at a specialist's office in San Francisco. I had never heard of Ocular Melanoma. I knew that melanoma was really bad, but ocular melanoma? And there was no way to know how far it had advanced. The only treatment was to remove the eye plus radiation, but no chemotherapy. After the surgery we came home, and lived each day as if it were a gift. We were told that if Jay made it for five years, that the cancer would probably be gone and had not spread. We were not that lucky. Three years later the melanoma returned with a vengeance. More surgery was done, and I brought Jay home from the hospital just before Christmas. We had no idea that it would be our last Christmas together. He felt good, and the kids came up and it was really nice, but very quiet.

We made arrangements to get married in the church, as Jay had wanted to do all along. It was a small ceremony. We went from the office to the church, were remarried, and went back to work!

Jay left the job on the lake, and worked with me at the tax office that tax season. He had moonlighted there all along, and he was licensed. It was a good thing to be together. We grew more dependent on each other, and we did not know how long we had left together. The cancer progressed, and it moved into other parts of his body. One day in early September he awoke in pain and so we got in the car and made a trip to the emergency room. He was admitted to the hospital and the oncologist came to talk to me. Jay would not be going home.

I lived in his room for the next two days, and called the kids to let them know. His daughters came to say goodbye and so did mine. He left very quietly early one morning. I was holding his hand, and one minute he was there and the next he was gone. Most of me went with him. I don't know how I got through the next few days. We had services locally, but he is buried at Arlington National Cemetery, as were his wishes.

I was thankful for the twenty-three years we had had together. It had held much joy, and some pain. We had fun, we argued, we got the kids to a point where they were on their own. I missed him more than words can tell. Somehow the word 'widow' just would not register.

I was sitting alone in the living room looking at his chair and I wanted to hit it. How could he do this to me? Just go off and leave me when we were just getting to a place in our lives when we could do all the things we had planned while the kids were growing up? What about our trip to Europe? We had tickets for a cruise! And to top it all off, I was angry about his car. It was the old Volkswagen. The gas gauge was broken, and I did not know if I could make it to the corner or down the street. I had no idea how much gas was in it. I yelled at his chair, and yelled and yelled. I went to bed, hiding under the covers, until I finally fell asleep.

Suddenly, there he was, standing beside the bed looking at me. "Sandy," he said, "you know that I always keep half a tank of gas in the Volks. Just go on with your life, and don't worry, I am fine!"

I awoke and flew out of bed. I just sat there wondering what had just happened. Only a dream, I told myself. The next day I took the car for gas, and there really had been half of a tank in it. After that things were better. Was it really him that I saw that night? Had he really talked to me? I don't know. Maybe? At least I knew I had to continue and that was what he would have wanted for me. I took some time off from my office, and tried to get on with things as best I could.

Being a 'widow' was a whole new experience. I found that maintaining a sense of humor was important here, too. About six months after Jay died I got a phone call from someone selling burial insurance and insisting that they talk to Jay. I did not want to say I was alone in the house, so I just said he was not available. That did not work. You know how persistent telemarketers can be. I finally asked her where she was calling from and she told me Virginia. I told her that she was closer to him than I was and if she really wanted to converse with him she could go to Arlington and dig him up. She hung up on me, but I was never bothered by that company again. Her reaction left me laughing.

I decided to go on the cruise we had booked for the honeymoon we never had. Many of our friends were going on the same cruise. We went to Hell on Grand Cayman Island (that really is the name of a town), took a raft trip in Jamaica, and dealt with a ship full of Italian tourists who had been on board for two weeks when we got there. I think the Italians took lessons in Rude-101. On one occasion, my friend had some peaches on her plate. We were at one of those shipboard buffets. A lady came over to her, said something in Italian, and took my friend's peaches! We started laughing so hard that we could not finish the meal.

I came home, went back to work, became involved in some civic groups and generally filled up my time, and the next five years passed quickly. I took two trips to Europe, trips Jay and I had talked about taking but we had always figured we had plenty of time to go after the kids were grown.

I was on a committee for the local symphony, and we were having a formal dance. I needed an escort, preferably one with a tux and one who knew which fork to use. A name came to mind, and after calling his daughter to see if he was dating anyone, I called and asked him if he would go with me. He said yes, he would be glad to go, and the evening turned out well.

We started seeing each other, and he told me he would have asked me out before but was afraid I would say no. Things progressed, and just like the old Prince Charming story, we fell in love. When Jay died, I swore I would never marry again, and now I had to rethink everything. I was invited to dinner at his house, and when I walked in, there was a large model train set. It took up the whole living room. It was wonderful! Almost like an omen that this was where I belonged.

We were having dinner one evening, discussing travels and trips and places we had been. He asked me if I thought Hawaii would be a good place for our honeymoon. I truly did love this person, and I knew that it was time to move on. I said yes. We were married at my mother's home six months later, and I moved into his house because it was larger than mine. Life has been an adventure. But the best part is now.

My tale is not over, and in ten years maybe I will write more. Who knows what lies around the next bend in the train tracks? I am still working, and keep thinking I should retire, but things might be boring without the IRS to gripe about on a daily basis. My husband works, too. We have two dogs, and lots and lots of grandkids and some great-grands, also. Life is good. I cannot end this with out the words—to be continued.

Now if you have read this far, you might be wondering why? This is just such an ordinary person, and an ordinary life. What interest could it possibly hold for someone else? But then, maybe reading about me may have made you think about your own life, and what you hold dear to you, and how lucky you are, so go hug your children, and tell your husband you love him. Those of us with "ordinary" lives are the lucky ones! Alllllllllllll Aboarddddddd!!!!!! A new day is here!!

To contact "Sandra": survivorsandi@aol.com

"Dolores's" Story

~Chapter 1~

Back in the 1950s, when I was born, the gringos were the bosses and the Hispanics or Mexicans were the peons. It was a white man's world in our town and we quickly learned our place within it. I was one of many young girls born into a town that was rife with class distinction, segregation, racial inequality and racism. It was an accepted way of life; the order of things.

The gringos filled almost all the important positions. The political climate was not open to the Hispanic populace to hold office. Not that there were any Hispanics aspiring to become the mayor or chief of police. Many Hispanics did not even vote. City Hall positions, judgeships, city mayor, police chief, etc., were not positions to be aspired to by our Hispanic class. Even most of the secretarial positions in the area were held by white females. Those Hispanic females who were fortunate enough to stay in school before I was born, took home economics instead of shorthand or typing. Hispanics occupied jobs such as waitresses, cooks, mechanics, store clerks, taxi cab drivers, warehousing laborers, gas station attendants, farm laborers, and so on.

All was tranquil in our small town, no tension or disorder. Even if the gringos did not mix with Hispanics unless it was for work purposes, both races respected each other and showed it by living peacefully together. They worked side by side and sometimes formed strong friendships. But everyone always understood each other's place within the community.

There was very little unfairness that I could see. Even the children that I went to school with that were white, tended to play with each other, form their own friendships and bonds, yet socialized amicably with the large Hispanic community. There were very few interracial relationships, but the few that I saw were older adults, usually an older white man married to a younger Hispanic woman.

I grew up in a small Texas town by the Rio Grande Valley. The Rio Grande divides the American and Mexican borders. Most border towns are filled with descendants of Mexicans who either crossed illegally, legally or became part of America when Texas became a U.S. territory. My family came from the latter. However it did not matter whether we were truly American born, we still exhibited the culture of Mexican ancestry that had been handed down through many generations. All the myths, beliefs, attitudes, ethics, and morality were served to us just as an integral part of our daily meals. Interestingly though, our family had very little Mexican ancestry...it is more a mixture of French, Italian, and even Aztec Indian...but we still lived the life of those considered Mexican in our community.

Even though the town was almost ninety percent Mexican or Hispanic, and ten percent white, it was the gringos who controlled the town. The Hispanic community was a community of malleable people, willing to accept that their place was beneath the others and they did not question why they were less significant than those above them.

Many of our own helped to keep that cultural mentality alive within our community. I remember growing up with my mother's sorrow for never being allowed the opportunity to go to school. My grandfather believed that women were required to learn how to cook, clean, marry and have babies. School, according to my grandfather, was a waste of time and only served to bring out unsavory character flaws in females.

My mother used to tell us the story that had sealed her fate to never finish going to school. Prior to this incident, being the youngest and most favored daughter, she had been able to beg and coerce my grandfather into allowing her to attend school. She enjoyed only three months of school before a young girl was found raped and murdered. This happened in her vicinity. They found the child's body in an open field that my mother and uncles crossed daily and that the children used to get to school. Once this happened, no amount of begging or crying would convince my grandfather to let her return to school.

So my mother's desire to acquire knowledge became a dream instilled in her children. She made a promise to herself that all of her children were going to have the opportunity to learn all she had been deprived of. It became an obsession for her to make sure we all graduated from high school.

Every time one of her children walked down the aisle to receive a high school diploma at our local auditorium, her eyes swam with tears of happiness and pride. And yet sadly, her own lack of knowledge led her to believe that to attain a high school diploma was to reach heaven on earth. She knew nothing about colleges and universities.

I was born into a family of five. I was the youngest in the family, the third daughter with two older brothers, a mother and an absent father. My oldest brother Rogelio, my oldest sister Leticia, my middle sister Beatrice, my brother Ramon, my mother and I, lived together in a tiny little house, while my father was away.

When I asked my mother where my father was, she would say, "Oh, do you see those airplanes up in the sky?"

I said, "Yes?"

She would respond, "Well your father is up there in one of them."

All five of her children, would run out doors and wave at our father every time we saw an airplane in the sky.

"Daddy! Daddy! Here we are!" we would wave and scream at the top of our lungs.

Our mother kept our dad alive with all the stories she told us about him. How much he loved us all and wanted to visit us. How hard he worked so he could send us that check we got at the beginning of every month.

I cannot remember the first five years of my life. I wonder many times why? I have concluded that they might have been the happiest part of my childhood. Therefore, nothing traumatic happened to cause me to have that part of my life etched into my memory bank. The only memories I have of those years are what my mother has shared with me. If her account of my life is correct, then indeed, I must thank my guardian angel for allowing my formative years to be so precious.

You see, my mother relates that I was destined not to walk. I took my first steps at the age of three. She says I walked so pathetically, that it made her cry. She had taken me to the family doctor because I seemed not to be able to take my first steps. The doctor told her I was going to be an invalid. She refused to accept this or to give up on my being able to walk.

She unknowingly practiced her own ritualistic physical therapy on me every day and night. She prayed every night that her child be able to walk. She believed in the Great Physician having the last word. So, my first steps were a blessing to her, even if it brought tears of sadness to her eyes to watch me struggle to walk on twisted legs.

She continued her brand of therapy, massaging my legs every night as she prayed over me to have the Great Physician heal me. I walked and do so today by the grace of God and the determination of my mother. Though it has always been a painful experience, I never let the pain I felt stop me from living a normal life.

My mother told me that this disability caused her to spoil me until I was five, when she finally saw me walk as normally as my brothers and sisters. The guilt she felt because of my disability made her give in to me constantly. As a child, she says I took advantage of it and threw a tantrum if I did not get my way. At this point, once she saw me walk normally, she decided she had to correct her failure as a permissive parent and train me to be a better-behaved child.

So, my first memory of my life comes when we moved into our brand new three-bedroom home. We had previously lived in our hellish little home of only three rooms, a tiny living room, one huge bedroom and an attached spacey kitchen that served as a bedroom also.

The kitchen was not originally part of the house. It had been a store once that belonged to one of my many uncles. He had earned his livelihood running a store until he died in his forties of a heart attack. The store had been a source of happiness for us kids. It was located only one house away from our home and we were sometimes allowed to go with our mother to help out at the store. My uncle was a single man, who I now realize, desperately wanted a family of his own. Since we were the closest family he could call his own, he sort of adopted the whole bunch. He gave us sweets all the time and this of course was against my mother's wishes. But my mother had learned her place in our society and that was that a man's word was more valuable than a woman's word. So she bowed to his wishes, as she bowed time and time again to several other requests that my other uncles made throughout her life.

Our uncle brought us bananas, watermelon, cantaloupe, grapes, and all sorts of fruits when they were in season. He would come in with Mexican sweet bread and we were allowed to dip our bread into milk and enjoy its full flavor. This was a rarity, for my mother was very keen on having good table manners.

When my uncle died, my mother was given the building and she had it connected to our house. We had previously lived in a two-room house, with an outside toilet. When my mother attached on the added room, she had indoor plumbing added also. We had moved up in the world! That was a great accomplishment and worthy of great pride!

I remember the one thing I hated about this tiny run down house; one minor problem that we hid from the world at large. The added room was built higher and larger than our tiny house. Consequently, when the room was added to the house, there remained a gap between both rooms large enough for insects and mosquitoes to come to join us in our habitat.

Mosquitoes found they loved to suck my blood! My legs were attacked mercilessly. You know the saying? "Every thing is bigger in Texas!" Well, I can attest that mosquitoes definitely are. My legs were a mass of welts and sores. I was very ashamed of my legs and all the scars I had from sore after sore. My mother tried to keep my sores clean and uninfected, but I scratched mercilessly during the night. She used several home remedies to fight the infection and to minimize the scars.

I remember once I went with chocolate paste applied to my legs to minimize the scar tissue. Week after week, daily, she would cover my legs in this chocolate paste to minimize scaring and to lighten the blotchy dark spots. My mother made batch after batch until she realized it was never going to take the problematic scars away. They all eventually faded, like my memories of those times.

To this day I can remember my hate for those dratted mosquitoes and my battle to wrench my legs away from them. I was generally known to not be able to kill anything, not even an ant. But an evil, horrendous side of me emerged when I battled a mosquito or a flea. Since they both liked to attack my legs, I armed myself with anything I could to destroy the enemy! I was a formidable enemy; I always won even if it was after they bit me.

~Chapter 2~

My father had made the Air Force his career. I saw him maybe three times in my entire life. The first time I met my father was when I was born according to my mother. The first time I actually remember meeting him, I was almost six years old. There was a knock at the door and I ran to answer it. I saw a man, his face shadowed by a cap, with a huge knapsack.

I ran crying, "The boogie man has come to get me! He has come for me! I didn't do anything wrong!"

My mother ran out to the living room of our three-room, wood-frame house, to see what was happening. She threw open the screen door and ran into the boogie man's arms to my disbelief and horror!

She invited him in as I cowered away, completely appalled that my mother would even let him in the door. She told me he was not the boogie man come to get me, but my father. I refused to believe her or get near him. That was until he took out a very beautiful shiny quarter and offered it to me as a gift. A quarter! I had never owned my very own quarter! I was lucky if I got to hold a nickel in my hands. The most that I had ever truly held for very long between my fingers were pennies for the candy machine. And this man offered me a quarter to come into his arms?

Young as I was, I was not convinced I was ready to get close to any boogie man even for a quarter! But curiosity and my mother's reassurances won out. Or maybe it was the greed of a young child to own her very own quarter. I kept thinking of all the candies I could buy with a whole quarter! And thus I met my absent father. The one my mother had kept so alive for me with tales of his job as an airman. The one who flew up in the sky and I waved to very frequently.

I asked him, "Did you see me wave and call to you the other day?" I remember now he looked confused, until my mother explained how we all would go out to wave at planes and say hello to him. He didn't answer me, but smiled a sweet, kind smile and I knew then that I liked him. It would be a long time before I truly got to know my father, who he really was and what I meant to him.

He stayed for a few weeks on leave from his assignment and I got to know what it was to have a father around. Until then, my life had been one where my mother was the only adult or parent that I knew I answered to. Suddenly this man seemed to have some control over my mother; the person whom I felt was as powerful as God. My mother would bow to his word, or send us to ask him for permission if we wanted to go outside to play. I was in awe of a male role model. Yet he smiled at me often, treated me with so much kindness that I felt good about it, even if I was rather shy around him.

I was not prone to shyness at the time. I was the youngest and was possibly quite spoiled, if it's possible to spoil a child when the mother is a strict disciplinarian. My first experience of his anger was when he directed it at poor Ramon for something that was my fault. I believe my father could not bear to spank me so he opted to spank my brother instead. According to my mother, he was partial to his daughters. In the end, it was worse punishment for I felt so guilty when I saw my brother's tears running down his cheeks. To this day, I have not forgotten the look of hurt in Ramon's eyes directed at me because he knew it was my fault and it was unfair he got the whipping I deserved.

You see, I had coerced my brother into jumping on the bed. It seemed we had invented the trampoline long before it came around. I got on the bed and jumped and whooped until I enticed him to get on. All the time I jumped and laughed he kept cautioning me, "You are gonna get in trouble if Mom catches you."

I cheered myself on until he was tempted to jump on the bed. He never got to jump. My father walked in as he was about to take his first leap. I was off the bed watching and waiting to cheer his jumps. I was appalled that my brother was caught.

You might believe that was not such a grievous crime to deserve a belt strap on my brother's bottom. Well, my mother was having an angry fit over it and so my father felt he had to take care of business. You see, coming from poverty, you learn that a bed is not just a bed. It is the only precious bed that you have had the luxury to own and sleep in. Therefore this bed should be treated with utmost care. Without this bed, there would only be the floor to sleep on.

All possessions were irreplaceable, and a child had to understand that nothing we owned should be battered or destroyed in child's play. For once it was gone, where would the money come from to replace it? One of many lessons a growing child of poverty had to learn as she grew up. I was not as quick to learn that lesson, as I was to learn the lesson of guilt.

For weeks, I tried to make it up to my brother for that beating. I let him win every time we played cowboys and Indians. I died time and time again at his command when he shot me in our games. Previously, whenever he said I died, I would argue that I got him first. If my brother wanted to play a certain game, and I wanted to play another, I deferred to his wishes. When there was only one pancake left to eat, I would not argue that it should be split between us as I had argued before, but give the precious pancake to him. On and on, I made sacrifices to make up for the beating he took in my stead.

In my defense I can say that I tried to tell my father it was me jumping on the bed but he could not hear me with all the ruckus my mother and he were making. So thus I came to find I had a real father and not the fantasy father in the sky riding all the airplanes.

I was too young to see that my father treated his daughters differently than his sons. I have only my mother's word to rely on. I do remember, however, that during this visit he went to buy both Letty and Bella some beautiful Easter dresses. Letty purchased a beautiful lacy white dress, while Bella got a lovely lacey pink dress. I recall not going to town with my father, when he took my sisters, and having a fit for being left behind. I am sure I was left behind because of my unruly and spoiled behavior. At the time I did not understand this of course, that I had only myself to blame for being left asleep. But I believe I was able to realize they had waited until I fell asleep, before going off shopping. My father had brought me a dress, but I was very hurt that he had taken Letty and Bella and not me. After throwing a mighty tantrum, he tried to calm me with comments, like, "You were asleep, but I bought you a dress."

So I ended up with a shiny, satiny taffeta, baby blue dress. It hardly had any lace on it other than possibly a little trimming. I was sorely disappointed that it was not lacey, like my sisters' dresses. Everyone tried to tell me what a beautiful dress it was and I don't believe I let them know how I truly felt. I am not sure if I never accepted the dress because it was not to my taste, or if it was because it represented being left out again, as I felt for the majority of my childhood years. Having a blue dress, instead of a white or pink, made me feel less of a girl. I never did care for blue after that. Needless to say, when I became a mother, I always wanted to dress my adopted girls in pink. To this day, all three of my adopted daughters dislike pink.

During this visit my father worked out the financing for a new home for us. Before he left, all the contracts were signed and workers contracted for the construction of a three-bedroom, wood-frame house to be built in front of our tiny little home. We watched as every day, beam by beam, the house took shape.

My father left soon after. He was not there when the house was completed. He had been on military leave and only for thirty days. Another six years would go by before I laid eyes on my father again. He came back to attend a funeral, someone important in his life had died; I cannot remember who it was, possibly his father? We were strangers again. I believe I was eleven or twelve years old and I kept a distance from him. I did not feel comfortable being around him. I was not comfortable having an adult male staying with us.

My mother seemed to change when he came home on leave. She was no longer the strong, aggressive mother. She became unsure of herself and the decisions she made. She stopped singing and even yelling or spanking us. Instead she seemed to spend a lot of time in whispered conversations with my father. Once or twice I felt sure they were arguing, but I could not tell because they kept their voices at a whisper and what they discussed a secret from their children.

And so our family was moving up in this poverty-stricken Hispanic society we lived in. We were attaining middle class-status and leaving poverty behind. Now we were moving into a brand new, custom built, three-bedroom house with all the amenities. We now had a rental unit to generate income. The little house had become an asset.

Oh the pride in my mother's eyes when she walked into her new home was something to see. She was a very proud woman and now she could add another accomplishment to her list. Her husband had come home to visit and was instrumental in getting her home built. She could now tell everyone who had doubted she had a husband what a wonderful man and provider he was. He supported his family with the military income he earned.

She told neighbors who asked how she always got a check in the mail every month from the government for the care of his family. As a little girl, I stood on the sidelines and watched my mother as with pride she related all her blessings to her friends who came to visit.

Hispanics spur each other on; they always want what the Joneses have. My mother had many acquaintances, few friends and many enemies. All seemed to be envious of her blessings in life.

Now a joke I heard comes to mind. Have you heard it? It goes like this:

There was once a vendor who set up his stand to sell shrimp. The vendor had all kinds of shrimp, Russian shrimp, Greek shrimp, Anglo-Saxon shrimp, Mexican shrimp, etc. Now, as the customers came to buy, they became curious why all the shrimp containers had lids on them except the containers of Mexican shrimp.

So one customer finally asked, "Can you tell me why the Mexican shrimp never have a lid every time I come here to buy?"

The vendor replied, "Sure, I can tell you that. You have but to stand and study those for a bit and you will have your answer." The customer looked at the shrimp, confused.

And so the vendor told him, "Notice how every time a Mexican shrimp tries to get to the top to get away, his fellow shrimps make sure to pull him down? That is why the Mexican shrimp don't have a lid. All the other shrimp help each other to climb to the top, except the Mexican shrimp," he responded. "Therefore, I never have to worry that a Mexican shrimp will reach the top and get away."

When I heard this joke I realized it was so very true. My mother had been one to live the life of the shrimp that wanted to reach the top and her envious neighbors seemed determined to bring her down. I had seen it with my own eyes, and lived it as I stood by my mother's side.

~Chapter 3~

The time came for us to move into our "mansion." My first true memory of my childhood starts here. My mother led me to a corner of the middle bedroom. I remember looking at the soft pastel green color, so warm and inviting. She handed me a piece of paper, not a coloring book for we could not afford one, and some crayons. She instructed me not write on the wall. What can you suppose a young child who has a blank sheet of paper to write on and a wall with so many little bumps to roll a crayon over will do? Well I must have enjoyed it tremendously since I went wild writing on not one wall but both walls in that corner of the bedroom. So the whipping I received for that later was at least worth a good time. This was the beginning of my mother's determination to reform my character. I had previously been given too much license to misbehave.

I had a lot of lessons to learn and catch up with. Suddenly, I could not always get my way or throw tantrums. If I threw a tantrum, I got a spanking. Where before my needs had been seen to, now I had to participate and carry my weight like the rest of the kids. I am sure I had never done chores before, but now I had to learn to do simple things. I don't think I did them very well because I was easily distracted.

As time went by, I was expected to join all the others in pulling weeds from the rosebushes my mother loved. She had a green thumb and all she planted seemed to flourish. Our yard was a garden of roses and flowers with a rich carpet of deep hunter green grass. When we sat on the grass, it was soft and cushiony, not scratchy. I was not born with a green thumb or the desire to garden. Weeding was an absolute bore to me and so I seemed to never get it right. My mother was a perfectionist who wanted the entire world to see a perfect family. We had a perfect garden, a perfect house, and she had perfect children, the type that were seen and not heard. Her home indoors was immaculate, no dust or trash or messes anywhere. We never sat on couches or beds. We learned that a bed was for sleeping at night, once up, you made the bed and dressed it up with a nice bedspread and did not touch it again until nighttime.

I soon attended school as my brothers and sisters did. I so looked forward to school and never once during those twelve years of school did I ever feel different. I had the freedom to be at school and not have my mother correcting my ill-begotten behavior!

I remember my first day at school. I can't remember my teacher's name but I can recall her Sourpuss face to this day. She instructed us where to sit. We had double seating desks that had a place for a student on the left side and another student on the right side. Compartments in the middle for our notebooks, divided each student.

I was paired with a fat, little, blue-eyed blonde girl whom I instinctively felt I could push around. We could not communicate since I spoke no English and she spoke no Spanish. So I made sure she understood my body language. She was given the left side of the desk and the top compartment, and I was given the right side and bottom compartment. Well I had figured out that without my mother around, there would be no stopping me! So I signed with my hands as I spoke to the little girl in Spanish, "the top compartment is mine!" When I heard her say some gibberish and point to the teacher, I ignored her, punched her side and threw her notebook on the floor. Then I promptly placed mine into her compartment. She started to cry and good old Sourpuss came to her rescue. She talked gibberish and instructed me with hand signals to put my hand out, palm up and proceeded to smack me with a ruler a few times until my palm turned red. She told the little girl to take the compartment on top. I waited for Sourpuss to turn around and I punched the little wimp on her belly this time. I heard her make a noise, something like ughhhhh, and again told her in Spanish, "this compartment is mine!" Sourpuss turned to make sure the sweet, little, fat girl was fine, and we both smiled at her.

I kept the compartment throughout the year in addition to anything the little girl brought to school that I wanted. She was obviously wealthy and I was poor, so she kept me supplied with pencils and erasers throughout the year. Of course I kept them in that compartment because I did not dare bring anything that did not belong to me home. My mother was a very righteous, Christian woman and would had taught me the error of my ways had she known I had taken anything that did not belong to me.

My first lesson in English was when my teacher, Sourpuss, asked me to identify the picture she held up. It took me a long time just to figure out what she wanted of me, since I knew no English. I was a quick learner, though, so I promptly said she held an apple, but in Spanish of course. She marched to my desk and asked for my palm and smacked it for saying it in Spanish. I had to try again and again and again. I did eventually figure out how the hell to say apple so I could take my cherry red hand back from Sourpuss. Can you imagine how difficult it is for a six-year-old child to figure out how to move her tongue and form the word apple when it's such a foreign thing to do? Well luckily I was smart enough to figure it out, but other kids were not so fortunate in the brain skill department.

Now I realize that I was unfortunate to be born stubborn and ambidextrous, and tended to lean toward using my left hand because Letty helped me learn to write and she was left handed. Sourpuss would have none of it. I was to learn to write with my right hand for that was the only hand acceptable. She took out the ruler and struck my palm or knuckles every time she found me using my left hand to write my assignments. To this day, I do not know if it was my sister teaching me to write with my left and Sourpuss forcing me to write with my right hand, that made me ambidextrous, but I kept that skill until I reached junior high and homework got so massive that I opted for my left hand instead. Another thing I still wonder about, "was it my last rebellious act against Sourpuss?"

I can remember those very significant teachers in my school life that had an impact on me. They showed me love and patience, without my understanding this. They will forever be held dearly in a special place reserved for them within my heart. Ms. Woods, Ms. Escobedo, Mr. Aguilar, Mr. Breeden, Ms. Pete, Mr. Trevino and many others throughout elementary, junior high and high school, will live in my heart until the day I die. As you can see, Ms. Sourpuss is also there but for quite the opposite reasons.

By the time I got to first high (as first grade was termed at those times) with Ms. Woods, I was able to understand enough English to get by. Sourpuss was left behind and I had succeeded to move up from plain and simple first grade to first high. I figured out many years later that this was the way for Hispanics to learn English. We repeated first grade if we did not know English. Those who were fortunate enough to have learned English before coming to school went directly to first high.

So, why, I always wondered, was a little, fat, blue-eyed girl sitting next to me? Later in life I determined they had to mix a few of their own in with a bunch of Mexicans to make it look like it was not segregation. The movement for equality of the races was on, after all.

~Chapter 4~

Even though within our community we were considered above poverty, the truth is, we were way beneath the poverty line. How can this be possible? Only in a world full of inequality could a poverty-stricken family be considered middle class. Those who owned homes, let alone a rental unit, were considered above the lower class renters. Property ownership was a class distinction, worthy of much pride to attain such heights within our class.

Many days the groceries my mother was able to buy to last the month, did not last as expected. We would go hungry many times. My mother was a miracle worker. She made food last unbelievably well. She was a fantastic cook and would mix plain ingredients and create a wonderful dish.

There were times that I was sent to the little store in the neighborhood that belonged to an old man named Don Juan. I imagine that he set up his store long after my uncle had passed away. I could buy two eggs for a nickel and five bubble gums for a penny.

I always bought bubble gum with my pennies because I could make gum last a long time. Once the flavor was gone, I would sneak into the kitchen and either added sugar or honey to sweeten it up. At night I would wrap it up in its wrapper so I could use the following day. Sometimes I was able to have bubble gum just about everyday of the week, if I was careful not to have it taken away or made to spit it out at school. One nickel always bought me a lot of bubble gum.

I remember now how loving my mother was. When food was plentiful she cooked a feast. She cooked her wonderful tortillas, set a beautiful table and called all her children to come to dinner. She never sat down to join us and none of us ever saw anything wrong with that. That was all we ever knew. Since we sometimes went hungry, when there was food we ate everything in sight. I never realized then that my mother had not set any food aside for herself. She ate whatever was left over, if anything. As an adult I have come to realize the enormity of her love for us.

She also took to sewing for the neighbors and was very skilled at it. If she only knew she was born to be a designer and not a seamstress. I was with my mother once when it was my turn to have shoes bought for me. I stood by her side as she studied a window that was full of mannequins dressed in beautiful dresses. I heard her say, "Yes, I can eliminate the collar, add a sash, put a zipper at the back and drop the buttons." She was mentally designing her own version of a similar dress. My mother never used a pattern.

Her designed dresses were always a hit with her customers. They would bring their cloth, zippers, thread and buttons and describe what type of dress, skirt or blouse they wanted and my mother designed it from scratch.

I remember when she would create a skirt and charge fifty cents for labor. Letty, Bella and I were all recruited when she had too many pieces to sew. We learned to hem very skillfully at a very young age. I did seem to be able to handle a needle with ease and always looked for my mom's approval for a job well done.

Letty was as skilled as my mother but my mother never expected her to use her skill to do any pieces that were on order. My sister used her skill to make herself her own dresses. Letty was a very beautiful and proud young lady. She was approximately three years older than me, but had the sweetest and most sensitive spirit of all. She was no match for me and I am ashamed to admit now, I was a true burden on her. I guess even while my mother worked diligently to curb my willful, flawed character, I was turning out to be a real hellion on wheels.

My mother and Letty created lovely prom dresses, Easter dresses, wedding apparel, hats, men's shirts, belts, etc. The most difficult cloths to work with were transformed into what I considered a masterpiece. I was always on the sidelines looking in. It seems that I was all thumbs for I seemed not to have the skills my sisters had. Every attempt I made to master some fine, ladylike skill turned out to be a failure. I was run out of the kitchen for ruining precious food. My mother would demand I leave the fancy cloths to Letty. I was not to touch them for fear I would get them dirty or somehow tear them.

I tried to keep up with my mother and sisters' abundance of skills. Letty could cook, clean, sew, bake, needlepoint, crochet, embroider, garden and so many other things. Bella was an awesome housecleaner and could make everything shine like new. I gave it all a try and found I ruined everything or could not master how to do it right. And so I was constantly banned from the circle of skilled labor they formed. My mother did not have the patience for teaching me skills, as her day was so full of demands to make ends meet. I don't think I saw my mother's face ever without that worried, strained look.

As for duties, I cleaned underneath our house, which was set on cement blocks. I disliked that duty but was something I could do without breaking anything more than a rake. I would crawl under and rake any debris that might have been blown there on a windy day. I also took the trash to the alleyway on the days the garbage truck was to come. I recall watching the men who hung onto the edge of the truck as they stopped at our backyard entrance and took our silver aluminum trashcans and emptied them into the huge truck, and then proceeded to just drop the cans on the ground.

I was happiest when I climbed a tree to sing my lungs out. I sang love ballads from long ago singers. The neighborhood could hear me screaming at the top of my lungs, "De piedra la cabecera, la mujer que a mi me quier-aaaaaaaaaaaa." Most of those singers were already dead even at that time. I had learned the songs when I heard my mother sing as she ironed all day long.

Once again, I failed at my singing skills, for my mother would yell for me to stop that horrendous noise I was making at the top of my lungs. That never crushed me; it only propelled me to sing more so I could practice how to do it right. I would sit at the top of my favorite tree limb and sing, "Tommy and Laura were lovers, he wanted to give her everything, flowers, presents, but most of all a weathering ring." I never knew why my sisters laughed at me every time I sang that song. That is, not until I figured out it was not a weathering ring…it was a wedding ring.

We had a special day set aside for ironing, one for washing clothes, and one for cleaning the house thoroughly. This was not like the cleaning that my mother did everyday, but more like a spring-cleaning day, where everything was scrubbed spotless. You see, my mother was not only fanatical at cleaning, but also needed perfection in anything she undertook.

There were days when even cleaning was fun. We had hardwood floors and we would have one day a month to apply Johnson & Johnson paste wax to polish the floors to a mirror-like shine. I recall I did not do as much of the applying on the hardwood floors. I did, however, get to ride the blanket that everyone pulled as I sat on it and polished the floor with my bottom, or the weight of my body. Everyone got to ride it while others pulled. We did this most of the day until the floor was shiny and we were exhausted.

When I was still young and illiterate, Letty and Bella would spell out what they did not want me to understand. So I remember making a song out of a word once that I did not understand. My sisters said, "Ask m-o-t-h-e-r if we can go to the s-t-o-r-e." I never even realized I should also learn the word store. I got hung up on m-o-t-h-e-r. Oh what a song I made of that word as I went around singing at the top of my lungs, "M-o-t-h-e-rrrrr" over and over, repeating the letters, up and down, my melody went for I was determined to remember those letters and learn as soon as I could what it meant.

I became truly great at spelling in elementary school and I have my sisters to thank! Lest you think this is no big deal, I remind you that I was a little Hispanic girl who walked into elementary without even knowing a speck of English. Now I managed to end up almost in the last group at most spelling bees. At the time I felt sure that I never actually won any spelling bee contests and ended up as second runner up because I lacked the skill. Now I wonder if maybe, I never let myself win because I had a mirror held up telling me I would always be second best. Not necessarily by my mother or family, but by the society I lived in. It was always some white kid who took the prize. I was learning to take my place within our society.

At some point my very active and aggressive Grandma, my mother's mom whom we all loved dearly, had a stroke and came to live with us.

She was paralyzed on the left side and had lost the ability to speak or take care of herself. Letty was very close to Grandma Henrietta. My mother was a diligent daughter and cared for her other's needs as well as those of her five children.

Oh, the regrets and shame I carry for my hellish behavior around my darling grandma! In her disabled state, she tried to help Letty when she babysat my brother and me but we would have none of it. We went wild, running from one door and through another, chasing each other and screaming, any time my mother left to run an errand. We played chase, the boogie man and hide and go seek. I would run real close to my grandma but far enough from her reach so she could not catch me as I ran by her. I remember the sorrow in her eyes now because she could not help Letty. When Letty tried to run after us to stop us, my brother and I decided to lock her out of the house. He locked the backdoor and I locked the front door. My mother came to find her sitting on the front porch crying because she could not get inside. She got a major scolding for being so dumb and we got a whipping. That was life in the fast lane for my brother and me. We made quite a mischievous pair.

There are many memories of our grandma. Before her stroke, we used to visit her all the time at her own home. She had a huge lot and we ran outside and played with the chickens, fed them and chased the roosters away. I remember eating wonderfully baked pies, cookies made from fresh picked fruits. She was very kind and smiled a lot at us. She and Letty were very close.

After the stroke, Grandma was paralyzed and she spent her once very active days sitting on a special armchair my mother had bought for her comfort. Other than when my mother bathed her, dressed her, combed her hair, and fed her, she spent her entire day just staring ahead of herself as if lost in her own world. Most of her children, my uncles, came to visit her regularly but it was my mother who saw to her every need.

Our grandma passed away when I was around ten years old. This was the first loss I had experienced and now I had full understanding of death. I did not take it very well and threw an emotional fit, not wanting to accept her death. I believe it may have been my guilty conscience for all I had done to make my grandma's life unbearable. I wanted time to make it up to her and now I had no more time to take it back. I felt like the worst sinner of all. My mother suffered a lot the loss of her only remaining parent. She wore black garments for years and stopped singing and laughing for a long time. I grieved for the loss of that side of my mother. It had been the one side that had brought joy to our home.

~Chapter 5~

For a time we did not own a television set but we were close to our next-door neighbors and they invited us every Saturday morning to watch cartoons with them. My mother did not approve of us being a nuisance to others, so she did not allow this. This was the one time I remember both my brother and I disobeyed her. We would slip out of bed quietly, get dressed and go next door to watch television anyway. I loved Mighty Mouse, the super mouse that always came to save the day. My brother loved Fury, the horse that always saved someone. We both loved Lassie, the beautiful dog that always was a lifesaver.

We finally got our own television set. I think my mother decided to get it to keep us at home and to stop having the same problem of spanking us every Saturday morning for disobeying her strict orders not to go next door.

We were so proud of our television set; it was a twenty-five inch black-and-white Zenith TV with a rich mahogany wood cabinet. My mother bought it on credit and paid five dollars a month on it. It was a source of great joy to the whole family. We spent hours watching special family programs. My mother loved Rawhide, and thought Clint Eastwood was cute. Another favorite of the family was Bonanza, where my sisters could not decide if Little Joe Cartwright or Adam Cartwright was the most handsome. The Waltons was also a show we watched and enjoyed as we all sat around on the floor watching television.

I recall one of my uncles coming for a visit and my mom proudly displaying our brand new TV. This was when I became aware of how disrespectfully my mother was treated by most of my uncles. After asking my mother what it cost, he told her that she had made a poor buy and it was not even a color TV. I saw my mother's face go from a happy, sunny, smiling and proud one to one of sadness and it angered me. As always, my mouth got me in trouble.

I looked at my uncle crossly and retorted, "Well if your television set is so much better then ours, what are you doing here? Go back to your house where you have it."

He looked thunderstruck and then I saw the angry brow frown with disapproval as he faced my mother and said, "Well it is obvious you are not doing that much better raising your children by how that one behaves! I can tell they will all become useless delinquents."

Even though my mother did tell me to be quiet, my uncle's comment about her children angered her and she said, "Well then maybe you should go back to your perfect house with that perfect TV and your perfect children." I was so proud of my mother for firing back that comment since she was always treated as if she was beneath them. Even if I got a spanking after he left, I felt it was well worth it. He ended up leaving and not speaking to us for years.

I might add that years later, my uncle's children were truly less than perfect and rather rebellious. They were into drugs, dropped out of school and his two sons ended up badly. One was murdered tragically at age nineteen, while the other son ended up with brain damage from the use of drugs. We were not glad this happened but my mother was proud that her children had a better end.

Hispanics enjoyed feuding, vendettas, quarrels, revenge and overly-heated arguments. Men liked to get drunk and quarrel over anything from jealousy to anyone staring too long at them. It was the way to show off their Mexican pride. Those of a higher class or who considered themselves more intellectual learned to curb this crude behavior. It was not a rare thing for families to break all communication between each other and remain distant from generation to generation. Grown sisters became estranged and very distant from each other without ever resolving the problems between them. They expected their children to carry the grudge against the other family members as a matter of loyalty.

This happened to us with my father's parents. We were never close to them because my father's mother did not like her daughter-in-law, my mother. I believe the story was that my mother was rather candid with her remarks and extremely clean, while my grandma on my father's side was not prone to cleanliness. She was Aztec Indian and filth did not seem to bother her too much. I do not mean to imply Aztec Indians are filthy, but my grandma could certainly live with Texas-sized roaches without a qualm. Whereas, my mother and her five kids could not stand to see a roach, especially within a kitchen! I do not have good memories of how my Aztec grandma treated me before the break between families occurred.

In our community, Hispanics discriminated against their own people. The darker the color of your skin, the more discrimination was directed against you. My Aztec grandma had a beautiful, half-white granddaughter who was a little younger than me. I could not compete with her fair skin and wimpy, lady-like behavior. Being fairly allergic to the sun, I burned to a dark crisp brown and my outrageous behavior did little to recommend me.

We visited her every Sunday after church and the most memorable thing I cherished was skipping all the way from church to her house, singing "Skip, skip, skipty, my Lou, skip, skip, skipty, my Lou, skip, skip, skipty, my Lou, skipty my Lou, my darlinggggg." My two sisters always walked ahead or behind me, very embarrassed to be associated with the ludicrous little girl screaming at the top of her lungs. I must add here that my brother, who was one year older than me, was also with us, and darker of skin than I, so just as badly disliked by our grandma. I was not as badly behaved when compared to my brother's unruly behavior! I think we fed off each other's dark side.

Once we got to my grandma's house, I did not receive much attention. I remember my cousin, crying and whining to our grandma, "She hit me!" and off to the outdoors I was sent and the door locked behind me so I was not allowed back in for the four hours of our visit.

My grandma called me names when she was mad at me and I am sure I annoyed the hell out of her. That was just the type of child I was. When I asked for water, she told me to drink water from the water hose outdoors. When I asked to use the bathroom, I believe I was told to use the one outside. I can't remember where that was, so I may have gone behind the bushes.

The break up between my mother and my grandma occurred when my mother found out we spent most of our time locked outside because my grandmother could not stand to have us around her. I recall the big fall out and never skipping to my grandma's house again. I was still young and never again had anything to do with that grandma. Since she had never showed me any love or concern, I did not miss her. Besides, my loyalty for our mother, who at this time was the only person who truly loved me, would never have allowed me to feel otherwise. If this woman despised my mother, then she was not worthy of any kindness from me.

I know none of the five of us kids missed that grandmother. My brother, Rogelio, was much older than me, and I did not actually know how he felt. I knew he had once been close to that grandma. He was the true reason for the fall out between my mother and my grandma. My grandma wanted to take my brother, Rogelio, away from my mother and raise him as her own. My mother was not the type of weak person to allow any such thing. She was a very protective mother and loved her children dearly. Besides, she knew my father, Grandma's own son, had suffered very much as a child from his mother, and she was not about to let her first-born child out of her sight. I don't even recall that he joined us on our weekly Sunday visits. I believe he rarely did. The rest of us were rather relieved the weekly visits to Grandma's house were over.

Sometimes I felt very isolated as the youngest child. Even though my brother was my playmate, there was a certain pairing up between my older siblings that left me out of it. My brother, Rogelio and Letty were buddies and confidants. They shared the same school life experiences and music, etc. Bella and my playmate brother, Ramon, also made a similar pair. That left me quite alone when they decided to go through this phase of partnership. I was a misfit. Whenever I tried to join either pair, I was gruffly told in so many words to get lost.

My sisters labeled me "voy contigo" which basically translates to "tag-a-long". They would say, "Shush, voy contigo is coming, we don't want her to hear our plan." That's why they took to spelling words out to each other. Of course that did not work for long as I was a very determined child and figured out that I could learn to spell to stop their little game. I was no shrinking violet who let the world around me beat me down! As a matter of fact, one of my mother's greatest lessons to her children was, "Where there is a will, there is a way". We were never allowed to say, "I can't do it" for my mother was determined that she must prove to us we could. I learned that if I truly wanted to get out of doing something, using up precious resources was my best way out. If I ruined something, she banned me from it because she could not afford to waste any of our valuable supplies or resources, whether it was food, paint, cleaning supplies, and so on.

During my time in elementary when I learned to read, I discovered the world of reading. We had to spend time with another teacher because our teacher was out sick, I believe. Ms. Pete introduced me to Heidi. Everyday, she read a chapter or two from a hard-covered book and I lived for those minutes of uninterrupted reading time. I was obsessed with the story and felt deep pain when it came time to wait another day.

Whereas, before discovering the world of books, all I looked forward to was recess time, where I ran wild and fought my way to whatever I wanted. Now I became obsessed with stories. I found a way to volunteer my time at the library so I could have first choice of any new book that came into our tiny library. I read all the Nancy Drew series, the Little House on the Prairie series, the Hardy Boys series and any other books that caught my interest.

I was fascinated with books, and soon found myself withdrawing into the wonderful world of words. I became a shadow within our home and I am sure my mother was relieved that her once wild and boisterous child had turned into a child she never knew was in a room. I hid from everyone to spend time with my library books and the writer in me was born. Soon I began to write short mystery stories because I never had enough books to read. I was only allowed two books every two weeks. My desire to read was so great that I sat by Letty as she read Spanish love stories to my mother. I became a nuisance as I asked constantly for her to tell me where she was in the story. Thus, I taught myself to read and borrowed Spanish romance novels from neighbors to satisfy my need to read. This was an obsession, to escape to the world of books.

There was really much to escape from. Our life was not easy. It was full of deprivations, sadness, and spankings. We lacked a father figure and yet always knew we had a father...he was just never around. My mother was a paradox. She was strong, harsh, proud, forceful, controlling and forthright. Yet the other side of her was full of uncertainty, self-doubts, fear, shame, guilt and dependency. Although my mother had never been physically abused as a child by her parents, she had an older sister ten years her senior, who was full of jealousy and spite. As my mother's main sitter, while their parents went to pick cotton or run the farm they managed, she was responsible for much of the abuse handed down to my mother. My mother was favored and spared while all the other children in this very larger family of twelve were physically abused. It was the norm during their time. So our mother passed on to us all she had learned from this very dysfunctional family life. Her inconsistent behavior made us strong, yet full of self-doubts. I wanted to escape this confusing world many times and chose the world of reading as my safe haven.

One of my favorite places to hide and read, believe it or not, was under my bed. The bed was by the side of a large window and I got plenty of light from outside until it grew dark. I spent hours hidden under that bed involved in adventures all over the world.

There were times my love of books got me into deep trouble with my mother. She was so active, always running around, doing something. She cleaned and scrubbed, cooked, gardened, sewed, washed dishes and clothes, tended to Grandma's needs and a million other things that she did in a day.

She would say, "Keep an eye on the beans cooking on the stove, I am going outside to take down the wash from the clothesline. Don't forget." She would come barging in some time later, "Can't you smell the beans burning on the stove! I told you to take care of them! Not to let them burn!" Smack!

"I told you to get your nose out of that stupid book and add water to the beans so they wouldn't burn!" Food was too precious to waste so recklessly during those lean years.

For some reason, I was born without the sense of smell. I could never smell anything unless it was burning or the smoke was in my eyes. Many years later, the doctor told me it was a lack of zinc that my body did not produce and told me to take some. I finally got my sense of smell, took one sniff at a bouquet of flowers, got a horrendous headache from the cloying scent and decided to forget the zinc. I felt better off not being able to smell. After all, I was old enough to throw burned beans away if I ever decided to cook any, and I was surely not about to smack myself. I had lived in a world without scents most of my life and I found it much more pleasant than when I could smell the scents around me.

So thus, as I grew up I began my love affair with the written word, and moved through many different authors, and books of all types, biographies, fiction and non-fiction stories. Whenever life was difficult, I escaped into reading and writing. Sadly, since my mother was always cleaning, one day she decided to throw away all the pile of papers stashed away in a box. That box had contained volumes of poetry and short stories written throughout my childhood and teen years. I still mourn for those pieces of paper that held the thoughts, dreams, tears and joys of my youth.

~Chapter 6~

I recall having long-lasting friendships. I had a girlfriend, Mary, who I met during my first years in school and we were a pair up until seventh grade. We had wonderful times together, playing with dolls and little dishes. Since I was a rather aggressive child, my friends tended to be meek and shy. I was their protector. Mary was a sweet, soft-spoken girl with beautiful long curling lashes, soft, curly black hair, high cheekbones and a lovely smile. She rarely said anything and when she did, she usually blushed prettily. How I wanted to be more like her! I was the complete opposite.

I recall being jealous when my oldest brother, who never seemed to care to spend much time around me, was being very sweet to Mary. I have a very painful memory of how he hurt my pride in order to show Mary she was smarter than me. Mary was rather intelligent, another reason why I enjoyed her company. Do you recall I said I was a champion speller?

My brother said, "So let's see who is smarter, can either of you spell 'schedule'?" I tried and misspelled it.

Mary spelled it right and blushed prettily as she smiled shyly at my brother. My brother filled her with praise as I felt a painful jab in my heart. I had always yearned for the love and approval of all my older siblings, something they seemed to tauntingly withhold. To my oldest brother's credit, he was the one sibling who was kinder and more fun than the rest. That's why this incident of showing me up to my best friend hurt so deeply.

I had my first boyfriend in fifth grade. I thought the boy looked like Elvis and I had a deep case of puppy love. Elvis was my idol. I spent hours singing at the top of my lungs all of Elvis' current hits. My sisters and I all had a case of idolization going on. I never did care much for the Beatles because they pushed Elvis off the pop charts.

Well, my best friend and I shared my first boyfriend. He went around with me until I dumped him because I noticed he was falling for my best friend's blushes when he walked me home from school. They went together until he started flirting with another girl, Rosa, who tagged along with us from school. I never really liked Rosa because she was as aggressive as I was and was trying to take my best friend away from me. So all three of us walked to and from school together and shared our first puppy love. The only thing that made me feel special was that I was the first girlfriend of the bunch and that I dumped him before he dumped me, as he did with both my other friends.

We played patty cakes with mud, Mary and I. We played tag and red light/green light. We drew squares with chalk I stole from the teacher's blackboard and hopped until we fell. We jumped rope and played jacks. I can't remember my friend ever having much to say but always doing anything I said. If anyone dared to push my friends around, they had to deal with me. I was sure our friendship would last throughout our school years.

We had now become three girlfriends who were always together to and from school; since Rosa never really stopped hanging around us. She became Mary's second best friend. I considered her a daily acquaintance. I guess you can say that even if we did become friends, there was something about her I did not trust. Maybe I was jealous that she wanted to take Mary's friendship away from me. But I had grown up with a very moralistic mother. She handed out bits of wisdom on rare occasions and I listened and took them to heart. One such bit of wisdom was, "if a person gossips about another person in your presence, remember that she will gossip about you with another person". Rosa was a born gossiper. She loved to share all the dirt about everyone we knew. She would have made a great columnist.

And so we were now in seventh grade. Mary and I always met by the gym to walk home together. Rosa most of the time joined us. Mary and Rosa had made it to the side of the gym where we always met before I got there. I was about to turn the corner to meet up with them when I heard Rosa say my name. My mother's advice and the fact I knew Rosa was a born gossiper made me hesitate. I listened.

Rosa was saying, "Well Dolores really thinks she is beautiful. I don't know where she got that idea. She walks around like she is real hot stuff."

I waited to hear what my one and only best friend would respond. Even though I was shocked at Rosa's comments, I was not surprised at her gossip. What she thought about me did not bother me, as I did not care whether I kept her friendship or not. It was my best friend Mary's response I wanted to hear.

"I know" Mary replied. "She is just a little pretty."

"Well, not to me," Rosa replied, "and she thinks she is so smart, but I think she is rather dumb at times."

"Oh. I had not noticed that," Mary responded.

That's all I needed to hear. I knew then that my long-lasting friendship was a myth. I rounded the corner of the gym and confronted them. Mary turned pale at the sight of me. Rosa had a smirk on her face.

"Well, I am sure glad I heard this tidbit," I sneered, "Obviously, Mary, you do not defend a friend like I do. You make a good pair, so from now on you won't have to put up with this friend. And for your information, I feel far from pretty, but I know I am not dumb. I am not dumb enough to keep you as friends! So from now on, we will never have to speak to each other again!"

That was the end of years of friendship with my one and only friend. It was very painful for me, but my mother had taught me all about pride and how to hold a grudge. If she could never talk to my grandmother, I could certainly never be friends with such disloyal jerks.

I carried the hurt deep inside and walked past them in hallways as if they had never existed. Rosa always smirked or made belittling comments, but I have to admit that Mary looked sad and embarrassed. I never heard her say much and I realize now that was basically who she was. A person easily swayed to and fro. I walked away from that friendship and never looked back. My best friends had become my enemies.

It was ironic that I lost my best friend because they accused me of believing myself beautiful. In my home, I had felt like the ugly duckling of the bunch. I thought I was rather ugly with my dark eyes, black hair and round face.

Even though we lived in a relatively small town with only one high school, we were able to graduate from school without seeing much of each other. They maintained their friendship throughout high school.

When we graduated, Mary's name caught my attention during our commencement exercises because she got a small scholarship for college. I was rather ignorant of anything that had to do with higher education so I thought that proved that what my brother had tried to teach me long ago was true. I was not as smart as Mary. She was truly more intelligent than me. Here she was, the only daughter of a single parent who held one of the most demeaning jobs in town and she had earned a scholarship.

Mary's mother worked in a factory beheading shrimp. She was a "camaronera" which was far beneath my family's stature. They rented a tiny little house while we were property owners and landlords. Rosa was even further down my stature; she was living in the projects, considered too poor to even rent without city or welfare assistance. Thus was the mentality of our community and my friends and I had learned our lessons well and taken our place within it.

Between junior high and high school I struggled with friendships. I had many friends but was too hurt to trust anyone to get close enough. I kept friendships light and when a girl began to cling and follow me around, I made sure to make myself scarce. My highly resourceful personality and real caring of others seemed to draw weaker females who befriended me. They may have seen a side of me they wished they possessed.

I never realized how deeply Mary had hurt me. That I had lost faith and trust in others to not hurt me through the act of friendship, I hid behind my tough exterior and pride. I decided not to look too close but instead to place all my thoughts on what lousy friends they had been.

Whatever the case, I was having none of close friendships or best friends. I met a friend named Trina then, but kept the friendship light. She was one of many who would on occasion join me during lunch hour to spend time with me.

I owned a little transistor radio and we would play it and listen to the top ten hits. We spent hours listening to tunes like, *My Girl, I Wanna Hold Your Hand, I'm a Believer*, etc. I had a following of girls who would come to look for me where I tended to eat lunch under a massive tree encircled by a bricked, elevated border. I sat down on the border to eat my lunch and listen to music. Many friends joined me. It still fills me with satisfaction, for I was a deeply insecure girl inside and rather shy and fearful of making a fool of myself in front of others. I imagine now it was all that silly pride or ego that seemed to be so important in our household.

My next-door neighbor and girlfriend, Angelica, was a year older than I was. Every time we played or walked to the store, all the neighborhood boys hooted and called out to her. This reinforced my belief that I was ugly. Not one of the neighborhood boys ever looked my way. It never crossed my mind that my brother was one of the most feared boys because he was known for his fists. He fought like a demon and rarely lost a fight. There wasn't a boy in our neighborhood who would dare take him on by getting close to his little sister.

On one such occasion, both Angelica and I went to the little store in our neighborhood to get some bubble gum. We loved to chew gum and blow huge bubbles. We would stand outside during the evening, in my backyard or hers and dream.

Angelica would do most of the dreaming and I listened. She had a crush on one of the singers in a popular group, Dino, Desi and Billy. I believe she liked Dino, and her cousin Bertha liked Desi, and I was given Billy as the last of the group. Well I never had much of a crush on Billy, but decided to be a good sport and go along with their game.

Angelica fantasized that we were a singing group of three females. She had us sing and act out as if we were really on stage. We were supposed to get to be Dino's, Desi's and Billy's equals. I felt more like one of the Supremes, but I never dared to burst her fantasy bubble.

One day, I recall Angelica and I contriving to go to Don Juan's store. It was getting dark and he would soon close his doors. As I said, Angelica was older than me, and a rather spoiled child. She wanted me to get permission to go. I knew how strict my mom was and she would never agree to let me go so late in the evening. I was terrified of getting into trouble with my mother, so Angelica said, "Fine, I will go ask your mother and then you go ask mine." I was puzzled but followed her as she instructed me to do. She knew something I had not learned yet—how to be conniving. She told my mother that her mom had sent her to ask if I could accompany her to the store since it was getting dark and did not want her to go alone. My mom agreed hesitantly and told us not to tarry.

"Now you go and tell my mother the same story," Angelica instructed.

I was not as good at lying as she, but I did a good enough job to get permission from her mother, also. Mainly, I believe because her mom was nowhere as strict or as sharp as my mom.

We were off to the store for some gum. I had this uneasy feeling that we were going to get caught. We made it to the store on time and bought our gum. As we headed back down our now darkened alley, a gang of neighborhood guys jumped out from the darkness.

One of the boys held me or tried to hold me still, while the rest ganged up on Angelica. I have a suspicion that they were pawing under her clothes. All the boys had their faces hidden with bandanas but all the neighborhood kids were friends of my brother. I knew them all, if not by face, then by voice.

I began naming them and saying, "I know who you are and I am going to tell my brother Ramon. You will regret it!" Then I stomped the foot of the boy who held me, very hard. He let me go and went off screeching that I had broken his toe.

I took off like a flash, screaming, "Just wait, I am coming back with Ramon! You will all regret you ever did this! I'm going for help, Angelica, I'll be back!" One of the guys was yelling, "Catch her! Don't let her get away and call anyone!"

All the time the thought that I had lied to my mother and she would find out, was going through my head. I knew I was in for a whipping but I didn't care. I had to save Angelica from those jerks.

When they saw I had gained lots of ground between them and me and that there was no stopping me, they let Angelica go. I waited for her as she ran to catch up with me. We were both stunned and scared witless. I asked her if they had hurt her, done anything to her. She just shook her head in silence. I was really too naïve to understand what the boys were after. All my mind could conceive was a stolen kiss. I believe now that it went much farther and she must have felt molested and degraded with so many of them surrounding her. Not to mention the terror she must have felt not knowing how to get away. I realize now she never really fought, or knew how to fight to get away from them. She was too much the lady while I on the other hand was as much a tomboy, and much more aggressive than a female should be, and it was because I had to be in order to survive my brother.

She never did tell me what the boys who crowded around her did to her, but I know she never spoke to another guy on our block other than my brother, Ramon. She hated every single one of them until the day we were grown and she moved away. I sensed she felt forever indebted to Ramon and me for being there to defend her. My brother always treated her with kindness and respect even though he was really into flirting with other girls. He respected Angelica because she was my friend and our neighbor.

I had grown up with Ramon as my brother and playmate. I had learned to be tough to survive someone as tough as he. It never dawned on me that everyone in the neighborhood feared him or befriended him because I never once feared or cowered from him. But then again, Ramon was my protector; he fought like crazy with anyone who dared offend any of his sisters.

~Chapter 7~

My sisters were growing up. Sunday afternoons became much more interesting when my sisters and I sometimes got to go to the movie theater to go see Godzilla. I was terrified of that awful creature but loved to be a part of the movie outing.

Bella got herself a boyfriend when she was fourteen, and he paid the dime for me to go to the movies with them. Of course our very strict mother did not know about the boyfriend and I was sworn to secrecy. We were not allowed to speak about boys or anything of that sort. For my sister to have a boyfriend would have gotten her in trouble with my mother. I was twelve years old and life suddenly became interesting.

Our town had a yearly celebration called Charro Days. It was usually held for two weeks in February and a carnival with lots of rides, games and food stands was a part of the celebration. Again, my mother's inconsistent behavior took place. She was very strict about what we wore, where we went, who we befriended, our language and good manners, but on the other hand she gave us permission to be out every single day during the Charro Days celebration. We had a curfew and if we were late we got a whipping, but were not grounded from going out the next day.

From the age of twelve through fourteen, I was very devoted to attending a church with another friend I had met at school. I loved going to Sunday night and Wednesday night services. It gave me freedom from home and something different to do with my time. I loved singing special hymns with my friends during the church service. Every time I attended church I prayed my mom would one day come to know Christ.

This part of my life ended abruptly when my mother heard gossip that I was not going to church to be inside the service, but instead, was known to be outside messing with boys. I had gone to my friend's house to catch the church bus with them. My mother was so enraged by this gossip she decided to go find me at my friend's house to bring me home.

It just so happened that we had been sent to the store to buy some Mexican sweet bread by my girlfriend's mother. There was a strict rule that my mother expected us to follow. When we were allowed to go somewhere, we had best never leave to go anywhere else.

My friend was one of twelve children. She had several brothers who were walking back from the store with us. As we all turned the corner to my friend's house, I heard my mother's angry voice insulting my friend's mother who was a Christian lady with a soft spoken, sweet way about her. My mother was calling her all sorts of names, demanding to know where I was. When she saw me turn the corner with a few boys in tow, she was livid. I was ordered to follow her home at once. I do believe I said, "What about church?"

One look from my mom froze me in my place. She marched me back home. I got the whipping of my life for being involved with boys. I was supposed to be sneaking out from church service to mess around with boys. This truly never happened for this was a time in my life when I had developed a close relationship with God. So close was that relationship, that I was praying that I could convince my mother that instead of the typical 'quincienera,' a Hispanic young girl's fifteenth birthday ball, I wanted a dinner celebration at the church. This request was out of the question for my mother, as she was not into church. I decided that if I could not have a church celebration, I did not want a celebration at all. After this incident happened at my friend's house, she prohibited me from attending church with my friend again. I cried and prayed but in the end resigned myself to my mother's will. I had spent a few years praying for my mother to go to church like all those sweet ladies I had learned to love. After this embarrassing incident I gave up. I became bitter and resentful. I began to pray a different prayer. I asked the Lord to take me away because I was not wanted or loved on earth, so I would be better off dead. I never again befriended that Christian girlfriend. I stayed away from her even when she searched for me at school. Eventually she realized that I did not want her friendship.

I had a conversation with God, where I told him that since my mother refused to let me go to church or do my fifteenth birthday dinner celebration at church, I would stop serving him. I would never try to go to church again and instead turned toward worldly things. I remember saying to the Lord, "If I cannot serve you then I will serve the other. From now on it's all about going out and having fun."

At this time in my life, as a young teen, I did not understand the complexities of life. What I do know is that there was a danger I knew nothing of in that Christian home. Even though my girlfriend's mother and sisters were all Christian, none of the males in the family were. In fact they were perverts in the real sense of the word. My friend's older brother would always smirk and make references to my growing breasts. I would blush hotly and run away from him. Then on one occasion, her father tried to molest me.

He was a big, heavy man. He came into the room where we were playing and sent her to wash the dishes. I was about to follow her there and he told me to stay there and wait for her. He closed the door and leaned on a piece of furniture, like a dresser. He asked me to come over to him. I had been conditioned to always mind my elders. I went but when he took me between his legs and began rubbing my body over his private, I struggled free and ran out the door, past my friend and all the way home. I never told anyone, not even my friend, but I did continue to go there before my mother stopped me. But I never again went indoors to play and always got to her house a few minutes before the church bus would come to pick us up.

There was a lot of rivalry between Bella and me. I sensed my mother's favoritism toward my sister. Bella looked so much like my father. She was a feminine carbon copy of him. I knew how much my mother loved my father. Our sleeping arrangements were such that I shared the bedroom with my mother. My two brothers had one bedroom, my sisters had the other, and my mother and I shared the third. This gave me a little more insight into my mother. Many times I went to bed and acted as if I was asleep and heard my mother's nightly prayers. They revealed her true heart to me as she spoke imploringly to the Lord. She always asked the Lord to watch over my father and protect him from harm.

Bella seemed to have a lot of influence on my mother's decisions. There were times when I would ask my mother if I could do something and Bella would argue against it. Once when I was in elementary school, I wanted to participate in the Charro Days Parade like she once had. She told my mother not to let me do it because she had done it and it was very tiring. After all, I had problems with my legs, and it would be too hard for me since the parade crossed most of the city's width. My mother did not let me dance in the parade.

Another time when I was in high school, I wanted to become an Eaglette. It was a group of girls who were trained to dance during intermission while the school band played at football games. My mother had said we did not have the money for this and I offered to work for the money as a waitress. Bella again opposed this idea and said I would get very tired with my legs being so weak. I was almost about to explode, but my mother surprised me and told me that if I raised the money for the uniforms and fees, I could go ahead and try out. I made it and it was the most exciting time of my life.

Twice in my junior high years, my brother showed me what he was capable of. Once, when a boy decided to walk me home and carry my books, my brother caught up to us. Rob was a shy boy who I didn't have the heart to reject when he asked if he could walk me home. My brother sneaked up behind us and yanked Rob to the ground. Rob paled at the sight of my brother and his angry face.

"Is he bothering you?" my brother asked.

I was embarrassed and ashamed. "Why did you do that?" I screamed in anger. "Look what you have done to my books!" They had scattered all over the ground where they had fallen. Rob's face was now a deep shade of red, because it was obvious he had no desire to get off the ground and fight my brother.

"He is my friend and I told him he could carry my books home!" I yelled at my brother. It was comical how my brother promptly helped Rob off the ground and straightened his shirt.

They both began to pick up my books and my brother said, "Sorry, just wanted to make sure no one was bothering my sister."

Rob gladly replied, "No problem, I understand." He never volunteered to carry my books home again, and I was relieved.

The second incident was more serious. My brother had a friend who used to come to visit him at our house. This guy was actually not a very nice guy. He would say inappropriate things that made me blush. When he said, "that's a pretty dress" and I said "thank you", he proceeded to add, "can I take a peek underneath it?" and I would blush deeply while he laughed at me. I told him a few times that if he did not stop I would tell my brother, but he laughed anyway.

Well, it did not take long before an incident occurred during school that my brother happened to walk into. All the girls had dressed for gym class in our required gym suit. It was a one-piece navy blue short set with metal clasps down the front and our school name embroidered above a front pocket.

Some of the girls wore it tight but I was not one of them. I seemed to attract hoots and catcalls anyway and that rather unsavory friend of my brother was one of many guys who sat close by and watched the girls heading out to the field. He would embarrass me by making some inappropriate comments about my body, inciting the others to do the same.

My brother turned the corner of the gym as his friend was making such a comment. That guy never knew what hit him. In a flash my brother had yanked him off the floor where he sat and was pounding his face with iron closed fists. The rather gangly weakling's face was soon covered in blood. The rest of the guys circled them and cheered the fight on.

I was aghast as I was every time I witnessed my brother's violent fights. I usually wanted to get as far away as possible from it, but my loyalty toward my brother kept me close. It wasn't long before someone said the principal was coming. They enforced the 'no fighting in school rule' strictly. Anyone caught breaking that rule was immediately expelled. I knew my brother could not be caught because he would face serious consequences at home. My mother was obsessed with the education of her children. She would not allow any of us any leeway to misbehave and get kicked out of school. I ran through the circle of guys who had formed around my brother and his friend.

I yelled at him, "Ramon stop! The principal is coming! You have to leave before he catches you!"

My brother fisted the guy one last time and bolted around the gym and out of sight. Our principal was rather heavy and it took him a while to get there. There was no trace of my brother, nor any of the circle of onlookers by the time the principal made it to the scene. The only one left was that obnoxious guy still sprawled and bleeding from his nose. They took him to the nurse's station and expelled him when he refused to reveal that Ramon had been involved in a fight with him. I never saw that guy at our house again. My brother's friendship with him ended after he heard what the jerk had said to me. That was the way it always was in our family, we always stuck together, loyal to a fault.

~Chapter 8~

The life in our Hispanic community was one of those who have and those who have not. For the most part those who were more fortunate than others tended to give a helping hand. As long as the person was respectable, being poor was not considered a reason for lack of respect but more a badge of honor. Often a neighbor who was having trouble getting food on the table for their children was offered plate after plate by a neighbor who had it a little better. One never forgot those who helped you, and always paid the debt back, even if it was many years later and was to a son or daughter of the person who had showed a kindness to you.

Gratitude was expected and those who did not show it, soon found out doors began to close around them. It was not necessarily expected that people feel indebted to anyone, but gratitude was a matter of being honorable. If you never had more than you had that day, people understood you were unable to return the favor, but appreciated that you had wanted to. My mother had neighbors so many times knocking on our door, asking for a cup of sugar, a few bucks to be able to pay a light bill or gas bill, a bar of soap, flour, etc. And just as many times I answered the door to receive two cups of sugar for the one cup borrowed, two bars of soap, and so on, with a kind speech of gratitude for helping the family when they found themselves in a bind.

Other times a mother and her children were given a place to sleep on our living room floor because the husband had abandoned the family and they had no where else to go. The woman would usually go out of her way to help with chores and still look for a job to get on her feet. A few over-stayed their welcome and were not grateful, but most got on their feet and my mother had a friend for life.

To this day, there are many women my mother helped who still love her and visit her. They have never forgotten how she helped them when they were at their worst financially. Even if they have moved to other parts of the United States, when they came to visit that small Texas border town, they stop to visit and say hello. They had tears of gratitude in their eyes, and pictures of the children who lived under our roof, now full grown, in their wallets. It warmed my mother's heart that she made a difference in their lives.

Such was the world I grew up in. I saw it happen time and time again. Much charity was extended within the community. Our family also received this type of help. A better, well-off family or relative would bring boxes of quality clothing to us to use or give away. My mother would gather us around the box and find what fit. What we could not use, she also sorted and gave to the poorest of the families on our block.

On the other side of the coin, there was also plenty of gossip and strife within the community. There were times that some sordid gossip would divide friends, and they would sever all communication for life. Many times it was a simple thing like hearing that a neighbor thought another's children were completely lacking in manners. That would begin years of anger and dispute between families, mostly between mothers and children. Men were generally working and kept out of the gossip mill.

Sometimes the children could have been close and played together daily. Suddenly, after an argument between adults, their children were not allowed to play with each other anymore. It was a matter of loyalty and of family sticking together.

Bella, my middle sister, lost a best friend that way. I remember how sad those two girls were because they went from best friends to not being able to talk to each other again. They used to walk together daily to their junior high school and back home. Suddenly, they could not even say hello. Bella and Eva used to be so close; they shared each other's clothes, styled their hair and wore their makeup alike. They almost looked like twins. It was the saddest thing to see their friendship come to an end.

Another belief that was predominantly ingrained during my upbringing was that we believed in ghosts, and in good and evil spirits roaming the earth. Families loved to sit around in a circle and tell tales passed on from generation to generation. La Llorona is a well-known tale of a woman who could never rest when she died because she had lost her children, and she went around looking for them, crying into the wind. My mother passed many of those tales along as we sat around our kitchen table, or on a hot muggy evening when we sat around in a circle on the soft green grass outdoors.

I also used to hear neighbors and acquaintances come and visit my mother and tell her of spells that had caused them an illness or the breakdown of their marriage. Sometimes they talked of potions they believed would heal the illness. My grandmother, as in many past generations, had a lot of home remedies she passed on to her children. My mother used some of these when we were ill, had fevers, earaches and things of that nature.

We had two cemeteries in our small town. One was located almost directly across the street from my Aztec grandma's home. The other cemetery was a few blocks away from our house. We had a lot of tarantulas that lived within the cemetery. During the nights we sat outside, we would begin to talk about them and spook ourselves.

We believed if you talked about them, you would call them and soon after we would all scream, as my prankster brother would say, "There's one!" It never failed, during that night a pair of tarantulas would make their presence known. They always traveled in pairs, male and female. All the girls would run inside screaming, sometimes the boys had to prove they were not afraid and stayed to kill the tarantulas. Lots of times my mother would take control and go kill the pair with a shovel so she could quiet down the house.

We always had people coming and going to our home. Mostly women and children in need called on my mother to ask for her help. She had a rental house, which meant homeless families in search of an affordable house for rent came to see if they could rent the small house.

Many of those who lived in that rental house, located in the rear of our home, became close friends for life. My mother always seemed to give in to the mothers who had several children that could not find a place because no one wanted to worry about the damage the children would cause. My mother had children herself and knew these families were desperate. She could not stand to think of a family being homeless. So she taught us to be concerned for others and give a helping hand when possible.

As a result, I always had many playmates around as I grew up and we all gathered in that circle during those warm, scary nights. We also had many friends in the neighborhood who came to join us at different times. Some of our previous renters had moved down the road but still remained our friends and would come and join us.

One particular story that my sisters and I have added to those passed down generations was one we personally lived ourselves. This happened when we were in our teen years. I might have been about fourteen. Letty had gotten her first car. It was an old Chevrolet station wagon. She didn't have a license but that was not unusual during those times. Many Hispanics went without them. Young, pretty, Hispanic girls usually got off with a warning if a policeman stopped and asked for a license. We were in the station wagon together and ran out of gas. There was a Shamrock gas station at the corner, right across from the cemetery. Both my older sisters were walking side by side and I was tagging along as usual. The cemetery was on a slightly raised hill and we were on the raised sidewalk approaching the cemetery entrance.

They were so involved in their conversation that they did not notice the lady in black. Since I had nothing better to do with my time, I noticed her. She was covered in black from head to toe. I could not see an inch of skin but did not think that rare as many Mexican women dressed this way over the death of a relative. They honored a loved one's memory for five years or more of mourning, by wearing complete black from head to toe. She crossed the empty street in front of the cemetery's gated entrance. I watched and wondered how she passed the sidewalk we were on and got past the gates. We were still a stretch away but I thought she walked rather strange, almost like floating.

I said to Letty and Bella, "That lady does not look like she is walking, almost like she is floating." They laughed at my comment and kept talking.

We approached the gates of the cemetery, just as I said, "What if the gates to the cemetery are closed?" We were now in front of the gates and as I glanced at the gates, I saw they were padlocked. I was watching the lady in black and she was definitely floating. I told my sisters, "All the gates are closed!" My sisters looked at the padlocks and begin to scream. "Run!! She's a dead person, she's floating!"

Bella, who weighed about ninety-eight pounds, turned and fled the way we came from. She sprinted away and was gone in the blink of an eye. My older sister Letty was a more emotional, nervous type person. She began to run but was not moving. Her fright had somehow frozen her, and she was running but not moving forward. I, in turn was already halfway gone, but turned around to see why Letty was not coming. I hesitated, and thought to myself, *Should I leave her there, or should I go back?* I yelled, "Letty! You are not moving!"

She cried out, "I'm trying, I just can't move!"

I turned back and went to her, took her by the arm and pulled her with me. Her feet began to move forward and we both ran toward Bella.

We were scared out of our wits, crying and laughing and in shock. We had never seen a real ghost. We had heard many stories about the lady in black who walked the cemetery. Now here we were on the wrong side of the cemetery and scared to death. We had run away from the cemetery and headed away from the gas station and it was getting dark now.

An elderly couple stopped and gave us a ride home. We told our mother what had happened and she said she had to treat our shock or we might become ill. Then once we settled down, she told us the story of the woman who kept roaming the cemetery. This was one of those legends passed down from generations. Our mother told us that back when the transportation system had first been set up to run in our area of town, the bus used to run down the main street and do a bus pick up/drop off where the Shamrock gas station now was. They had finally changed the route and had the bus turn two blocks away from the original stop because bus drivers kept complaining or quitting or refusing to drive that route. All their bus drivers that ran that route claimed that a lady dressed completely in black and covering her face with a thick black veil would get on the bus and just sit. The lady in black never got down on any stop but would just disappear off the bus. The drivers said the lady never said a word; and that even her hands were covered with black gloves. My mother said the route was changed in order to keep bus drivers employed to run that route.

One of my uncles was a taxi cab driver. He told us that cab drivers had shared similar accounts of receiving a call to pick up a lady where the gas station now was. When a cab driver arrived, the lady in black would get into the taxi, hand the driver an address. She never said a word but would disappear before the cab driver would get her to the address on the slip of paper. Some of the drivers that had this happen felt that they had to get paid for this fare. So they drove to the address and knocked on the door. An elderly lady dressed in black would come to the door. When the driver would tell the lady about the woman in black that had disappeared before she got down, the elderly lady said it was her daughter who had died many years ago. She would always pay them the cab fare and tell them to please continue to bring her to her home. The elderly lady said her daughter was harmless, had just been too young when she died and could not rest.

Previously, even while I had heard the stories and legends about ghosts, I was skeptical. But after seeing the lady in black with my own eyes, I never doubted that there was some truth to many of these legends.

My mother recounted stories my uncles had told her of things that had also happened to them. One uncle related that he had been drinking at a bar and decided to go visit my mother. He walked down the railroad tracks that were close to our home and noticed a lady dressed in a very fancy sequined dress. She had an unbelievably shapely body; the dress hung down to the ground. My uncle was well known for two things; he was a drinker and a womanizer. He was also very good looking and had no problem getting involved with women. He decided he was going to try and catch up to the lady with the lovely body and long shimmering hair. He got pretty close all the while calling out to her to wait for him.

She never answered or slowed down so he sped up until she was at arm's length. He took the last few steps to touch her shoulder. When he did, he felt a cold chill generating from the touch. She turned around at his touch and he almost passed out from fright. She had no flesh according to my uncle. Her face, which was covered by a shimmering scarf, was nothing but a skeleton. He shrank back and ran as fast as he could to our house. He banged loudly on the door until he woke up my mom at an ungodly hour of the night. My mother said she had never seen him so frightened and shaken. She scolded him and told him that's what he got for flirting and messing with any woman in skirts. He promised her he was going to change now and never flirt with another woman unless he had her face-to-face, which made my mother laugh all the time. She mentioned that after that incident, he moderated his flirting and womanizing ways. He settled down and not long after his life became a series of unfortunate events until he died. He died of grief for losing one of his sons in a drowning incident. My mother said he could not live with the idea that his young son was gone. His son had only been thirteen years old. My uncle actually died of a heart attack, but my mother said that he died of a broken heart helped along by the alcohol.

~Chapter 9~

Latinos, Chicanos, Hispanics, Mexicans, all the names that describe my race, are an interesting people. Culture beliefs are so deeply instilled within them that few really get to know who they really are. Their true self-identity is never released or allowed the freedom to surface. I was one of many who became a mirror of who I was taught I should be. Does that make sense?

We are taught that loyalty is like the oxygen you breathe. Without it, you will die a painful death. Pride is ranked second only to loyalty. Pride is an interesting thing in my culture. I learned that pride was a jailer, the one that imprisoned me and did not allow me to be who I was meant to be in this life.

We were a working family. We all did what we could to earn a few cents to help our mother out. I started babysitting at the age of nine. The lady who rented our little house that sat in the back of our own lot would hire me to watch her son. I gave my mother every cent or quarter I earned.

Letty was making potholders and I would go out in the neighborhood to sell them and bring the money to my mother. Ramon would work with a neighbor fisherman who had only one leg and needed assistance to do the hard jobs. They would go off on weekends to fish for oysters and then bring them to the fisherman's home and bottle them to sell. Ramon gave my mother every penny he earned, also.

The only person I don't recall working and bringing in money was Bella. But she stayed home and helped our mother around the house with all the chores. And she did help my mother with hemming skirts and dresses. She also did much of the work to free my mother's time for sewing.

When Ramon and Jimenez, the fisherman, were not at sea bringing in oysters, they worked as carpenters. My brother was Jimenez's assistant. It amazed me that this one-legged man was some times seen on top of a roof putting on shingles. Ramon would help him up and down a ladder, and once up there, assisted Jimenez by bringing up all the tools and materials he needed.

Later, when Ramon was a teen, he worked at a gas station and brought in a lot more money to help out. He went to work right after school and into the evening.

There was no law that mandated employers to request a social security number at that time. It was easy to hire underage children and illegal aliens in our community. But there were always random sweeps for illegal aliens at different places of employment.

I went to work at the age of twelve for a lady who had a small restaurant. I washed dishes, shaved ice for flavored ices, waited tables, and cleaned the community restroom in the establishment where she rented space. My work hours were from nine in the morning until nine at night. I was paid one dollar and fifty cents for all my efforts. I gave my mother every cent, proud to be of help to her.

There was one thing that bothered me greatly about leaving work at nine at night. I had to walk a long stretch of road that was without lights and full of brush next to the railroad. I also learned that adults lied. The only adult I had been around for most of my short life was my mother, and I never heard a lie. Sometimes her blunt honesty made her more enemies than friends.

When the restaurant owner hired me, she talked to my mother and promised that she would always walk me past the railroad tracks. Yet shortly after, the lady told me she would stand at a far distance and wait for me until I came up on the other side of the railroad crossing. She would be able to see me by the light of the ice plant. She was an elderly lady with swollen legs and feet and did not want to walk more than necessary. She told me not to tell my mother or I would not be able to work for her anymore. I wanted to help my mother so badly, that I agreed.

So when I got to the darkened wooded railroad crossing area, I would run so fast, that I would sometimes forget to breathe. I was terrified of the dark and was sure that someone was going to grab me from behind at any second. This feeling only propelled me to run all the faster and not stop until I got to the other side where an ice plant lit up the whole street.

I learned to trust my mother's word above all else because it seemed every time I dared to lie, deceive or do a bad deed, what my mother had told me would come true. It never failed. I felt guilty for participating in this deception because my mother never failed to ask me if the elderly lady had walked me past the railroad. So I had to repeat the lie every Saturday. She was always waiting for me to get home and I am sure could see my agitated state. Once I crossed the railroad, our house was but a few houses away.

I knew that I should never have been a part of that lie when my worst fears came true. It was one of many Saturday nights when I found myself running as fast as my legs could carry me. A naked man walked out of the bushes. I was terrified almost to the point of insanity when he seemed to be approaching me. The only thing I am thankful for is that I was so lost in fear that even if I saw him completely naked, I never recalled what I saw. I ran, still hearing his voice coaxing me to stay. I will forever be thankful I did not have Letty's problem of running in place when she went into shock.

What could I do? I did not even dare tell my mother what had happened. I was more terrified of being caught in a lie and what my mother would do to that elderly lady. So I kept the secret deep inside me. Luckily, the following day, the neighbor across the street called the police to report she had seen a naked man on the railroad tracks. Her backyard faced the railroad and he had exposed himself when she was out hanging her wash on the clothesline. They searched the area and did not find him, but soon other women and children begin to report spotting him. My mother decided to walk with my brother to get me at the end of my work day, for she did not feel an elderly lady could be of much protection for me. I was so relieved I had not had to quit working, for I felt a wonderful feeling every time I handed my mother my little contribution for our food. I saw in her eyes for a moment a sense of relief.

You see, I had been the one to find the job in the first place. The restaurant was located next to the neighborhood bakery. I had been sent to buy some fresh French bread and saw her ad on the window for help wanted. I never regretted the job, only the late night scary sprint to get home.

A lady who lived next to the establishment bumped into me once when I was coming from cleaning the bathroom. She asked me what I was paid and when I told her, she offered to pay me the same for a few hours of babysitting. I agreed and my work hours changed to babysitting from noon to six in the evening. I loved coming home during daylight hours.

You would think I would be happy with the change, but there was a problem. The child I babysat was grossly overweight and very spoiled. He cried non-stop and I had to hold him throughout the hours I babysat. By the time it was time for me to leave, my back, head, and arms were hurting so badly. I was completely exhausted but in a different way than when I had worked all day non-stop at the restaurant. This job did not last very long and I was glad not to go back.

The lady who rented our little house and worked as a waitress at the local Rexall pharmacy and restaurant came home to tell my mother they needed a waitress right away. I believe there had been a sweep of illegal aliens and were very short of waitresses. They had lost a couple of ladies during the sweep. They hurriedly dressed me up in a white pleated skirt and white blouse. I was twelve and on my way to my first real job. It was summer and I worked every day but Sundays throughout the summer earning thirty-five dollars a week!

That was a blessing for us. It helped pay for the mortgage on the house and bring food to the table. I could also buy left over pies that were not sold that day. My mother and I were hooked on them. This was the first time I had tasted lemon meringue pie. I worked all summer and I finally saw my mother's face less filled with worry. She did not sew until dawn or was not as nervous or stressed. I never thought to keep a dollar; it all went to my mother for our care.

I was only twelve but must have appeared much older. I was not very self-confident and did not believe myself beautiful. I did not smile much, and my large brown eyes looked sad. I am sure that, added to my maturity and ability to work so hard, made me appear older than twelve. So when I started to attract male attention, I did not know what to do with it. My mother did not allow discussions of boys in our home and I did not feel close to my sisters. I had no one to ask or confide in.

I found myself with three older men who wanted to date me, walk me to the bus stop, and flirted with me every chance they got. I was scared to death of men from all I had heard my mother say. All I wanted was for them to leave me alone but I did not have the skills or confidence to say so. They fought with each other attempting to assert their right as my boyfriend. The one I did like to talk to, Pedro, was taken by Immigration on a following sweep. The other two were much too forceful in their flirting and scared me, making me want to hide. I felt so lost with how to handle these two very assertive young men that I began to hide in the bathroom during my breaks and made sure I was with other women during lunch.

At one time they had an all out fight during lunch because David wanted to sit next to me and did even after I had told him no. He made a joke and said, "Yes you do, you are just playing hard to get," and plopped his body next to me. Alberto, who waited behind David to ask the same question, decided to be insulted for David's behavior and proceeded to yank him off the seat. This was one time all the other waitresses either left to run errands during lunch or were working because we were short on help that day.

The two men fought and rolled on the floor and threw punches left and right. I kept begging them to stop. They knocked a full barrel of potatoes over and I panicked. I was sure the loud banging noise had been heard downstairs in the office area. I did not want to lose this valuable job over their fighting. It was when I burst into tears that Alberto stopped long enough for David to throw a punch that stunned him. I could not believe he would take advantage of this, so I went to Alberto to help him up and help him wash his bloody face. From that day on, I did not talk to David again. I walked away every time he tried to talk to me. Alberto started to walk me to the bus stop every night because it was late when we left work and he did not want me to walk to the stop alone. There were several male bars along the way and it was not safe to walk the downtown area when it was so deserted other than the bars.

He sometimes sang *Strangers In The Night* as we walked down the street. He said that we were strangers but that he would use these walks so we could get to know each other. All he ever did was hold my hand as we walked. I learned to trust him because I sensed he truly acted like a true gentleman with me. I worked there and we continued being friends until a law was passed that all employers must require social security numbers from all employees. At the time you could not apply for a social security number until the age of sixteen or that is what I was told by my mother. I had to quit and the money that helped so much was gone.

Several years later, when I was fifteen, I ran into Alberto at a dance. He was with his fiancée. I could not believe he came to ask me to dance when his girlfriend went to the bathroom. He told me he was getting married soon, but said, "If you tell me right now I have a chance with you and you will marry me someday, I won't marry her. Will you marry me?" I was shocked speechless, blushed furiously and told him that would be a terrible thing to do to his fiancée.

He answered, "I have always loved you and I told her all about you. She would be hurt but she would understand. When you left work, I did not know where to find you and your friend would never give me any information about you."

Again, I did not know what to say or do. I never believed I was loveable, and even as he talked, all I thought was, *He does not mean anything he just said, he is just a hopeless womanizer.* It was incomprehensible for me to believe that any man would love me or see anything worth loving in a simple, rather ugly, Hispanic girl. I would never believe he still cared for me after so long of not seeing each other and to leave a fiancée almost at the altar? I was sure he was not serious and my kind heart would never even consider doing that to any other girl. I did notice his fiancée had come out of the bathroom before we stopped dancing and after he sat down with her she seemed upset. She would turn to give me angry looks, daggers shooting from her green eyes.

They left soon after and he turned one last time to wave goodbye and blow a kiss. Again I blushed furiously at such a display of emotions directed publicly at me. I never saw him again, but to me he was a wonderful memory of a good friend. I never felt any stronger feelings than those of friendship for him, and had always told him so during our walks to the bus stop. So I received my first proposal at the age of fifteen.

~Chapter 10~

The only reason my mother imposed any boundaries on our comings and goings was because she feared what the neighbors would say. That was her argument to us any time we asked for a little later curfew on special dates, like the prom, or certain school events. We could never stay out anywhere, because "What will people say?" was her natural response. Her pride that she was a good mother and we were good girls restricted us all. We could never consider spending a night out at a friend's house. The only good thing was that it was not a practice in our culture to have overnighters. No one ever seemed to spend time at anyone's home overnight that I was ever aware of.

Two incidents come to mind that had a grave impact in my life and how I would feel about my father. The first happened when I was younger. During a time of great sadness and depression for me, I searched until I found one of his few letters to my mother and got his address. I wrote him a letter and asked for his help. I was so young and naïve, but I asked him to please allow me to come and live with him. This was a time when I felt very unwanted and useless to do anything around the house like both my skilled sisters could do. I never received a reply and I told myself it had to be the letter got lost. I felt sure he would have called or written otherwise.

I found out as an adult while working with attorneys that mail for a military man always got to them. Even if it took years to track a military man down because he might have been transferred time and again, correspondence would eventually get to them. I realized that my father had received that pathetic letter from his youngest daughter crying out for help, and he had simply ignored it. It was then I realized I did not truly have a father. It had all been a fantasy, a lie my mother had made us believe because she needed to believe it herself. I was not bitter toward my father, he was really a stranger to me, but I was very hurt. I felt sure it made sense that my father cared little for his youngest child, for she was not loveable.

The second incident was when a law was passed that made military men responsible for sending child support to their families on their own. Prior to this law, the military automatically deducted a percentage of a married man's salary to send to his family for support. For as long as I could remember, we got a check once a month for one hundred seventy-five dollars for our support. When the law changed, my father never sent a dime for our support again. That was the very time when it became so critical for all of us who could work, to find work immediately.

Those were very trying times for us. We had always been poor and my mother made every penny count. Now without our monthly support, we had no income whatsoever. My mother was forced to swallow her pride and go to the local welfare office to ask for help. We received food stamps and a small monthly check for the first time in our lives. My mother was devastated and hurt terribly with our father's abandonment. I shared the same bedroom with her and heard her prayers and her crying during the night.

Letty was a senior that year. My mother was determined that Letty would go to her prom night and have a prom dress. This was the first time I saw my sister rebel and try to confront my mother. She did not want to go and did not want to learn how to dance. I believe Letty was trying to save my mother the worry of the expense it would take to go to the prom. My mother got my sister a beautiful hand-me-down dress. Letty was as proud as my mother and refused to wear it. It became an all out battle, with my mother raging and my sister crying. I thought the dress was beautiful and that my sister looked like the identical picture of Mary had a Little Lamb. It was a white, ruffled dress, one tiny ruffle after another from waist to the floor. It was strapless and my sister looked beautiful in it.

My mother got Letty's next-door neighbor friend, to get her a date because Letty refused to ask anyone. I believe my sister had been asked to the prom and had turned down any invitations. Even though she was very shy and self-conscious, she was very lovely and many boys her age were interested in her. She had an awesome body and the tiniest waist.

The day came and Letty was dressed and ready. Her escort came with a corsage in hand. Letty had resigned herself to going but she looked very sad. The young man had a crush on my sister so I am sure he was elated to take her to the prom. To me, every young man must have had a crush on her, for she was lovely, sweet and intelligent.

My mother found a way to make sure Letty had everything needed for her senior year and graduation. She got her high school ring on credit at the local Zale's store and found the money for the graduation picture and invitations. All in all, every obstacle my mother conquered had cost her a grave effort to achieve. She suffered and raged and cried as I watched silently on the sidelines.

Here I must tell you a story before I go on. Letty was not much different than my mother, with one exception. She suffered just as much but her pain turned toward bitterness against my father. She would not forgive the abandonment that turned her senior year into such a nightmare for her. A few years later, Letty would mete out her own revenge for justice against him. When she went to work in an attorney's office, she got her boss to bring charges within the military system for abandonment of his family. My father lost two stripes, which reduced his pay drastically and set his career back a few years. He was so angered he wrote my mother a letter that we would never see him again.

True to his word, I never saw my father again. The next time I heard from him, was when we were all grown and he served my mother with divorce papers. I was the only one who, even if married, still lived in our home town. Everyone else had married and moved away and both my brothers were in the military service. My sisters had followed their own spouses who were also in the military. It was the seventies and after the Vietnam War, there were very few young Hispanics not in the military during those war years. Many had continued to stay in the military after the war.

My mother was heartbroken to have received divorce papers after so long. All of us had finally realized that our parents were separated and that was our family secret. Her pride would not allow her to admit in public that her husband had abandoned her. Now he had filed for divorce and all the world would know he had not only left her, but divorced her as well.

I was working for attorneys as a secretary and they helped my mother deal with the response to the petition for divorce. They contacted a law firm to represent my mother and responded to the divorce. I was going to Arizona to accompany my mother to court. My father's attorney was to advise us when the court hearing was to take place. All we had left was to wait.

We waited months and heard nothing. Finally one of the attorneys I worked with called to speak to my father's attorney. He informed him that the divorce proceedings were dropped when my father passed away a month or so later. He felt sure he had sent a letter to my mother's attorneys to notify them.

To this day, I am puzzled over my reaction to the news of my father's death. When the attorney I worked for said, "Well it looks like you and your mother have nothing to worry about now since your father is dead and your mother was the legitimate wife up to the end."

I felt an inexplicable pain in my heart and a need to cry aloud. I had too much pride and reserve to breakdown in his study, so I turned and ran straight to the bathroom. I locked myself in a stall and the tears gushed down my face in torrents. I kept asking myself, *Why are you crying? You hardly knew him!* But I could not stop the tears; I was shuddering and crying loudly, scaring myself all the more for this emotional response. The attorney sent another secretary to check on me, concerned that he had blundered in sharing the news so callously. I finally got myself under control and went back to the office.

The attorney apologized. I told him it was not how he told me, but that the information that my father had died months before and of the concern for myself in having to tell my mother, who had never stopped loving him. I went home immediately to tell her.

I had my emotions under control again; the flood of emotions had disappeared as quickly as they had come. When I told my mother, my concern and feelings were solely about her and what she felt. Her eyes moistened but she said in her resigned voice, "Well, it was over long ago. I just never knew when I married your father that the day he died, I would not be at his funeral." She was able to maintain her pride, and sorrowfully told everyone her husband had passed away.

Time passed and more than a year later, I went to the post office to pick up mail for the office. I usually did not do this but our other secretary was out ill and the mail needed to be picked up daily.

When I arrived and went to the postal clerk, he stared at me for a while before he asked, "You would not by chance be related to Letty Bontemayor?"

When I said, "Yes, we are sisters." He proceeded to tell me how relieved he was to find that out.

"You see, I went to school with your sister and used to see her here almost daily. When I saw a letter for an old post office box addressed to your sister's mother, I kept it rather than return it to the sender as undeliverable. I thought I should ask your sister first before returning it. Now I have kept it so long in my drawer, I am concerned that I will be reprimanded if I send it back now. It's an important letter from a government agency. Will you take it?"

I thanked him and let him know my sister had left town to join her husband in Maine. I noticed he was disappointed to know she had married.

I read the letter after I called my mother and told her about it. It was a date-sensitive letter that requested my mother to prove she was married to my father. It appeared another woman was claiming all survivor benefits as the sole wife of my father. He had a young son with her that she claimed was the only child my father recognized.

I was shocked and furious. I promptly took the letter to one of the attorneys I worked with to read. He advised me to immediately write a response to the letter and to send a copy of the marriage certificate along with the utility bills and tax records that were still under my mother and father's names. They required a documentation of my parents' marriage years.

I spent a week gathering strong information to prove my mother was the legitimate wife. I wrote an extensive account of their married life. Also included in the letter was information on all the children of this marriage and their birthdates.

A few months later, my mother received a letter, awarding her all widow's benefits other than the burial reimbursement costs, which went to the woman who claimed she had buried him. Also included in the letter was an explanation that since all of my mother's children were adults, none qualified for dependent benefits other than the son of the woman claiming to be his wife. My father's youngest son was six years old and lived in Arizona.

My father had died at the age of fifty-three. My mother always claimed that he died because he did not really want a divorce or to break off ties with his children. She felt sure the other woman was pressuring him to divorce my mother, so that she could marry him and receive the widow's benefits.

In any case, since my father had died more than two years prior to the award of the benefits, there was an accumulation of money that now belonged to my mother. She also received a monthly retirement pension for the rest of her life or until or if she remarried. My mother would never go hungry again. It seemed that now that all her children were grown, and she did not have the need of so much money to live, that she was to have it.

I had helped my mother get a job as a janitor at the plant where I worked before joining the attorneys. She was able to quit the night shift job and stay home and rest. She was fifty-seven and had worked hard all her life to bring up her children. She now had the money to go buy a dress and not sew one for herself or anyone else. Her cupboards were full of food supplies and treats she had never been able to afford to buy us. This brought tears to her eyes and many times said she felt guilty to enjoy such wealth because her comfort came about with the death of our father. I understood, but could not feel the regret that she felt.

None of my other sisters or brothers cared much that our father had died. They were more than happy to know that our mother would never suffer with poverty again for as long as she lived. All of us knew she would never marry again; she was too devoted to a man who did not deserve it. She told us he was the only man she had ever loved and had no desire to ever replace him, even if he had been willing to replace her. I marveled at her love and lack of bitterness for a man who had abandoned her and her five children to hunger and poverty. The last time he had visited, I recalled my mother was still a very beautiful woman with her flawless skin. (Letty was the image of her, and she was the beauty of the house). Many times as a child, I recalled as I walked with her to town or to the store, so many men attempted to flirt and get to know my mother. She never gave any man a chance to get close. She rebuked them and told them she was a happily married woman.

~Chapter 11~

During my junior high and high school years, I began to attend what we called "get-togethers". They were usually birthday parties held in a garage or living room area with parents either gone or in their bedroom, as a group of kids danced to music on a record player. I was allowed to stay out until ten-thirty at night on a school night. I went to those parties often. I also went with my sister to what were called "shindigs", promoted dances with live music groups. We didn't have any money to pay for the entrance fee, so we would work at whatever we could find to get the money. These public dances happened once a week on Tuesday nights.

Once, Bella wanted to go really bad but we didn't have the money. So the day before the dance, we went to work in the fields, hoeing tomatoes to earn the money. I was not much into being in the outdoors. My legs were always in constant pain and I didn't do well in the hot Texas sun. It was summer and temperatures could sometimes reach a hundred degrees Fahrenheit. I went only because Bella would not take no for an answer. I was terrible at picking cotton, and worse at working in the tomato fields. I got into an argument with the supervisor because I felt he was treating us inhumanely. It was very hot and he would not allow us a water break; nor could we stop working before he was yelling at us to get back to work. Well, I knew my mouth would soon get me in trouble.

The supervisor told me I was useless and did not know how to work. Oh my, I thought I was hearing my mother talk to me but this time I could answer back! So I went off on him telling him that he should be reported for how he worked people. He told me to get back to work but not bother coming back to work for him. Bella kept telling me to be quiet or we might not get a ride back home or get paid and this only set me off more. I was raging that he better pay me for the slave work I had already done, or he would be sorry. The man never said another word to me but gave me the most hateful looks imaginable. He paid us and took us back with all the rest of the workers in the back of a truck. It really didn't matter to me that I did not know how to do this job. My hands were full of blisters where I had not known how to hold the hoe tight enough so it would not slip back and forth. Bella's hands fared better.

We went to the dance and Bella looked beautiful with her dark tan, while I had gotten burned and it hurt. My blisterered hands were even worse. I refused to dance because that meant my hand was held and the blisters would hurt all the more. Bella danced the night away, apparently the tomato incident all but forgotten.

In high school, I finally befriended Trina, whom I had met in junior high. She eventually became my very best friend. I loved her deeply and enjoyed spending all the time I could at her home. I developed an almost close case of hero worship for her mother. It was the first time I was around a mother who was very expressive in her love and so willing to share her wisdom. I learned so much from her and the advice she handed down to Trina while I was there. Our bodies were developing and any questions we had, Trina could easily ask her mother and she shared her wealth of knowledge with us. Trina's mom was also a camaronera but she was also a very savvy businesswoman. She had many rental houses she owned and kept a healthy income coming in to support all her children. She was a widow with a large family. Trina was the youngest, born before her dad was killed in the war.

Once again I let myself believe in friendship. Trina was not at all like Mary. Even though she was very naïve and non-aggressive, she was also very assertive and talkative because she was brought up rather spoiled. She was the baby of the house and pampered by all her older brothers and sister. They bought her beautiful dresses and I rivaled her with the wonderful dresses that my mom especially made for me now that I was in high school.

Trina had a stronger personality than Mary ever had. She let me know how she felt. Once I loved her dearly, I became fearful of her judgments toward me. She seemed to have plenty of judgments regarding behavior and I wanted her approval. Most of the time we had fun and she was forever coming to me for help or advice. If anyone bullied her, they soon learned she had a fearless defender in me. This was our culture; the weak looked after the stronger to help them survive. Hispanic teens loved to fight. Boys were into physical fighting to prove their manhood. That is why many joined gangs and lost their way. They were trying to show the community how tough they were and proud of it.

We were teenagers now, and went to dances together. Trina had another neighborhood girlfriend. Janie was kind of nutty, but nothing like Rosa. We became good friends and there was never any rivalry over our best friend. We began to notice boys and boys noticed us. Janie wanted to date a twin brother, but he was not interested. His best friend, Johnny, became interested in me and so asked his best friend to have Janie set up a blind date for him. Janie begged me to go out on the blind date because the twin would not go out with her otherwise. Janie was known as "easy". Both Trina and I tried to rein in her behavior but could not. As time went on she became more promiscuous but we never stopped being her friend. Even though in our community, good girls did not associate with "fast" girls because it might damage their reputation, we cared too much for Janie to leave her friendless.

I agreed to the blind date after much debate because both my friends promised he was not ugly. I met the person who was to be the love of my life. Or so I thought at the time. By this time the ugly duckling had obviously turned into a swan because I had many boys after me. In the span of my single life I received nine marriage proposals before I accepted the proposal from my husband. Johnny came with baggage. But I fell hopelessly in love with him, something that he did not reciprocate. A month later he broke my heart when he broke it off and returned to his ex-girlfriend. I came to find out that the reason he was attracted to me was because I reminded him of her, with my bronzed clear skin, large black eyes, and dark hair. I submerged myself in four years of deep depression over him. To this day, I cannot understand why I fell in love with this creep; maybe it was because he was the first and only man who rejected me instead of it being the other way around.

I cried constantly and my school grades went from As and Bs to Ds and Fs. I stopped smiling and lost all desire to go to dances. My family, as we always did, showed their loyalty and concern as they rallied to help me through my depression. My sisters encouraged me to go out while my mother went from scolding me for my lack of pride, to encouraging me to go out more and more. I was in a deep haze and did not care what happened to me. I went out and held my head up high when I happened to bump into Johnny, but inside I was crying. This was a very hellish time in my life.

Bella made sure we went to the Tuesday shindigs where I met several young men. One of them, Eddie, seemed to really want to get to know me. I was still in a haze, my broken heart hurting. I have always wondered who it was that Eddie thought he fell in love with, for I seemed to be a shell of a person. All the life had gone out of me. I smiled when I thought it was expected, answered if I was asked a question, but mostly went around in a silent emotional stupor without a smile.

I met Eddie at the first shindig for the summer season and then did not return to another dance for weeks. Bella and my mother tried very hard to convince me to go every week with Bella, but I refused. I just did not have the energy to attend a dance and dance with guys who wanted to get to know me, when I had decided love was a painful affair. I had no idea that Eddie was going to every single shindig looking for me.

I was finally coerced into going to the last few dances and it was rather comical what occurred that night. Bella, Trina, Janie and I were standing in one of the entrances into the hall. Sam, a guy who liked Trina, had just said hello to us and was standing nearby.

Sam was facing me as Eddie walked up to him and said, "Hey Sam, I am looking for a special person, can you help me look for her tonight? Tell me if you see her? I met her during the opening shindig and have not seen her since."

"Sure, if I know her. Who is she?" Sam asked.

"I really like her, Sam. Her name is Dolores."

Sam looked straight at me, cracked a smile and decided to pull a prank. "Oh, really? What does she look like? I know several Doloreses from school."

"Well, she has beautiful long black hair and dark eyes," Eddie answered.

"Well, that sounds like almost every girl I know," Sam smirked.

I was blushing, completely embarrassed, for my friends had all gone quiet, obviously listening to the conversation.

"No, Sam, this girl is so sweet and special; I think I am in love with her."

I think Sam knew I was about to bolt. My friends all had knowing smiles and were staring at me.

Sam said, "Oh! *That* Dolores. Well, all you have to do is turn around and I bet you won't have to search much longer."

Eddie quickly rotated to face our group and his face turned a deep red as he realized I had heard the conversation. I was just as embarrassed. The music started and he walked over and took my hand and we headed toward the dance floor for some privacy. He seemed elated to have found me again and went on to tell me how he had come to every single dance looking for me. We stayed together for the rest of the night simply because he seemed to be afraid I would disappear on him again, and because I did not know how to tell him I would rather be with my friends.

The first thing he did was, he made sure that he got my phone number. He told me he had poured through the yearbooks trying to find me. I told him I had missed school the day the pictures were taken so I was not in the yearbook. He said he found my sister Bella and was sure it was me. I laughed, for many people did confuse Bella and me. The only difference between us was that Bella weighed ninety-eight pounds while I weighed one hundred and seventeen pounds.

So Eddie was a determined young man who began to call and ask me out. We went to the movies, to dinner and to dances together. I truly did not want to go out but could not stand to hurt him by telling him so. My mother and sisters seemed to be ecstatic that I was dating again. Eddie and I saw each other through the summer and into the new school year. This was during the Vietnam War and he was a sophomore in college. I was a freshman in high school.

On one of our many dates, he told me he was going to join the Air Force. The war had been difficult on everyone in the community. I had gone to plenty of funerals when young men we knew had been sent back home in a coffin. It saddened me to know he wanted to go off to join the war, but this was not the first young man I knew that was headed that way. What he said after that shocked me more.

"When I go off to the service, I would like to know that you will be my fiancée. Will you accept my engagement ring?"

I was only sixteen and not sure what I should say, but yes was not it. I believe he sensed my shock. So he continued to try to convince me why this would be good for us.

"I would love to marry you, maybe after a year or two down the road. Meanwhile, we could be engaged and you can wait for me while I go off to war."

I was still speechless and continued to look down without saying a word. When he finally asked me to say something, I looked at him and said, "But I am only sixteen! I haven't even graduated from high school. I don't know how to do anything at home." I finally looked at him.

He looked very sad but as I expected, very proud, when he said, "I understand. The answer is no. But I want you to think about it. Don't give me an answer now, but later. I'll take you home now."

I never went out with Eddie again. When he called I told him I could not marry him and that seemed to end the friendship. He had given me a record with my name engraved on it when we first began dating, and to this day, any time I hear the song "Elusive Butterfly" I remember him. He told me that all the time he looked for me he played that song because I was his elusive butterfly.

~Chapter 12~

As it seems to always happen, I was a victim ready to be found. My lost love was always on my mind. I fought the memories but could not fight the depression, the sadness, or the emptiness. So, instead, I did what Johnny had done to me. I met someone that reminded me of him and went on a date. It was the biggest mistake of my life.

Tony supposedly fell in love with me and never again left me alone. There were no stalking laws back then, but he was a stalker through and through. He used everything in his power to force me to stay in the relationship. I never loved him, but that did not matter to him.

I stayed with him for four years because I did not have the strength to fight his determination. I was deeply depressed and simply did not care enough to protect myself. At sixteen, I had learned how much pain a naïve young girl could experience.

To make matters worse, my very best friend, Trina, fell in love with a boy from my neighborhood. Our families did not like each other. She became completely besotted with him. I did not like him for I knew his family was a very troubled family that Trina should stay away from. I cautioned her, even begged her to be wary. Well, you know how love is. All my warnings fell on deaf ears.

When they grew closer together, he finally gave her the ultimatum, "I want you to choose between Dolores and me. I don't want you hanging around with her if you are my girlfriend." Trina came to me in tears.

I knew he did not like me. Trina and I had discussed this many times. She had tried to make us get to know each other and accept each other. We were having none of it. We already knew each other too well from the neighborhood. Our Hispanic pride forbade either of us to back off. To be honest, all he held against me was that too many boys were always hanging around me. I just knew they were the snobs of the neighborhood. His father was a cop and they seemed to think they were better than the rest of the families in the neighborhood. My brother had a reputation for fighting, which he had earned honestly. So Ramon had tainted our family's reputation, and we were therefore known as troublemakers. I was never in fights, but was known to be rather aggressive when I felt it was necessary.

So Trina tearfully told me one very gloomy day, "I'm sorry, I love him. What can I do? He is going to break up with me if I keep you as a friend!"

I said what any good friend should, "Then do as he says," I responded. "I understand."

"He said I can't even say hello to you if we pass each other down the hallway. You understand, don't you?"

"Of course, don't worry. I won't say hello or talk to you ever again. Goodbye and I hope you are happy," were the last words I said as I quickly walked away. I was heartbroken. This, I believe was all the more reason I could not fight off my stalker boyfriend.

I gave up on friendship then. I knew there really was no such thing as best friends. I had learned that people used that as a convenient way to attach themselves to someone and use them in their best interest. Well, I was done with that.

Throughout the years, many considered me their best friend, while I only considered them a friend. I insulated my heart from experiencing any more disappointments. I found many times over that I was right. There were many other girlfriends who considered me their best friend and soon after they confirmed it, the friendship ended when it was in their best interest to do so.

I did leave a slight door open, which was called faith. But now I never took a person's word for it, when they said they were my "best friend". I had matured in this area of my life. I looked toward their actions and kept a cautious distance. I learned to give my friendship without needing that extra closeness that could only spell trouble or pain.

The following years were dim years for me. I existed from day to day without much joy. Tony was a major part of my existence. It was a time of breaking up and making up again. He took me dancing just about every date because I refused to be alone with him where there were no people around. Bella and I had become friends and we double-dated everywhere together. I was no longer the nuisance or unwanted sister. We shared friends and many experiences together. We kept secrets and covered for each other to stay out of trouble with our mother.

The first time I tried to break up with Tony, a month into the relationship, I was shocked at his reaction. He begged me to reconsider or he would just kill himself rather than live without me. We were on our way home, walking and about four blocks from my home. It was evening and darkness had fallen. He ran into the middle of a normally busy street and knelt down in the middle. He swore he would not get up and off the street unless I took him back. Had I been more experienced, I would have walked away from that scene and let him figure out what he would do with his life. It would have saved me years of pain to come.

I was a naïve, innocent, kind girl who believed in God and that suicide was wrong. I could not stand to watch a human being hit by a car and killed because I did not do anything to get him off the street. A car would be coming any minute, and it would be too late. I begged him to get up and finally agreed that I would not break up with him. I had to promise him I meant it.

That was the defining moment of our relationship. After that incident, he was always figuring out ways to control me. He knew I did not want to be involved because I was still in love with Johnny. I was such an honest trusting fool; I thought if I told him the truth, it would make him see I was not good for him.

All my life I had felt unworthy of anyone's love and now I was suddenly faced with a person obsessed with keeping me as his girlfriend. I did not understand why he did not see me as others in my childhood had seen me. I didn't have experience with males, other than my brothers, who were always off at work.

Tony was always begging me to love him and I felt so guilty that I did not. He was very good at manipulation. He made me feel like a terrible, mean person who hurt him purposely. I was so depressed that I rapidly accepted my badness. He refused to listen to me when I told him we did not have a future together. He would counter that with a comment of "when we get married."

He figured out how easy it was to get me to agree to anything so long as my mother was not hurt. He became sickeningly sweet with my family. He realized how much control my mother had over me, how much I needed my mother's approval. So he began to use that against me.

I did not realize that he planned to make sure I lost my virginity so I would have no choice but to marry him. I had met Tony around September or October and by late February I was pregnant. It was then that I realized I was never going to get away from him.

I did not even realize what had happened. I felt it was my fault. I recall coming home that night after our date, getting in the shower and scrubbing so hard my skin turned a deep red. It was the classic scene I was to see later in life, over and over, as Americans became more aware of date rape. By the end of my shower, I was on the floor of our shower stall, silently crying brokenly, copious tears running down my face. I felt so dirty and bad. I just could not get myself into the large bed I shared with my mother. I was sure I was contaminated and my mother did not deserve to have me in the same room with her.

I was so under his control mentally that I blocked out the memory of me telling him to stop, pushing him away. I forgot the horrified feeling of the painful experience. I wanted to forget his grunting as he fought to control me to be able to finish the deed.

Tony was a good manipulator. Everyone thought he was God's gift to me. My family thought I was horribly spoiled and pitied him for his lot in life. What a master of reverse psychology he was! They saw me trying to break off the relationship. They saw him begging and pleading for me to stay with him. They did not know all the times of forced sex or the demeaning comments he made about me being worthless trash that not even a garbage man would pick up! He had taken my virginity, which in our community was the only precious thing a girl had of great value. If you were not a virgin until marriage, then you were worthless. He made sure I did not forget that every time I tried to leave him. In the end I stayed with him because it took too much effort to try to leave.

Over the four years of our relationship, I tried over and over to break it off. He went from threatening to tell my mother that I was a cheap whore, to again threatening to kill himself. If he felt I needed extra convincing he said he would make sure everyone knew we had sex and that he would destroy my reputation in our town. Our society treated unwed girls very harshly. They not only gossiped about her incessantly, but also ostracized her.

Shame controlled my every move. That first time we had sex, I became pregnant. I was seventeen, scared and horrified. He gloated but stuck to me even more so. I went to Bella to ask for help. We could not go to Letty because she would have judged me as a failure. Bella helped me through this crisis. Tony wanted to get married, but I cringed at the thought of marrying him for life. I decided I would leave town and give the baby up for adoption. He had no choice but to agree.

My mother had recently had a stroke in her late forties. Her health was very delicate. I felt sure that if she found out I was pregnant, it would kill her. I let Tony know if he dared tell her and something happened to her, he would never see me again.

For the first time he was unsure what to do. I could tell he wanted to use my pregnancy to force me into marriage, but I adamantly refused. You see, he blackmailed me any time I tried to leave him and swore he would tell my mother what a whore I was. I was terrified this would cause my mother a stroke and she would end up dead or like my sweet grandma had ended up—paralyzed. I let him know, "If you tell her and this happens, then I have no further need to stay with you. Not to mention that both my brothers will kill you." So I went away to San Antonio to have my baby and give it up for adoption.

I think now what a gutsy or naïve girl I was. I boarded a bus to San Antonio, Texas, without knowing where I was going to stay. I thank God he protected me. Once I got there, I asked a cabdriver to take me to a decent but cheap hotel. I had a little money from both my sister and Tony. Bella had graduated and was now working at a Hagar's sewing factory. Tony had gotten a work-study summer job.

I became pregnant in the latter part of February, so I was into my fourth month of pregnancy when I arrived in San Antonio in June. It turned out the cab driver was a greedy swine. He drove all over town running the meter until he figured out what my problem was. He offered me a room as a rental in his home with his wife and children. He took me there and asked me to wait in the car while he went to speak to his wife about it. She was a beautiful, meek Mexican-born lady. All I ever remember about her is her sweet smile and long suffering looks. I believe she was in the United States illegally and that is how this man controlled her. Not to mention she had a young son from this man.

I stayed with this family and became close to the lady's daughter, Maria. She was the swine's stepdaughter and he treated her horribly. She was a tough girl, very streetwise and gutsy. She had to be strong to survive that household. Her mother did not have the strength to stand up to the man. I wondered later if he perhaps physically abused her, like he abused Maria. Maria told me she was so glad I had come to live with them because he had stopped beating her since I came there.

The first time I saw how she was treated at the table, I was horrified. Maria took it so well; his treatment never even disconcerted her. He never allowed her to sit at the table with the family or me, whom he considered a guest. She was forced to eat only the leftovers, once we had finished eating. That made me feel very uncomfortable; I never wanted to eat too much for fear there would not be any left for Maria. She was forced to eat moldy bread, and just tear the moldy parts away. I was shocked and began to feel her mother was really a pathetic person to allow such treatment of her daughter. I had been born to a very strong, aggressive mother who felt there was a solution for just about any problem in the world. It was a real awakening to now live with such a weak mother.

Maria always made herself scarce when her stepfather was around. As always, my mouth got the better of me on several occasions. He could not mistreat her in my presence and expect not get my angry retorts on her behalf.

I noticed that if Maria was around, he reprimanded her for being in the way and if she was not around, he yelled at her to stop being so lazy and make herself useful. Well, I just had to let him know she made herself scarce because I overheard him tell her to stop getting in the way. We did not like each other, but we tolerated each other because he wanted my rent money and I needed a place to stay.

Both Maria and her mother begged me not to anger him. But I could not believe how this child lived. I suspected that what Maria had not told me but implied, was that her stepfather visited her during the night before I got there. It was not that she confided in me, but more her practical remark about no doubt she might already have a growing stomach like me, had she not been so fortunate to have us share the room.

Maria decided my problem was her problem and set out to find a solution to my dilemma. She found an adoptive family for my baby, the next-door neighbors. They had never been able to have another child after their first daughter was born. They wanted a baby badly. Maria was a true problem solver. She had learned to survive by solving her own problems, so she was an expert at it. All seemed to be going well. The adoptive parents wanted me to get to a doctor immediately and would pay all expenses if I would sign over my parental rights to them. I was happy that my baby would have a good, loving family.

The only thing I found wrong with them was that they spoiled their daughter and gave her anything she asked for. Coming from a family that always went without and never could afford to get everything they wanted I saw this as a positive thing. This did not last long.

The asshole found out about the deal and decided there was a profit to be made so he ranted and raved that he wanted a finder's fee! Maria advised me to leave. She told me now that he had the idea he could make money on my baby, he would not stop. So she and I set out to find an unwed mother's home where I could go.

To this day I will always support the Salvation Army. They saved a seventeen-year-old runaway and helped her deal with a pregnancy, a product of her date rape. They helped place her baby for adoption through the legal avenues. I went there on foot, once I got off the transit bus on the right street. I walked twenty-eight blocks with my suitcase in my hand. My feet were swollen beyond shape by the time I got there. But once I found that I was safe in that unwed mother's home, it didn't matter.

School started and I attended school there. Our records showed that the unwed mothers attended Madison High School as if our classroom was an extension site. I finally felt safe for the first time in years. I was with many girls in the same situation.

My mother did not want me to stay away. I was supposed to be visiting a friend for the summer. I insisted I wanted a chance to attend school in San Antonio and to at least let me attend one semester. Bella, who had such influence over our mother's decisions, supported my argument. My mother reluctantly agreed.

The Salvation Army people told me they had contacted the welfare office in my hometown to get them to pay for some of the costs of the home. All other expenses were to be paid by the prospective adoptive parents. It was a closed adoption and I was kept out of most of the decisions being made. I was so easily handled since I had never been allowed to make any decisions in my own home. My mother was a complete authoritarian parent. I thank God I was in good hands and that decisions made were in the interests of both me and my baby. I was still in that dazed, depressed state and had no real coping abilities at the time. They told me there was no going back because I would have to pay the family back for all the costs of having the baby if I decided to change my mind. The Welfare Department would become involved in deciding if I would be able to care for the baby should I decide to change my mind.

My mother's health was of the utmost importance and I was sure that I would not change my mind.

I had a healthy, full-term baby boy in the latter part of 1970. The hospital messed up and brought the baby to me, unaware I was giving it up for adoption. They never let the girls from the home get attached to their babies. I named him Noe. As I held Noe in my arms, my heart melted. I loved him the moment I held him. For the first time I thought, "I don't want to give him up!" and cried.

I had not signed the papers yet, so as soon as I went back to the home, I called my sister, Bella. She was stunned and immediately told me I could not change my mind.

"Think of Mom," she told me. "Don't do this to her. Her health is still very delicate. What if she has another stroke if you tell her?"

I cried so much my face was covered in tears and they were soaking my pajama top. I went back to my room and sunk into such a deep depression. I would not talk to anyone, or eat anything. I believe they called my sister because she came that weekend, forced me out of bed, got me dressed and took me outside for a walk. I finally accepted that there was no other way.

It was the 1970s, and good girls did not have children out of wedlock. My mother's health would not be able to sustain the embarrassment and ridicule of the neighborhood or the shame I would bring to the family.

I left a part of myself with that child and then proceeded to erase all memory of his existence. So much so that I even forced my mind to forget his actual birth date. I remember taking the hospital band, placing it in a deep pocket of a wallet, hiding the wallet at the bottom of a box filled with childhood mementos and sealing it. I never searched for it again, until years later when the pain had lessened. I couldn't find the box or wallet. I might have erased his birthday, but never Noe himself from my mind. Throughout my life, I have prayed that God has kept him safe and blessed his life…a mother's prayer, without a doubt.

Well, I was disillusioned with love and friendships…and in God. The only difference when I returned home was that I was much tougher. I had gone away from home and met many girls of different races. I had learned that nothing terrible had happened to me while I lived and shared my life with plenty of "bad girls." Instead, I enjoyed their company, their spontaneity, their self-esteem and even their careless disregard for breaking the rules.

Some came from wealthy families and were spoiled rotten. Getting pregnant was a way to get back at their wealthy, working parents. Others were not as fortunate, but the one thing I did realize was that every single one of those girls could argue and fight with their mothers. They could say no, and some even cussed their parents out. I was shocked and horrified but I realized that a bolt of lightning did not strike them down.

I remembered Louise, a beautiful, sandy-haired girl who had a deformity. Her right leg and arm were enlarged. I marveled that even with her deformity she had such personality. She was always smiling and would suddenly start singing at the top of her lungs, "Eli's comingggggg" and begin to do a spontaneous jig down the hallway. She had decided to name her baby Eli.

I met Donna, who came from a nearby town close to mine. We were very much alike, so we became good friends. We all had duties to do, and I volunteered to clean floors since I felt very inept in the kitchen. Donna enjoyed the dishwashing duty, which I could never understand. We always met after our duties to study and watch TV. Donna came from a broken home, a single mother who was brought up in a gang-infested area. She was not very bright, mostly because she had skipped too much school to hang out with her boyfriend. He had dropped her the moment he found out that she was pregnant. Her mother was on welfare and the Welfare Department had helped them send Donna to the unwed home for young girls. Throughout my stay there, I helped Donna with her homework and helped her get caught up. She was behind in both her English and writing skills.

I met another young girl...Sandra. I was cleaning floors when I overheard the head nurse scolding her. Marcy, the head nurse, was a wonderful person. I adored her and looked up to her always. I could not believe her angered tone toward Sandra. Sandra was crying and apologizing. I trusted Marcy enough to come and stand at the door, a frown very apparent. She told Sandra she was to stay in her room until a decision was made. Marcy asked me to sit down and told me that she would tell me what it was about because all the girls would have to be informed and a decision made whether Sandra would be leaving. She had been out without permission with her boyfriend and had contracted gonorrhea. Marcy asked me to be careful and not use her bathroom from this day forward. Then she explained to me how this venereal disease would more than likely harm her baby. I was shocked and horrified. I had never seen Marcy lose control and be so emotional. She had tears in her eyes. She truly cared for the girls and the coming babies.

Once I left the home, the little girl afraid to disappoint her mother was gone. I would still follow my cultural upbringing; it was too ingrained within me. But I also felt a strength to fight back and never let myself be made a victim again.

The first to encounter my changed attitude was Tony. I told him, "You will not touch me again; I will not ever again risk getting pregnant." Of course he thought nothing much of my ultimatum. He was sure things would be as before. I continued, "You head out anywhere to neck and I will be out of that car even if the car is moving!"

Of course, he thought I was bluffing. It did not take long before I proved him wrong. He could not believe that I was willing to get out of a fast moving car, but I made it clear, "I would rather die than get pregnant again!"

It took years to get over the sadness and depression generated by relinquishing my baby son to strangers. The relationship between Tony and me deteriorated…but he still refused to let go. It amazed me that Tony never asked about the baby. When I returned he acted like I had never been pregnant or gone away. I never saw him sad or troubled about giving up his flesh and blood.

He was now being unfaithful and all I cared about was to catch him at it to finally get out of the relationship. He had decided to sleep with a girl who lived four houses away from mine. His older brother was living with this girl's oldest sister. The two sisters lived alone in a rental house on the same block I did. Tony's sister, Teresa accidentally slipped up and did not realize I had caught it. I waited to make sure there was no doubt.

He dropped me off at midnight one night and he waited till I got inside. As soon as he drove away, I went out to watch him drive straight to her house. She greeted him in her nightie and they walked inside. Throughout the night, I went outside to check to see if his car was still parked at her door. I wanted to have irrefutable facts to confront him with.

During the sleepless night, I cried out to God and begged him for help. I asked him to please put love in my heart for this man, if I had to marry him. Otherwise, I asked God to have him fall madly in love with someone else and leave me alone. If I was to find someone to share my life, I asked God to pick him for me, for I had done a terrible job so far, and could not trust myself anymore. I asked for forgiveness for the words of rejection I had spoken as a young, confused child.

I confronted Tony with the facts, and told him to leave, that we were through. I returned his promise ring and any gift he had ever given me. I wanted nothing from him. I am sure he left thinking he would be returning, like so many other times. But I felt a sense of peace and freedom. Something I had never felt before.

Two weeks later he called to say he had met a beautiful girl named Lola, and he was madly in love with her. But Tony had a lot of anger toward me for my constant rejection. He said, "I finally found someone worth being with and now I don't want to spend my time with someone as worthless as you."

He meant to hurt me, of course. I couldn't wait to hang up. I dropped the phone on its cradle and ran around with the most joy I had felt in years. "Thank you, God! Thank you, God!" I cried aloud. "He found someone else! You answered my prayer!"

My mother came out of the kitchen to see what the ruckus was. I acted the part of the angry, spurned lover. I felt free for the first time since I met Tony. I began to smile again, my faith in God restored.

~Chapter 13~

I went out with my girlfriends and connected with an old friend. We had been in school together and he had a crush on me until he met an older girl that he fell in love with and married. They had a little girl together. Now, a few years later, he was divorced and had full custody of his little girl. His ex-wife had left with a man and abandoned my friend and their child. I had always considered him a good friend. He let me know he had thought of me often after his marriage fell apart. I went out with him a few times and he told me he was going back to Houston where he now lived. He had been in town visiting his family and letting his parents enjoy their grandchild. He asked me to marry him and go to Houston with him and be the mother to his little girl that she so desperately needed. I was so tempted, but I remembered that I had left it in God's hands. I cared for him but there was no love on my part. I suspected even if he felt he could love me, he wanted to make a family for his daughter more than he wanted me for his wife. I told him I could not leave my mother but would think on it. He left, called a few times but we both knew it was not meant to be.

Something very interesting happened during this time. I stumbled across Johnny at a store. My heart still raced at the sight of him. I kept my distance but felt him staring. I went home and called up my girlfriends to make plans for the night. When the phone rang, I was stunned to hear Johnny's voice. He said a quick hello before he asked, "You still have that boyfriend?"

After a slight pause I said, "If you are referring to Tony, no, we broke up some months ago."

He asked me out and I could not believe the bitterness that came rushing forward. I was not the naïve young girl anymore. I laughed and responded, "You think I have been sitting around for four years waiting on your call? I must have really made a fool of myself if you thought that!"

He grew curt and said, "You don't need to be rude! You can just say no."

I laughed again, and said, "Well I have plans to go out with my girlfriends and they are a lot more trustworthy than most guys that I have had the misfortune to get involved with. And where is your ex-girlfriend? Oh that's right, I heard through the grapevine she dumped you for someone else? She got herself pregnant while you were away and came to your house to return your engagement ring?"

There was a long silence and then he said, "I don't want to talk about her ever again. You have changed from the nice girl you used to be. Well, I see you are busy tonight, maybe another day?"

I told him not to bother to call again; I would be busy every night from now on. I readily agreed with him that I had changed. I was no one's fool anymore. We said a definite goodbye.

A few weeks later, I was asked out on a date. Manny was the man God had chosen for me...I felt it from the moment we met. He was sweet and a true gentleman. He was somewhat shy and reserved, and on our first date, I talked the whole night. When he took me home, I walked inside, closed the door and leaned against it. I took a deep breath and realized my throat was hoarse. I was mortified when I realized I had talked non-stop. I thought to myself, *I have surely given him a headache and he will never call me again.*

Later during our relationship, he told me that he had in fact gone straight to his best friend's house and told him he was in love. He told his friend he was crazy about me and couldn't wait to see me again.

Manny told me that he had always liked me since high school but knew I had a boyfriend. God is awesome! He not only answered all my prayers, but he had Tony be the one who told Manny I was free.

Apparently, Manny's best friend was a mutual friend of Tony's. Tony had dropped by for a quick visit while Manny was there. He suddenly said, "I got to go, Lola is waiting for me."

Manny caught the name and asked, "Lola? I thought your girlfriend was Dolores?" Tony let him know that we had broken it off some time ago when he had met Lola.

Manny couldn't wait to get to work the following Monday to ask me out. God had even placed us in the same factory and the same area.

We dated regularly and eventually exclusively. He had been seeing another girl who worked at the same factory and it was rather awkward to break it off, because the girl was truly in love with Manny. He had not given her any reason to see their casual dating as more than a friendship, but as it often happens, one cannot always control one's heart.

My heart was joyous and yet heavy during the first few months we dated. I felt I would soon have to break it off because of my past. When I did let Manny know I did not want to continue dating, he grew very quiet and then asked to know why. He said he felt he deserved at least to know why. I told him I could not tell him, it was not something I would confide to anyone.

He wouldn't let it go and insisted that I could tell him anything, that I would have nothing to fear. So eventually, when I noticed the tears of sadness in his eyes, he wore me down. I took that leap of faith I never knew I had within me, and I confided in him about the rape. He listened patiently as he held me in his arms and said, "If it's because you are not a virgin that is no reason to break up."

I told him there was a lot more to it than that. He encouraged me to tell him everything. When I did, all he felt was anger toward Tony for all I had suffered while forced to endure four years of a relationship with him that I had not wanted.

I was truly happy to have the burden of my secret lifted off my shoulders. We continued to date and soon after, he asked me to marry him. I was stunned and the first thing that came to my mind was my very uselessness in doing things around the house. I had never been able to learn to be as capable as my sisters were.

I answered him, when he asked, "I can't marry you! I don't know how to cook! As a matter of fact, I don't know how to do anything but wash clothes!"

He laughed and said, "Well I know how to cook so we won't starve."

I said, "Yes," and was amazed that he planned a big wedding to prove to me how much I deserved it and to undo all the horrible things Tony had said and done.

He said, "I want you to wear that white dress down the church isle that you deserve to wear." I was in tears because he made me feel so cherished. And for the first time, I realized I was not the worthless whore Tony had convinced me that I was.

Three months from the day he asked me out, we were engaged. He did the ceremonious "asking the bride's hand in marriage," by bringing his parents to a formal dinner he and I planned so our parents could meet. He got nervous when it came time to ask for my hand in marriage and had to be prompted by his mother, which made us all laugh as he turned bright red. But he eventually got through the speech and my mother agreed to let me marry him. When he placed the engagement ring on my finger, I felt for the first time a sense of completeness.

Nine months from the day Tony and I had broken off, I was dressed in a beautiful, white wedding dress, headed for the church to marry Manny. We married at my church of attendance, with bridesmaids and grooms, maid of honor and best man at our side. Our reception was held at our local community center with more than eight hundred guests in attendance. We hired a live Latin band for dancing, as was the custom.

The only cloud over our wedding was Tony. The day before the wedding, he called begging me to not marry and to take him back. He said he had always talked about me to Lola and she had finally told him that he must still be in love with me and to do something about it before I married.

I panicked for a moment before the peace and security Manny had instilled in me with his loving kindness took over. I told Tony it was over and no amount of threats would change that. He tried and I told him to do whatever he pleased, but to make sure to hide if he caused my mother any harm.

He showed up at the wedding reception and begged my older brother to let him in. He promised that he would not cause trouble…that he just wanted to see me for one last time. Both Manny and I were very angry at my brother for letting him in. All my brother said was, "Well hell, I did not know what to do with a crying man in front of all those guests other than let him in!" Again, I realized Tony had used manipulation to get his way. But that night, my past was buried forever and I would never again feel as worthless as I had during that sad episode in my life. I had God back in my life, and the sun was shining on my life. I no longer felt the isolation or darkness weighing me down.

~Chapter 14~

I wish I could say life was all sunshine and happiness after I married Manny, but I doubt any couple can say that. I was faced with the same problem my mother had faced with her mother-in-law. She was not happy that we had rushed into marriage. Of course everyone's first thought was that I must be pregnant. Had they only known how very much I had decided that I would never find myself unwed and pregnant again. Manny was a gentleman and once he knew my past problems with Tony, he would never have forced the issue of sex.

I had been brought up to be grateful and I was so grateful to Manny for his love and acceptance of me that I was determined to win my mother-in-law over. I refused to feud with the woman who had given Manny life. I knew how much his parents meant to him and that I was the intruder in the family. It was up to me to win my mother-in-law over. So I was patient and determined to hold nothing against her. She loved her children and did not have an easy time of letting any of them go. Sometimes it was painful to sit through her careless remarks toward me and my inabilities to be a real wife—one that could cook and do all the things females are suppose to know how to do before they get married. I kept a lot of what she told me to myself and did not worry Manny with it. There were times when he overheard or she directed her remarks to both of us and he was not as tolerant of her as I was.

I sensed that Manny loved me enough that had I said, 'I don't want to see your mother again', that it would have ended the problem. But I could not do that to her or to Manny. He didn't deserve to end up paying the price for marrying me. It took years of long suffering to win my mother-in-law over. It was not until she saw how happy her son was that she finally opened her heart.

And even though I may not have learned to cook, I learned how to do everything else. I kept a clean house, worked full time, went to college, devoted every moment I could to our sons, once they came along.

She realized I was not taking advantage of her son, but that I carried a lot of the burden myself. It took years but the day came when she told me, "The daughter-in-law I felt sure was a mistake, turned out to be the best one, and those I thought were good turned out to be problems." I smiled when she said that, for I knew we had finally come to respect each other.

By then she had seen me stand by her son through difficult times, whether it was illness or loss of employment. She saw me encourage him to go to college and to move toward buying our homes rather than renting. She began to call on me if she had a legal problem so I could advise her what to do.

We have become good friends now. She knows when she needs a shoulder to lean on, that I am there for her. She has confided things to me that she has not told her own children. We enjoy reading and working out puzzles together. When my sweet father-in-law, whom I considered the father I never had, became ill and eventually passed away, I went back home to be there to help them out. I took my sweet father-in-law to any medical appointments because he was refusing medical help and I seemed to be the only person he would listen to. We cried together and held each other when that sweet man finally lost the will to live. He was a proud man to the end, always saying there was nothing wrong with him.

As for Manny and me? Well, we spent years getting to know each other. During that whirlwind courtship, I don't believe we had the time to do so. Manny's stubbornness and pride put a lot of strain on our marriage, but I am sure I was equally as difficult. I learned to give in to the little battles and save my energy for the crucial ones. I made sure to let him know that I refused to be stubborn to the point of ignorance as many in our culture did.

We fell in love and out of love many times over. We have dealt with infidelity issues, parenting issues and marriage crisis issues.

I had so much growing to do. After our marriage I found I could not get pregnant. What an irony! Now that I could have a child of my own to keep, I could not conceive. I had no way of knowing how much damage my childhood trauma had caused. As much as I wanted to make it all go away, I realized early in our marriage that I had to face some of those issues in order to find happiness. I have no idea how I figured this out, but it might have been my constant reading and searching for answers. I began to read self-help books and psychology books.

My desire to have a child propelled me into chaos. I feared I would be an abusive mother. I was sure I would spank my own children and not listen or understand them. I had to face my painful childhood head-on. So I began to immerse myself into parenting issues. I was attending church and my mother and I had become close enough for me to talk to her about my feelings. I remember confronting her about my childhood spankings and how crippled I now felt in being a parent. I was sure that was one reason I could not conceive.

My mother was hurt when I told her what those childhood years of pain had done to me and she eventually asked for my forgiveness. At first she insisted she had been a good mother. It was not until I told her that this was not about blame…I realized she had done the best she could, considering the abuse she had witnessed and suffered from her own sister. She was able to understand how much I loved her and felt she had been an awesome mother…she was just a mother who had unfairly been saddled with the total responsibility of raising five children. I blamed my father for not being there to help her with the strain of parenting and the financial support that was necessary.

Once my mother and I faced the physical abuse issue together, I felt a great burden lifted from my heart. It took three years and a miracle from God, but I finally conceived my first son. By then, unknown to me, I had pushed Manny away with so much anger and pain, that he had gotten involved in an affair that lasted close to a year. He terminated it without me ever knowing about it. I did not find out until twenty years later. It still amazes me how naïve and gullible I was; so very trusting. Once he gained my trust, I gave it so completely it was easy for him to deceive me.

In any case, he had terminated this affair and was determined to make our marriage work. So after I became pregnant, he finally reached some happiness and stability in our marriage. But always, I seemed to be driven by unknown monsters. I never felt it was enough. I had to be a better mother—he had to be a better father—we had to have a better home—I had to have a better job—he had to have a better job—he had to get an education—he had to get a degree—I had to get an education—I had to get a degree…and the never-ending list went on. Manny tried to sometimes attempt to satisfy my requests. At other times he just refused and became a stubborn mule that refused to budge.

I believe this is what drove Manny to have an affair in the first place. He felt a loss of control within our marriage and chose to grasp control in some way. By the time I found out about the affair, even if I felt all the feelings of betrayal, there seemed to be no reason to beat a dead horse, since it had happened so long ago.

Now I convinced Manny to join the service so we could gain the veterans benefits to help us buy our first home. We were still living in that small Texas hometown I hated so much. Two years into the marriage he joined the Army and six months later I followed him to North Carolina. This was when he made a choice to end the affair and agree to leaving our hometown as I wanted. I was still having problems with my mother-in-law and I felt sure we needed distance in order that we not end up enemies. She was supportive of this plan because she wanted us to buy our own home.

Our first son was conceived while we were in North Carolina and we tried desperately to have another. We wanted to have our children while he was in the service. I again had trouble getting pregnant and it took me until two months before Manny was to leave the service for me to conceive. He refused to stay in so I could have the baby while he was still in the service. He hated military life and throughout his stay in the military our marriage suffered because of it.

When I finally learned about the affair he had ended, I wondered if the reason he was so bitter in the military was because he regretted making the wrong choice and staying with me instead of that other woman.

We returned to our hometown to try again. I was still driven by my inner demons. So, pregnant as I was, I enrolled in college and took a full load. I made the dean's list that year and found out what that was, for the first time in my life.

My mother-in-law was one of the lucky women of her time who had actually been educated and pampered during her childhood. She was my source of information for she was also very driven to have her nine children get an education. She saw how I felt about getting a degree and took me under her wing. We slowly got closer, learning to appreciate each other's strengths. When I achieved the dean's list, she was the one I went to and she made me feel so proud of my achievement.

Manny sometimes felt railroaded when my mother-in-law and I joined forces to get him to do something we felt was for his own growth. We were able to coerce him through three years of college until he said, "No more!" If I had trouble getting him to see buying a home was the best thing, I went to my mother-in-law who readily took my side and got Manny to acquiesce.

All this effort for me and Manny to grow did not stop the demons within me. I was never satisfied. I did not know what I lacked but something propelled me forward. I believe I would have continued this way until I drove Manny away had I not somehow found some answers. I realized I was living my mother's life in a sense. I had to be in control of every decision regarding the children, the finances, our education, our jobs and our future. This is all I had seen as I grew up. My mother had been my only role model. I basically had unmanned my husband. When he made a decision I criticized it, fought it, countered it and many times changed it. My husband grew more belligerent and stubborn, a trait he was already born with. He learned my weaknesses and I learned his. We then used our weaknesses against each other. I gave in and lost many times because there was one thing I could not stand, and that was screaming or fighting. It took me back to my childhood years. Manny figured this out early in our marriage and became an expert at raising his voice in front of the children to win an argument. I wanted our two boys to grow up in a stress-free environment. I did not want them to be impacted by verbal abuse or out-of-control anger as I had seen in my young life.

So I found ways to win the most important battles and let go of those that weren't as important. I took on more responsibility than I should have in order to have control over the decisions. Any of the children's needs were my responsibility. What they wore, where they attended school, what doctors they saw, and when they ate, slept, and woke up. Manny was marginally involved with them even if he was a good father. He played with them and when they grew older they often wrestled on the floor where he always let them win.

I always took the highest paying jobs I could find, even if it meant working twice as hard or long. I typically earned more than Manny, which I now realize was my way of showing him that I did not need him, if he were ever to abandon me and the children. I have since realized that there were plenty of abandonment issues I never dealt with regarding my father.

Throughout our married life and our children's lives, I was hovering over them and protecting them from their father's possible abandonment. I failed to see that Manny was not the type to leave. He had been brought up in a two-parent home, where both parents had stuck it out regardless of what problems they had faced. By the time I realized this, both my boys had not developed the best relationship with their father, and Manny had become a remote and unapproachable father.

Of course, Manny was not a saint. He had plenty of issues of his own. One big issue was infidelity. As all typical Hispanics, he had a roaming eye. He liked the ladies and kept that secret very well hidden from a very trusting and gullible wife. I was too involved in staying in control of my own issues that I did not have the energy or desire to figure out what Manny was into or what was lacking within him. Even though he chose to be unfaithful, it was always just a passing thing. He never searched for anything lasting, after that long affair at the beginning of our marriage.

The interesting thing about our marriage together is that what usually drives most couples to divorce, is what drove Manny and me closer together. If we struggled financially, or faced a different crisis, we came together to talk it out and work it out.

There was a period of unemployment for Manny and it threw him into depression. He truly could not stand being a kept man. I was working to support the family and he was angry and belligerent during those days. His self-esteem plunged very low until he finally landed a career position that he has kept to this day. It amazed me how quickly he recuperated from his low self-esteem the moment he was employed again.

When Manny faced a health crisis in 1988, and was diagnosed with cancer, we clung together. He had to undergo an operation and radiation treatments. He took time off from work for a few weeks, but soon returned to work even while taking his radiation treatments. I saw my husband for the first time at his weakest, yet he refused to give up and stop working. So I acquiesced and worked hard to lighten the load anywhere else I could so he could get himself to work and back. Doing that wiped out all the energy he had within him.

I was obsessed with being a good parent and read books and attended classes to learn what the experts were advising at the time. The boys were fairly well behaved, stable kids and soon learned that Mom hurt more when she needed to spank them than they did. They took full advantage of it.

I had set a rule for myself in order to be in control. I was to spank no more than two times and always on the bottom. I hardly ever had to spank my youngest son because he was intelligent enough to figure out that if they listened and followed the rules, a spanking was never necessary. His older brother loved to test the waters, while the younger brother learned from his older brother's mistakes.

I had a whole ritual of what would happen if I felt the boys needed a spanking. First came the scolding lecture, then they were sent to their room to think about what they had done and I would be up later to administer the whacks to their bottom, usually with a belt. I never spanked them hard because it hurt me just to think of spanking them. When they grew up they told me they usually went to the bathroom and stuffed their bottoms with lots of toilet paper so it would not hurt. They planned making a lot of crying and screaming to make me feel real bad because they knew how much I hated to spank them.

Manny could not understand my obsession with being a good parent, or why I never felt I was doing it right. He seemed to have no problem thinking that kids would grow up fine on their own, with only the necessary rules to keep them out of trouble. I felt that that was uncaring, and an act of a lazy parent. In the end parenting for us became one of the greatest pitfalls in our marriage.

The day came when the boys told me they needed some space and were no longer young kids to be overprotected. Of course, they were still in elementary. Steve, our eldest, was headed for seventh grade and Pete was in fifth grade. Manny told me I needed to let the boys have their space.

We talked about how we both felt that we really weren't done parenting and that we would both love to have a girl. I brought up the idea of adoption. We talked it over with the boys and Manny was willing if the boys were okay with it. The boys felt this would give them the space they needed and would keep their mom occupied with an adopted sister, so they were all for it.

So we went to a foster/adopt agency meeting and, after a lengthy process, were certified to be foster parents. Once we fostered for a few years, if the placement of a child was successful, we could proceed to adopt.

We wanted two sibling sisters between seven to ten years of age. We were told babies were almost impossible to get and if we wanted a child it was better to go for the older kids. That seemed good to us. We felt sure that a sibling set would help the children adjust better.

Well, after a few months' wait we got the call for possible placement. It was a group of three sibling sisters, the youngest one was five, the middle one was seven and the oldest was twelve. It was not what we had requested, but after talking it over we agreed to accept them into our home. What courage, an experienced foster parent would have thought, when in truth taking in three sisters was complete ignorance! We had no idea that all of the years of parenting our boys meant nothing when parenting a child from the system.

The agency cautioned us about the twelve-year-old, Anna. They felt she had tendencies toward being over-protective and difficult with regards to her younger sisters. Vanessa, the middle sister was supposed to be a joy, helpful, friendly and well behaved. Lydia, the youngest was said to be adorable and loving. It amazes me today to see how very little the system knew about these children.

Anna and I had a talk regarding our roles with the girls. I told her they would be safe with us and I wanted to be a mother to them so very much. She would never have to worry about her sisters for I would do that for her. I just wanted her to be a young girl her age and be happy.

Anna gave me a beautiful, sunny smile and agreed. I never had one battle or confrontation with her regarding the girls' care. She trusted me completely. She became a joy to the family. Even though she had many emotional issues and seemed to get along fine with the boys, she seemed to crave acceptance. We readily gave her that by including her and treating her with the respect and most freedom we gave our boys. She had a real problem with equality of the sexes when she joined our family. She was determined to prove to everyone that men and women were equal in every aspect. She camouflaged her stubbornness and willfulness behind what she called debates. She said she loved debating and would sometimes spend hours debating any issue with anyone in the family who was willing to go for hours with her. Our oldest son and Anna enjoyed challenging each other.

Our home became lively, noisy and full of laughter. It terrified our boys to have three such alien beings invading their home, and they took refuge in their rooms a lot of the time. But they also loved them and were very protective of their new little sisters.

Steve and Anna became good friends, mainly because Steve loved to be adored by a younger sister, while Anna was in a state of adoration over her oldest, handsome and smart brother. She found out that he could challenge her in her arena of debate and win the argument. For years, they debated and grew close as a brother and sister. Sometimes they went weeks without talking to each other because their debates had turned into fights when Anna refused to give in to Steve's point of view. She was growing stronger in accepting rejection from others and not feeling the terror of abandonment within her. Steve gave her plenty of practice in this by throwing her out of his room and a few hours later allowing her to go back and play a board game with him and Pete.

Our home became a house of rules and consequences. There was a rule for everything you could think of and a consequence for every misdeed that was done. No one was allowed into someone else's room without that person's permission. The same applied to using anything that belonged to someone else. Anna thrived on boundaries even if she fought them every step of the way with her debating qualities. She was a lovely child whom everyone seemed to love, for her heart, though badly bruised before she got to us, was still a heart full of love. She became very close to Manny, her dad, but confided all her fears and sad moments with me. We both knew that she was truly a blessing that God had sent us.

Vanessa was an interesting child. She was not one to wear her emotions on her sleeve like her older sister Anna did. On the surface she was as sweet as candy, but her deeper hidden personality was not so mellow. She was a grudge holder, jealous, envious and whiney when she did not get her way. Yet, she was also readily helpful and pleasant. I yearned to get to know this daughter more deeply for she was not an easy child to get close to. She kept her heart very guarded and distant.

Vanessa, I soon learned hid a second agenda when she was helpful. It was her means of controlling her environment. When she helped, she did things her own way and I soon learned that meant always the opposite of what I had told her to do. It took her a while before she realized she did not have to help in order to be loved. Once she discovered this, she never volunteered to help unless asked. She had little self-esteem and needed constant reassurance. Yet she was such a sweet-natured child, always shying away from conflict and so easy to love.

Pete noticed her fragility and became her knight. He was watchful of her and always had a ready smile of encouragement if she seemed to need one. His protective nature over Vanessa helped her slowly become more self-assured, knowing she could run to Pete when she was afraid. He never let her down and had such a matter-of-fact way of dealing with things, that she trusted him.

When we took vacations, Steve and Anna paired off to ride the scary rides. Pete would dutifully stay with Vanessa, who was too young for the scarier rides, and rode with her on those she could handle. It was wonderful to see how well our boys had accepted the girls as their own sisters. Their facial characteristics were so much like our own; people had a hard time believing they were not our own biological children.

We struggled through the system, slowly gaining more rights over the girls and eventually terminating all parental rights so they could be free for adoption. The biological mother, though not at all able to parent, going from boyfriend to boyfriend, drinking and partying, still did not want to give up her rights as a mother.

Lydia, our youngest daughter, was a complete and unexpected surprise. She had so much spunk and fight in her, and she was angry at the world. Her life had been disrupted one too many times. She did not trust anyone, including us. She had been the little terror of the house with the previous foster parents and had not learned much there. At five, almost six, she did not know even the basic skills of wiping her bottom. She would not dress herself, or comb her hair. She fought everyone who did anything she did not want them to do. Getting her dressed and combed in the mornings was an all-out struggle. She fought and kicked and hit until she got her way.

Both Steve and Pete were horrified of their littlest sister and did everything they could to stay as far away as possible from her. She was very coy and manipulative, yet aggressive. She had never learned that there was any other way but her way.

Our home became a battle ground with Lydia. She opposed everything we tried to teach her. At her age, she felt she knew better than anyone what was best for her. Both her sisters tried to stay away from her even though they did spend quality time playing together. The minute Lydia became rebellious and aggressive they wanted no part of being around her. This only angered Lydia more and made her more aggressive.

I attended class after class to learn how to deal with such an out-of-control child. She had attachment disorder and all the girls had ADD (Attention Deficit Disorder). All of them had control issues, abandonment issues, trust issues and low self-esteem.

It was hard to believe Lydia had low self-esteem for she also had traces of narcissistic behavior. Her biological mother was diagnosed as narcissistic and also had ADD. It was hard for me to understand how a child who demanded the world cater to her every whim could have such low self-esteem, but I was told that she did.

The first year they were with us, they wore me out with their demands. Lydia expected so much of a mother and when I did not cater to her whims she retreated back into the world of doubt and distrust. After a year of utter chaos, I set my foot down and said no more!

I set up a system of accountability for the kids, and timeouts became the way to assert my rights as a parent to say no. Lydia sometimes had to be dragged or carried to the timeout chair, but she eventually learned that all the kicking and screaming only made the timeout ordeal last longer.

Slowly our home got back to some sense of normalcy. I learned that the girls were stubborn, and their distrust of others made teaching them new skills ten times more difficult than teaching our own boys. Just teaching them to brush their teeth daily, flush the toilet at every use, eat slowly and with utensils, took me years to do. Constant reminders, repeating the same instructions over and over until they finally accepted it. We set up a star reward system, whereby when the girls achieved a set goal they earned a star. Rewards were handed out weekly on Saturdays, and could be anything from a double-scooped ice cream cone to going to the movies or having a special night out.

Anna soon learned that college was not meant for rich kids only. She was amazed and came to tell me that her teacher had told her she could go to college and verified with me if this was true. They always had to check any information with more than one or two sources. I told her it was so and I would hope that she would go to college when she completed high school. She went around with an awed look for a few days, talking about how she was going to college when she grew up.

Anna was so good with younger children; she decided she would be a teacher. We worked with her to stay focused and bring up her grades. She had believed that she was dumb and as we encouraged her, she found she had strengths that she was not aware of. She was an excellent math student, and once she got her teacher's positive reinforcement, she worked hard at being at the top of the class in math.

I loved to read and so it was not long before all three girls went around with a book in their hands. We would sit around and share the stories we read, recounting them out loud to each other.

Being a parent to them was not easy. They took so much, and left me little time or energy for myself. But in the long run, they were worth every effort as I saw them blossom into beautiful, self-assured, strong, independent young ladies.

We were strict about homework and grades. We let all our children know we expected them to be able to attend a university so their grade point average needed to be up there. The girls listened more than the boys did, since they were amazed that one day, they were going to be in college.

Anna said no one from her biological family had ever even graduated from high school and she was going to be the first one to attend college. The younger girls idolized their older sister and wanted to do everything she did. Anna was such a fantastic older sister to them; it was easy to see why they loved her so. She was the only person they truly trusted without reserve.

Anna had loved the movie "The Little Mermaid" and she knew every single word and phrase to it. She could imitate some of the characters, Sebastian in particular. She would entertain her sisters by doing imitations and I would hear them laughing as Anna would pucker her lips and say, "Now you got to pucker your lips like this." This was a part of the movie where Sebastian was teaching Ariel, the little mermaid how to kiss. I would sit with them and laugh at her antics.

So our children grew up, Manny and I had finally reached a point in our marriage that I no longer pushed him to grow if he did not want to. The girls had taken care of using up all my energies, so that I had none left to worry about Manny or me.

Anna graduated from high school and was given a four-year scholarship by our school district to become a teacher. All she had to do in return was teach two years for that school district. We were so proud of her. She was so proud of herself. Though she had not totally become self-assured, she had learned that she was a valuable, loveable individual and could do anything she set her mind to do.

Well, love decided to come Anna's way, which, I am afraid, put all her college plans on hold for she fell deeply in love with her young man and soon was planning a wedding. It was a grand scale wedding because the groom's parents wanted it that way. We bought her wedding dress and she was the most beautiful bride I had ever seen. Her long black, waist-length hair hung in ringlets down her back. My sister, Letty, who had always loved crafts and was an excellent seamstress, made the most beautiful headpiece and veil imaginable.

Our girl had reached adulthood. She now has a wonderful, loving husband and a beautiful little son of her own. Oh the joy I feel in my heart when I see her loving tenderness toward her child. For in her actions, she lets me see she indeed learned all I wished to teach her. She had two examples of motherhood, and she honors me by following my example.

Vanessa seemed determined to always be seen as the good little girl. She felt that was the only way to be loved or not abandoned. As time went by, she became obsessed with being perfect. Her handwriting had to be perfect, her grades had to be high, and her bedroom had to be very organized and clean. She moved things around the house, like scotch tape, stapler, hammer, screwdrivers and things of that nature. We found that if we needed to know where anything was, all we had to do was ask Vanessa. This sort of control was important to her. She arranged all the cupboards and utility drawers to know what was in them. Sometimes this was helpful, other times it was annoying. The family learned to deal with it because it was important to Vanessa to have this control over her life. As she became more self-assured, she became less of a perfectionist. The day came when she didn't care to fix her drawers or her room and I missed the perfectionist child she once had been!

Vanessa worked at never doing anything wrong. She was the perfect little girl and teen until she got to her senior year. At that time, she had a bad case of senioritis, and was fortunate to have gotten a high enough GPA (Grade Point Average) that she graduated with high honors in spite of it.

She received scholarships along with grants to get her started at the local university. She has grown to be a lovely, very capable young lady. She is studying to be a forensic psychologist. She is an amazing young woman with very little ADD and a lot of focus. She is so much like Pete in many ways, her buddy as they grew up. Pete always learned from Steve's mistakes and Vanessa has opted to learn from Anna's mistakes. She has determined not to have a boyfriend until she obtains her degree so she will not get sidetrack on her career goals and degree. I am so proud of her determination to succeed. She is definitely worth all the sacrifice and tears I cried as I worked with her to get her to adulthood.

Lydia was the most challenging child of the three. I can't say there weren't times that I did not regret accepting three sibling sisters instead of two. Yet, I learned to love Lydia very much and could never see myself letting her go. My own mother loves Lydia dearly and prayed for us constantly. Lydia had attachment disorder, which meant she could not trust or get close to others. She had an extremely guarded heart and would never allow anyone close enough to hurt her again.

So, my mother said I had ended up with a hellion of my own. She said Lydia was very much like I had been as a child. The same behaviors I had exhibited were now being reciprocated by Lydia. My mother was very glad that I had gotten my just reward and adopted a Lydia. Lydia was rebellious and obstinate. One time she was throwing a tantrum and kicked my knee out so badly, I have had arthritis ever since and have trouble walking on it in winter. Poor Lydia now feels so remorseful when she sees me limp during winter. One of the many deeds she wishes she could undo.

She has grown into a beautiful young lady. People who meet us say she looks so much like me and cannot believe she is adopted. She is spunky and full of life and very intelligent. She loves to write poetry, and even though she is only a junior, she has already earned a scholarship for college from the governor for high-star test achievement. She wants to get a degree in child psychology. Her desire is to work with disadvantaged kids or as a probation officer, helping guide them to better choices in life.

Manny and I are very proud of our children and love all of them equally. Even though I have always had to explain to the girls that as we have five different fingers in our hand and each one performs a vital function, so is the love we have for each of our children. For the girls, needing to know they are loved as much as our biological sons is very important.

Life has been good to us as a whole. We have remained married for over thirty years. I have never forgotten my little Noe, and when the time was right, he was the main reason I became a foster mom. I took in abandoned children from the foster care system to make up for the one child I could not have.

I can't say our marriage has been a bed of roses, but it's been a good one. But it is true that time does heal all wounds and maturity does come with age. So I welcome the passing of time, for with it comes wisdom as well as the fruits of all my labors.

To contact "Dolores": survivordolores@yahoo.com

"Lynetta Marie's" Story

~Chapter 1~

Yes, I'm a child of the fifties, born in the heartland of America. And yes, I was abused: physically, mentally, emotionally and sexually. Of course, all of that made me what I am today. The most unsettling part of what it made me is that I seem to have become a perpetual victim. But I'm working diligently to change that. However, a lot of good came out of it, also. And they weren't all "bad" times.

I was born right up the street from my grandmother's house in your typical small Kansas town about fifty miles south of Kansas City. What a great place for a kid to grow up. Main Street naturally ran through the heart of town. The middle of our town is a square, which in most small towns contains the county courthouse, but we had a park with a bandstand in the middle and all the community gatherings took place there.

The first four or five years of my life were happy times. I remember so many things, but they are all jumbled and disjointed memories: like the Model T Ford that we had that my daddy kept so shiny; our apartment over the drugstore in Kansas City; one Fourth of July when I decided to see if the sparkler stayed hot after it went out; making cinnamon toast on the space heater in the kitchen because we didn't have any "modern" conveniences. Then I remember suddenly, my little brother, Gary, and I were with Grandma and Grandpa Rush, and I was starting school in Paola.

Grandpa always planted a garden, so we had lots of fresh corn, potatoes, squash, onions, and tomatoes all summer long. We spent a lot of time canning every summer, too. It was a lot of work, but it was worth it. We may not have had much money, but we surely had enough to eat. All of the canned goods were stored in the root cellar under the house. And that's where we would go if the weather got bad and there were tornadoes in the area.

Every Saturday morning, my brother and I were allowed to walk, by ourselves, to the movie theater, which was eight blocks away. Everyone knew everyone else and who was married to who and who lived on the "right" side of the tracks, so we were safe.

My brother and I each had a quarter to spend. With that puny little quarter we got into a double-feature movie, with a newsreel and a cartoon, plus we had enough for popcorn, candy and a soda pop. That's where I fell in love with all the cowboy stars especially my favorite, Hopalong Cassidy. But mostly, I fell in love with their horses.

    I don't remember the movie we saw with Daddy, but I remember a type of cartoon where the audience was asked to Sing-A-Long. The song was Swiss Miss, and we "followed the bouncing ball", which bounced along the words to the song on the screen: "I miss, my miss, my Swiss Miss misses me. I miss the kiss, my Swiss Miss gives to me. . . ." I also remember Daddy taking us to a neighborhood bar so that I could sing for the people in there. Daddy stood me on the bar so everyone could see and hear me. I just soaked up all that attention. To me, my daddy was the greatest man who ever lived. I never once quit believing that one day my daddy would come back and rescue me from all the horror that followed. It was the lifeline I kept groping for.

    Of course on Sundays we went to church. At least Grandma, Gary and I did. I don't believe I ever saw Grandpa go to church until his grandchildren started getting married. Church was a place for social gatherings and hearing the news, potluck suppers and Christian Youth Fellowship, and camp every summer. And Wednesday night was choir practice. Having come from a musically gifted family, I was lucky enough to have inherited my mother's singing voice. And that musical inheritance and background came into play throughout my life.

    Finally, the end of the war came. I stood at the front room window watching all the people going crazy and simply said, "Now maybe my daddy can come home." Grandma cried. She knew that my daddy wasn't coming home because my mom had divorced him. That's why my brother and I were living with Grandma and Grandpa. I didn't know until I was grown up what a son-of-a bitch my dad had been. My mother never once said a bad word about my dad. I was grown and had children of my own before I learned the truth, and my dad was the one who told me.

~Chapter 2~

Now comes the hard part. While Gary and I were living with Grandma and Grandpa, Mom had run off to California with her best friend, Rose Penney. While they were there, my mom met a Marine named Delbert Upshaw from Michigan and she fell in love. Up to this point, other than a swat on the butt from my grandpa, or a switch from the Spirea bush across the legs wielded by my grandma, my brother and I had never been severely punished for anything. That changed. We were now part of a new family, the head of which was a Marine and all that the military mindset entails.

Mom came and got us, and we went back to California with her. From California, we moved to Battle Creek, Michigan, where Del's parents and the rest of his family were. And I was left with Del's family while my mom and little brother went on to North Carolina with Del, until he could be mustered out of the Marines. This was the time in my life when I learned what real punishment was. Not just a swat on the butt from these oh-so-religious people. Oh, no! Any infraction of the rules was promptly corrected with several lashes with a razor strop. Have you ever seen one of those? Thick, thick leather and it hurts like hell across your back. And yes, it was across the back that I got it.

Then Mom and Del came back from North Carolina with my new baby sister. Oh, how excited I was. A sister to play with named Sheila. And we got our own house across town from the rest of his family. A year and a half later, I had yet another baby sister, Sue Ellen. Poor Gary. He was outnumbered.

Having a very strict, military-type dad, my brother and I had chores to do. At eight years old my job was to do the supper dishes every night. I had to pull a chair up to the sink to be able to reach it. And Lord help me if I broke anything. I remember one night that Mom and Del were out. I conveniently forgot that I was supposed to do the dishes, even when the sitter reminded me. But, of course, later on in the evening I realized how much trouble I would be in when Del got home and they weren't done. The sitter had no compassion for me. I had waited too long, and it was bedtime. Not to worry, folks. The dishes did get done that night. When the folks got home, Del just dragged me out of bed and made me do every dish in the house, the dirty *and* the clean ones.

And he was really good about saying, just before he beat the hell out of us, "This hurts me more than it does you." Yeah, right! You never questioned Del if he said "No." Another lesson quickly learned. If you did, you would wake up clear across the room with bruises and an aching body.

This is also where the sexual abuse started. I clearly remember one afternoon when I was about eight years old, Dad decided to tell me the facts of life and how excited I was, mostly because I had his undivided attention. And you'll notice at this point in the story, I have finally started calling him Dad. I had refused for the longest time to call him anything but Del. I don't remember exactly what Dad said, but it was all about how babies are made. I do, however, clearly remember asking him to show me. And he did, or at least he tried. He actually tried to penetrate me—a thirty-something-year-old man and an eight-year-old child. I have always thanked God that he wasn't able to do it and didn't try to force it. I believe the memory that I asked him to show me how it was done made me think that I had to be guilty as sin, and that it was my fault that he continued trying to get me in bed for the rest of my life.

And that wasn't the only abuse. Of course, there were the sessions with the razor strop (yes, he had one, too). But I really think the emotional and mental abuse were even worse. Those scars go much, much deeper and hurt longer. It included the constant ridicule of my clothes, hair and makeup (when I got older). Never seeming to be able to do things quite good enough to suit him. I simply cannot remember ever having my dad tell me I did something well.

Sixth grade came and we were growing up. Some of my classmates had even started to develop breasts. I was so envious and ashamed of my flat chest. We had a film one day about the changes that were, or about to, take place in our bodies. It was basically a film about reproduction, although it didn't really explain a whole lot about the actual sex act. And we got some literature to take home with us to discuss with our moms. Fat chance! I wasn't about to talk to my mother about sex or anything else. I was too afraid that I would let it slip what Dad was trying to do to me and then I'd be in real trouble! But, I had no problem showing all the boys the literature on our way home from school that day. Made me the center of attention, didn't it?

I was not happy about Dad always pinching me on the boobs or rubbing my bottom as I walked by, or goosing me; I was especially beginning to get more and more uncomfortable with waking up and finding him kneeling next to my bed trying to put his fingers in me. But I was afraid to tell Mom. He would always say, "Go ahead and tell. Who do you think she'll believe? Me or you?" And I just knew it wouldn't be me that she would believe. And if I pushed it and said I was going to tell, he would get the most evil and mean look on his face and I knew I was in for it. So I kept quiet.

When playing with my buddies, Robbie and Teddy, across the street at Joey Teasdale's house, I was more than willing to show my friends what I had learned from my dad. And when Joey, who was much older than all of us (he must have been all of ten or eleven) suggested that I show everyone how it was done, I was more than willing to let my friend Robbie help me with the experiment. After much grunting and groaning, we decided that it wasn't all that it was cracked up to be (no pun intended). It was very disappointing, but again, I had been the center of attention. I was unaware that my virginity was still intact until I was nineteen years old, when I actually did lose my cherry. Not only did it surprise the hell out of me, but guess how the recipient felt? But, there I go getting ahead of my story!

Ahhhh! The simple joys of youth—Hide and Seek; Red Rover; and Duck, Duck, Goose. And sneaking into the field of cantaloupes next door to eat stolen, hot cantaloupes. I really did not like them but those stolen fruits were deeeelicious!!

My piano lessons started when I was about eight. And I hated practicing. Oh, I wanted to be able to play, but it was going too slow, playing "Row, Row, Row Your Boat" and the scales over and over. Mom soon discovered the carrot to making me practice willingly. I had received a bicycle for my eighth birthday and from that day on I was mobile. I went all over town on that bike. But—if I wanted to go off on my bike, I first had to put in an hour of practice. Practice problems solved.

Mom and Dad would often have friends over to play cards and party well into the wee hours. The mornings after, Gary and I would have a high old time (literally), sipping the half empty drinks and beers, and pretending that we were smoking the cigarette butts left all over the house. I remember how absolutely awful that booze tasted. I couldn't understand why anyone would like it. But it made me feel grown up.

I used to have a terrible temper. That temper would always show up whenever Gary and I were left alone together. On Saturday mornings I wanted to do nothing at all until I had heard my stories on the radio—Let's Pretend and the Green Hornet. One Saturday morning, Gary just wouldn't leave me alone or be quiet, so a battle ensued. At one point, Gary threw a butcher knife at me. I grabbed the closest object, which happened to be a baseball and let it fly. Did I tell you the living room was complete windows all across the front of the house? You got it! I broke one of the windows. Oh, my God! We were both petrified. We were really in for it now. Let me tell you something, you never saw two kids work any faster polishing, sweeping and shining every surface that we could find. That house was a miracle of clean before the folks got home. Of course, all our hard work was to no avail. I got another "this hurts me more than it does you" lecture and a red butt for all our trouble at trying to make amends.

Then a terrible thing happened. Being only twelve at the time, my memory is really sketchy, but the family was front-page news in February of 1951. It seems that Calvin and Minnie (Dad's parents) had been quarreling for some time and had been talking about getting a divorce. Del's sister, Francine, and her husband who still lived at home with the folks, came home from work one day and found her parents dead on the kitchen floor. After the investigation, it was decided that Calvin had shot and killed Minnie while she stood at the kitchen stove, and then killed himself. Calvin had wanted custody of Dolores, their youngest, in the divorce and Minnie refused. He must have just gone berserk. After that I always carried the fear with me that my dad would do the same thing to my mother one day. That made it even more difficult for me to fend off his sexual advances, because I was afraid of what he might do to my mother if I kept refusing him.

I was not allowed to date at all until I was sixteen, and then I had to take my little sisters on my dates with me. As you can imagine, I didn't have too many boyfriends willing to take on that burden. Later I realized that the reason Dad did not let me date anyone alone simply had to do with the fact that he wanted me for himself.

~Chapter 3~

I guess the sudden loss of both of his parents was more than Dad could handle and he had to get away from all the memories. Shortly after the death of his parents, we all packed up and moved back close to Grandma and Grandpa Rush. Now I figured that things were going to be all right after all. We were going home! We drove back to Kansas and that was one of the fun times that I remember. We were too poor to have a fancy car with a radio, so we had to amuse ourselves. Playing poker with car license plates, seeing how many different state license tags we could count, and singing. Dad didn't have too shabby a singing voice himself, and knew the neatest songs: "Who's that a-knocking at my door? Who's that a-knocking at my door? Who's that a-knocking at my door,' cried the fair young maiden." I never did learn all of that song. At a certain point, mom would say, "Delbert!" And that would be the end of that. How was I supposed to know they were naughty songs? They had such happy-go-lucky melodies and were fun to sing.

One Saturday while Mom was grocery shopping, Dad came into the bathroom while I was taking a bath. He had been watching me through the crack in the door and thought I was masturbating. (I was exploring my body.) It got him all excited and he wanted to help me with it. I managed to talk him out of it and he didn't touch me, but he did sit on the edge of my bed and jacked-off in front of me. After that episode, I can't count the number of times I would wake up in the mornings and Dad would have his hand under my sheets trying to put his finger in me! That's why, when I made my bed, I always tucked in the sheets and the blankets. Then when I went to bed, I would roll as close as possible to the edge and clamp my arm down on top of the blankets on the other side of me to hold the sheets down tight so he couldn't get his hands on me. That way of making my bed carried over into my married life, even into my late twenties.

Every summer, my mom would somehow scrape together the necessary funds so Gary and I could attend church camp. The first time I went it started out horribly. I had never been away from home, and I got homesick—big time! But it soon passed, and I had a wonderful time. We were busy from dawn to dusk, and dusk is when the memories get brighter—sitting around the campfire roasting hot dogs and marshmallows, telling ghost stories and scaring everyone to death. And Lordy, did we sing. The good Lord had gifted me with a beautiful singing voice that I used to my advantage every chance I got. But, strangely enough, I never even considered making a career out of singing. There's just something about singing around a campfire at night that is magical.

The summer of 1951 was the first time that I had seen my real father in years. Mom sent Gary and me to California for a visit. Daddy Brian was still in the Army and was stationed at a base somewhere close to Marysville, California. While he was in Alaska, he had remarried and had two more children, another boy and girl. This was also my first meeting with his other family: his wife, Bernice and the kids, Scott and Sally.

The most fun that summer was the swimming. I think it was a lake, but it could have been a pond. I do know that there was a big raft out in the middle of it. I was taken with one particular fella, and I was bound and determined to make him notice me. I'm sure that he was too old for me, but I was in love. I saw him sunning on the raft when we arrived, and I immediately jumped in the water and swam out to talk to him. It was really hot that day, so he jumped in the water to join me and we went under the raft for a little shade. He was really nice to me, considering the age difference. He never talked down to me at all, but he never took advantage, either. The conversation, of course, got around to what I did in school, and when I mentioned singing, he asked for a sample. Of course I was more than happy to show off my talents. I probably sang half a dozen songs or more. I thought I was singing just to him. Imagine my surprise when I realized that there was applause coming from the beach. You know how sound carries over the water, right? Well magnify that with being under a raft built on fifty-gallon oil drums. I had been serenading the entire base!

Back at home Dad decided that he wanted to be a farmer, so he moved us all to a farm in Parker, a little spot in the road that didn't have much more than a post office, general store, bank and the consolidated high school. Gary and I both immediately joined the 4-H Club and started learning all about farm life (like we didn't already know).

After moving into the house that had only electricity and just a pump for water in the kitchen and an outhouse in the back, Dad immediately set out stocking the farm with animals. I bought myself a pair of baby Muscovy ducks for twenty-five cents. I wound up with a duck and a drake. They grew up quickly into a beautiful pair. The drake had a wingspan that I'd be willing to bet it was four or five feet across. I could always tell when Mom went to the outhouse and forgot the broom. I would hear her screaming at me, "Lynetta!! Come get this God-damned duck!" I would go running and find my mother standing with the door of the outhouse partially open and my drake, with his head lowered, wings spread and fluttering, hissing at mom to beat all get out. For some reason, he had taken a dislike to my mother and would chase her all over the barnyard if she didn't have her broom with her to beat him off.

Now, let me tell you about my first horse—Lady. She was beautiful and gentle, and was going to be "My Friend, Flicka," "The Black Stallion," and "Black Beauty" all rolled into one. I couldn't wait to ride her the day that Dad brought her home. She was everything I ever wanted but he said that she had been abused and we had to be careful.

One crisp fall Sunday morning, Gary and I decided on a double ride. We threw on the old blanket and the saddle. Lady had this cute little trick she pulled when you first put the saddle on. She would take a great big breath and hold it so that the cinch wasn't really tight when she exhaled. We were onto that little trick, though. All we had to do was wait a minute until she couldn't hold it anymore, and then, quickly tighten the cinch again when she exhaled. I jumped on and Gary quickly hopped up behind me.

We rode down the little dirt road for a bit, and then turned into a cornfield that had been recently harvested and all there was left was dry, brittle cornstalks. Of course, when I turned Lady's head back toward the house, she started to hurry. All of a sudden we realized that there was a problem. We were slipping to the side, saddle and all. It was so funny that all we could do was laugh, as we kept tilting farther and farther to the left. We finally both let go and jumped, and Lady immediately stopped when the reins hit the ground. It was absolutely hysterical. The saddle had a ring on both sides so all the while that that we were cinching her up on the left side it was coming loose on the right!

I was beginning to mature at thirteen and my body was changing. I had started my periods that summer before we moved to the farm. When I went to the bathroom at one point, I noticed a dark red stain on my panties. I rushed downstairs to show Mom, really excited because I had finally made it! When I showed her, what did she say? "Well, you know what it is, don't you? Go get one of my pads." Darn! I had wanted some kind of recognition for becoming a woman! Or at least a rough discussion on what sex was really like. Not from my mom. No way. I thought that she just assumed I already knew all about it, but now I realize that she was embarrassed and just didn't know how to tell me.

As well as the outside chores, it also became the responsibility of Gary and me to keep the house in order and I began cooking for a family of six. Of course, my mom had been teaching me to cook all along, as well as my grandma when I was with her.

I was now a freshman in high school and would again be meeting a whole new crop of kids. Parker had a consolidated high school that served several of the little towns in the county. Our farm was only a couple of miles from town, and Gary and I often walked home from school on the good weather days.

~Chapter 4~

One of my classes was typing and I had found another thing that I did very well. My fingers would just fly over those keys on an old black Remington or Underwood typewriter with a bell when you got to the end of the line so you knew when to throw the carriage and start the next line. My teacher told me the reason I was so good at typing probably had something to do with all the piano lessons and having to milk the cow.

The worst time on the farm came the next year. My uncle raised Pointer hunting dogs and had given Gary the runt of the litter, which he named Pup. She was his and he was going to train her to hunt with him. They were together all the time out in the woods. Sadly, though, Pup came down with distemper and we didn't even know it. The vets didn't have all the inoculations for dogs and cats that they have now. Pup survived the distemper, but it left her with a constant, spastic twitch and she could never stand still, which rendered her useless as far as a hunting dog. My 'wonderful' stepfather made Gary take Pup out into the woods and destroy her. He made my twelve-year-old brother take his beloved dog out into the woods and put a bullet in her head!

Dad and Mom decided that they had had enough of farming. So we moved back close to Grandma and Grandpa Rush at the end of my sophomore year. Most of our animals didn't make the move, but Lady and the ducks did. I slipped right back into the groove with my old friends from junior high. However, my body had developed quite nicely, and all the curves were in all the right places. That was a blessing and a problem. I began to be noticed by the boys, but it also increased the attention I got at home from my dad. It was becoming more and more of a fight to keep him away from me.

One evening, after Mom was already in bed, Dad started badgering me again about letting him 'show me how love should be made.' This time I really argued with him. He even went so far as to ask me if, should he leave my mother, would I go with him. Then he started feeling me all over and I struggled until I got away from him and ran upstairs to my mom, determined that this time she was going to listen to me. I was sobbing so hard, she had trouble understanding what I was saying but it finally got through to her. I was insisting that Dad wouldn't leave me alone and I wanted to leave and live with Grandma and Grandpa.

By this time Dad had come storming upstairs, and he and Mom got into it. I rushed back downstairs where Gary was standing, frightened at all the screaming and yelling. I glanced back up the stairs where Dad had started back down toward me, with Mom right behind him yelling, "Leave her alone!" Dad had that mean and vicious look again and I was really scared this time. I was frantically trying to remember where all the guns in the house were so that I could get to them before he did.

Dad was halfway down the stairs, but something Mom said got his attention and he turned, grabbed her by the ankle, yanked her feet out from under her and started dragging her down the stairs on her butt. About this time Gary went running out the back door. I didn't know where he was going until about fifteen minutes later when the phone began ringing. Gary had run all the way to Grandma and Grandpa's house (which was about three miles) and Grandpa was calling to find out what the heck was going on. I guess that scared Dad enough to stop the craziness. And Grandpa came to get me so Gary and I could stay with them for a time while Mom and Dad worked out the problem. Fat chance! Either my Grandpa and Grandma never figured out what was really wrong, or they just didn't want to admit it, just like my mom had done. She had to know why I was upset. I had made no bones about what Dad was doing to me. But she chose to overlook it and forgave him. I guess he made her believe that it wouldn't happen again. Sure. If you believe that, I have a bridge I'd like to sell you in New York.

At least the blow up and subsequent talks got things settled down—somewhat. And we went back to the same old things. Child abuse and sexual molestation were not discussed in the fifties. Wives and children were still considered totally at the mercy of their husbands and fathers. The man's word was law, and the authorities did not step in.

The best job Dad could find was at the railroad shops in the next town, and he decided that we should live close to his work, so he found us a little house just a few blocks from school. Mom went to work in a little restaurant in town called "Mom's Café", and they could both walk to work if they wanted to. This was a nice little house and Dad had picked right for a change. There were two bedrooms accessed off the large living room area, a separate dining room and a small kitchen and back porch. Two bedrooms and six people is still a difficult equation. To begin with, my sisters and I got the second bedroom, and Gary had a pair of bunkbeds in the dining room.

Mom decided to teach me how to be a waitress. She didn't want me to be a waitress all my life, but she wanted me to have the experience just in case I fell on hard times when I got on my own and couldn't find any work in my chosen field. There's always a job waiting tables somewhere to get you by. And she was right. There were several occasions when that early waitress training saved my buns. (Oh, no! Not another pun!) So Mom and I would get up at three o'clock every morning (keep in mind, I am now fifteen years old), drive down to Schuyler's Bakery downtown to pick up the sweet rolls and doughnuts and then open the restaurant. I worked the breakfast crowd until eight o'clock, and then skipped across the street to catch the Greyhound bus to school over in Paola.

I didn't quite make it through the entire junior year. Working and going to school in another town was just too much for me. I did, however, make it long enough to participate in the operetta. That year we did "The Mikado" by Gilbert and Sullivan. This time I got one of the female leads. I was Yum Yum (I love that name). Yum Yum was engaged to KoKo. There was one scene where Yum Yum and KoKo had a meeting in a garden and we were sitting on a bench. My character, of course, being a shy schoolgirl and proper Japanese maiden, was sitting as far on my end of the bench as I could. When Matthew got up to come over and try to kiss me, I fell off the bench!

~Chapter 5~

Now things are starting to get interesting, as I am an upper classman and, again, the new kid on the block. However, it's not exactly the same because I've been hanging around with my new classmates for some time now, since we live in the same small town and I go to church with a lot of them. I still didn't have too much freedom. During the summer, I worked in the refreshment stand at the drive-in theater. Since we no longer lived on the farm, our chore list had changed. Gary and I were still doing most of the housework, because both Mom and Dad were working. (Hhhmmm! What's wrong with this picture? I'm working and going to school.) Senior year was filled with activities more than class work. Between the music competitions, senior play, lunch-hour sock hops in the hallways, senior trip and finally being allowed to date freely, I was busy all the time.

The scariest incident with my dad occurred about this time. There was a big Rush family reunion in Oklahoma. I remember begging Mom not to go or to take me with her, but she said I had to go to school and off she went. I shared the second bedroom with my two younger sisters and we all slept together in a double bed. There was a closet between Mom and Dad's bedroom and our bedroom, which we all shared. Of course, that meant there was access between the two bedrooms by coming through the closet. Sure enough, after Dad thought we were all asleep that night here he came into our bedroom and started moving Sue Ellen and Sheila into his room. While he was taking one of them in there, I jumped up and put on my clothes, then went out and tried to wake Gary, but I couldn't get him to stay awake. Dad caught me and dragged me back in the bedroom, threw me on the bed and then it started. I thought he was going to strangle me. I don't remember what stopped him; it may have been that Gary finally made some noise or one of the girls came back and tried to get in bed. I carried bruises for the longest time on my neck from that night. Mom was gone just long enough that the bruises had faded by the time she came home, or they were hidden behind my sweaters and blouses so she didn't see them.

It was just about this time that I met my first love. I don't know about men, but a woman never forgets her first love. His name was Donald Davidson and he was from another little farming community. He had beautiful clear blue eyes, sparkling white teeth, and a tan that was to die for. I couldn't believe he was interested in plain old me. I had a nice body, yes, but I never considered myself a traffic stopper like some of my classmates.

Donald was an ace athlete. He could do it all—football, basketball, baseball. He was such an incredible baseball player, that I just knew that he would go on to be a professional baseball player. However, some choices that he made rendered that only a dream. He didn't have a car yet, but he would hitchhike the twenty miles from his home to my house on Friday nights so that he could spend the weekends. That may sound strange, considering the type of guy my dad was, but I do believe that Dad thought he was going to catch Donald and me in a compromising position, and then I would be at his mercy. Little did Dad know, but it was that very thought that had kept me a virgin for so long. I just knew that the minute I went all the way with my boyfriend, Dad would be able to tell and then I would no longer have any argument to keep him away from me.

Mom got some very sad news toward the end of my senior year. Her best friend, Rose Penney had fallen asleep with a cigarette in her hand and had died in the fire. Rose's mother, knowing how Rose always felt about my mom and me, inherited everything from her daughter, and in memory of Rose, sent me a five hundred dollar U.S. Savings Bond for graduation. With that savings bond I bought my very first car, a 1949 Plymouth, four-door sedan that was a yucky green color, but it had a beautiful gray cloth interior and a real wood dashboard. I just loved that car.

Senior prom and graduation came and went and Donald and I were together almost constantly. When Donald's dad learned that his son was dating an "older" woman from another town, he had nothing good at all to say about me. He was sure that I was going to get myself pregnant and that his dream for Donald's professional baseball career would be down the drain.

Two weeks after graduation, I finally got a job at the State Mental Hospital in the typing pool. Since I was such a fast typist and completed my assignments before the other girls, I also was assigned to help out in the hospital's post office. So I became acquainted with all of the doctors and nurses on a more personal basis. I turned eighteen in August of 1956, and the first thing I did was apply for a room in the employees' dorm at the hospital. I was earning an incredible one hundred and ninety-one dollars a month in salary, and I could rent a room for the measly sum of fifteen dollars a month. I was all grown up and I could now escape from the attentions of my dad. I was sure that as soon as I left the house, things would be better for my mother and my sisters. How very wrong I was, but I didn't know that at the time. I had my own room, my own car, a steady boyfriend and a job that I loved. I was on top of the world.

I quickly graduated from the typing pool, to secretary for the Geriatrics Unit at the hospital. There I had more personal contact with the patients, as well as with the staff. I also now had a room in the new employees' dorm, which was right next door to the Geriatrics Building. It was about this time that I decided, since I was over eighteen and no longer lived at home, that I was in love and sure that Donald and I were going to be married. So, I decided it was time I learned what all the excitement was about in the sexual department. I knew everything there was to know about it, except for first-hand experience.

I was all set to do the dirty deed. I dressed very carefully for that date, choosing an outfit that would be easy to get out of. After the movie and dinner, I drove to our favorite parking spot and we moved into the back seat for some heavy necking. I quickly removed my panties and prepared myself. We were both breathing heavily and, I thought, ready to go. Well, hell! Donald was afraid. Remember what his daddy had said? I was going to get myself pregnant and then we would have to get married? Talk about throwing cold water on someone. Here I was all hot and bothered—on my back in the back seat of a car with the love of my life poised to make me a woman—and he kept repeating, "Are you sure it's safe? Are you sure you won't get pregnant?" I was furious! I was so indignant that I jumped up, got dressed, gave him his ring back and drove him home. And that was the end of my love affair with Donald.

Mom and Dad took me to the city and negotiated a brand new, black 1957 Ford Fairlane. Plain vanilla. No frills. I even had to pay extra for a sun visor and armrest for the driver's side and a radio and ashtray. I now had a brand new car and a new job. I got another promotion, this time as secretary to the whole Psychology Department in the Outpatient Clinic of the hospital. I was secretary to six psychologists.

One night I was getting ready to go out dancing, and while I was filling up the car at the gas station, Donald showed up all of a sudden. He didn't know what to do and wanted my help. He had started dating Katherine Warfield after we broke up and it seems that she had gotten herself pregnant. Awwwww. How sad. And what a lot of balls Donald had asking me for help after what his father had said about me doing that very thing to trap him into marriage. I just looked at him and said, "Good luck!"

At Dad's insistence, Mom and I both applied for a job at Bendix in Kansas City. Of course, that meant I had to give up my independence at the hospital and move back in with the folks; which, of course, meant that I could count on being harassed by my dad on a regular basis again. When I had moved out, they gave Gary the second bedroom, and put the bunk beds in the dining room for Sue Ellen and Sheila. When I moved back in, I took the top bunk and the little ones got to share the bottom one. Again, I had the old problem of waking up with Dad trying to get his hands under the covers to get to me. Being on the top bunk made it a little more difficult for him, though. I still tucked in the sheets and blankets and then scooched over close to the edge to anchor them, and I also kept the rail up that was to keep younger kids from falling out.

I had started dating an old classmate, Lenny Eissenagle, and we were getting pretty serious. He was a tall, lanky, freckle-faced redhead and was absolutely adorable and funny as hell. My love affair with Lenny was doomed to failure from the start, but I never expected it to end the way it did. He had joined the Army right after high school and long before we had become engaged. He was stationed in Oklahoma so we didn't get to see a lot of each other. I spent more time going out with my girlfriends than I did with Lenny. I was faithful, in that I didn't date any other guys, but I was beginning to chafe at the bit and I was still a virgin…now going on nineteen. During one furlough Lenny and I had a big fight because he wanted to go out with the guys instead of spending time with me. So, I went out with the girls…again.

I got home at a decent hour and I vaguely remember hearing what sounded like screeching tires and the crunch of an automobile accident just as I fell asleep. I awoke early the next morning with Dad again trying his little tricks. I mumbled like I was still asleep and moved closer to the edge of the bed to make sure he couldn't get his hand under the blankets. All of a sudden he shook me roughly and had me sitting straight up in bed crying, when he said in a loud voice, "Get up! Lenny Eissenagle was killed last night!"

Oh, dead God! That crash I had heard was what had killed my fiancé. I desperately tried to remember everything that we had said to each other the night before, hoping that nothing I said had led to his death and praying I hadn't said I didn't love him any more. He wasn't even driving the car. My sweet friend, Don Holford, had been driving and of course, they had been drinking. There was another car involved, but they were never caught. If losing Lenny wasn't enough the day of his funeral, his sister, JaNiece, came at the request of their parents and asked me to return his class ring so he could be buried with it. It broke my heart all over again but I gave it up.

I guess I went a little wild after Lenny was killed. I drank a lot and spent most nights at the Hilltop or Ray's, dancing and trying to forget. It was only through the energy and strength of youth that I was able to maintain my job, but I was beginning to have trouble with my fellow carpoolers because I was often late picking them up, and one by one they deserted me. It was at Ray's that I met Raymond Canfield.

Another "out-of-towner," Raymond was from Olathe. He was very sure of himself and had seen me dancing at Ray's almost every weekend. He'd checked around and heard all the stories about me so he was sure that I would be easy. He was surprised when I turned him down the first few times that he asked for a date, but he was even more surprised when I refused to have sex with him. About a month into our relationship, I decided that the time was right and gave in. Raymond was surprised when he realized that I was really a virgin and he was my first! Then we made love on a regular basis until I became totally insensitive to it. I finally knew what it was all about and I felt like Peggy Lee—"Is That All There Is?"

Raymond became totally possessive of me. Whenever we went anywhere where we might run into one of my old boyfriends, he would make me stay in the car until he went in to see who was there before letting me go inside. However, it was beginning to wear on me and didn't bode well for the relationship.

I had to make some changes in my life again. I was bored to death working at Bendix, so I started looking for another job and found one as secretary to the credit manager of Waggener Paint Company. The all-male-but-me carpool often stopped about halfway home to have a beer and play pool at a little roadside tavern. This didn't set too well with Raymond when he found out about it, so I finally got fed up and told him to take a hike.

It was at this new job that I met my first husband, Wilbur Edmund Coleman. Will was about three months younger than me and wasn't much taller, maybe five foot four to my five foot two. Like Lenny, Will was redheaded and freckle-faced. He worked in the shipping department, which was on the first floor of the plant, while I worked for the credit manager and was on the third floor, so we didn't have a conflict as far as working together. Will didn't impress me in the least, but he persisted and I finally gave in and we started dating in May of 1958.

Very early in the relationship he took me home to meet his family. And what a family it was! His dad was named Carl, but everyone called him Shorty because that was what he was. Will's mother, Martha, was a real piece of work. She caused endless problems in the family, but she became my staunchest supporter in later years. She never forgot my birthday or any other holiday. I could always count on her sending me some little something, even if it was just a trinket. And all four of my sons call her Grandma Martha even though only my oldest is really her grandson. And, of course, Will's sisters, Maryann and Carlene, completed the family unit.

Will soon asked me to marry him and I accepted. We originally planned a spring wedding but for some reason, we both decided that that was too far away and changed the date to October 18, 1958. Of course that started tongues wagging, with everyone thinking that I was pregnant and that was why we had to move it up, but that wasn't the case at all. We just decided we didn't want to wait so long. I never even asked my folks to pay for my wedding because I knew they couldn't. Will and I paid for the whole thing ourselves. My cousin, Patty Lynn, whose wedding I had sung in just the year before, was taking a class in cake decorating, so she offered to make the cake. The biggest expenses were the flowers and the photographs. I chose to be married in the church that I had attended in my hometown, and my high school music teacher agreed to sing for us for nothing.

I made my attendants' dresses and my grandmother and I, with some help from Mom, made my wedding dress in white satin with a chantilly lace overskirt, a satin panel in front, and long princess sleeves that came to a point on the back of my hands. The dress had tiny little covered buttons all the way up the back and on the cuffs of the sleeves. And my cousin let me use her tiara and veil. So we were set in the clothing department.

The day before the wedding Dad made one more try. He didn't touch me, just talked to me in the sickeningly sweet manner that he had when he wanted something. He told me that I really needed to let him show me what love was all about so I would know what to do on my wedding night. I very graciously (Geez, I was about to throw up—how could I even keep a straight face) refused and told him that I wanted to go to my husband just the way I was. Inside I was laughing hysterically. I had already been with my husband. I was about to break free of Dad at last. Famous last words!

I guess Will and I had just a little too much togetherness. We got up and had breakfast together, we drove to work together, we worked together, we had lunch together, we drove home together, and we ate supper and then went to bed together. That works for about the first year.

Then you realize that you really don't have anything to talk about because you already knew what happened at work. You were there!

But that wasn't the only thing. I turned my paycheck over to my husband and he paid all the bills and provided me with a place to live, food to eat and took me out occasionally to dinner—usually McDonald's. In addition to my working, I did all of the household chores and thought that I was keeping him happy in bed. I wasn't really all that satisfied, but what did I know? But, there I go again, getting ahead of my story.

The president of Waggener Paint had given Will a raise as his wedding gift. I found out later that he gave Will a raise simply so that Will would be making more money than I was. A wife simply couldn't be the major bread-winner. It went against the grain. So, between us, we brought home about five hundred dollars a month. Not bad for two kids starting out in the late fifties.

Sadly two months after Will and I were married and just before Christmas, my paternal grandmother died. I had just discovered that I was pregnant with my first child and it really saddened me that she didn't live long enough to meet her first great-grandchild. Daddy Brian flew in from Okinawa, and Will and I picked him up at the airport for the trip to the funeral. It had taken Daddy Brian some thirty-six hours to make the flight on the Military Air Transport System planes and had to come in a roundabout way.

I learned a lot about my real father on that trip. We had to make a stop at a liquor store on the way to the funeral in the middle of the state, because my father needed to replenish his supply. He told us that he had had seven fifths of Seagram's VO when he left Okinawa, but he had run out. Seven bottles of whiskey in thirty-six hours? I'd had no idea that my father drank so much. It was then that I realized that I never ever saw him sober. He was a "functioning alcoholic." It was also at that time that I found out what caused the break-up of my parents' marriage. That's when he told me about bringing the girlfriend home to our apartment in Kansas City all those many years ago.

~Chapter 6~

Things went along pretty smoothly for Will and me for a while. It was all new and exciting and we were expecting our first child. Plus, Will was a master at stretching pennies. I, of course, had the fifty-seven Ford when we got married. Will had a Volkswagen (did I forget to tell you about how difficult it is to make love in the back seat of a Volkswagen? No? Well, take my word for it) and he traded them both in for a Kharman Ghia, the sports model of the Volkswagen. It was something that he had dreamed about for years. However, it was not very comfortable for me the more my pregnancy progressed. It was what my granny called a "step down" car because you had to step down to get into it. Try that when you're eight or nine months pregnant. Not fun.

This was in the days before Women's Lib had taken hold in the country. I was required to quit my job when I entered my fifth month of pregnancy. In order to make ends meet after I had to quit, Will took a second job at a service station. What with Waggener Paint, the service station and school, I didn't see very much of Will anymore. And it was very lonely.

Then, the family problems started. The family doctor at that time was Dr. Curt Gruder, an osteopath who had been the Coleman family doctor for several years. So he became my doctor also. The doctor's wife, Lois, was his assistant. Shortly after Christmas, Will's dad decided that he preferred the doctor's wife to Will's mother, so two families were torn apart. I guess that was the straw that broke the camel's back, because Martha just seemed to go completely bonkers when Carl left her.

I had a surprise visit that summer when I was pregnant from Dad's youngest sister, Dolores. She had recently married a man almost twenty years her senior. We had some real heart-to-heart conversations during her short visit. She shocked me when she asked if Dad had ever tried to do anything to me sexually. I didn't admit anything at first until I found out why she was asking such a thing. After the death of Dad's parents, Dolores was given into the custody of her sister, Francine, and Dad got custody of his next oldest sister, Brenda. It seems that Francine's husband, Rob, had tried a little hanky panky with Dolores and she had gone screaming to Francine. That's when Dolores learned that her big brother, my stepfather, had forced both of his other sisters to have sex with him. Francine and Brenda both! That explains why Brenda so promptly got herself pregnant—so she could get married and away from Dad.

My first son was due to be born on August second. I had always been told that first babies are either two weeks early, or two weeks late (old wives' tale, ladies). On the evening of August 3, 1959, when Will came home from work at the service station about ten thirty that night, he patted my tummy on his way to take a shower and came to a dead stop. "Gosh, your stomach is as hard as a rock. Do you feel okay?" he asked.

"I feel great," I replied. "I have done a lot of cleaning today, though, and should probably be very tired. But I'm wide awake and ready to dance the night away," I joked.

"What kind of cleaning?" Will asked, concerned. "The apartment was already spotless. What could possibly have taken up any of your time today?"

Anyone out there know what the "nesting urge" is? Yup. I was subconsciously getting my nest ready for my baby. My body knew better than I did what was about to happen. Will called the doctor who told him to get me to the hospital I was obviously in labor. At midnight, I changed my mind. I was suddenly in hard, active labor and Kyle Daniel Coleman made his appearance into the world at six twenty the next morning—the morning of my twenty-first birthday!

It wasn't long before it became apparent that the apartment wasn't going to be big enough for us, so we found a nice little rental house in Overland Park. I was so happy being married, having a home of my own and having Kyle that it took a while for it to sink in that my "chores" had just increased ten-fold. Now not only did I do all the housework, laundry and meals, I had the added burden when I went back to work, of getting Kyle ready for the babysitter's.

Within a year, there was some bad news at my job. They had merged with another company and were closing down the Kansas City office. Most of the management people were okay...they would be relocated, but us peons were out in the cold. So I was looking for work again.

It took me at least a month to find a job and things were getting pretty tight at the house. After about a year, we bought a home of our own. As I said earlier, Will was going to school to be a CPA, and was moving up in the company. I always said that Will could stretch a dollar farther than anyone I ever saw. We had been married about three years and had a new car every year, our own home with new furniture and a beautiful piano, and boats. Will just loved going to the Lake of the Ozarks for vacation.

Will's mother, Martha, was getting worse and worse. She had moved into what she called the "little house," the house that she and Shorty had lived in when they first got married. They had kept it and rented it out when they bought the bigger house. She had quit taking care of herself and Carlene. We tried and tried to get Martha to go get some medical/psychological treatment, but she was just in denial. We finally had no choice and filed suit against her for custody of Carlene. Martha had a good lawyer, and they made a deal that Martha would sign herself into the Osawatomie State Hospital for ninety days and we would take care of Carlene while her mother was getting treatment.

It was during Martha's stay in the hospital that I ran into my first love, Donald Davidson, again. He was head of the Physical Therapy Department on the men's ward in the Main Building at the hospital. Not quite what we had expected him to do with his life. Oh, remember that Katherine got pregnant and they had to get married? Well, poor

Katherine. She carried that baby boy for two years! Yup. She had tricked him, all right.

Carlene and Kyle were getting along great. Will bought me a little red mixed-breed puppy that looked like a purebred miniature Dachshund I named Heidi. We were very much the "normal American family." Sure. (Too bad you can't hear the sarcasm). Martha was very smart to sign herself into the hospital. When the voluntary commitment period was up, she was free to walk out, regardless of whether the doctors said she was cured or not. And she did. She never did complete the treatments, but she survived. I guess we all survive in one way or another.

We had a birthday party for Carlene and I lost my precious Heidi. Will had taken Carlene over to Martha's for her birthday visit and I was standing at the kitchen sink cleaning up when I heard this horrible screeching of tires and a thud. I ran screaming out into the front yard. Carl went out into the street, picked Heidi up and brought her up the driveway and laid her down. I was sobbing uncontrollably and was totally useless. As much as I loved Heidi, I knew Carlene had loved her more, and I was frantic with worry about how it would affect Carlene when she came home and found Heidi had died.

That afternoon, we scoured the newspapers until we found an ad for miniature Dachshunds, and we looked at all of them until we found the one that looked most like Heidi and brought her home. When Carlene came back from her mother's she never knew this Heidi was a different dog.

Things were beginning to go very sour in my marriage, but I didn't know it. It seemed to me that we had a fairly active sex life, but then I had nothing much to compare it to. I had had only two partners before I married Will and I was really rather staid and straight-laced in that area. In the four and a half years that Will and I were married, we seldom experimented with exotic positions or enhancements, and I'm sure that we never engaged in oral sex because I would not do it as it reminded me of what my dad had tried to get me to do and it disgusted me. Unbeknownst to me, Will was finding his excitement elsewhere. There were little warning signs (had I known what to look for) so it came as a shock when I found a long, light brown hair caught in the trim on the passenger-side car door. For the past ten years I had kept my hair cut in the short, curly Italian style that was popular back then because of the movie star, Gina Lollabrigida. Plus my hair was definitely not light brown. It was dark red!

That was my first indication that another woman had been in the car with my husband. I was indignant, outraged, hurt, shocked—you name it. I immediately moved into the spare bedroom and refused to have anything at all to do with my husband. I demanded a divorce and I stood my ground. Ahhhh, the foibles of youth. I wished many times over the years that I had had the good sense to talk things over with Grandma Rush. She would have given me the straight scoop. But I ignored all of my better instincts. I had been wronged. And it was over. Will moved into an apartment. I was alone in the house with Kyle.

I found a good job at the Faultless Starch Company. And my boss, Dennis J. Small IV, was just what the doctor ordered to bolster my wounded female pride. (Good thinking, Netta. Throw your husband out and go after someone else's? That makes a lot of sense!) But I didn't stop there. Every chance I got I was at a party, drinking up a storm and taking on all comers. What the heck, I said. If I'm going to have the name, I might as well have the game, right? My dad had done a good job of convincing me that I was a slut, and Will seemed to go along with that thinking. I had never been unfaithful or given either one of them any reason to doubt my morals, but that didn't make any difference.

Shortly after Will moved out, I was having a doozie of a migraine. It was Will's weekend for Kyle, so I was home alone. I had just shut myself in the bedroom with all the blinds down making it as dark as possible and took some codeine tablets to stop the pain, when there was a knock on my door. It was Dad. He said that Mom had sent him as they were worried since they hadn't heard from me and I wasn't answering my phone. I groggily opened the door to let him in and he could see that I was sick. I was wearing only my bra and panties with a lightweight bathrobe, and the codeine was kicking in, so I was very out of it. I mumbled something about being okay but having a bad headache and I turned to go back to bed.

Dad followed me into the bedroom and sat down on the edge of the bed but I really didn't hear what he was saying. I was trying to sleep. He started massaging my back and shoulders and even though I didn't want him there, it felt good and seemed to be helping my pain. Before I knew it he had climbed onto the bed with me and had straddled my legs, all the time keeping up the delicious, pain-relieving massage. I was so groggy that it took a while to register with me that rather than massaging my neck and shoulders, his hands had slipped lower down my back until he was massaging the small of my back and upper buttocks and had actually worked my panties down and was about to finally do what I had been fighting against all those years.

When I felt the head of his penis probing between my legs I was immediately awake and bucked like a green-broke mustang. It took Dad so by surprise that he wound up on the floor beside my bed. If I hadn't been so angry, I would have been laughing uproariously at the sight of him sprawled at my feet with his pants down around his knees. I was up and screaming like a banshee, ordering him out of my house and threatening not only to do bodily harm to him, but to banish him from my house forever and to keep him from ever seeing my son again.

Will and I had a very "amicable" divorce. We used the same attorney (my mistake). I got the house, all the furniture and the piano (including all the payments, plus having to buy a car), and he took his clothes, the new car and the boat. We were divorced in late January 1963, and on February 15th he drove across the state line and married his little girlfriend. Then they moved to California into the house that Will and I had looked at to buy by the summer before. The reason for the move to California was Will's promotion to General Manager of the new plant Pratt & Lambert had built there.

The next few months are mostly a blur. I had to buy another car when Will moved out and I got a "fun" car, a Volkswagen convertible. Really sensible vehicle for a single working mother, right? Well, gee, guys. I was only twenty-four! While I had not married all that young, I really hadn't had my "fling."

The sexual revolution was in full swing in the mid-sixties, so I was making up for lost time. The good Lord was really looking out for me during that period, because I got myself into some really bad situations that could have had dire consequences. Even though I was fairly selective, and would stick with one guy for as long as the attraction lasted, some of those guys were, well, not very nice to me. But that's what I was used to. I knew how to cope with those kinds of guys. The ones who were nice to me, I didn't know how to handle. It didn't dawn on me for many, many years, that in order to participate in all those wild parties and sexual escapades, I had to get very drunk. Otherwise, I had too much common sense.

Fortunately for Kyle and me, Grandma Martha decided to move herself and Carlene in with us. I was glad for the company, really. And it gave me a live-in babysitter when I realized that I was struggling to make ends meet and had to take a second job. And that job was as a cocktail waitress/bartender.

It soon became apparent that I was not going to be able to maintain the house, the car, insurance, etc., etc., etc. Oh, Will sent his child support regularly. But it still just wasn't enough. So Grandma Martha and Carlene went back to the "little house," and I put my house up for rent and moved into a much smaller one-bedroom apartment. I had to have a new car. I was still in my "fling" mode, so I got a 1964 TR4, British Racing Green with a white convertible top. I soon had to move out of my little apartment. My landlord seemed to think I should be giving him more than rent money. What's with these men, anyway?

About a year after the divorce, I got a call from Will's sister, Maryann, asking me to meet her for coffee because she wanted to talk to me. What she wanted was to tell me that Will's second marriage hadn't worked out, that he was in town and wanted to see me to see if we could get back together. So I had the meeting with Will, and we decided to give it another try. At least, that's what I told him I was going to do. But I had a lot to do before I could move to California, so Will went on, and I said Kyle and I would drive out about a week later.

I made arrangements with the renters of my house to make their rental payments directly to the bank to pay my mortgage, then I packed up everything and put it in storage, except for Kyle's clothes and mine. Sheila begged to go with me (she was between husbands, I think, and living back at home with the folks with her son and daughter). It was an awfully long trip to take by myself with a small boy, and I knew I could use help driving, so the three of us set out for California in my little TR4. We made the trip in good time and pulled into the driveway about a day and a half later at the house Will and I had chosen a year before!

Will's attitude toward marriage had changed. We now had a maid who came in twice a week, so I didn't have to do all the housework. And he sent his business shirts to the laundry. Yes, being with Will then was very, very different, but I was, too. Will did his best to win me over, but after about three months, when we got word that the renters had moved out of my house and had not made any mortgage payments for the entire time that I was gone, I jumped at the chance to go back to Kansas City. That was probably the second biggest mistake I ever made in my entire life.

When I walked into my house I was dismayed. Half of my furniture was gone and while I knew they were putting in a carpet, they had assured me that they didn't tack it down. Wrong! They had ruined my beautiful hardwood floors. I had no choice but to lay tile to cover the damage, since I couldn't afford to have the floors refinished. That was just the first of the many slaps in the face I got when I arrived home.

Kyle started kindergarten that September in 1964. I started drinking a lot more, trying to escape the reality of my failures. Will came back to Kansas City the end of November, but I was unaware that it had to do with my house. Even though we were divorced and I had been awarded the house as my separate property, Will's name was still on the mortgage and they had contacted him when I got so far behind in the payments. Will took care of it without telling me.

We had a long talk and I asked him to take Kyle with him back to California until I could get my finances straight, which I thought would be accomplished by the end of the school year the next June. Will agreed, and I put on a happy face for my son, waving goodbye and not knowing that I would not see him again for over three years. Now I was totally alone in that big house. I put all my favorite sad records on the stereo, grabbed my bottle of scotch, and quietly started getting drunk. I drank and cried, cried and drank.

Then I got a call from Jack McGinnis (my dad's new boss at another company) and he could tell I was crying, so when he asked me to go with him to a party, he wouldn't take no for an answer. He came and got me. Around one or two in the morning, the subject of Jack's office in Houston came up, and Jack said that he and one of the salesmen were leaving for Houston to check some things out and invited me to go. I said, "Why not?" I didn't even go back to the house to get some clothes. Jack said we could pick up whatever I needed after we got there.

And that's how I got to Houston, Texas. In Jack McGinnis' fire engine red, brand new Cadillac convertible. I was astonished as it got daylight and I saw that the grass had gone from being brown and dried up in Kansas, to green and it was getting warmer the farther south we went. And it seemed like most of the trees still had leaves. Two weeks later, I went back to Kansas City, gave all of my furniture away to my sister, Sue Ellen, who had just gotten married (at sixteen) and had had a baby, threw all of my clothes in the Corvair and hot-footed it back to Houston.

~Chapter 7~

The first two weeks I was in Houston, I did give in to Jack McGinnis' advances and we had a short affair. I rarely made it out of bed. Then I started coming to and knew that I wanted to stay in Houston, so I started talking about getting a job and a place of my own. Jack offered me a job at his office. The salary wasn't much, but it included an apartment, which was close enough to the office that I could walk to work, and the bills were included with the rent. But as far as I was concerned, as soon as I started working for him, there would be no more hanky panky. Either I failed to make that clear, or Jack refused to believe it. I was unaware that when he showed me my new apartment, that he had obtained a key of his own. But that didn't become apparent for a couple of months.

I really enjoyed the new job. I had never been in direct sales before; I had always been a secretary. Now I was an office manager who supervised the telemarketers and even participated in the "closings." I also had signature power on the company checkbook. For Christmas (with Jack's consent) I gave myself a bonus and bought a black, miniature poodle for about a hundred dollars. I named her Angelique after the heroine in a series of books I had been reading. I found a tiny little dinner club called La Riveria in the middle of downtown Houston. I had been there on several occasions by myself and after a few drinks, could work up the courage to get on stage and perform with the band, The Billy Holeman Trio. But more about Billy later.

I soon had a rude awakening as to what my job entailed. We were expecting McGinnis to come into town soon and I was the first to see him the day he got there. When I went home for lunch I found him in my bed and all of his clothes in my closet. I shouldn't have been surprised but I was. I quietly picked up my purse and went back to work. Later that afternoon when he showed up at the office, I told him we needed to talk. At dinner that night I asked him how he got into my apartment and he very simply told me he kept a key when he rented the apartment for me. I very carefully explained to him that I just didn't mix business with pleasure and as long as I was working for him that there would be no personal relationship. It just got too sticky when people did that. He seemed okay with that, at least that's what he led me to believe. And he removed all of his clothes from my apartment and checked into a motel.

The next day at the office McGinnis called a meeting and announced that I was being promoted to administrator, and that we needed to hire another woman so I could train her to take over the job I had been doing. Along with the new title, I was getting a substantial raise in salary. I was ecstatic. I had no doubts now that I would have all my finances back in order and be more than ready to get Kyle at the end of the school year.

We soon found a replacement for me, but I had no idea that the whole time that I was training her that she actually was my *replacement*. It didn't take very long to train her, and I was soon ready to start performing my new duties. However, McGinnis was gone, and no one seemed to know exactly what those "duties" were. It soon became apparent to me exactly what had occurred, when the first of the month rolled around and my apartment manager started bugging me to pay the rent. When I handed over the reins to my replacement that included signature power on the checking account, so I was no longer in charge of paying bills. When I asked her what the deal was and why my apartment rent had not been paid she directed me to Jim Sedona. McGinnis had dumped the job of telling me that I was no longer gainfully employed on Sedona. I was in shock.

Here I was eight hundred miles from home and the only friends I had in Houston were at the office. Crying and screaming wouldn't help since Sedona was only following his orders, and McGinnis had conveniently absented himself so I couldn't find him. I had no choice but to pack up my Corvair and move out. I had no money to get another apartment, so I wound up living in my Corvair for two weeks. That was exciting—not!

I called Will and told him the situation. I asked him when he was going to send me the balance of the money on the trade of the TR4 for the Corvair and he said he'd get it to me right away. I told him to send it to the office, and then I called Sedona to tell him to expect it and I would be over in two days to pick it up.

I found a job as a waitress right away (thank you, Mom!). Then I got the check from Will and was able to rent a small one-bedroom apartment about a block down the street from a little strip club called The Closet where I had been spending my evenings just to be with people. Well, making a dollar or two an hour plus tips just wasn't going to make it. I had to find another job, or a second job. The owner of The Closet offered me a job as bartender/waitress and I jumped at it. I was again working two jobs and things were looking up. At least I was able to make bills.

On the nights that I wasn't working at The Closet, I still spent my time there and one night I walked into the poolroom there and proceeded to drink the bar dry. My friend Sally got me home. That was the first time that I had suffered an alcoholic blackout. It scared me so bad that I drove to downtown Houston and signed up with Kelly Girls so I could get a job that didn't entail being around booze. They put me to work the very next day.

The next seven and a half years of my life contain some unbelievable highs and lows, ecstasy and pain. But, as Garth Brooks' song says, 'I could have missed the pain, but I would have had to miss the dance.'

I had become very good friends with my next-door neighbors, a couple originally from California. They said that they had just the man for me. My neighbors finally got their friend and me together. As nice a guy as he was, he was much too old for me. I was attracted to him, but I was twenty-seven; he was in his mid-forties. I shied away from older men. Didn't need another daddy, don't ya know? His name was Allen Adam Morley and he was called Al for short. He was prematurely gray, with blue eyes and a dark complexion.

I was still a regular visitor at the La Riviera where I could sit in for a set or two with Billy Holeman and his band. Billy got another gig at The Clubhouse, another little hole-in-the-wall on the back of a shopping center in Houston. Then, after hours, we would all go to one of the "after hours" clubs in town where a lot of local musicians would all congregate and have one big happy jam session until three or four o'clock in the morning, sometimes even later. They played it all: rock and roll, jazz, rhythm and blues, even country and western. There were many nights I would get home at four or even five, take a catnap, jump up, shower, get dressed and rush off to work. How in Sam Hill I did that, I'll never know. Sure as heck can't do it now!!!

On one such morning when I was at the Kettle by myself, Al came into the bar with a group of people, and took up the corner booth. He nodded to me and then started talking animatedly with a very nice looking young man who was with him and they both kept looking back at my table. The young man looked vaguely familiar to me, but I just couldn't place him at the moment. Then the young man headed straight to my table.

"Hi," he said. "I'm Nick. Did Billy tell you what we've been talking about?"

"Uh, not that I recall," I stuttered. I was having trouble concentrating on what Nick was saying. I had an almost instant reaction to him. He was about five foot eight, very slender, dark hair, blue eyes and dark complexion. Then he cleared up my confusion with one simple statement.

"Al's my dad. He told me that you were the singer Billy has been talking about."

Bingo! That's why Nick looked familiar to me. He looked exactly like a younger version of his father. And where I had been mildly attracted to the father, I was wildly attracted to the son. We sat at the table in the restaurant talking for hours. Nick was just starting in the music business and had decided he needed to pair up with a girl since girl/boy duos were a hot item on the country and rock scenes. I was willing to discuss singing rock or rhythm and blues. So we talked until I took him home with me and we became a couple. A week later we were in the studio with Billy Holeman, Denny Walters and Hank Finn, the original Billy Holeman Trio. We reworked a song Billy had written for a girl named Linda, and my children's favorite song was born, "Lynetta."

I was in charge of putting Nick's songs on paper, creating the score and then mailing a copy to us certified mail, return receipt requested, which we never opened. That was the least expensive way of ensuring that no one else could steal our music before we could record it or get it published and registered with BMI. I often jokingly said that the only reason Nick married me was because I could immortalize his music in writing.

The warning signs in our relationship were there early on, but I ignored them. Nick often "forgot" when he was supposed to come home, and would show up way too late for us to make our commitment for dinner or whatever. Or he failed to show up to give me a ride home from work, claiming that he didn't understand or got too busy. He was a delivery truck driver, for heaven's sake! And what was wrong with the telephone? That's all I ever asked for, just a little consideration so I wouldn't stand around waiting for something that was never going to happen. But I let it pass. Shame on me!

Within a month, I knew that I was pregnant and Nick insisted on getting married. This would be the second marriage for both of us. So on September 7, 1965, I became a wife again. And I learned that my husband's real name was Andrew Adam Morley. He had chosen the stage name of Nick Allen, because several people had told him that he resembled the actor, Nick Adams. We moved into a four-plex with his dad and his sister, Gladys (whom we affectionately called "Happy Butt." Gladys . . . glad ass . . . happy butt. Get it? Oh, never mind.) Billy had introduced us to his would-be manager, such a forgettable character that I've forgotten his name. He got us several gigs at area nightclubs and a spot on a local television production.

After one particularly good session one night in a club with Billy and the guys, Billy invited us to a jam session in the Montrose area where a few local musicians were congregating. There was another fellow there who sang under his real name, Kenny Rogers. I have to confess that I was not impressed with Mr. Rogers at that session as he was non-communicative and verged on being downright rude. This was, of course, before he became so well known as part of the New Christy Minstrels.

Then before we could really work on promoting the record and maybe even doing more, the bane of Nick's existence appeared. His name was Bill Junior Mooney and he had been instrumental in getting Nick into the printing business and into country music. Bill and his wife, Bettie, had been singing for a long time in Kentucky and had most recently formed a band called The Blue Notes. Bill had also purchased a small print shop in Covington, Kentucky, right across the river from Cincinnati, Ohio, and offered Nick a half interest in the place. So a month after getting married, cutting our first record, and appearing on television, we were off to Kentucky.

I hope any native Kentuckians will forgive me but I spent the most miserable year of my life there and for the longest time as far as I was concerned Kentucky did not exist. Bill and Bettie had arranged for us to take over a small apartment on the first floor of the house where they lived upstairs. Since my husband was now half owner in a business, I was under the mistaken impression that I could now become a stay-at-home mom. Fat chance. What Bill allowed Nick to take out of the business was barely enough to buy groceries or pay the rent. I had no choice but to try and find a job. Being pregnant I knew that I would not be able to find a permanent job. Thank goodness for Kelly Girls.

Nick found us a bigger place (hah!) in Newport, Kentucky, which was actually the back of an insurance business. There was a living room, a small kitchen/dining area, and the bedroom in which a double bed just barely fit. But the bathroom was in the basement. We had no yard, our front door opened directly onto the company's parking lot, and we had no back door. Since I was pregnant, the owner of the company had given me the key to the back door of his office in case I needed to use the telephone.

We settled into a kind of routine, going to work, coming home, getting dressed to go out and perform. When I was three months pregnant I went to the doctor for the first time to get a check-up and had the rug yanked from under my feet. I was not three months pregnant, I was *five* months. That meant that the baby I was carrying could not possibly be Nick's! I was devastated. I had unwittingly saddled the man I was growing to love more and more every day with someone else's child.

I drove around for about an hour after that appointment, crying and thinking. I finally decided that there was nothing to do, but to get it out on the table immediately. There was no way I was going to go through the entire pregnancy and then try to make Nick think everything was hunky dory and that I had just had a premature baby. Nick didn't seem to be bothered by the fact that he wasn't the father of my child. To him, it was just another "history repeats itself" episode. It seems the same thing had happened to his father with his second wife. We made a promise at that time not to tell the rest of the family, but that as soon as the baby was old enough to understand and we thought maybe eight or nine years old would be the right time, then we would explain it to him or her.

One bright spot in this year of utter desolation was Dick Cheeseman. He was the owner of one of the bars that we frequented. There are legions of Dicks in the world—frustrated musicians who finally give up on making it in the entertainment world, they buy their own bar so they can perform any time they like. And they are very generous in allowing would-be artists to practice.

By December I was beginning to feel very pregnant and didn't feel comfortable getting up on the stage any more, but I went along. That's when I really began to love my husband. I finally understood those girls who were so crazy about Elvis. Sitting in the audience and listening to Nick would just send chills through me.

Then it was New Year's Eve, and the band had a gig in Dayton, Ohio, at an American Legion party. It was a bit of a trip and since I wasn't performing, I begged off. I never could sleep until Nick got home so I polished the apartment. Then I ironed. Then I read. I expected him home at two, maybe three, depending on how long they kept them. Then it was five. I was frantic with worry. He finally strolled in at five-thirty in the morning of New Year's Day. I asked him how the gig went and why it took him so long to get home.

He nonchalantly said, "Oh, we didn't get the gig." When I asked why not, he explained that two different people had hired bands and the other band got there first. I asked him why he had not come home then and he said that they went out to celebrate New Year's Eve.

"But, why didn't you come and get me?" By this time I was sobbing uncontrollably. He was getting exasperated now. He couldn't understand why I was so upset. He reminded me that I did not want to go out. "I said I didn't want to go sit with a bunch of strange people while you guys were on stage performing. I never said I didn't want to go with you to celebrate New Year's."

He said that he didn't want to discuss it anymore and was going to bed. I was left standing in the kitchen, tears streaming down my face. I just couldn't believe he had been so callous and unfeeling as to celebrate our first New Year's without me. I simply couldn't get to sleep at that point, so I sat at the kitchen table and wrote a song. Then I wrote a long letter to Nick's mother that I never sent. Nick found the song, but not the letter. He made some comment about why I couldn't write a happy song. Why were all of my songs sad? Hmmm. I wonder why he couldn't figure that out? So, just to show him that I could, I sat down and wrote a song based on a popular phrase of the day, "That's the Breaks!" which became my children's second favorite song. My boys always called it the "doodle doot" song, because that was the majority of my part in it.

Our relationship suffered a great deal after the New Year's fiasco. At one point, I was so upset and just knew it wasn't going to work, I snuck into the insurance office late one night and called Will in California. I was ready to throw myself on his mercy if he would just take me back long enough to have the baby and then I would get out of his hair. What a fool I was!

I was taken aback when a woman answered the phone. I almost hung up. But I asked for Will and she said, "Just a minute." I guess I don't need to tell you that Will had finally gotten married again and that it was his new wife who had answered the phone. So I didn't tell him what I had been about to propose. I was too embarrassed. I did let him know that things weren't going that well but that we were working it out. Kyle was already in bed asleep, so I didn't get to talk to him that time.

I tried to make the best of what I had gotten myself into. My baby didn't come on the second of February as predicted. He decided to wait until the seventh—when there was about three feet of snow on the ground and it was colder than blue Billy blazes. I was just about to drift off to sleep when a popping noise woke me. The popping sound came right after the baby had given me a good hard kick. My water was about to break. So I punched Nick to wake him up and we slid all the way to the hospital in the snow.

Nick had been waiting beside the bed until I woke up so he could tell me that we had an eight pound ten and a half ounce baby boy. And since he had already had a son named Andrew Adam Morley, Jr., he wanted to ask me if it would be okay if we named our son Nick Allen Morley. I was very touched and told him that was perfect.

When Nicky was a month old, I got a release from the doctor to go back to work. The very first weekend after I went back to work, when I got home Nick wanted to know if I wanted to go out with him and Bill and Bettie. "Nick, we don't have any money," I said. "We have to wait until next week when I'll have my check from Kelly Girls."

So, he wanted to know if I minded if he went with them as I did not want to go. I just saw red and I wasn't going to stand for it any more. "Okay. If you think we can afford for you to go out with Bill and Bettie, get enough money for me and to pay a babysitter, because I'm going out, too, but not with Bill and Bettie."

Where he got the money from, I don't know and I don't care. The fury raging through me lasted long enough for me to carefully put on my make up and my best party outfit. Then I headed for Dick Cheeseman's, the only place where I felt comfortable going alone. And boy, did I party. I did my darnedest to stay out later than Nick did, but I just couldn't do it. I'll tell you one thing, though. He never did that again.

Then I was forced to make a decision between my dog and my baby—or rather, my dog and my husband. Nick had really never liked Angelique. And when he saw her jump up on the couch so that she could lay down next to Nicky with her head on his stomach, he flipped out. There was no getting around it. He insisted that I had to get rid of the dog. He contended that she was jealous of the baby and would wind up hurting him. I insisted that she was just crazy about the baby and would protect him. Nick put his foot down and I lost. So I advertised for a good home, and gave her away. I cried buckets.

It soon became apparent that we were going to have to get a bigger place. Our tiny bedroom barely held a double bed. We had to climb over the bed and around the bassinette to get to the dresser now. This time we got a third floor apartment, which was really a converted attic and I lucked out to find a babysitter on the first floor. We still didn't have a pot to piss in nor a window to throw it out of, but our marriage was gaining ground...I thought. It was really a chore going to the grocery store and carting the groceries up all those stairs. It was even more of a chore to carry the laundry down to the basement so that I could do the wash in the big stainless steel sinks. Did you ever try to wash a pair of men's jeans by hand? What a bummer. Anyway, back to the story.

We were beginning to make a little headway. I very carefully sat down every weekend and planned the week's menus and bought only what I needed to make those meals. I scrimped and scraped and finally got enough together to buy a black and white television.

I didn't get to the doctor soon enough to get birth control pills and was soon pregnant again. Our next baby was due to be born approximately six weeks after his brother turned one year old.

~Chapter 8~

Before I knew it, it was June, and time to make arrangements to bring Kyle home. It took a few calls before I actually got to talk to Will. Cheryl always answered the phone and said she would have him call me, but he didn't. Then one night he finally answered the phone when I called, and my world came crashing down around my head. He simply refused to send Kyle back to me and he wouldn't discuss it—just hung up. I felt betrayed. I had never had the slightest inkling that Will would be that cruel. I cried for days. Then I finally got mad and called the folks to ask them to find me a lawyer in Kansas. I was going to have to take Will back to court. That was the beginning of a continuing battle that lasted three years. The divorce had taken place in Kansas, so it still had jurisdiction. I lived in Kentucky at that time, and Will was in California with Kyle.

To take my mind off my custody battle, Nick suggested that we get a puppy since I had been harping on it for a while now. I could never stand to be without a dog for more than six months at a time, and Nick figured that if we got a small dog now, that Nicky would grow up with it. So, we started searched and ended up with an Italian Greyhound that I named Bambi. Things had been going so well for us the last couple of months, so it took me completely by surprise when Nick nonchalantly threw into one of our conversations that he was going to go on a road trip to Alabama with Bill and Bettie. There was no discussion on it. No preambles. Just flat out, "I'm going on a road trip." And the unspoken end of that sentence was, "without you!" Talk about a kick in the teeth. We were just beginning to make headway again and money was not quite so tight that we couldn't take a little trip once in a while or have a night on the town. Not to mention the fact that I was about three months pregnant again. I could see that he had made up his mind and nothing I said was going to change it. I just accepted it, because I was numb (or is that "D-U-M-B!").

Nick left the next day while I was at work. I came home to find the television I had worked so hard to pay for gone, along with everything and anything else that he thought he could hock. And all but one or two of the pictures in my modeling portfolio had been torn to bits and scattered all over the living room. But that wasn't the worst part. A few days later the landlord came up to tell me that my rent check had bounced. There was no way I could have bounced that check. Oh, yeah, there was. In addition to taking everything of value from the apartment, Nick had cleaned out the checking account on his way out of town.

Fortunately, the landlord generously offered to let me pay a little extra each payday until I could catch up on the missing month's rent.

About six weeks later, Nick called from Alabama begging me to let him come home. I hesitated and then said, "All right. But we are going back to Houston as soon as you get here, or I'm going back to Kansas. I am not staying here anymore." He agreed and within a day he was back home with his tail tucked between his legs. My first question was, "Where's my television?" He looked surprised that I hadn't figured out that he'd had to sell the television to get the money for his bus ticket back to Kentucky.

The next day I gave notice. Within the week, we had packed all of our clothes and a few kitchen items and shipped them to his dad in Houston. I gave the key to the Chevy to my landlord to make up for any shortage in rent, and we bought tickets on the train to Houston. There was only one problem—Bambi. How was I going to take her with us? There was no way that I was leaving her behind, and to buy a crate and pay to ship her was almost as much as the tickets for the two of us. My solution was to buy a small ditty bag with a zippered top. I carried her on the train and set her on the floor by my feet. Then I would collect the newspapers people left laying around in the dining car or lounge and I would carry my ditty bag into the bathroom with me and let Bambi do her business, get her some fresh water and just in general stretch her legs. She never made a sound the whole thirteen hundred-plus mile trip to Houston. Everyone in our car knew she was there, except the conductor. Then as we were pulling into Union Station in Houston I opened the bag and took her into my arms to carry her out. When the conductor realized that she had been on the train, he was livid. Who cared? I was home!

We were all really tired after what amounted to three days on a train, so we just went to the apartment Nick's dad had rented for all of us. Now I was really happy to be back in Houston. However, I was again looking for a job and pregnant. Which meant it would have to be Kelly Girls again until the baby was born. I found a long-term assignment with a frozen food distributor as secretary to the general manager. Nick was able to find a job with a print shop and I sighed a great big sigh of relief.

Bright and early on the morning of St. Patrick's Day, we drove to the hospital and the nurses started the Pitocin drip in my arm. They didn't have to leave it in long at all because I went into hard labor almost immediately and approximately two and a half hours later Shane Patrick Morley made his debut—almost exactly thirteen months after his brother Nicky. The apartment soon became too small with three adults, a toddler and a baby so we went looking and found a nice little house. We were still doing our music and I was making all of our costumes. The only professionally-made costume we ever had, was a few years later when we had matching electric blue sharkskin outfits made. My outfit included a very short skirt and a pair of slacks with a vest. And Nick's was a Western style suit. All of the pieces had white kick pleats. Remember this sharkskin suit. There's going to be a test later.

Just when things seemed to be getting better, life has a way of yanking the rug out from under you. The first heartbreaker that year was while Nick and I were at work, Al watched the boys during the day because he was between jobs. He called me at work because Bambi had jumped off the front porch and was hit by a car. She wasn't killed, but one of her back legs was broken.

Then in the summer of that year, 1967, after battling for over two years, the Kansas court finally issued the orders for Will to return Kyle to my custody. I was ecstatic. My son was coming home. I hadn't seen him for almost three years and he would soon be eight years old. We made all the flight arrangements and got the bedroom ready for Kyle. His flight was due on Saturday, but on that Thursday evening, there was a knock on the front door and I was presented with a summons by a deputy sheriff. Will had filed for change of custody in the California courts. I was in utter despair. My boy still wasn't coming home and I would have to go to California and fight some more.

Along with all of that, Nick's drinking was getting worse. I had quickly learned that alcohol has a way of making you forget lyrics and your timing gets way bad, so I drank instant tea when performing. Unfortunately, Nick didn't think it was necessary to stay sober when he performed. And if he blew it, I was the one who suffered on the way home—all the ranting and raving, name calling, pushing and shoving. He hadn't hit me—yet. So I put up with it and tried to calm him down. After one particularly bad screw up that he had made on stage, he started yelling at me before we made it out the door. I was afraid to get in the car with him that night, but I was about twenty miles from home and didn't know what else to do. I started to get in the car but before I could open the door, Nick peeled out of the parking lot and left me standing there alone. Okay. Now what? I didn't have any money on me, and Billy and the rest of the band had already left. Thank goodness, Norman was still there. Norman was a mutual acquaintance who was currently sleeping on our couch in the living room. The next day, as always, Nick was apologetic and things were good again.

Soon it was time for me to go to California to continue the fight for Kyle. I made the train trip to Kansas City to drop the boys off with my sister, Sheila, and her new husband, and then I continued on to San Diego where my aunt lived. The first thing we did when I got there was go to a lawyer my aunt knew to see what I needed to do to get my son back. After listening to my story and reading the orders from the Kansas court, he tried to talk me into kidnapping my own son, but as Kyle had not seen me in three years I felt that that was not a good idea for Kyle. The lawyer told me to try to work it out with Will, and then get back to him as far as what I needed him to do.

So we went back to my aunt's house and decided to go to Los Angeles the next day to try and talk to Will. When we got to Los Angeles I called Will at the office and told him I was in town and wanted to see my son and to talk about the custody suit. After the initial shock of learning I was that close, Will agreed to a meeting and told me that he would meet me at his house when Kyle got out of school.

Aunt Teddie and I arrived at the house before Will got there. Carol graciously invited us in and served us some refreshments. Then she excused herself to go call Will and let him know we were already there. About thirty minutes later there was a knock on the front door. I glanced at Teddie. Surely it couldn't be Will. He wouldn't have to knock on his own front door, would he? It was a process server. Carol showed him into the living room and I was again served with the change of custody papers Will had filed in California. You'll have to forgive me right now if this gets a little disjointed. As I write all this down, I'm crying so hard that I can hardly see the screen. It's really a little like living it all over again. Two seconds—that's all it took. The process server walked in, handed me the papers and walked out. I think I collapsed into a sobbing mess. "He's not bringing Kyle home, is he?" I tearfully asked Carol. To be so close and then learn it was all for nothing was just more than I could bear.

"Yes, he is," she said, and walked back into the kitchen to make a call. I was crying uncontrollably. Then she came back into the living room. I was finally getting myself back under control and resigning myself to going home without seeing Kyle. In just a few minutes, Will walked in the door—alone. He came into the living room and stared at me.

Then he said, "I'll be right back," and he walked out the door. We moved out onto the patio. Carol tried to make things a little easier by telling me how well Kyle was doing in school and some of the activities he was in. She went back in the house to get some snapshots and school pictures and gave them to me. By the time Will got back with Kyle, I almost had it together again. When Kyle walked out of the patio door, he hesitated for just a minute. He looked at me and then at Aunt Teddie, and I could see the confusion in his face. So I took a couple of steps toward him, bent down and opened my arms and he came running. A great weight was lifted from my shoulders and a feeling of peace settled in. I don't remember much about the rest of that visit except that Kyle never left my side. It was finally time to go back to Aunt Teddie's and I went back with the understanding that I would be back the next weekend to celebrate Kyle's birthday.

Once back in San Diego, and having no idea how long this process was going to take, I again went to my old standby, Kelly Girls and started working so I would be able to contribute to the household while I was staying with Aunt Teddie. Not to mention the fact that I had to get enough money together for a lawyer and for the trip home. I certainly couldn't expect any help from Nick. The following weekend, I rode the train up to spend the weekend with my son. By mutual agreement, we didn't discuss the custody issue. We just tried to make it as joyful an occasion for Kyle as possible. We went to the zoo and had a really glorious day. Our agreement not to discuss the custody issue was nullified when I got a call from Nick as we were sitting down that night for Kyle's birthday supper.

He wanted me home right away. I asked him just what the emergency was. Oh, not much. Simply that there was this girl in Kentucky claiming that he was the father of her child and she was coming to Houston with the baby. This baby was just a month older than our son, Shane. Jesus, Joseph and Mary. Just how much more of this crap was I going to be able to stand? I told Nick that it would be at least another week before I could come home, simply because I would have to work to get train fare.

When I finished my conversation with Nick, I looked at Will and Carol and told them that we needed to talk privately as soon as Kyle was in bed. When I was sure that Kyle was asleep, I explained what Nick had conveyed over the phone. They were both shocked. The next day, when Will put me on the train to go back to Teddie's, he tried to talk me into moving to California with my two boys but without Nick. I looked at him blankly for a minute and then realized exactly what he was asking when he took me in his arms and began kissing me. Oh, no. I wasn't interested in that kind of arrangement.

After agonizing and praying for God to lead me in the right direction over what to do for the next week, I finally came to what I felt was the best decision for Kyle. Will and Carol were speechless when I told them that I felt that it would be best for Kyle to stay with them since I had such a lousy situation at home and didn't want to put him through that. Even though it was breaking my heart, I really felt Kyle would be much better off in the stable environment he had with Will and Carol right then, than to come home with me. Will was certainly much better off financially than I was, and I could see that Carol really cared for Kyle and he cared for her, too. So I told Will to have his lawyer draw up the papers and basically reverse the original orders giving him custody and me visitation rights. I had to go back to Houston and try to salvage my marriage to Nick. Although I would always have a big hole in my heart, I prayed that I had made the right decision for Kyle

I first headed to pick up Nicky and Shane and then on to Houston. Talk about mixed emotions. I was grieving over my decision about Kyle, happy to have Nicky and Shane back in my arms, anticipating seeing my husband again, and dreading what was facing me when I did. I didn't have much time to really think when I got back to Houston that Sunday morning because Barbara and her two children were due in that afternoon. I could see that Nick was really in a dither about the mess that he had gotten himself into. It was pretty obvious that he loved the boys and me, while at the same time he felt obligated to do something for Barbara and this baby if it turned out that he was really the father. I told him that we would just have to play it by ear until we could figure out what to do.

Against Al's advice I went with Nick to the train station that evening to pick up Barbara and her children. I clamped a hard hand down on my basic instinct to walk over and slap the crap out of her when she got off the train. But after the first few sentences out of her mouth, I realized that she was just a scared shitless, unworldly, totally out-of-her-league, little girl. She wasn't even eighteen years old and already had two illegitimate children. I gave Nick my best "shame on you" glare behind Barbara's back as we headed for the car and home. Yes, you heard me right. I said home. I was taking my husband's mistress home with me

We weren't in the house very long before something was said, and I finally lost the stranglehold I had on my temper and my basic instincts took control. I believe Nick had asked me if it was all right if he moved into an apartment with Barbara, because he felt that he needed to be with her and the baby. Excuse me! What about my baby? Oh, but remember me? I just lost it then and ordered them both out of the house and out of my sight. Then I locked myself in my bedroom for most of the rest of the night, until little Nicky knocked on the door wanting supper.

It only took a week for Nick to come to the conclusion that he had chosen the wrong path and he came crawling back. His finally realized his place was with me and our two boys, not with a young girl and the result of a few stolen one-night stands when he was unhappy with me in Kentucky. He called and asked if he could meet me after work and talk it over. So we met and I agreed to let him come home. The marriage was doomed from the start. I had just put a bandaid on it for the time being.

Shortly after Barbara went back to Kentucky, Sheila came for an extended visit with her two children. Husband problems, I think. But it wasn't very long before her husband Phil followed her, and they rented the house just two doors down from ours. In the midst of all that mess I had found a job that I really liked with an engineering firm in downtown Houston that was to be my work home for the next four years. Nick was still working for the tire company in the print shop, so we were doing well. We cut a few more records in a little studio. We kept Billy, but the other members of the trio had changed and we added a popular disk jockey, Jim Black, on the keyboard. We now had a new manager named Mark McCollum who was a real go-getter.

We began getting jobs all over with Mark as our manager. Mark also produced a country and western show at the Houston Theater in the Round, which included, along with yours truly, popular artists like Mickey Gilley and Jerry Lee Lewis. But my most memorable meeting with a country star was in 1969 on a tour bus outside the auditorium in Austin, Texas. A co-writer friend had always claimed that he knew George Jones personally and he proved it by taking us to meet George and his wife, the First Lady of Country Music, Tammy Wynette. There's a picture floating around somewhere of me on that tour bus sitting on George's lap with a very pregnant Tammy grinning beside us.

But alas and alack. All the golden opportunities we had failed to produce that "instant stardom" that Nick was always so sure was just around the corner. It may have had something to do with the fact that he never really worked for it! He expected Colonel Tom Parker or someone like him to be sitting in the audience when we performed and there never was. Or maybe it was his drinking. Or maybe it just wasn't meant to be. And the longer it took for us to be "discovered," the more he drank, and the more he drank, the more he screwed up on stage, at work and in our marriage.

Then we decided to try one more time for a daughter, and in short order I was pregnant. In the meantime, I became interested in obedience training and had enrolled a new Italian Greyhound, Smokey, in a dog class. That was the beginning of an interest that has lasted over thirty years. I still train with the same teacher. Smokey and I were beginners together and after training for a few months, I showed Smokey at my first dog show—I was six months pregnant and it was raining. Poor little Smokey. In those days, the obedience rings were always outside.

On the evening of January 13, 1970, I was having trouble sleeping. Sure enough, just as I was able to drift off to sleep, I was awakened by the beginning contractions. I woke Nick, loaded the boys into the car and we dropped them off at Sheila's. Thirty minutes after making it to the hospital, Scott Edward Morley came into the world, yelling for all he was worth. What? Another boy? At first I was upset, because we had hoped for a girl, but as soon as Eddie was in my arms, all thoughts of a girl were gone.

A friend of Nick's introduced him to a developer who had purchased a farm and was creating a neighborhood by buying old houses, moving them in and remodeling them. We got a really good deal on a beautiful four-bedroom house. I loved that house. It was the perfect place to raise a family. The elementary school was only four or five blocks down the road and they had just built a new high school. We had plenty of room to handle my dogs, of which we now had four IGs, and we adopted a little female Dachshund that someone had left behind. So I had another Heidi.

Unfortunately, Eddie was always sick. It seemed he forever had a cold. He was six months old and still hadn't had his immunization shots, because the doctor wouldn't give them to him when he was sick. One night when Nick was passed out in the bedroom, and my newest girlfriend, Sammie, had come to live with us, Eddie was running a really high fever. Sammie and I tried everything we knew to bring my baby's fever down, but we were getting nowhere. We finally realized that there nothing more we could do so we headed for the Texas Children's Hospital about twenty-five miles away at the Texas Medical Center.

Eddie wound up in the hospital for a week with bronchitis and middle ear infection. Some member of the family had to always be there, so Sammie and I took turns. She would stay during the day while I was working, and then I would take over at night. Nick would come to visit during his lunch hours. The first few nights I didn't get any sleep at all. I had to keep touching Eddie to make sure he was alive, because I couldn't hear him breathing.

When things were going halfway normal, we continued playing music when we could. On one occasion we hired one of the neighbor girls to watch the boys. We had made arrangements for the babysitter to spend the night so it wasn't necessary for us to take her home when we got back. Just before I fell asleep, I realized that Nick was not in bed. So I went looking for him and found him in the living room in the dark, sitting on the couch where our young babysitter was sleeping. I was too tired to think there was any hanky panky going on there, I just told him to come on to bed and he did.

A few months later all hell broke lose. We received a foreclosure notice in the mail, which took me totally by surprise. That's when I found out that Nick had been taking the mortgage payment check out of the mailbox, and then he would withdraw the same amount of money from the bank, so it appeared to me that the bill was being paid. Then he used that money for his own spending money. In addition, our babysitter's father paid Nick a visit when I wasn't at home, demanding that Nick own up to the fact that he had violated the neighbor's minor daughter who was now expecting a baby.

Nick managed to find several boys that the girl had been seeing, who admitted to having sexual relations with her so her father really couldn't prove anything against Nick. But I knew. Just as sure as I'm sitting here, I knew. And I also knew that the end was coming fast because I just didn't care any more. I didn't care what he did. I no longer had any trouble falling asleep at night when he wasn't there. I didn't sit up all night imagining all sorts of car wrecks, or drunken brawls. But I did care that I was losing my home. And there was nothing I could do about it. We had to move again.

I found us a house inside the Loop where I could catch the bus to work right there. It was a tiny little two-bedroom house with just a living room and a kitchen, and we had to sell most of our furniture, including my piano. The worst part about it was the backyard was right up against the feeder road for Loop 610 with all the traffic noises.

The arguments were beginning to escalate. One night when Nick had made a special idiotic fool of himself getting up on stage and almost falling flat on his face, then totally butchering a song, he was ranting and raving at me as I was driving us home. He was upset that I had allowed him to get up on the stage in that condition, even though I explained that he would not listen to me. Then, just as I was getting onto the exit he backhanded me. He knocked my glasses almost clear off of my face, and at such an angle, that I was having trouble seeing the road—especially with the force of the slap knocking me silly. I had to stop the car to get my bearings back. It startled me so, because that was the first time he had actually hit me. Oh, there had been lots of shoving and threats, but he had never actually hit me. I got really scared—then I got really mad.

The farther I drove, the louder and crazier he got until I just pulled over to the side of the road, threw the keys at him, and got out of the car and started walking. He jumped out, insisting that I take the car and that he would walk. So I did—I left him there. I drove home, approximately five miles, and picked up the kids on my way.

About two hours later, the front door banged open and an enraged Nick came charging in. He yelled and screamed foul names at me, the boys were now all awake and crying, and then I got really scared. Nick went into the kitchen and came back with a butcher knife. He was yelling, "If you want me gone, why don't you just kill me?" raised the knife and brought it down hard on the coffee table right in front of me and it stuck, standing straight up and quivering. Much like I was quivering inside. I really don't remember how we made it through that night, but Nick must have calmed down after that outburst. And so, life went on.

~Chapter 9~

New Year's Eve 1971. My first New Year's Eve with Nick was bad and the last one was just as memorable. Fortunately, New Year's Eve that year was a Friday, and I didn't have to take time off from work. I left Thursday night to drive to Dallas and be matron-of-honor for my friend, Sammie. Just before heading back to Houston after the reception, I changed into my blue sharkskin outfit with the white kick pleats because Nick and I were supposed to be on-stage at the Winchester Club that night, along with Glen Barber, Mickey Gilley and Jerry Lee Lewis.

Of course the place was packed when I got there about eleven and I had trouble finding a parking place. As I started down the side of the building to see if there was any room to park in the back, I swerved to miss something white that came out of nowhere and landed on the ground. I couldn't see what it was, just a white patch. I finally found a place and hurried into the club. When I walked in, Glen Barber pointed over to the area on the side of the stage where I finally located Sheila and Phil. When I asked Sheila where Nick was, she said that he had felt sick as he was drunk, and had gone outside to throw up. We all rushed outside and sure enough there was Nick. He had walked between two vehicles, leaned forward and threw up. Then he collapsed face down into all the mess. That's what I had seen when I drove in, the flare of the white pleat in his jacket when he fell.

In February of 1972 my friend Alice gave me the best news. The law firm where she worked had an opening if I was still interested. Oh, I was interested, all right. So I interviewed at Boston, O'Rourke, David & Fitzgerald and got the job as secretary to one of the name partners, Mark Fitzgerald, who specialized in real estate and corporate law. I had to take a pay cut, since I had no legal experience, but before my three-month probation period was over, I had proven myself and my salary was raised to where it was originally.

Within a month after starting, tragedy struck our family again. Nick got a call from his ex-wife in Chicago telling him that while on a school outing, their youngest son had fallen through the ice with some other boys, and he had drowned in the icy waters of that lake. I had to get an advance on my next paycheck to buy a plane ticket so that Nick could rush to Chicago to attend the funeral of his son. That made two children that he had lost. Their first son, Andrew, had been born with Hydroencephalitis (commonly called "water on the brain") and had only survived for six weeks. After a few days of not having heard from Nick, I started calling his family. I learned that Nick had taken advantage of the situation and decided to make it a vacation and visit all of his relatives in the Chicago area. Nick had known when he left that we were about to be evicted from the house because the landlady found out about all the dogs. I jumped on Nick for not coming back and helping me with the money and the packing.

Fortunately, the early seventies was a boom time in the real estate business, and the other real estate lawyer in the firm had a housing development, which still had the original house on it that he was willing to let us rent. It was only one bedroom but the front entry hall was more than big enough to hold bunk beds for Nicky and Shane, plus Eddie was still in his crib. The original owners had kept two acres in front, and had built two new houses, shutting off driveway access to the old house. So it was pretty tricky getting back to it. We had to literally drive through the pasture to get to the house.

The best part of the deal was that the property had originally been a dairy operation and the dairy barn was still there. It was the perfect place to keep all the dogs because I was getting quite a collection of them. I think we had somewhere in the neighborhood of twelve or thirteen dogs at that point, counting the puppies and the strays.

This is the period of time when our marriage deteriorated daily. One night when he came home drunk, I opened the door and he almost fell on his face. He went into the bedroom, grabbed his guitar and tried ripping the strings off with his bare hands. When that didn't work, he started swinging it like a bat against the doorframe until it was smashed to pieces. What finally stopped him was when he tried to put his fist through the kitchen wall. Bad move. This was an old house. We're not talking sheetrock...we're talking lath and plaster. That wall was solid as a rock and Nick broke his hand.

As much as I loved living in the country, I knew that it wasn't a workable situation without transportation, so I started looking for another place. Our babysitter, Virginia, had a neighbor who owned several houses, all within a few blocks of Virginia. The house that I picked was a two-bedroom and in 1972, it cost me ninety dollars a month rent.

I found homes for most of the dogs, but it still left me with five. Soon after moving there, I told Nick that I wanted a divorce and I filed in June. He finally agreed and signed the waiver but he had nowhere else to go and asked if he could stay until he found one. He would be gone for days at a time, but then he would come back for a place to sleep and eat. When he was gone (with the car, of course), I would have to get up, get the three boys, who were two, five and six, dressed and walk with them the five blocks to Virginia's house. Then I would catch the bus into downtown to go to work.

One night Nick showed up at the house. I was in the kitchen fixing supper when I heard Nick cussing up a storm and a yelp from one of the dogs. I rushed into the living room to find that Nick had kicked little Princess out of his way and she was staggering all over the living room, obviously injured and in pain. I grabbed Princess and ran out the door with the boys and raced to the vet. There was no saving her. Nick had broken some of her ribs, which punctured her lung.

That was it as far as I was concerned. I told my lawyer that I wanted the divorce finalized right away. Since Nick had stayed in the house for a couple of months after I had filed, my lawyer said that we would have to re-file, and he had just re-filed the papers in September. This was the middle of October and the sixty-day requirement had not been reached. I told him that I had to have the divorce right away so that I could keep Nick out of the house to protect my children and my animals, so we went to court the next morning and got the divorce. However, since the sixty days had not elapsed, the judge granted the divorce but would not sign the papers until the sixty days were up. I was given all the furniture (and the bills to go with them) and Nick got his clothes and the car. I was also granted a hundred and fifty dollars a month child support. When I gave Nick a copy of the papers, he handed me fifty dollars and demanded his visitation for that weekend. After that first fifty dollars, he never paid another penny in support.

One of my old friends whom I had dated a few times was also going through a divorce and we were using each other for moral support. He loaned me a Dodge Cougar to drive until I could get a vehicle of my own. The night of October 22, 1972, is a date that will live forever in my memory. I had been to dog class with the three boys and my two Whippets, Dancer and Sunny. I pulled into the driveway about eight thirty, and was just heading for the shed in back to put the dogs away when Nick comes roaring up and stops right across my driveway, blocking it. He comes barreling out of the car yelling at me, "Whose car is that? Where have you been? Who are you screwing around with?"

Now really, folks, I'm standing there with three little boys and two dogs. How could anyone (except Nick) think that I'd been out screwing around? Before I could even answer, he reached out and backhanded me with a half-closed fist across my right jaw, knocking my glasses off into the grass. I felt something crack in my jaw and I couldn't see anything but stars. Then he punched me in the stomach and I doubled over. The boys are crying, the dogs are barking, Nick is screaming and not one neighbor stuck their head outside the door. I'm scrambling around on the ground, trying to find my glasses when Nick grabs me and hauls me up on my feet so he can hit me on the other side of my face, this time with a closed fist. I herded the boys up onto the front porch and considered going in to get to the telephone, but then I realized that I was safer in the yard. At least I had some running room. I was more concerned about the boys and the dogs. As I was turning back after getting the boys on the porch, he grabbed my hair on both sides of my face and started banging the back of my head against the side of the house. I felt some of my hair rip out as I struggled and finally managed to get away from him.

I yelled at the boys to stay on the porch and I started running across the street to the convenience store. I made it into the store and started begging the startled clerk to please call the police, that my ex-husband was attacking me. Then Nick came in and it started again. All I could think of was the damage that he could do in the store and I would be responsible. I screamed at the clerk to please call the police and I ran outside. Of course, all of the kids and the dogs had followed me across the street.

While I was trying to round them up and get them back to the house, I heard Nick cussing at the dogs and turned around just as he kicked at Sunny. That's when I finally went after Nick! As we say down here in the south, "I was all over him like white on rice." Then he started running from me! We got back to the house just as two police cars pulled up. One of the officers took Nick to the side and the other talked to me. I told the officer that we were divorced and that Nick didn't live there but since the judge had not signed the papers, I couldn't prove that we were divorced. They told me that if I still felt the same way the next morning, to be at the police station at eight o'clock and file charges on Nick. What they didn't tell me was that if I had insisted on filing charges right then, they would have had to take Nick in. But we're talking about 1972 here, people. The police didn't get involved in domestic disputes. It was a family matter and none of their concern.

They let Nick go and then I started looking for my dogs. Dancer had stayed close, but I couldn't find Sunny. I put Dancer away, put the kids in the car and drove all over looking for Sunny but I never found him. I was afraid to stay in the house for fear that Nick would come back, so I drove until I came to a motel and I checked in with the boys.

The next morning early, I went back to the house, got the boys ready and took them to Virginia. I called my boss and told him what had happened and what I was going to do. Then I spent several hours at the police station, going from one department to the other filling out paperwork. When it got down to the last thing I would have to do, which was take the papers to the desk so that a warrant would be issued for Nick's arrest, I asked them how long before he would be picked up because I was afraid to go home. That police officer sat there with his bare face hanging out and said, "Well, the warrant officers are so busy, it could take anywhere from two weeks to a month."

"Are you serious?" I asked. "This man just tried to kill me. And you're telling me he won't be picked up for a month?"

I got up and walked out, and I went to the office. All of my co-workers were aghast when I walked in the door. Mark hadn't told them why I wasn't there and I hadn't tried to hide the bruises, because I wanted the police to see what Nick had done to me. Hubert O'Rourke, the partner who specialized in family law at the firm, told me that I should get a restraining order on Nick. "Sure," I said, "and I have a bridge I'd like to sell you if you're interested," I continued sarcastically. "Restraining orders only work on people who obey the law. Nick could care less about a piece of paper."

Within a week, there was an incident where a young woman had taken a restraining order out on her ex-husband and he had broken into her apartment while her father was there visiting and had killed them both, along with himself. I went to work the next day and dropped the newspaper on Hubie's desk with the report of that murder-suicide circled in red. "That's exactly how much good a restraining order would do me."

I tried to put the attack out of my mind and get on with my life. I tried to put all of the pain and hurt where no one could find it. But I guess God wasn't through testing me yet. I threw myself into my job and to raising my kids, but I was only thirty-four years old. I still needed adult conversation and companionship. The firm had an impromptu get together almost every week. At five o'clock on any given Thursday, Mark would give me the key to the bar and asked me to fix him a scotch and water. If I was through with my work, I could fix one for myself. Gradually, everyone would wind up in the conference room drinking. Everyone could call their significant other to come and join us—especially if the party graduated to a restaurant where they also had a bar.

About a month after the attack by Nick in my front yard, one such party started to celebrate the birthday of one of the young associate attorneys. I was a little bit late getting to the party and there were about a dozen people grouped around a table, including a couple of black men whom I didn't know. A couple of times, one of the young black men wound up dancing with me. He said his name was John and that he was helping his friend, Tim, celebrate. I was just having a good time and also socking away the scotch. When it got close to closing time, the party started breaking up and we all started drifting back up to the street to our cars. I was again driving a rental vehicle until I could find a car for myself. As everyone pulled out of the parking lots, I noticed that John was left standing alone. "Hey! John," I called. "Did Tim leave you behind?"

"Looks like it," he said.

"Can I give you a ride somewhere?" I asked. And he got into my car. He directed me south down the freeway and had me take the Scott Street exit. Now, I had been in Houston for almost ten years and knew the northwest side of town like the back of my hand. I could get around the rest of it, but Scott Street I had never been to. It was a black neighborhood and I did not know where I was. So I followed his directions and we soon wound up in a deserted area. It was then that his real intent became crystal clear. He pulled the pick out of his Afro hairstyle and brought it right up to my eyes and told me to take off my panties. Then he slapped me across my face and my still sore jaw when I didn't move fast enough to suit him. I was numb. I was still sore from the beating I had taken from Nick, especially my jaw. I was trapped in a car in an area of town that I knew nothing about. It was also a rental car that I was responsible for and I was afraid to try to jump out and leave it behind. Besides, where would I run? I didn't know where I was.

Without going into all the lurid details, suffice it to say that he raped me. I did not struggle, I did not fight, and I did not participate. I simply turned my mind off and concentrated on surviving. Needless to say, I sobered up in short order. When he finished, he ordered me into the passenger seat and he took the wheel. He drove to another part of the neighborhood to an all night café and made me go in with him. I was the only person in the place who was not black. I know I must have looked a fright, but I didn't care. I was still in survival mode and I definitely didn't want anyone else to find me attractive. He ordered a meal, but I refused food and just ordered coffee. After what seemed like an eternity, we finally got back in the car with him driving again. He finally drove onto the feeder road of the freeway and I knew vaguely where I was. When he pulled up to a stop sign, I jumped out of the car and started running toward the freeway with him running right behind me. Praise be to God! What do I see coming down the exit? It was an absolute miracle. It was a Houston Police Department squad car. The lights came on and it was all over.

I did not report the rape. I simply told them that he had assaulted me, as I did not want to go downtown and file charges. I just wanted to go home and they let me. I don't know what they did with John. Oh, his name wasn't even John. It was LeRoy something. The next day at work I asked Tim about his friend John. It shouldn't be a big surprise to anyone, although it was to me, but John was not a friend of Tim's. He had just crashed the party. Fortunately, I never saw or heard anything from John/LeRoy again. And I was finally able to get past the incident and go on.

~Chapter 10~

I got a better job at Langley Smith, a much larger law firm than Boston O'Rourke. My luck was a little better there. Johnny, my boss, and I hit it off really well right from the start. So well, in fact, that I must confess, I broke two of my cardinal rules: not to get too friendly with my boss; and never date a married man. I was soon able to get a three-bedroom duplex right across the street from my friend, Jodi's house. Shane and Nicky started school and one of the stay-at-home neighbors watched Eddie for me. Since we were living about twenty-five miles from downtown, I had to leave the boys alone for about a hour until the school bus came, but I didn't see anything wrong with that. They were eight and nine years old, and I had been staying at home alone with two baby sisters from the time I was eight. They just had each other to take care of for an hour. After school, they went to Jodi's.

We had just walked in the door one day to find that the dogs had decided to take the trash out for us. You didn't know I could train dogs that well, did ya? Well, I can't. They had just taken it out of the garbage can and scattered it all over the living room and kitchen.

We just barely had time to get a drink of water before I had to begin to pick up the trash, when there was a knock on the door. I opened the door to find a social worker from Child Protective Services standing there. It seems that someone had turned me in for neglecting my children, and CPS was there to investigate the charges. I was stunned, to say the least. I was too stunned to be angry—that would come later. But as a result of that accusation, I was forced to find a caretaker for all three boys who also had the facilities for getting Nicky and Shane to school and back. More expense and time I couldn't afford—time to move closer to my job.

I didn't choose the Ironwood Apartments because it was so close to The Clubhouse, but it didn't upset me that it happened that way. I didn't even have to drive there, or go out on the street to get there. I just had to walk through the complex and across the back parking lot of the shopping center. I usually went out only on the weekends when Nick had the boys, but I must confess, there were times I waited until the boys were asleep and went anyway. Not something that I'm proud of.

I was fortunate in my choice of living space to find a babysitter just upstairs in the same unit. Brenda and Richard were originally from Wisconsin and had a boy and a girl just a little younger than my three boys. As well as watching the boys for me, we became friends and I spent a lot of my weekends upstairs in their apartment.

The boys were beginning to give me a few problems by getting into trouble; nothing major, just little incidents. But then there were incidents when they would do something so considerate it would make me cry. For instance, one day when I had very little in the house to fix a meal, they went out and collected cans and bottles to cash in, and they brought me the money. It probably wasn't more than a couple of dollars, but I was so touched that they even came up with a plan to contribute to the family finances.

Little did I know that the family finances were about to take a big turn for the better.

~Chapter 11~

Okay. Now let's settle down and get our life going forward. I found an ad in the paper that I just knew was my job. A law firm was looking for a secretary with experience in the corporate and real estate fields. And they wanted a fast typist who was a good speller. Okay. I had all that. And the applicant also had to have experience with an IBM Mag Card. Whooohooooo!! That was my job. It was tailor-made for me.

    I called Tom Lakiotis, gave him a synopsis of my experience, and we made an appointment for me to come in for an interview the next morning. After a very short interview and finding out I was available for work immediately, Tom hired me on the spot. Tom was Greek, with a very volatile temper. At one point when I tried to quit after one of his tirades, and in fact had accepted another job offer, he called me into his office and asked what my new salary would be. I really wasn't going to be making that much more money, but I pumped it up a couple of hundred dollars in an effort to make sure that Tom couldn't or wouldn't match it. But he did. So I stayed. I settled into a routine. But I was still hurting for money. I was very close to having my phone turned off, and due to the antics of my boys, I was about to be evicted, again.

    Then the first week of November, I got a call from Frank Romano, one of Tom's oldest friends and clients. He had just been in the office meeting with Tom about one legal matter or another and had called me almost as soon as he got out the door. Frank asked if I would like to meet him for a drink the next day. I hesitated. Frank was very married. In addition, he was much older than me, and I never dated older men.

    I explained that he would not be able to call me as my telephone was being shut off and he said that he would handle it. He said that he would call me the next day at eleven. The next day, my phone was still in good working order, and Frank called close to eleven. I decided, what the hell, why keep giving myself away? Besides, I needed the money. We made a date to meet at a service station close to his plant. Oh, did I forget to mention that Frank was a millionaire? He owned his own manufacturing plant that made parts for the air conditioning business. And he had a mansion in one of the most prestigious sections of town on Memorial Drive.

    I left my car parked at the station and got into Frank's. He immediately drove to the nearest motel. Well, so much for the romance. However, the motel had no vacancies, so he drove to another one. And another one. There was some kind of convention in town that had all the hotels and motels full. But he wasn't out of ideas yet. He took me to a dinky little house not far from his plant. It seems that it had belonged to his former brother-in-law, which he had used specifically for assignations of the sexual kind. (I wonder if that is why he was now Frank's *former* brother-in-law?)

    How I got through that first time with Frank, I really don't know. I was shaking in my boots. This was not some spur of the moment thing that had evolved after a couple of dates. Or even a one-night stand after a night of drinking and carousing. This was pure, unadulterated, planned sex. Well, since he was married, I guess I can't really say it was unadulterated, now, can I?

When I got back to the apartment and Sammie, I was foaming at the mouth. Being unaccustomed as I was to having sex for money, I had not been able to come right out and ask him for the fifty dollars. And I guess he forgot about it. But my phone was turned off the next day and he had tried to call me, so that reminded him that he hadn't given it to me and I hadn't asked for it. Monday morning at work, I received an envelope delivered by a messenger service and it contained a crisp, new one hundred dollar bill. I was now officially a "kept" woman.

The affair with Frank started gathering steam and we were seeing each other almost every day at lunch, in addition to two or three times a week in the evenings, when he was supposed to be at some meeting or another. Soon Frank started talking about divorcing his wife. I told him that he didn't need to do that on my account. I was happy just being his mistress. Then, before I knew it, school was out and it was time to make my semi-annual trip back to Kansas for a visit. After Dad had graduated from the osteopathic school, he had quit his job as an electrician at the telephone company, and they had moved to the Lake of the Ozarks where he intended to hang his shingle. Unfortunately for him, he failed to pass the medical board examination and was never able to legally practice his new profession. Quite frankly, I gave a big sigh of relief that it worked out that way. I could just see all kinds of medical malpractice suits filed against him when he started molesting his patients, and he would have done that, I have no doubts whatsoever.

Every day that I was in Kansas City Frank called me, no matter where I happened to be. I had left all of the numbers for where I would be visiting. My mom said, "I think the man is in love, Netta. When are you going to do something about it?"

"Well, there's this little problem. His divorce isn't final yet, and he hasn't asked me," I replied. Both of those problems were resolved when we got back to Houston. Frank's wife had found out about me during the divorce proceedings, and tried to have me subpoenaed as a witness, but I avoided the process server.

I finally decided to leave Afton Village Apartments before I was asked to, and got an apartment at the French Village. Frank decided that I needed new furniture for my new apartment, so one Saturday morning after an especially satisfying rendezvous, he took me to a furniture store and I picked out bed-room, kitchen and living room furniture. The bill was right at two thousand dollars for all of it. Then Frank bought me a tri-color Sheltie. Something I had always wanted. Shelties are the very best obedience dogs. Frank had also bought me an Oldsmobile station wagon, which came in handy with the boys. Once I had started seeing Frank on a regular basis, I did not date other men. But that doesn't mean I stayed at home pining away for him. I still went out on the weekends when Nick had the boys.

Frank then decided I needed a bigger place. So we went house shopping and found a nice three-bedroom house with a fenced yard. I was really afraid to rent that house. It cost way too much for me to afford it on my own but Frank insisted. He said, "You have money now. Act like it." Yeah, like I had this really big bank account I could access at any time. Not! Maybe that was part of my problem with Frank. He had a champagne pocketbook, and I still had a beer mentality. And I really didn't have the money. He did. I didn't have access to it without asking him.

For four and a half years, I was totally ignorant of what was going on. I really loved Frank and things were much better for me financially. What I didn't realize was, I was his wife, and I was my children's mother. And never the twain shall meet. Oh, yes. He considered me his wife. Even though we did not have a formal wedding in front of a priest or a judge, I was his wife.

He introduced me to everyone as his wife, and when his mother asked on our first trip to see her, what she was supposed to call me, he said, "She's my wife, Mother. That should be obvious."

It was about this time that I got word from Kyle that he was getting married to a young girl that he had gone to school with in California. I was so excited. My son was getting married and I could be there. They were getting married on base and then, after a short honeymoon and Christmas in Kansas City, he would be going to his first duty station in Greece. I was a little excited about seeing his father again after such a long time, but I was in for a shock. Will had retired on disability a year previously and his diabetes had taken control of his life. When I saw Will again after so many years, I couldn't believe my eyes. We were both just barely pushing forty, and he looked at least twenty years older than that. The diabetes was really taking a toll on him.

Within a year of the marriage, Kyle wrote to tell me that he and Tammy were divorced and she had, in fact, married another Air Force man they both had known in California. In fact, the man she left my son for was the man who had loaned them his little white MGB for their honeymoon trip. He had been a part of their wedding!

Frank was a great believer in going out to dinner with friends and family—his friends and family. We had standing dates every Thursday, Friday and Saturday nights with one couple or another who had been his friends for years. On those nights, he would give each of the boys about five dollars so they could go buy dinner at McDonald's, and we would go to some ritzy place and spend two hundred dollars just on one bottle of wine. I had nice clothes, shoes and purses to match. I had fur coats. I had lots of nice jewelry, the real stuff. He had a ring made for me that matched one he had and he considered it my wedding ring. Of course, it wasn't exactly the same as his. His had two diamonds totaling almost three carats, and mine simply had two small chips in it. He said that I wasn't old enough for big diamonds. I had a maid who came to the house twice a week. We traveled all over the country, but mostly back to Massachusetts a couple of times a year to see, you got it, his family. We would fly the boys to my real father in West Virginia, or drive them there and drop them off, then continue on into New England.

When I first got together with Frank, I was spending a lot of time teaching in the obedience classes, at least two nights a week. He even went to some of the classes with me early on and he got interested in it, so the first thing I knew, we were looking at buying an Afghan Hound puppy from one of my fellow trainers. Frank had decided that he wanted to join me in showing dogs, although he was leaning more toward the breed ring competition than the obedience. I tried to impress on him how much work was involved in preparing an Afghan for the show ring but he was set on an Afghan. So we arranged to have second pick of the litter when my friend's Afghan had her puppies. As with everything else I liked to do, I had put my dog interests on hold to please Frank.

At a show in San Antonio, Frank spent most of his time in the other building watching the breed ring competitions and especially when the Afghans were in the ring. On the way home from the show, Frank informed me that he had changed his mind. And the reason he had changed his mind? There were too many gays and lesbians who showed dogs. Well, of course there were. The dog world was one place where they were unequivocally accepted as equals.

For the family cookouts, Frank would provide the steaks for everyone, and the rest of us brought the side dishes. When I finally pitched a bitch about never seeing my friends and family, always his, he relented and invited my family for one weekend. It was on one such weekend at the property when it was only us and the boys that my past came up and bit me in the ass. Nicky had turned fourteen that year, and Frank had gifted him with his own dirt bike (at least Frank said it was for Nicky). We were sitting outside. Frank was reading and I was doing needlework, when my boys all rushed up talking at the same time. The boys still saw their dad on occasion, and on one such occasion, he had told Shane and Eddie that Nicky was not really their brother at all. He didn't tell Nicky, though. Shane and Eddie got mad at Nicky for not sharing his bike enough to suit them, so they decided that it was a good time to inform him that he wasn't their brother.

I was so unprepared for that discussion. And I was kicking myself all over the place for not having followed through with my promise to myself to sit down and talk to Nicky when he was about eight. I never even considered that Frank would take it as a sign that I had been lying to him all along, keeping secrets, and what else might I have been lying to him about? I honestly wasn't keeping it a secret. I do believe that incident was what triggered the beginning of the end as far as Frank was concerned.

At the next family get-together at the property, Nicky was involved in an argument with Frank's granddaughter, Angela. She insisted that she was allowed to ride Nicky's bike, because it wasn't Nicky's bike, it was her bike. Her grandpa told her so. When I asked Frank to settle the argument, he just looked at me and said the bike was there for all of the children to ride it. It didn't belong to just one of them. I just stared at him. "You gave that bike to Nicky for his fourteenth birthday. What do you mean it belongs to all of them?" I demanded. Frank just turned and walked away.

Not long after that revelation, I got a call from the school that Eddie and Shane both were involved in some kind of mischief. I don't really remember what, only that I had had to leave work and go get them. A week later we were all having dinner at Frank's favorite Mexican restaurant. While in the men's room, Eddie had helped himself to a handful of matchbooks that were there for the customers. It was apparent to me that my boys were acting out in order to get my attention. Something was very wrong and I needed to spend some time with them to get to the bottom of it. After the first incident, I had begged off from our Friday night date with Frank's friends to spend time at home with the boys. Then when it happened again the very next weekend, I told Frank that I needed a weekend with the boys and I took Shane and Eddie to the beach for the weekend and some one-on-one time. That did not make Frank a happy camper. My boys were interfering in his lifestyle. When the boys and I got home from a fun-filled weekend where a lot of things got thrashed out, I didn't notice that all of Frank's things were gone from the closet and our bathroom. I just noticed there was something different about the house. I didn't notice until I got a call from Frank asking me to meet him at the apartment he had kept on Memorial Drive. When I got there he very matter-of-factly informed me that it was over. He could no longer handle my kids and my dogs. He said that he was just too selfish to share me. What an understatement!

I was speechless. We had had no real arguments. There had been no disagreements of any kind that I could remember. He never indicated that he was unhappy with the way things were going. I had just had to cancel two dinner dates and spend some time with my children. What the hell kind of reason was that for ending a relationship? I was especially surprised that Frank said it was my kids and my dogs. When he first brought the up marriage I had argued against it. I hadn't really thought that he wanted to take on three small boys and I was perfectly content to remain his mistress. But he insisted that he wanted us to be a family. So it wasn't like I had suddenly decided to say, "Oh, by the way, I have these three children." And although I had been totally involved in the obedience classes when we met, I had only had one dog at the time. The other dogs Frank had bought for me, so I now had a total of three dogs at that point.

There was no changing his mind. Frank told me that he would continue to pay the rent on the house as long as I kept my bank account where he was on the board of directors. He would also continue to maintain my car and pay for my gas, provided I always took it to the same Shell station on Memorial Drive where we always went.

My life on Easy Street was over.

~Chapter 12~

I was a complete and total mess when Frank left me in 1981. We had chosen a lovely Victorian-style house to build on the land. We had also picked August eleventh to get married, which was approximately halfway between our birthdays. For about nine months after Frank pulled the plug on me, I got up and drove downtown to work, managed to make it through each day, and the minute I got in the car to start home I'd start crying. I was not really much of a parent at that time. As soon as I got home, I hurried into my bedroom, shut the door, and cried. Oh, just an observation here. I discovered that divorce or separation is the greatest diet in the world. It didn't take long to get back to my slim, trim hundred and ten pounds, because I couldn't eat...I couldn't sleep. My saving grace was the fact that the last assignment that I had taken had been with my old firm with my favorite boss, Mark Fitzgerald. I wasn't actually back working for Mark, I was just a floater, but it was my "safe" place. In order to spend more time with the boys, I was working nine to three with no lunch hour, so I didn't leave for work until after the boys left for school, and I was home shortly after three when they got home.

Eddie went into a slump after Frank left, and I made an appointment with a psychologist to get him some help. Eddie had heard me tell someone the reasons Frank gave me for leaving, and Eddie took the blame for the break-up of the marriage and my resulting deep depression. After three months of therapy, I saw no change in Eddie and I discontinued his sessions and concentrated on putting our lives back together.

Kyle had returned from Greece a year prior to Frank's abandoning me, and had been stationed in San Angelo. So we had been seeing each other on a fairly frequent basis. Late one evening I got a call from Kyle. He had just received word from his stepmother in California that his dad had died and Kyle asked me to please get him a flight out of Dallas and he would drive to Dallas to catch the flight.

I was very glad that I was in a position to help Kyle. And I felt some small justification for having made the decision to leave him with his dad all those many years before. Will lived long enough to see his son graduate from high school and get married. Will died a month or so before he would have been forty-two years old.

In January, Mark's current secretary got married and asked me if I would be willing to cover her while she was on her honeymoon. I was delighted to have my old job back even though I was just covering that position. Mark was still using the real estate and corporate forms that I had set up on the Mag Card system. The Rolodex on the desk still had cards with my handwriting from almost ten years before. It really was like I had never left there.

But I realized that Frank's support was not going to last forever, and I needed a permanent job with all the benefits. So I asked the administrator to consider me for the next permanent position came open. I also started checking with the other attorneys I knew to see if they had anything opening up, and I got a job offer from one of them. Then I pressured the administrator because I preferred staying with Boston O'Rourke.

One day, Mark's secretary wanted to talk to me before I accepted the other job. When they got back from their honeymoon, her husband found out he was being transferred to Dallas. Mark was going to need a new secretary. She had told me before she told Mark about having to leave. So, almost nine years to the day that I had originally gone to work for Mark Fitzgerald, I was back at my desk.

I finally realized that Frank was never coming back. He had refused to talk to me when I tried to call. Then the deposits stopped appearing in my checking account, and I got a letter from the insurance company that the beneficiary had been changed on the one hundred and fifty thousand dollar policy Frank had "given" to me. So I filed for a divorce. I finally took Grandma Rush's advice and got mad.

I try not to get mad because I internalize my stress, which results in physical problems. Over the years I had had episodes where all of a sudden, this high-pitched ringing would start in one ear or the other. They were few and far between and didn't last long, so I never mentioned them to any doctor. This episode was different and made it difficult for me to concentrate. The ringing continued off and on for the rest of the day. I woke up about three o'clock the next morning, knowing that I was about to throw up. I sat up, put my feet on the floor, and promptly fell on my face. I was so dizzy that I couldn't get up. I literally had to drag myself into the bathroom and pull myself up to the commode to make sure that I didn't have a mess to clean up. After throwing up my toes, I staggered back to the bed. It seemed like the worst hangover I had ever had. I finally was able to navigate a little, and had my niece, Shelly drive me to the emergency room. They gave me a prescription for some Antivert to counteract the dizziness, and told me to see an ENT specialist on Monday.

I was feeling a little better by Monday morning, but still couldn't drive safely so Nicky took me to the ENT specialist in the professional building right next to the hospital. The doctor said that he thought it was Meniere's Disease (a chemical imbalance in the inner ear) but wanted to run some tests to make sure. When the results confirmed his diagnosis he sent me directly to the hospital. I did not pass go; I did not collect two hundred dollars. I had lost all of the hearing in my right ear. There is no cure for it. It is a stress-related disease, which usually affects older men. With the advent of more women into the work force, it had started appearing in women in their thirties and forties. The doctor told me that I would regain some of my hearing in that ear, but not all of it, and would have a constant ringing in that ear forever.

I had been in the hospital for four days when Frank called and he was livid. He had just been served with the divorce papers. I was really groggy from the meds but I was hurt that he wasn't concerned that he had to call me at the hospital to chew my ass off. I was released from the hospital after five days, and went back to work the next Monday. I walked like a drunk because losing your hearing affects your balance. But I got stronger every day. And I eventually regained more of my hearing in my right ear. As it got close to the end of the sixty-day waiting period to get my divorce, I happened to see in the newspaper that Frank had been issued a marriage license. What? He's in the middle of a divorce and he's getting married? Now you do realize that what we had is known as a common law marriage but if you remember, just before the shit hit the fan we had set the date to get married and everyone believed that we already were married. But that didn't faze Frank. He had money, don't you know. He had decided that we were married, and then he had decided that we weren't. So the little bastard went ahead and got married before we ever went to court for the divorce.

I found a really nice lease/purchase house in a new subdivision. Much more upscale than anything we had had before—and much more expensive. Nicky would be a senior when school started that fall and Eddie in eighth grade. Shane had been put back a couple of times and he was getting close to the age where he would no longer be allowed to continue high school if he didn't make it this time. Then just after New Year's, Nick called from Florida. Shane announced that he was going to go live with his father in Florida. (But I had to buy his bus tick.) Nick had promised Shane that he would help him get his GED, so it would not be necessary for Shane to continue school. I gritted my teeth, put a hold on my tears, put on a happy face and my son on the bus to Florida. Then I cried all the way home.

Kyle called to tell me that he was getting married again. He lived off base in a little two-bedroom house he had purchased for him and Chelsea. In February of 1984, Nicky was turning eighteen. I planned a big surprise party for him and invited all his high school friends from both high schools that he had attended. His birthday was really not until Tuesday, so having the party the Saturday before would make sure that he didn't suspect anything. All of the invitees arrived before Nicky called and a more surprised kid you never saw.

Eddie went to Florida for two weeks to spend with his father but on Father's Day, the boys called me from Florida—they were ready to come home, Eddie *and* Shane. And they wanted to come home that day. It seemed that they had had a particularly rough week with their dad's bingeing, and at one point they had to sleep on the street because Nick had passed out and they were locked out. When Nick broke Shane's new stereo that was the straw that broke the camel's back. I called the bus station, prepaid tickets on the next bus to Houston, and was waiting for them when they arrived.

Kyle and Chelsea announced that they were expecting a baby early the next year, and I was about to become a grandmother. On December fourteenth, tiny premature Skye Alexandra Coleman made her debut into the world. I finally had my girl!!!

I had been pushing my lawyer to take Frank's deposition so that we could finalize the divorce. I wasn't asking for much—I wanted the hundred and fifty thousand dollars he had promised me, and I wanted him to give Nicky another dirt bike. Then, before I knew it, we were negotiating a settlement. Frank was offering to settle for twenty-five thousand and I had to pay my own lawyer. As usual, I was in desperate need of money. I needed whatever I could get, so I took the settlement and started looking for a place that I could afford. I found an acre of land, with a three-bedroom doublewide on it. Being the eternal caregiver, and wanting to help my friend Sammie get on her feet, I bought a brand new single-wide trailer for myself to also go on the property, and I let Sammie and her youngest, Bonnie, have the doublewide with the understanding that if she maintained the payments that it would be hers. So in August of 1984, we all moved to the country. Sammie surprised me with a house warming/birthday party right after we all got moved in. I don't think I had ever had a surprise party before, and I was really touched.

I was soon struggling trying to keep my head above water. Sammie had failed to uphold her end of the bargain on the doublewide and had moved into an apartment. I couldn't pay for both homes so I voluntarily gave the newer singlewide back to the finance company and we moved all of our belongings into the doublewide. And life settled down for a while.

Nicky was well on his way in the Air Force and only came home occasionally on furloughs. Eddie was barely maintaining his grades in high school, and Shane was working construction with one of our neighbors. Most days when I got home, my house would be overrun with teenaged boys. I didn't mind until the day I came home and found them brewing mushroom tea in my kitchen. That's when I exploded and put my foot down. I had already had to put Eddie in the hospital and have his stomach pumped when I came home and found him totally out of it on some pills that he had taken. He was not trying to commit suicide, just trying out the pills to see what kind of high he would get.

My boss, Mark, asked me to move to Austin with him to work in the new branch office of the firm. So, I contacted the finance company on the doublewide and gave it back to them. We finally decided on a duplex close to Lake Travis, and we were soon settled in. Eddie did well at his new school and it was soon evident that he would be able to graduate. Shane was tired of being a busboy and took a job as a cook trainee under the tutelage of a French chef. It looked as though Shane had found his calling. His boss was impressed with Shane's natural ability and was talking about sending him to a fancy cooking school.

I got a call from Kyle to let me know that my second grandchild was going to make an appearance on April sixteenth and Kevin Anderson Coleman was a roly-poly armful. Nicky called from his duty station in Wyoming, to tell me to start planning on being in Cheyenne in December, because he was getting married. Nine months later, Nicky called me to tell me that Angie had gone into labor and Chad Allen Morley was born. The grandkids were coming fast and furiously.

Shane and Eddie both had jobs and Monica, one of the girls the boys had known, moved in with Shane. The Austin office closed and I was moving back to Houston, but they wanted to stay in the duplex and between the three of them they assured me that they could handle the bills on it—famous last words yet again. Shane foolishly became involved with some teenagers who were breaking into the fancy lake homes and stealing items like electronics. And they got caught. Shane had not participated in the actual break-ins, but he had helped transport the stolen goods from one point to another. Unfortunately, Shane was no longer a teenager and even though he had never been in trouble before, the judge came down hard on him. I had to get a loan on my 401K to pay an attorney twenty-five hundred dollars to represent him. Shane was given probation and about a hundred and eighty hours of community service.

Then I found out the boys had not paid any of the bills and they called to tell me that they were being evicted from the duplex. The lights had been turned off and when I tried to get a phone connected in my new place, I was told that I would have to pay off over seven hundred dollars owing on my phone in Austin! So I had to go get the three of them plus all of my remaining stuff and bring it to my new home. Eddie, knowing that I was about to find out about the lights and the telephone immediately enlisted in the Navy and was gone before you could say, "Scat." I do have to say, though, that Eddie eventually paid back approximately four of the seven hundred dollar phone bill.

It's a good thing that I had gotten a three-bedroom house, because soon after Eddie left for the Navy, Sammie and Bonnie showed up again looking for a place to stay. Sammie soon had a job bartending at a neighborhood sports bar. Monica was working at Pizza Hut, and Shane was working at Grandy's. Unfortunately, the first day Sammie was at the house after we all went to work, she left the gate to the backyard open, and we lost our foundling Afghan. Shane and Monica started going to classes to get their GEDs and when they completed the course, I bought him a cheap car. It wasn't much to look at, but it worked, and it was all I could afford. Then they decided that they wanted to have their own place, so between Monica's folks and me we scraped up the money for deposits on electricity and telephone, and they moved into their own apartment. I was alone.

That didn't last very long. After about three months of not paying their bills, Shane and Monica had to move back in and they kept losing their jobs. They were each so jealous of the other one that they would stay home from work if the other one had a day off. Monica also had another problem. She was pregnant and the baby was due in October. About midnight on October thirtieth, Monica went into labor and Savanna Dee Morley was born about seven thirty the next morning.

A former partner of the firm who did family law, John Volcek, had gone out on his own the year before, and was looking for a new secretary. I called him and after a few weeks, we decided to give it a try, so I went into Mark's office and resigned after almost nine years. Kyle, who was still stationed in Germany, contacted me to let me know that Chelsea had taken Skye and Kevin back to her folks in New Jersey, supposedly for a visit. After she got there, she had called and told him that she wasn't coming back.

When Savanna was about seven months old Monica left and moved in with her sister. I do not know what caused the rift between her and Shane and I stayed out of it but I was nominated to pick Savanna up for weekend visits, which I was delighted to do. Then Monica and Savanna disappeared and Shane couldn't find them. Her family wouldn't tell him where she was. He would eventually learn from other sources where Monica had been, but it was always after she had already moved on. He found out that she had married an old boyfriend who was in the service and they moved to Killeen and then they were in Germany. Shane never stopped looking for his daughter, but since he didn't have much money, he was always too late when he learned their whereabouts.

Then came the killer. Shane had not performed the entire amount of community service hours that he was obligated to do to the court's satisfaction, so they sentenced him to six months in a military boot camp in Austin.

Shane called me from his probation officer's office where he had gone for his regular meeting, telling me that I had to come and get my car because they were taking him back to Austin in handcuffs.

~Chapter 13~

When I first went to work for John, he had a paralegal and a receptionist. I was the secretary/timekeeper/billing department. Then he had to let them go and I was now a "one girl" office. I had to do it all. (At least I got to move into the big window office the paralegal used to have.) And I loved doing family law. I had been divorced three times. Talk about "been there, done that!"

Mom had had two strokes and a heart attack the year before, and had never fully recovered. She was ambulatory but her speech was affected, and her thinking processes had suffered. Dad started asking me to move in with them to help out because he was not doing well with her. He really started pushing it when he fell and broke his shoulder, but I just really didn't want to go live with my parents again.

Then in early March, Eddie called me from California. He had met someone and they were getting married in a couple of weeks because they were madly in love, but also because they were expecting a baby in October. The end of April 1991, I was working away at my desk when the telephone rang and when I answered it I heard, "Nick's dead." It was my son Nicky. "Dad was killed in a shooting accident a couple of days ago. The Florida police and Grandma Alveta have been looking all over for you. They finally located me through the American Red Cross."

It was the call that I had been expecting for twenty years. And I still felt like I had been kicked in the stomach. The last time that I had seen Nick had been four years ago. It seems that Nick had been living in a transient camp for some time. The other man involved was an old "friend" of Nick's and they had run across each other earlier in the day. The other man was now living in a home with a woman and invited Nick to come over and visit. The man said that Nick had complained about being hassled by some teenagers, and so this guy was going to show Nick how to use a gun. (Sure! Nick already knew how to use a gun.) They were sitting around a campfire and then the guy said that they started working on how to disarm someone, and were practicing taking the gun away from each other and in the process, the gun went off and Nick was shot in the face. The deputy sheriff wasn't taken in by the man's story. For one thing, he kept changing his story. On top of that, he couldn't remember what he did with the gun. The guy had been arrested and was in jail at that point.

It was really hard for me to make the call to Shane while he was in jail, but there wasn't any other way I could do it at that point. I informed the prison authorities what I was about to tell Shane, and there were a lot of people there with him when I told him his dad was gone. Of all the boys, Shane was the closest to his dad. I know it was really a blow to find out he had lost him in such a horrible way. Even sadder was the fact that Shane would not be able to go to the memorial service in Chicago. The memorial service was videotaped and Nicky brought me a copy. He also had taped all of our records while he was there and gave me a copy of it. While I was watching the video I could hear our records being played in the background. That's when I lost it. I had not heard those songs for almost twenty years. And the sadness I felt at the waste of such a talent was more than I could bear. Nick had had such promise, but he just couldn't leave the alcohol alone. On the very day that her grandfather had been killed, Alexis Kay Morley was born. Nicky now had a boy and a girl. And Amber gave birth to Eddie's first child, Brian Edward Morley, that October.

Dad had a stroke, and there was just no getting around it now. I had to move into the folks' three-bedroom, singlewide trailer. Ninety-nine percent of my belongings were now in storage. I took just enough clothes to have a variety, my make-up and bath items. Mom let me have one drawer in her dresser, and just enough room in her closet for about seven or eight outfits. Mom was really in bad shape when I moved in and she was constantly hooked up to oxygen. She never got dressed, just stayed in her nightclothes all day long. She would get out of bed, creep slowly the fifteen feet to the living room to her recliner and sit there all day watching reruns of old television shows eating candy. Dad waited on her hand and foot. Until I realized that was part of her problem. When he would start to get up to do something for her I just stepped in and made her do it herself. I started making her get dressed as soon as she woke up. Pretty soon, the oxygen tank was left by the wayside and she was joining us at the table for meals.

Being the only employee that John had was finally getting a little heavy for me. So I talked John into hiring my sister, Sheila, to help out with filing and scut work. That would give her some money coming in and would certainly help me out. One morning after she had come to pick me up, she came in to get a cup of coffee. I gave Mom and Dad both a quick kiss goodbye as I left.

"How can you do that?" Sheila said, the disgust evident in her voice.

"Do what?" I asked.

"Kiss Dad after what he did to you."

"Oh." I thought for a minute. "It's kind of complicated—like Dr. Jekyll and Mr. Hyde. There are two sides to Dad. One side was a teacher of common sense things, and the other an idiot pervert. I loved one and I hated the other one. I think, now that I look back on it, that I'm madder at Mom than I am at him." She asked why and I told her, "Because she didn't protect me, and I know that she knew or at least suspected. And she definitely knew when I was fifteen and told her what he was doing. And she still didn't do anything about it. And now I can't even talk to her about it. She's like a child. Like a three-year-old child just starting to put sentences together. She can't carry on a conversation or comprehend what you're trying to tell her most of the time."

I went to get Shane when he completed his "boot camp," but adding another adult in that singlewide trailer made it mandatory that I had to find another place. Mom was progressing and looking better every day. I didn't think it was necessary for Shane and me to remain that close to be able to keep an eye on things. I began driving through the neighborhood after work with Shane and we looked for a new home. One night, we came upon some people moving out of a house. The next day I signed a lease with the owner. It was a little house, but there were four bedrooms and room for the dogs.

Summertime was approaching. All kinds of things happened in 1992. Sadly, Gary called to tell me that our father had passed away. Mom took Daddy Brian's passing very hard, so maybe it was fortunate that the strokes had left her comprehension at a child's level of understanding and she was not able to fully understand that he was gone.

About the same time, Nicky informed me that he had been selected to go to Officer's Candidate School and after he graduated as a Second Lieutenant he was going to the Orient. I was really excited about it but Angie wasn't. She told him she wasn't going and that she wanted a divorce. I couldn't believe it. I would have given my left tit to be able to go overseas, whether I liked the guy I was with or not.

I bought a new 1992 Ford Escort station wagon. Early the next year, I noticed a "For Sale by Owner" sign in the front yard of that to-die-for farmhouse across the street. I just had to have that house. The owner wanted two thousand dollars down and take over the payments of four hundred dollars a month. I borrowed against my paycheck for the downpayment.

Right after I made the deal on the house, Eddie called to say he was coming home and could I please come pick him up at the bus depot the next morning? Amber and the baby were not coming. It was becoming more and more apparent that Eddie had inherited his dad's drinking problem—a time bomb ticking. Eddie had had a few incidents while he was in the service, but always scraped through by the skin of his teeth. This time he hadn't been quite as fortunate—Eddie had stupidly made threats against the baby.

Amber and Eddie worked things out and she came to Houston, bringing two-year-old Brian with her. It was a happy time for all of us—in the beginning. Then Eddie's problem with alcohol escalated. Before Thanksgiving rolled around, Amber had returned to California taking Brian with her and, we learned later, was pregnant with a daughter, Brittanie, born the next February and whom I have yet to see.

Eddie stayed drunk for several days after Amber left him. He pulled all of their pictures and personal things out of the attic and started burning them in the burn barrel in my backyard while nursing a bottle of beer or three. I finally stood up and roared when he tried to take my picture of Brian down off the wall and add it to the stack. He finally went to bed and passed out. I started drifting off to sleep, but one of the dogs started howling. When I went to check on him, I saw through the window that the backyard was on fire and there wasn't that much backyard between the burn barrel, the house, and the trees behind my property. I ran upstairs screaming for Mark and Eddie, and they both ran downstairs and out into the backyard stark naked and put the fire put out. It would have been funny if it hadn't been so sad.

Sheila and I got an emergency call one morning from the home Health Nurse we had hired to care for the folks during the day. She had found Dad on the floor beside the bed that morning and she had called an ambulance to come and get him. He had obviously had a stroke during the night and had tried to get out of bed, but his right side was paralyzed and he fell, landing on top of his right arm. There is no way of knowing how long he was there before the Home Health Nurse arrived at eight that morning. But he was in danger of losing his arm from lack of circulation. While he was in the hospital and later in rehab, we had to make other arrangements for Mom. Sheila found a senior day care facility that had structured activities and when we picked her up at night we would take her to visit Dad. I just remember that she had to have twenty-four hour care so someone had to be with her at night.

Before Dad was well enough to come home, Sheila and I, and our other siblings, Gary and Sue Ellen, all discussed what needed to be done. It was obvious that Dad could no longer care for himself, let alone himself and Mom. And none of us could do it either. There was no choice but to find the best nursing home that they could afford. Since they were rapidly becoming mentally incompetent, we needed to have them sign powers of attorney so that Sheila and I could take care of their property.

Everything started falling apart all at the same time. I don't know what happened with Sheila and Morgan, the attorney she had been working for, but she was out of a job and he was apologizing to me for not being able to get along with her. Then I got the dreaded "we're coming to get the car" call anyone who has ever been late with a few installment payments always hopes won't come, and I had no choice but to give up my car. I was on foot without my own transportation for the first time since I was eighteen years old.

Then Sheila started calling me everyday at work after she had had a few too many beers, complaining about Morgan's treatment of her and I'm sorry, but after living with an alcoholic for seven and a half years, I have a "thing" about talking to drunks—you can't reason with them and they never remember the conversation anyway. So, I would hang up on her after I told her I couldn't talk. I remember she said something about a returned check on Dad's checking account and I called the bank to see what stupid thing I must have done, straightened it out and forgot about it.

Finally, when I wouldn't talk to her on the phone, she sent me a fax on the firm's fax machine, which was used by everyone in the office and I don't know how long that fax lay there before I found it. In very sloppy handwriting these words were scribbled: "Netta. If you don't call me, I'm going to assume that you have been stealing from the folks. The mail is now being forwarded to Dad and the checking account has been changed. Don't write any more checks!!" I didn't call, simply because I didn't know what she was talking about. Then I started getting demands from Sheila and from Dad for Shane to return his truck to him. I reminded my father that he had given the truck to Shane for the work he had done, but he kept insisting he wanted his truck back. We had no witness to prove that Dad had given Shane the truck. Then I got a call from my brother, Gary, insisting that Shane had to give the truck back to Dad. That was it. I made Shane drive the truck down to the nursing home and park it, and for another year, I continued paying off the twelve hundred dollars that I paid to have it fixed. I later learned that Sheila had sold the truck. Probably to pay expenses for the folks, but I was never told.

My wonderful friend, Jodi, offered me the use of her old Cadillac, which was just sitting in the driveway gathering dust. I began getting bad vibes at work from John. Nothing I could really put my finger on, more a gut feeling. Then I got a call from John that said he was on his way back from the courthouse and he needed to talk to me about something. At three thirty on a Friday afternoon, less than two months before Christmas, I was out of a job. John said he was sorry, but his financial advisors had told him he needed to cut expenses and he needed a secretary that he could pay less than me. Even though I was expecting it, it was still a big shock. I had just been in the new house a little over a year and besides the mortgage and taxes, had been trying to finish the inside. I had had my car repossessed earlier that year and had finally been able to give Jodi back her Cadillac when I found a Ford Bronco II that I could afford. My sister wasn't speaking to me and my sons couldn't hold a job. I think it's fair to say I felt like I had been dropped into a deep well full of caca.

  I didn't cry until I got out into my truck. My truck! Oh, my gosh! How was I going to keep up the payments on the truck I had just bought? There was surely a very dark cloud hovering over me.

~Chapter 14~

I hit the bricks bright and early on the first of November, but as you might imagine, there were no jobs available that close to Christmas. I wasn't too worried, yet. I still had two weeks' severance pay coming. About a week before the next payday rolled around, I started calling John to see when I could pick up my check. He never called me back and his new secretary wouldn't talk to me. The closer it got to the fifteenth of the month, the more worried I got about John keeping his word because I hadn't even had a nibble as far as a new job was concerned. Finally, I called John's secretary on the fifteenth but I didn't ask to speak with John. I asked her to give him the message that I would be in the area sometime after lunch and would be coming by to pick up my severance check. And then I hung up without giving her a chance to say anything. I appeared in his office reception area at one o'clock. He came out all smiles and took me back to his office.

  I got the entire nineteen hundred dollars, half of my usual monthly salary with no taxes or anything taken out. And as soon as I left his office, I went to the bank and cashed it. And my second stop was at the TEC (Texas Employment Commission), where I signed up for unemployment. It was only a thousand dollars a month, but at that point I was scratching for anything I could get to keep my head above water. I had managed to maintain the mortgage, and I had explained the situation to the dealership where I bought the truck and they were willing to work with me (at least they said they were). I finally signed up to do temporary work with one of the agencies downtown. At least they would pay me enough to get me gas and grocery money. That, combined with the unemployment, should help me make it through to the end of the year and I was sure I would be able to find another job in January when the job market opened up.

Then I got a call that Mom had been taken to ICU in the hospital in Baytown and I rushed over to see what was wrong. Of course, Sheila was there with Mom when I got to the hospital. It was such a relief to see Mom standing up at the side of her bed talking, that I didn't even think twice. Mom saw me and cried out she was so happy to see me. I gave her a big hug and then hurried over to Sheila from habit to give her one, too. It was like hugging a block of ice; stiff, hard and cold. I turned back to Mom and didn't say any more to Sheila. Sheila told Mom that she was going to go get coffee and let us talk.

I didn't stay very long, because I knew it would be uncomfortable when Sheila came back. I talked to the nurse on duty and found out that they had put Mom in the hospital to build her back up nutritionally because she wasn't eating right. She was having trouble swallowing, would sometimes choke, and the food was ending up in her lungs, which would cause pneumonia if it wasn't stopped. The doctor had suggested inserting a feeding tube. The four of us had discussed it at great length once before and had all turned thumbs down on that option. Now, though, I doubted that I would be consulted in any decisions since I had become the bad guy, and if the three of them decided to do something, my agreement or disagreement would not carry any weight.

I got a temp-to-perm assignment through the agency at one of the more notorious sweatshop law firms in town the middle of January, and I gave a great big sigh of relief. If I really squeezed my money, and took every overtime assignment I could get, I would be able to pull myself back up. But that little black cloud was still giving me fits. One afternoon when I pulled in the driveway, the boys were telling me about this stupid wrecker driver that kept going back and forth down our road. Eddie was expecting to have his car picked up because it had died on him, so they were laughing at that driver who was too blind to see the car he was supposed to pick up, right in our front yard.

"Hey!" Shane hollered. "That jerk is really confused. He just picked up Mom's truck and is headed out the driveway." Shane and Eddie went racing out the door to tell the wrecker driver that he had made a mistake, but the driver just sped up and peeled out of my driveway. It all happened so fast; I just stood there dumbfounded. Then I ran next door to Denise's house and asked to use the phone because the stupid driver had picked up the wrong vehicle. Not! I discovered that he had picked up the right vehicle. It was my truck he was after all along. It seems that the dealership I thought I had made arrangements with to work with me until I got a fulltime job, had decided they had waited long enough. It took me a week to scrape together the money to pay all the arrearage and get my truck back.

Just before Mother's Day 1995, Mom was again in the hospital. I went to see her a couple of times early in the mornings on my way to work. She never knew I was there. I don't know if she was asleep or in a coma. I couldn't tell and I didn't try to wake her, other than softly calling out, "Mom?" and touching her arm or her cheek. The doctor must have finally swayed the others, because she was now sporting a feeding tube. But she was never conscious when I went to see her. On the Thursday before Mother's Day I stopped to drop off my card to her and she looked ever worse than before. I could tell that whatever they were trying to do wasn't working. I kissed Mom on the cheek and turned away with tears streaming down my face. I even forgot to leave the card. That afternoon, Sue Ellen called to tell me that Mom had passed away.

For all intents and purposes my mother had been gone since 1989. She was never the same after that second stroke. But even when it's expected, the loss of your mother takes a toll. Regardless of your relationship with your parents, when they are gone it's a wrench that shakes you to the core. And even though I was fifty-six years old at the time, having already lost my father a few years before, I felt abandoned—a fifty-six-year-old orphan. I suppose that sounds silly and childish, but that's the way I felt.

I knew that Sheila, Sue Ellen and Gary would be taking care of all the arrangements so I called Grandma Martha. I was sure that she wasn't on their list of people to call, although she had been a part of our lives for thirty years. She was retired and was living in an assisted-living complex in a small community. She insisted that I come and stay with her for the sad business I had to get through over the next week.

I had only been working at Hurst Robbins since January and I knew that I didn't have any benefits yet because I had just become a permanent employee but there was no way that I was not going to go home for my mother's funeral. My bosses were very sympathetic and understanding and told me to take as much time as I needed. Grandma Martha met me at the airport and insisted that I drive her car as long as I was there. When we got there, she decided she wasn't ready to face the ordeal of seeing my mother in her casket. They were so close in age that I guess she didn't want to face the reality of her own mortality.

I was shaking when I walked into the funeral home, but there was no one there to hold my hand or point me in the right direction. As I was looking around trying to figure out where my mother was, a family friend, Jimmy Danforth, came out of one of the side rooms to my left wiping his eyes. When he saw me he came right over and put his arms around me and gave me a big hug. That's when the tears finally came. I was home. I was loved. And I had support.

Jimmy went with me into the parlor where my mother was, and after a few minutes, left me alone with her. I stayed there by my mother for a few minutes, stroking her cold hand and saying my goodbyes. One of the funeral directors finally saw me and came to talk to me. I gave him the plant Martha had brought and he found a prominent place for it on the floor by the casket. Then I remembered I had left Martha sitting out in the car, and we had lots to do before the viewing scheduled for that night and the funeral the next day. I kissed my mother's forehead, and went out to start putting the pieces back together.

All of the clan gathered for the viewing, including a lot of the people who had gone to school with Mom and my real father, Brian. At the funeral service the next day in the church that I had attended as a child, Sheila's son, Philip, who was in training to become a Baptist missionary, gave the eulogy. And a fine job he did of it with one little omission. He never mentioned Mom's marriage to my father. I really didn't think much about that omission, because Philip never knew my father. But my Aunt Teddie was a little upset. She said it gave the impression that Gary and I had been the result of immaculate conceptions. But then, Teddie had always had a soft spot for my father and was quick to come to his defense.

~Chapter 15~

I was settling into a routine at Hurst Robbins and finding my niche with the new group of people. I loved working with Christine, but wasn't too sure about Roland, my other assignment. Then, it seemed that Mr. Hurst, who was the head of the firm, had been so impressed with my work the few times that I had done some overtime for him, that he decided he wanted me in his section. And whatever Jay Hurst wanted, he got. I was transferred to his section to work for an associate, but everyone knew that if you worked in Jay's section, you worked for him first. Then if you had any time left over, you worked for your assignment and if it meant overtime for you to do it that was okay.

I got a call from Aunt Teddie wanting to know how Dad was doing. When I asked her what she meant, she informed me that he had fallen at the nursing home and was in a coma. She said that she had received the call just before Christmas. No one had bothered to call me. The nursing home was supposed to call me whenever anything happened to Dad, good or bad. I was on the list as primary and that was the rule. I should have been notified. They had always called before when something happened. As soon as I got off the phone with her, I called the nursing home and raised hell, wanting to know how my dad was and why they hadn't called me. They gave me the name of the hospice where Dad had been taken, and explained that the primary had been changed on the sheet and that Sheila was now the only one they were supposed to call. By the time I found out where he was and before I could even get there, Dad passed away without ever regaining consciousness. Eight months after Mom's death, we also lost Dad. A memorial service was held at the nursing home and he was buried in the Veteran's Memorial Cemetery. I did attend the memorial service, but I have never visited his grave.

The stress of working in Jay's section was beginning to take its toll on me. After five months of being jerked back and forth from secretary, to only being allowed to answer the phones, and then back to word processor for the entire section, my health was suffering. In the five months that I had been in the section, Jay had fired his secretary three times and then called him back the next day. He verbally abused everyone on a daily basis, but I was only ostracized in print—his daily "Procedures" memos.

After belittling my work and telling me that I was anything but a good secretary, he transferred me to another section. I was to work for Jim Stout. I would be on probation for three months and if I violated any of the rules of that probation, I would be out on the street. He asked if I had anything to say and I simply said, "No." But inside I was jumping up and down, and laughing. I was so happy to be out of there!

Mark and Eddie had a falling out and we didn't see Mark anymore. Eddie had transferred to the Waffle House in Baytown and had finally settled on one girl, Misty, a young, seventeen-year-old high school student who worked with him at the Waffle House. Soon, Misty had moved into our house and said that it was all right with her parents, because she hadn't lived at home for a couple of years now. Wanting to be sure, I double-checked with her mother, who said she could stay and it would be okay as long as she finished school.

One day I spotted an ad in the classifieds for my friend, Kathy's position with Jay, the tyrant boss. I went in to work and asked her if she had seen the paper and she said yes. I told her to check the classifieds. Suddenly a little while later I was called into Jay's office. "By telling Kathy that there was an ad in the paper for her job before I could say anything to her, you've created a problem," he said, almost foaming at the mouth. There was a lot more of the same crap, and finally he asked for my resignation.

I said, "Fine. Let me tell Jim," I said, as I stomped out the door. There was more of the same crap from Jay, although he toned it down for Jim's benefit. Jim backed me up for about twenty minutes and he finally caved in. Jay left, with a self-satisfied smirk on his face. As I walked to the door, the tears finally came, and I just looked at Jim and said, "You are all going to be sorry one of these days that you didn't stand up to that lunatic." I cleaned off my desk and went home. Within two years, my prediction came true. The firm fell apart when Jay had eight sexual harassment suits filed against him.

Misty was just about to graduate from high school, and she and Eddie were expecting a baby toward the end of November. Then Eddie was offered the job as restaurant manager at a store in Wisconsin. After much debate and soul searching, Eddie decided to accept the offer and off went Eddie and Misty to the cold country of the north leaving Shane and me in the trailer. Shortly, Shane and Fonda decided to become a permanent pair, and Fonda moved in with us until they could find a place of their own.

It looked like I might finally get all of my birds out of the nest and be able to have a life of my own. But, no. I guess it just wasn't time, yet. No sooner had Shane and Fonda found a really pretty place, when Eddie and Misty decided that they had had enough of the Wisconsin winter and came back to live with me in the trailer.

I had a very special birthday that summer. Nick's new assignment was at Langley Air Force Base, which he had been fortunate to get because it meant that he could live in Newport News, Virginia, close to Chad and Lexie. And, will wonders never cease? Kyle had actually retired from the Air Force and was living in Fairfax, Virginia, so he could be closer to Skye and Kevin. So my two oldest sons were again living in the same state.

Finally, in September, I was allowed to go back to work for Mark Fitzgerald. I had a lot of special conditions that I had to agree to before that could happen. For instance, I was not to practice criminal law (excuse me?); I was not to have any problems with my car (and just how was I going to control that?); I could not wear short skirts and boots (to which Mark replied, "For Christ's sake. She's a grandmother!").

Thanksgiving was about a week away. Misty would soon be telling us it was time to go to the hospital, but we were going ahead with our plans for a Thanksgiving dinner. One evening Shane's old girlfriend, Monica, called. I couldn't believe it was her. She was calling to ask if we might not like to have Savanna for Thanksgiving. Holy cow! Just like that, after having disappeared with my granddaughter and staying gone for seven years, she was nonchalantly asking if maybe we might like to see Savanna. Savanna had been seven months old the last time we had seen her. When I hung up, after getting all the pertinent information from Monica, I was shaking, laughing, crying, shouting, and running around the house! I guess you could say I was a little euphoric. I didn't know what to do first. Call Shane, drive to Monica's, have a drink—oh, no. I forgot. I don't drink anymore. I finally settled down enough to call Shane and give him the news and the information. He took it from there.

Shane and Monica made arrangements to meet and discuss things before the actual meeting took place between Shane and his daughter. It seems that Monica had acquired a drug problem during the years that she was gone and her husband, the one she insisted was the real father of Savanna had finally kicked her out. A year after their divorce, he had filed for a modification and took custody of their son away from Monica, but he didn't ask for custody of Savanna. He didn't even ask for visitation rights with Savanna. It was clearly apparent why he did not. The pictures that Shane brought home from that meeting with Monica showed an exact duplicate of my son. There was simply no denying the fact that Savanna was Shane's daughter.

Needless to say, that was one of the happiest Thanksgivings I have ever had. The day after Thanksgiving, Misty went into labor and Kalynn Nicole Morley was born.

I was getting antsy. Here I was almost sixty years old, and my children were still living with me. I desperately needed a place of my own. Living with Eddie was becoming more of a chore each day, because his alcohol problem was out of control. And each time I saw him with a beer in his hand, it was like having a flashback, and his father was there.

The next day, I called my old friend in the real estate business, Jodi Hadley, to start looking for a place for me to rent somewhere out Highway 290 close to her. She didn't have to look too far. Her current boss had several houses in a little subdivision that he wanted to sell. Jodi talked me into looking at the property and discussing it with Freddie, because he was willing to owner finance, due to my not-so-great credit.

I fell in love with the house the minute I walked in the door. It was only eleven hundred square feet, but it had three bedrooms and two baths, plus it had a cement patio and the yard was fenced.

~Chapter 16~

At home for the New Year after spending Christmas in Virginia, I had a few episodes in the middle of the night when I would wake up and my heart would be pounding and my chest felt tight. I had one of those episodes about three o'clock one Friday morning and seriously considered having Shane take me to the emergency room because it scared me, but I was so tired I couldn't stay awake. It bothered me enough so that the next morning after I got to work, I called my doctor and he freaked. He wanted me in his office now! The EKG didn't indicate any problems, but there were one or two little squiggles that, combined with my symptoms, made my doctor concerned enough to send me immediately to a cardiologist that afternoon. After another EKG and an ultrasound, they still couldn't find any evidence of heart problems, but the cardiologist wanted more tests done, so he told me to check into the hospital right across the street and he would do a stress test the next day.

Early the next morning, after being punctured again for more blood work, I was rolled down to radiology and they started the stress test. I passed the stress test with flying colors. But the cardiologist decided from one blood sugar reading that I had diabetes and had given me a prescription for insulin. I never filled that prescription because I was just as certain I did not have diabetes.

I got up bright and early Sunday morning ready to clean up a storm. I had been in the house for almost a year, and still had boxes in the garage that hadn't been unpacked. It was time I took care of that so I could put my car in the garage where it belonged. I started dragging boxes in from the garage two or three at a time. Then I started unpacking, putting things away, and cleaning up the mess I made as I got one box finished. About two o'clock, it was time to take a nap. I still had boxes scattered in the kitchen, but I was making headway and the garage was beginning to take shape. I just needed a little "power nap" to re-energize and I could finish it all that day.

About thirty minutes later I woke up with a God-awful feeling that there was an elephant sitting on my chest. It went away in just a few moments, but I was convinced that it had been a mild heart attack. I called Shawn (Sammie's oldest and my god-daughter) and told her what had happened. She screamed, "Call 911! I'll be right there." I told her to just get there.

I was fine and joking around with her. Then, as we sat there talking, it started. My chest got tighter and tighter, and the elephant came back. I do not remember any pain in my arms, just the elephant on my chest. I picked up the phone and dialed 911. Shawn was freaking. Since the Rosehill Volunteer Fire Department was only two blocks from my house, they were there in about two seconds. The first tech in the door gave me a baby aspirin to swallow and started checking my vitals. Then they put me on the gurney and took me out to the ambulance. Surprise, surprise, surprise! Guess who just happened to be at the hospital? My new cardiologist. Since he was there and I had recently been to see him, the hospital decided that he was my doctor and he wrote the orders for my care. The next day, the cardiologist came in to talk to me. He wanted to do an angiogram, you know, where they put this catheter in your arm and go in and look at the inside of your heart. I told him that I would have to think about it.

I was sure at that point that I had, indeed, been having a mild heart attack when I walked into their emergency room the night before the stress test, and they hadn't caught it. On top of which the doctor diagnosed me as having diabetes and the next day I had a heart attack. I called one of the girls at the office and had her look in our insurance directory for the name of another cardiologist, preferably one at St Luke's Hospital downtown, which was renowned for heart type problems. She found me Dr. Spencer with the Baylor Heart Clinic. He made the arrangements to have me transferred to the Methodist Hospital. I can tell you this. The minute they wheeled me into the Hospital, I felt this great weight being lifted. I knew everything was going to be okay.

The boys and Shawn were in and out all day, and Nick had called Sheila. Now, remember, Sheila hasn't spoken to me for almost four years. Nick said when he called to tell her I had had a heart attack, she started giving him some grief about why she hadn't had anything to do with me recently, and he just told her, "Get over it. She's your sister and she's had a heart attack." It worked, because Sheila called and asked if I wanted her to be there. I didn't even hesitate to tell her not yes, but hell yes! So, Thursday morning, when they wheeled me into surgery, I had three of my boys, my sister and my god-daughter in the waiting room pulling for me.

And then it was all over. They wheeled me back into recovery and later that afternoon into a private room. I had to stay completely still without moving my right leg because of the pressure bandage they had on the incision. When the anesthetic started wearing off, the pain in my right leg made it almost impossible to stay still. In the middle of the night they had to change that bandage. The pain then was excruciating.

They released me the next day and Eddie and Misty came to get me. Eddie and Misty had moved into the house while I was in the hospital, ostensibly to help take care of me when I came home, but really because they had no where else to go. Eddie's drinking was getting worse and worse. And I was in no shape to have that kind of stress, but there wasn't anything I could do about it. I was too weak, both physically and emotionally. When he's not drinking, Eddie is the most considerate, kind and gentle man you could ever ask for but when he's drinking, all hell breaks loose. I knew I didn't need that stress, but I was also really afraid to be alone at that point. After I got home I received a delivery of an envelope from one secretary who had taken up a collection, sent me a Peace Lily plant and then sent the envelope, which contained the balance of what she had collected, about sixty dollars. That helped a lot.

Things were bumpy at home, but we were managing. It was really cramped though, with three adults and a toddler and I could just imagine how it was going to be when the baby came. If I thought my garage was a mess before, you should have seen it then, with all of Eddie and Misty's belongings added to the pile. I didn't quite make it to the hospital for Kyle's birth. In the twenty minutes it took me to get to the hospital, Kyle Bradley Morley had been born October 24, 1999, and brought the total number of my grandchildren to ten.

A few months after Kyle was born, I was lucky enough to find a job for Misty at Hicks McMahon as a file clerk, but she didn't give up her job as a clerk at Mervyn's. It was necessary that she work two jobs because Eddie's drinking was making it impossible for him to hold down a job. In the meantime, Shane and Fonda were in the middle of a custody battle for Savanna. Monica's drug problem had reared its ugly head again and Shane had decided to fight for custody of his daughter because he found out that Monica had been sentenced to some time in jail, and she had left Savanna in the care of her stepfather. The four-year relationship between Shane and Fonda fell apart and within a few months Shane was dating a store clerk, June Kendall, and as the trial loomed closer, they decided that they should get married to give him a better standing with the court. Eventually June and Shane both quit their jobs at TA and came to live with me.

While Eddie was in rehab, Misty had taken the kids and moved back in with her folks, so I had the room for June and Shane. Then when Eddie completed his time in the rehab center, he came back to the house but Misty and the kids stayed with her mother, only coming over for the weekends. Needless to say, it got kind of hairy on the weekends with five adults, a toddler and a baby in an eleven hundred square foot house.

It was the beginning of the year 2000. Shane had accepted a position as maintenance man in an apartment complex, which included an apartment as part of his pay so June and Shane were now in their own place.

Unfortunately Eddie hadn't prevailed yet in his battle with demon rum. He fell off the wagon again after seven months of sobriety. It was the straw that finally broke Misty's back. She moved out for good that time, and I found out later that she has been going to therapy, as it threw her into such a deep depression. June and Shane didn't make it very long either. The custody battle for Savanna was settled when Savanna indicated after three years of saying that she wanted to live with her dad that she was going to stay with her mother. And once June discovered that she was pregnant, she ceased being a wife and eventually moved back home with her parents after only eight months of marriage. Tristen Alexander Morley was born in January of 2001.

Kyle, retired from the Air Force, has moved back to California to stay with his stepmother and is going to school. Nick is also going to school at the request of the Air Force, and has been attending the University of Alabama in Birmingham for the past two years. Shane moved back in with me and got his job back at TA. Eddie finally got so bad with the drinking that I had to kick him out of the house and in self defense have not been helping him this time. I finally realized that I was ruining my own health trying to help everyone else.

~Chapter 17~

In closing, I would like to share with you an email I received recently from one of my sons after a particularly trying time just after Thanksgiving a couple of months ago. It seems that in spite of all the things that I have done wrong, there were one or two things that I must have gotten right to have triggered this comment from my son, Nick.

>Hi Mom,
>
>Glad you got the cards. I still can't believe that this sort of thing is still happening to you after all these years. Hurry up and finish the last nineteen years (ha, ha) of your (book) life before another week goes by and you have to add another Chapter. What I remember most about growing up with you was watching how you started each day anew, as if you hadn't been physically or emotionally beaten the day before. If there's any greater lesson in life, it's learning how to move forward. No matter how great a challenge I face each day, I always remember how you picked us up and moved on with life as if no set back was ever going to hold you back.
>
>Love you always, Your Son

Then, there was the conversation I had with Shane on the way home from work one day. It was the day I was certain that Eddie had most probably used my bank debit card without my permission (and I found out the next day that I was right, to the tune of about a hundred and fifty dollars and with bank fees, it totaled about four hundred dollars). "I don't know why he thinks he had such a bad childhood," said Shane. "I think we all had a good childhood. We didn't have any money, but we always had clothes on our back, food in our stomachs and a roof over our heads. You were always there and we knew you loved us. I think you did damn good job, considering."

I couldn't speak for a moment. I had no idea Shane felt that way. Shane is the eternal pessimist and normally never says anything positive.

"Well, I did bring home a lot of different men," I said quietly.

"Yeah. But you were looking for a daddy for us. You were looking for a relationship. You weren't just some slut sleeping around," was his emphatic reply.

And on an even brighter note: approximately two years ago, I got an email from my brother with the name of a man who had contacted him by way of the Internet. Through one of those "classmates" sites, I suppose, or maybe my brother's genealogy connections. The man claimed to have gone to school with us in Parker, but said he really remembered me more than my brother. So Gary forwarded the information to me.

The name Rod Marshall did not ring a bell with me. But that's not all that unusual. After all, I only went to school in Parker for two years. After a few tentative email conversations, in which he mentioned the Ranch Pond where all the kids went swimming, and some pictures that he had taken of me and a couple of other girls at that pond one day, I still didn't hear any bells ringing. I finally received the pictures. He was in a couple of the pictures and I finally knew who he was.

Even though he was a year behind me in school, we had been in band together, we were in 4-H together, and if I'm not mistaken, in 1954, the summer he took those pictures, I was beginning to grow a little fond of him. But fate had stepped in when his folks sent him to Denver to visit his uncle. While he was gone, my folks decided that farming was not their cup of tea, and we moved back to Paola and I was nowhere in sight when Rod came home to Parker. The friendship was lost as we were just kids, miles apart now. The emails have been flying back and forth furiously for the past few weeks. Recent pictures have been exchanged and some discussions of the old days and all the days in-between. It has been almost fifty years since we saw each other, but that is about to change. I have reservations to fly to Arizona for a visit next month.

And if you want to know how the story ends, you'll just have to read the sequel in another Pearls of Wisdom upcoming edition.

To Be Continued As Years Go By

To contact "Lynetta Marie": SurvivorNetta@yahoo.com

~Updates From: *Pearls of Wisdom:* ~

Book One

"Peg"

The legal hassles to get the boys back from Georgia took almost three months. It was not a fun time in our lives. In the middle of September, just before I was to fly to Georgia to pick them up, I had a heart attack. Let me warn all you women out there that symptoms of a heart attack for women can be much different than for men. Do not ignore symptoms that you assume couldn't be a heart attack. My main symptom was a pressure in the glands in my throat that I ignored for a day and a half. Fortunately, I got into the hospital in time and had a stent inserted and was home after only three days in the hospital.

About a week later I flew to Georgia and retrieved the boys. I can't say enough about the Center for Missing and Exploited Children and the Georgia Center for Missing Children. My flight and lodgings were paid for; I was picked up at the airport and driven to get the boys, who had already been taken from their father a few days prior. Unfortunately, the boys' father and other relatives had used that three-month period to brainwash the boys and it has been quite a struggle undoing the damage they did. I think the worst thing they did was to instill a form of reverse bigotry in them. They now think their black side is the best part of them and have made remarks against whites. This is not how they were raised; they were raised to be proud of all aspects of their nationality. Both boys have done well in school this past year; the older earning several awards and being on the Honor Roll. They are both very active in sports and excel at them.

The final custody took place September 8, 2004. We received permanent custody of them then.

Maggie's and Fernando's relationship moved into the boyfriend-girlfriend mode but did not last. Maggie graduated from high school in June 2004. I was bursting with pride when she was awarded nine scholarships to college; more than any other student in the two high schools in town has ever received. She began college in January 2005, to obtain a nursing degree. She was also written up in the local newspaper for coming to the aid of three separate car accident victims within a five week period and rendering aid until paramedics could arrive.

I still have problems with my knee. Due to the heart attack they won't do the knee replacement surgery.

We have recently moved to a magnificent house with a panoramic view of the water and mountains. We found black toxic mold in our last house, which made everyone sick; Maggie even had to be transported to the hospital by ambulance because of it. I had a stroke of luck when I found this house and we moved two weeks later. I now have a bedroom and bed of my own again. The bedroom is large enough to accommodate my art studio, too—with plenty of room to spare. This house is almost twice the size of our last house—and it's dry and clean. I keep thinking I'll wake up and find out it has all been a dream.

I have quit selling on eBay on a regular basis. Since the boys came it has become too much of a hassle. Also after having the heart attack I realize we don't always have all the time in the world to do the things that gives us pleasure. So even though I'll be poorer financially (I should be used to that by now), I plan to take up my painting again and start enjoying what time I have left whether it be painting or sitting on my rear-end watching "While You Were Out" (that carpenter, Andrew Danjumbo is hot!). Hey! Don't count me out—I'm still on this side of the grass, you know.

SurvivorPeg1@yahoo.com

"Concetta"

My mother has been put into a nursing home in Denver, Colorado, by my sister who had kept her a prisoner for a year, and still my sister continues to keep us apart. She has placed a 'password' with the nursing home so that anyone wanting to see or talk to my mother must know the password. That is how she continues to keep us apart, and until I can afford to take this to court to prove that I have the real Power of Attorney, she will continue to be able to do this and get away with it. I have gone to the senior abuse association of Denver, Colorado, but to no avail. They talked to the daycare center when my mother went there and decided that it was just a family argument between two sisters. They never spoke to my mother, nor checked out the many things that I had told them.

Now my mother is beyond the stage of being able to bring her back to New Jersey, as moving her would be detrimental to her health situation, but had she been allowed to come back home, maybe it would have helped to prolong her life in a home situation that she begged for. Well, maybe I cannot afford the attorney, who wants over five thousand dollars as a retainer to prove my POA is the real one and to get the courts to appoint a non-biased third party to protect my mother from my sister, but I can do other things. I have contacted Dateline, 20/20 and all the rest of the TV shows in the hope that this story will get out and that my sister will get what she deserves. Maybe then my mother and best friend will be able to talk to me again. All I can do is pray. My mother does not deserve this.

Her daughter, Concetta Junior.